THE TRIAL OF THE HAYMARKET ANARCHISTS

THE TRIAL OF THE HAYMARKET ANARCHISTS

TERRORISM AND JUSTICE IN THE GILDED AGE

Timothy Messer-Kruse

First published in 2011 by
PALGRAVE MACMILLAN®
in the United States—a division of St. Martin's Press LLC,
175 Fifth Avenue, New York, NY 10010.

Where this book is distributed in the UK, Europe and the rest of the World,
this is by Palgrave Macmillan, a division of Macmillan Publishers Limited,
registered in England, company number 785998, of Houndmills,
Basingstoke, Hampshire RG21 6XS.

Palgrave Macmillan is the global academic imprint of the above
companies and has companies and representatives throught the world.

Palgrave® and Macmillan® are registered trademarks in the United States, the
United Kingdom, Europe and other countries.

ISBN: 978–0–230–12077–8 (pbk)
ISBN: 978–0–230–11660–3 (hc)

Library of Congress Cataloging-in-Publication Data

Messer-Kruse, Timothy.
    The trial of the Haymarket Anarchists : terrorism and justice in the Gilded
    Age / Timothy Messer-Kruse.
        p.   cm.
    ISBN 978–0–230–11660–3 (hardback) — ISBN 978–0–230–12077–8 ()
    1. Trials (Anarchy)—Illinois—Chicago—History—19th century.
    2. Haymarket Square Riot, Chicago, Ill., 1886.   I. Title.
    KF223.H3774M47 2011
    345.73′025230977311—dc22   2011011011

A catalogue record of the book is available from the British Library.

Design by Integra Software Services

First edition: August 2011

10 9 8 7 6 5 4 3 2 1

Printed in the United States of America.

Transferred to Digital Printing in 2013

CONTENTS

ACKNOWLEDGMENTS

It sometimes can be considered a backhanded compliment to be recognized in a book that is contentious or iconoclastic. There are many people whose assistance and aid I want to appreciate but without associating them in any way with my conclusions or opinions. No one who helped me along the way knew what I was up to or where my research was heading. I alone am responsible for any errors, omissions, or distortions present here.

Crucial steps in this project were possible only because of the cooperation of Russell Lewis, Julie Katz, and Debbie Linn of the Chicago Historical Society, and Vincent Giroud, Morgan Swan, and Timothy Young of the Beinecke Rare Book and Manuscript Library at Yale University. Joanne Hartough, Director of the Interlibrary Loan Department of Carlson Library, found many essential items for me over the years. Barbara Floyd, Director of the Canaday Center for Archival Collections at the University of Toledo, has been an indefatigable and reliable colleague.

The chemical analysis featured in Chapter 1 was performed by Jeffrey Dunn and Pannee Burckel at the Instrumentation Center at the University of Toledo and by James O. Eckert, Jr., of the Department of Geology and Geophysics at Yale University. I am indebted to them for their cooperation and hard work. This research was supported by a grant from the University of Toledo Office of Research. Many thanks to Richard Francis of the Office of Research for his support.

Special thanks to Dorothy Brown, Clerk of the Circuit Court of Cook County, and Phil Costello, Archivist, Circuit Court of Cook County, for their gracious assistance and for making their well-maintained collection of nineteenth-century legal records available to me.

I deeply appreciate Leon Fink's interest in new approaches to the field of labor history. Emily LaBarbera-Twarog helped in the preparation of an earlier article for publication in *LABOR: Studies in Working Class History of the Americas*.

Over the years I have benefited from the many conversations I have had with my colleague Peter Linebaugh, whose informed skepticism and deep knowledge of history has forced me to probe ever deeper into the Haymarket sources. Mark Lause's collegiality and his encyclopedic knowledge of nineteenth-century radical movements distinguish him as a truly great scholar but I appreciate him also as a fine friend. Gregory Miller has politely listened as I tried out all my more far-flung theories on him. I've benefited from the criticisms and comments of James Green, Bryan Palmer,

Melvyn Dubofsky, Beverly Gage, and Allen Ruff, though I probably didn't take them as they were intended.

A very special thanks is reserved for Hank Browne, who not only let me have the run of his Chicago apartment during research trips (which was just across the street from a police precinct station that stood at the time of the Haymarket bombing), but was a constantly constructive critic of my work.

Deborah MacDonald and Stephanie Rader may not realize that their day-to-day efficiency in running their offices allowed me to steal more time than I should have for this project. A number of graduate assistants, including Rachel Constance, Michael Brooks, and Jerald MacMurray, slogged books back and forth from the library, copied articles, and assisted in countless small ways.

This project would not have been possible without the keen understanding of the nuances of the German language and the efficient translation skills of Jason Doerre and Claudia Schneider. Geoffrey Howes graciously offered his expertise on antiquated German constructions and consulted on the difficult and mysterious "fugitive letter to Ebersold." Noreen T. Hanlon expertly translated some important documents from French. Michael Bryant guided me through the nuances of meaning in the reporting on the McCormick strike in the *Illinois Staats-Zeitung*. Much of the research into previously untapped German language sources was supported by the Office of Sponsored Programs and Research and the College of Arts and Sciences of Bowling Green State University (BGSU). The staff of the Jerome Library at BGSU, especially Mary Keil of the Interlibrary Loan Department, were able to track down many obscure titles for me. Thanks to Cynthia Price, Donald Nieman, Simon Morgan-Russell, and Roger Thibault of BGSU for their consistent support. Thanks also to Griffin Messer-Kruse for his help in converting a stack of century-old industrial time sheets into usable data.

Many librarians and archivists assisted in tracking down rare and ephemeral materials. Thanks to William J. Shephard of the Catholic University of America, Bill Gorman of the New York State Archives, Joanie Gearin of the National Archives Northeast Region, Frederick J. Augustyn, Jr., of the Manuscript Division, Library of Congress, John Reinhardt of the Illinois State Archives, Ella Molenaar of the International Institute of Social History, Amsterdam, and Julie Herrada of the Labadie Collection, University of Michigan Library. Thanks also to Lewis Clayton and Diana Sykes of the Clements Library, University of Michigan, for their help in reproducing the cover art and to Kate Alexander for her graphic design. Chris Chappell had the patience to give me the rare opportunity to revise and resubmit this manuscript several times. I hope the results are worthy of the chance.

In the end, it is the love and unconditional support of my family that gives me the courage to venture into such turbulent waters and risk being misunderstood.

Introduction

ON MAY 4, 1886, A RALLY WAS CALLED TO PROTEST THE SHOOTING OF STRIKERS at the McCormick Reaper Works by Chicago police the previous day. The meeting was organized by self-proclaimed anarchists, members of a small but growing movement that included both recent immigrants (primarily German) and a few native-born radicals who viewed the law as hopelessly biased in favor of employers, the republic as a sham, and capitalism as an evil so great that its immediate and violent overthrow was a moral imperative. This protest meeting, which took place near a widening of Randolph street on Chicago's west side known as Haymarket Square, was poorly attended by even the anarchists' standards. At about half past ten at night, as the sky darkened, chill winds picked up, and the crowd dwindled, nearly 200 policemen marched shoulder to shoulder, sidewalk to sidewalk, down Desplaines avenue up to the parked wagon that served as an improvised speaker's platform. As Police Captain Ward commanded the gathering to disperse, someone on the east sidewalk threw a bomb that landed in the center of the tightly packed ranks of police. The bomb exploded at the feet of patrolman Mathias Degan. The force of the explosion threw dozens of policemen to the ground and sent thousands of shards of metal whizzing faster than bullets in all directions. One of these jagged missiles, about the size of a thumbnail, ripped through Degan's thigh and severed his femoral artery, leaving him helpless to staunch the blood that poured out over the wooden paving blocks of Desplaines street. Thirty-five-year-old Degan was the first to die, orphaning his young son, as his wife had died from illness two years earlier.

Policemen closed ranks and scattered a heavy fire into the crowd. Though the immediate scene of the bombing was cleared of protesters in minutes, skirmishes were witnessed in the area for some time after the initial riot. A reporter for the Chicago *Times*, waiting at the Desplaines street station to speak with the chief of police, who arrived at one in the morning, saw police chasing a group of men in the glow of the electric lights from the Lyceum theater. According to the *Times*, "Suddenly a shot was fired toward the officers, and they commended a fusillade after the flying socialists." While the worst rioting occurred on the near west side, there was sporadic violence in other parts of the city throughout the night. In the lumber district in the southwest section of Chicago, a machinist for the McCormick company, presumably one who had not headed the call to strike, was beset upon by a mob and beaten unconscious.[1]

The Desplaines street station was turned into a field hospital. Wounded policemen were helped and carried first to the 30 beds available in the quarters upstairs, but when that overflowed, men were laid on tables and benches in the squad room on the first floor. Ten doctors and six priests proved too few for the number of casualties filling the building, and five nurses were summoned from the Illinois Training School for Nurses. Surgeon's probed, lanced, sewed, and sawed away until "pools of blood formed on the floor and was trampled about until almost every foot of space was red and slippery." Medics were so busy with the severely wounded that two cops were seen bandaging themselves: Officer McCormick wrapped his arm and Officer Gordon bound up his fractured foot.

Injured rioters were taken down to a dark room in the building's basement. The body of the one rioter found dead in the street was placed on a table in its center, where the others couldn't help but look upon it while waiting for someone to attend their wounds. Eventually, eight men suffering bullet wounds—three shot in the legs, two in their shoulders, and three hit in their back or sides—were gathered there. A gravely injured man found lying around the block from the riot was bundled into a patrol wagon and taken to the county hospital.

All through the night wounded men showed up at drugstores in the neighborhood for quick treatments. A man with an entry wound just below his left nipple and another in his right leg staggered into Ebert's Drugs on Madison avenue. Though the bullet had passed dangerously close to his heart, a group of friends took the man home to recuperate. With the assistance of several physicians, Ebert extracted bullets from five other men that night, including one that he tweezed out of a man's neck. Druggist John Hieland, whose shop was closest to the riot, reported having dressed the wounds of about a dozen men. Barker's Drugs was visited by three men suffering bullet wounds. Vogeler's Drugs reported treating a man with a bullet in his head. Reporters noted seeing men being bandaged out on the streets and wounded men riding in streetcars.[2]

In addition to Mathias Degan, at least 22 policemen were struck by fragments of the bombshell; five of them eventually succumbed to their wounds. John Barrett, an iron molder who left the trade for the police the year before, was pierced by a fragment that destroyed his liver; he died within 48 hours. The next to die was former teamster Timothy Flavin, who married on the day he left Ireland for America. The bomb must have fallen just behind and to Flavin's right because he took shrapnel above his right ankle, in his right shoulder, through his right hip, and in two places through his back—his lung and abdomen. Riddled in so many places, Flavin died of blood loss on May 9, with his three children at his bedside. One piece of the bomb scooped out a large run of bone from Officer Thomas Redden's left leg, while another lodged in his elbow. Redden, a 12-year veteran of the force, died ten days later from infection. Nels Hansen, a Swedish immigrant in his second year on the force, was struck by shell fragments in each knee and in the right thigh, left elbow, left ankle, and back (under his ribs). Surgeons attempted to save Hansen by lopping off his right leg, but the cure may have been worse than the injury, as septicemia finished him off on June 14.

At some point after the bomb exploded—some eyewitnesses said that it was immediately, others claimed that there was an eerie moment of quiet immediately following the bombing—the police and some of the protestors began shooting at each other. A bullet pierced Officer George Mueller's left side just under his armpit, bored through his intestines, and lodged just above his hip. Mueller lingered in agony for two days before dying. Patrolman Michael Sheehan took a bullet in his back that passed through his kidney and died after a surgeon attempted to remove it five days later, infection having set in. Timothy Sullivan was shot through his thigh and suffered a dangerous case of "blood poisoning." Although he survived, he had repeated bouts of illness that were attributed to his wound, and he died two years later.[3]

Twenty-three officers suffered injuries dire enough to disable them; worst affected among them was Jacob Hanson, who, when told that his leg had to go, said, "All right, doctor, it's an old friend of mine, and I'd hate to part company with it, but if we must part I can't kick, I guess." Lawrence Murphy was saved the trauma of amputation as the bomb had completely removed his foot. One year later, 12 men were still listed as "unfit for duty," and 11 were declared permanently disabled and retired from the force. Officer Daniel Daly suffered a head wound that left him paranoid, unable to sleep at times. His erratic behavior so alarmed his family that they twice committed him to the state asylum at Kaukakee. Ten years after the bombing, Daly had another of his spells at his sister's house, during which he swallowed a handful of carbolic acid and died five hours later.[4]

In turn, several dozen of those who had come to hear the anarchist speakers, either as protestors or curious bystanders, were shot, many as they fled. Carl Kiester was shot and killed somewhere near the corner of Desplaines and Randolph. Mathias Lewis and Charles Schumaker were shot in the riot but died days later—Lewis living until May 9 and Schumaker surviving "in great agony" until May 10. All told, at least seven policemen and three civilians were killed near Haymarket Square that night of May the Fourth.[5]

After an intense investigation, eight men were brought to trial, though the bomb thrower escaped the police dragnet. These eight anarchist leaders were charged as being members of a conspiracy to kill police officers that night. Under Illinois law aiding and abetting a murder carried the same legal penalty as directly performing the deed. Among those tried were the three men who addressed the crowd that night: August Spies, editor of the anarchist newspaper *Arbeiter-Zeitung*; Albert Parsons, editor of the anarchist journal *The Alarm*; and Samuel Fielden, "Red Sam," a teamster who earlier that day had delivered a load of stone to Waldheim cemetery, the same gothic field where his comrades would be buried a year later after the state of Illinois hanged them. Also implicated in the planning and preparations for the attack on the police were other anarchists of a lesser prominence in the movement. Michael Schwab and Adolph Fischer worked with August Spies putting out the *Arbeiter-Zeitung*—Schwab as assistant editor and Fischer as chief compositor. Oscar Neebe was a partner in the Acme Yeast Company and a director of the Socialistic Publishing Company that employed the others. George Engel was a toy merchant and one-time editor of the ephemeral *Der Anarchist*, a four-page sheet published in the belief that Spies' newspaper was too mild. Louis Lingg was a factory worker and the youngest of the accused, only 22 years old, and the most recent immigrant, having lived in

America just nine months. After a lengthy trial and appeal hearings before both the Illinois State Supreme Court and the U.S. Supreme Court, Spies, Parsons, Fielden, Schwab, Fischer, Engel, and Lingg were sentenced to death, while Neebe was given 15 years. In a rare move, both the prosecutor and presiding judge later supported a motion to commute the sentences of Fielden and Schwab to life imprisonment. The day before his sentence was to be carried out, Lingg cheated the hangman by smoking a small stick of dynamite that had been smuggled into his cell. On November 11, 1887, Spies, Parsons, Engel, and Fisher were executed. In 1893, Governor John Peter Altgeld pardoned the remaining three convicts.

The Haymarket bombing and trial marked a pivotal moment in the history of American social movements. It sparked the nation's first red scare, whose fury disrupted even moderately leftist movements for a generation. It drove the nation's labor unions onto a more conservative path than they had been pursuing before the bombing. It contributed to a string of legal decisions that served to restrict the civil rights of workers and empower the federal government against them. It also began a tradition within the American left of memorializing the Haymarket defendants as martyrs to the cause of the eight-hour day, of free speech, and of labor generally. Novelists and playwrights have dramatized their story. Poets have edified it. Artists memorialized it in bronze statuary. Activists founded labor's most widely observed holiday, International Workers' Day (May Day), upon it.

Since the late 1960s, historians have followed suit and enshrined the Haymarket affair as a landmark in the chronology of American social history. A bibliography of published works on the case contains 1,513 entries, and many more could be added as this reference work is now nearly 20 years old.[6]

Today, a popular and scholarly consensus concludes that the eight self-proclaimed anarchists who were convicted of the deadly bombing were innocent, the trial was a sham, and the whole episode was a prime example of the biases of the American government and judiciary against the labor movement. One of the most-read college textbooks describes it this way: "The trial was a farce. No one in the prosecution team knew or even claimed to know who threw the bomb...Nor did the prosecution present evidence that tied any of the eight accused to the bombing."[7]

Such a consensus took nearly a century to achieve, though. Well into the 1970s, labor activists and "defenders of law and order" disputed the facts and meaning of this event. Since the nineteenth century, each May Day brought with it to Chicago competing marches of policemen and union leaders, each side remembering their fallen heroes and blaming their deaths on the lawless acts of the other. Each year, on May 4, cops marched around a 20-foot statue of a policeman that stood on a granite plinth in the center of Haymarket Square and read the names of their fellow officers who had fallen in the line of duty, defending the city from the terror of the anarchists. On the same day, labor leaders gathered at their martyrs' graves in Waldheim cemetery and remembered their sacrifice at the hands of a corrupt judicial system doing the bidding of the city's merchants and industrialists.

But as the twentieth century drew to a close, the once bitter debates over the meaning of the Haymarket Riot—one side preserving the memory of fallen police heroes

valiantly upholding the law and the other remembering the railroading of labor leaders to the gallows—came to an end. Having survived several bombing attempts and
two actual bombings over 80 years, the Haymarket policeman's statue was quietly
removed by the city in 1972 and hidden out of public sight in an interior courtyard
of the police academy. On the other side of town, in 1998, the National Park Service
declared the anarchist martyrs' graves and memorials in Waldheim cemetery to be a
"National Historic Landmark" marked by an official government plaque that reads,
"This monument represents the labor movement's struggle for workers' rights and
possesses national significance in commemorating the history of the United States."[8]

   In 2004, with no opposition, the Illinois state legislature allocated 300,000 dollars
for a work of public art to commemorate the place where the Haymarket Riot had
occurred. With a unity unthinkable a generation earlier, the city government, the
Chicago Federation of Labor, and the Fraternal Order of Police cooperated in the
selection of a design for the monument, and officials from all three organizations
were on hand to offer speeches and congratulate each other when it was dedicated. All
sides now endorsed the interpretation cast on bronze tablets circling the base of Mary
Brogger's sculpture. "*In the aftermath, those who organized and spoke at the meeting—
and others who held unpopular political viewpoints—were arrested, unfairly tried and,
in some cases, sentenced to death even though none could be tied to the bombing itself.*"
Only the artist herself expressed any uncertainty about the meaning of this event.
When asked by a reporter whether her sculpture of abstract human figures standing
amidst pieces of a wagon was meant to show people building a wagon or tearing it
apart, Brogger replied, " . . . I didn't want to make the imagery conclusive. I want to
suggest the complexity of truth, but also people's responsibility for their actions and
for the effect of their actions."[9]

   Much of this startling shift in the public memory of this event was due to the
influence of academic historians. In 1936, Henry David published the first scholarly monograph on the subject, adapted from the dissertation he wrote at Columbia
University. In *The History of the Haymarket Affair*, David's conclusion about the justice of the Haymarket trial was strident and certain: "Parsons, Spies, Fielden, Neebe,
Engel, Fischer, Schwab, and Lingg were not guilty of the murder of Officer Degan
in the light of the evidence produced in court. A biased jury, a prejudiced judge,
perjured evidence, an extraordinary and indefensible theory of conspiracy, and the
temper of Chicago led to the conviction. The evidence never proved their guilt."[10]
Half a century later, in 1984, the foremost American scholar of anarchism, Paul
Avrich, published his prize-winning history of the Haymarket case, which immediately became the standard source for all references to the event. Like David, Avrich
concluded that the trial was not only unjust but perhaps the most unfair legal proceeding in all of American history: "Although Haymarket was by no means the only
instance where American justice has failed, it was nonetheless a black mark on a legal
system that professes truth and fairness as its highest principles . . . As a barbarous act
of power it was without parallel in American legal history."[11] James Green, author of
the most recent book on the Haymarket affair, whose title, *Death in the Haymarket*,
even casts into the passive voice the murderous act itself, called it "a sensational show

trial" that "challenged like no other episode in the nineteenth century, the image of the United States as a classless society with liberty and justice for all."[12]

Such criticisms of the trial revolved around a long list of alleged legal irregularities. The defendants were denied their petition for separate trials and were tried as a group. The jury was handpicked in an unconventional and biased manner. Evidence seized without warrant and of dubious provenance was allowed. Witnesses were coerced or bribed, and their inconsistent testimony was given credence over the more believable exculpatory statements of defense witnesses. A biased judge allowed the prosecutors to festoon the courtroom with the inflammatory banners and flags collected by police from around the city. At every turn, the judge showed his favoritism to the prosecution and arbitrarily denied routine motions of defense lawyers. Underlying the whole proceeding was a legal theory that allowed the Haymarket anarchists to be convicted even though the identity of the actual bomb thrower was never proven and the perpetrator never arrested. As a final act of unfairness, after all the evidence was in and both sides had rested their cases, the judge issued instructions to the jury that allowed the anarchists to be convicted for their words rather than their deeds.

Ten years ago, while I was teaching a labor history course, one of my students raised her hand and asked, "Professor, if it is true, what it says in our textbook, that there was 'no evidence whatsoever connecting them with the bombing,' then what did they talk about in the courtroom for six weeks?"[13] I had no answer for her because I had never thought of the question this way. Everything I had ever read on the subject had emphasized the utter lack of credible evidence. I lamely replied that I recalled that there was contradictory police testimony as well as some witnesses who were later shown to have been paid by the prosecutor's office, but beyond that I couldn't say.

For days afterward her question pulled at me. I began to look at the case more systematically, rereading the standard accounts but this time doing so while keeping my student's provocative question in mind. I was initially struck by how few facts seem to be positively known about the case. Historians, it seemed, could not even agree upon how many policemen were killed and whether they were even killed by the bomb that was thrown that night or by the frenzied fire of their fellow police officers. Upon reading Avrich's *The Haymarket Tragedy* more closely, I caught a brief reference to the fact that police officers discovered bombshells in the home of one defendant, Louis Lingg, the man who later killed himself in his jail cell. Wasn't that some sort of evidence?

It was then that I discovered that the Chicago Historical Society had recently completed a major digitization project for their Haymarket collection and that the entire transcript of the trial was available over the Internet. I spent days reading through the compelling verbatim testimony, and to my astonishment, discovered a trial unlike any I had ever read about. In what was the longest criminal trial in Illinois history up to that date, I found a judge very different from the bigoted and corrupt hanging judge who had been described as having shown open contempt for the defense and favoritism toward the prosecutors at every turn. I read the testimony of eyewitnesses who alleged firsthand knowledge of a bomb conspiracy, one even claiming to have seen an anarchist leader, August Spies, light the fuse. I read the reports of chemists who found similar compositions of metal alloy in both the bombs found in Lingg's apartment and the fragments recovered from the bodies of the slain officers. Surgeons detailed the nature of the wounds caused by the bomb, wounds that were easily distinguished from those caused by bullets. I was astonished to find obvious and glaring contradictions in the testimony of defense witnesses, whose stories later became the basis for historians' skepticism of the more consistent accounts of scores of police officers. So overwhelming was the prosecution's case that the defense opened by conceding that one of the defendants had manufactured bombs the day of the protest and that their other clients had indeed conspired to violently resist the police and thereby spark a "general revolution." August Spies, testified in his own defense and boasted of keeping bombs and explosives in his newspaper office to "experiment" with.

Though I was not able to give a full answer to my precocious student's question before the term was over, I had gone far enough into the sources to unhinge every certainty I had about the facts of this case. How was it, I wondered, that the universally accepted interpretation of this landmark event could be so wildly different from the record of the trial itself?

The answer lies in the fact that nearly all our contemporary knowledge of this event predominately rests on sources and accounts produced by the defenders of the anarchists or by the anarchists themselves. The leading historians who have written comprehensive accounts of the Haymarket bombing and trial drew their facts not from the full verbatim transcript of the trial, a daunting record thousands of pages long (and prior to 1998 accessible only in the reading rooms of several archives), but from the widely available *Abstract of Record*, a brief version of the proceedings accommodated in just two volumes.[14] Of the 118 witnesses heard by the jury in July and August 1886, the abbreviated testimony of fewer than half, 51, appears in the *Abstract of Record*. Even in those cases, the exact format of the questions and witnesses' verbatim responses to them are lost and only a selective interpretation of the gist of their testimony is preserved. More problematically, historians have uncritically relied on the *Abstract of Record* even though it was abstracted, edited, and published by the anarchists' own defense team.

Besides the *Abstract of Record* the source most cited by influential historians of the Haymarket trial is the most partisan version of the event, *A Concise History of the Great Trial of Chicago Anarchists in 1886*, by Dyer D. Lum. The author was a leader of the effort to win amnesty for the condemned anarchists, and his account of the trial was published while that campaign was in full swing. At the time Lum wrote *A Concise History*, he was also serving as the interim editor of the *Alarm*, the anarchist paper whose editor, Albert Parsons, was one of the men on death row.

The most frequently referenced work on the trial is Paul Avrich's prize-winning book, *The Haymarket Tragedy* (1984). In the four chapters of Avrich's book that primarily deal with the facts of the Haymarket trial, 93 of his 229 citations, or 40 percent of the total, cite contemporary anarchist publications, the memoirs of the accused, the accounts of the trial by defendants' attorneys, or the history of the trial published by Dyer Lum. Anarchist sources are twice as numerous as references to Chicago's daily newspapers and excerpts from the official records combined. Prosecution sources, which exist in quantities far more voluminous than those of the defendants, total fewer than one-quarter of Avrich's sources. In fact, Avrich relies more heavily on Dyer Lum's history of the case than he does even on the limited abstract of trial testimony, the *Abstract of Record*, which he consulted in place of the full trial transcript.[15]

No new troves of forgotten papers discovered in some dusty attic were needed to completely rewrite the history of this most-written-about event. All the combustible material needed to put the torch to a century of scholarship was there lying about in plain sight, simply ignored. Some of the most revealing information about the beliefs, social life, organization, and aspirations of Chicago's anarchists is contained in tens of thousands of pages of trial transcripts, police affidavits, and official reports that have long been discounted by scholars because they were viewed as part of the machinery of judicial murder and thereby not credible.

In describing the legal process that condemned seven men to the gallows and one other to 15 years in the state prison, I tried not to apply contemporary standards of justice and criminal procedure to an era that had not yet adopted them. In order to truly understand what the trial meant to people at that time, it is necessary to interpret it by the legal standards of their own day. For example, it obscures the meaning of the proceedings to fault a judge for failing to exclude evidence obtained in a warrantless search when the exclusion rule that mandated throwing out the "fruit of the poisonous tree" was a twentieth-century innovation. Generally, the existing accounts of the trial are laced with such presentism.

The conclusions reached by the method I have followed will be difficult for many to accept—that Chicago's anarchists were part of an international terrorist network and did hatch a conspiracy to attack police with bombs and guns that May Day weekend. That, by the standards of the age, the trial was fair, the jury representative, and the evidence establishing most of the defendants' guilt overwhelming. The tragic end of the story was the product not of prosecutorial eagerness to see the anarchists hang, but largely due to a combination of the incompetence of the defendants' lawyers and their willingness to use the trial to vindicate anarchism rather than save the necks of their clients.

My aim is not to prove that the police and the courts were right and the anarchists and their supporters wrong. Rather, I hope to understand the revolutionary anarchist movement on its own terms rather than in the romantic ways that their martyrs have been eulogized. The evidence uncovered by the police in their investigation and subsequently aired during the trial provides a new means to understand what it was that the bomber and his or her accomplices hoped to accomplish, to get inside their heads and view the world through their eyes, to see them as actors not victims.

CHAPTER 1

THE INVESTIGATION

FORENSIC SCIENCE HAD NOT YET BEEN INVENTED when Chicago's detectives attempted to determine who was responsible for the Haymarket bombing. Fingerprints, ballistics matching, and blood typing were not perfected until the early twentieth century. The first textbook of criminal investigation, Hans Gross' *Criminal Investigation*, was published in German five years after the explosion. Sir Arthur Conan Doyle had not yet popularized the close scrutiny of physical clues, as Sherlock Holmes would not make his literary debut until 1887.[1] Almost every prisoner incarcerated in this era had been convicted solely on the basis of some witness's or victim's testimony. Circumstantial or physical evidence of any kind was rarely brought into courtrooms, except where a torn skirt or a bloody knife could arouse the disgust, anger, or sympathy of a jury.

Police did not make a systematic canvas for physical evidence amid the refuse scattered about Desplaines street as such a procedure had not yet been invented. There was, therefore, no reason to limit access to the crime scene, and police were only concerned with preventing more outbreaks of protest; they kept crowds from gathering but allowed souvenir hunters to comb the street. Under a bright morning sun, traces of the previous night's violence were evident. Bits of cloth and flattened hats lay in the gutters. Splotches along the sidewalks and street planks were stained a dull red. A stream of the curious "composed largely of such as stand outside the jail at hangings" passed through the block, gaping at the broken windows and the debris. Young boys took their penknives and pried slugs out of the holes peppering doors, posts, and walls. Several artists set up easels and began preparing their illustrations of the great riot, and at least one photographer ducked under his hood and recorded the scene, though it seems his pictures have not survived the passage of time. One reporter counted up the holes punched into a telephone pole and arrived at a total of 107. The only evidence police retrieved from the scene was a stripped bolt that they suspected had fastened together the two half-shells of the spherical bomb.[2]

Worried that the escalating violence of the past days might still worsen, police initially focused their efforts not on catching the culprits but on securing control of the city. All police and detectives were kept on continual duty and assigned to the two great hotspots of the city: the near west side and the lumber district. By eight in the morning a squadron of more than five dozen police was assembled at the Desplaines street station and marched the length of nearby Lake street from Jefferson to the river, a stretch of streets that fronted a number of saloons and meeting halls frequented by radicals. Officers were posted at each corner and no one was allowed to linger or gather as they moved along the sidewalk. A squad of officers raided the Canal street workshop of C. H. Bissell, a gunsmith who was rumored to have sold arms to the anarchists. Police carted off a stack of 90 of Bissell's muskets for safekeeping in a guarded armory.[3]

Fearing more riots like the one at the Haymarket, the police department issued to each man a larger second sidearm, a .44 caliber cavalry pistol. Just in case even this additional firepower was not sufficient, a special squadron composed of war veterans was organized and outfitted with Springfield rifles. Patrol wagons were dispatched throughout the coming days to disperse all gatherings, menacing or not.[4]

Such preparations seemed justified on Wednesday evening, the day after the bombing, when two patrolmen noticed some men acting suspiciously on a bridge overlooking the St. Paul freight houses, a focal point of ongoing railroad strikes. The officers ordered the group to move on and then followed for a short distance until one of the men pulled a pistol and shot a round into the sky before ducking into Henry Schroeder's saloon. Officer Madden dashed in after him, grabbed him by the lapel, saying "You're the man I want," and dragged him toward the door. The man under arrest pulled a .38 caliber snub-nosed "bulldog" and fired once into Madden's chest. Madden grappled with the man and shot him twice, first in the groin and then in the head. Both men clung to consciousness during the bumpy ride to the county hospital. Madden's assailant told police that his name was John Laffelhardt, but they later discovered that his real name was Reinhold Krueger. His anarchist comrades called him "Big" Krueger so as to distinguish him from his younger brother August, or "Little" Krueger. Big Krueger died of his wounds two days later, while Madden survived.[5]

The police and city officials began their investigation into the bombing with the assumption that the attack was the result of the coordinated efforts of several conspirators and not the act of a lone terrorist. When a couple dozen sleepless detectives and policemen gathered at the Central Station early that Wednesday morning, Lieutenant Shea told them to begin by arresting the principal speakers from the meeting held the night before: Spies, Fielden, and Parsons.

Fielden was the first to be found a few hours later. When police burst into his home, they found him lying in bed and nursing a bullet wound to his knee. Like all the other men sentenced to death but one, Albert Parsons, Fielden was an immigrant, though the only one not from a Germanic country. Fielden grew up on the outskirts of Lancashire and like many other working class children was pulled to labor in its vast cotton mills. He joined the Methodist church and emerged as a good preacher and a popular young man, one of his mates from Sunday school recalling that "the time that he left the place of his birth to seek his fortune in America ... the send-off that he got and the good wishes expressed for him were something unusual for a man about 22 years of age . . . " But there was not much fortune to be found, and Fielden tramped from job to job, making hats in Brooklyn, washing cloth in a Rhode Island spinning mill, chopping wood for a farmer in Ohio, dredging an Illinois canal, driving stakes on Mississippi railroads, and stevedoring along the Louisiana levees. Soon after the great fire he settled in Chicago, where he worked his way up from a common laborer for the city parks to the owner of several teams of horses that he used to haul stone and pull a scraper that extended city streets into the surrounding prairies. The crowd of policemen with their drawn guns surrounding Fielden's bed-side looked down on the wounded man under the sheets as a dangerous threat to the public order; little did they know that their hard gazes also fell on a man who had as much claim as anyone to having actually built the city.

After a few years in Chicago, Fielden hired hands to drive his wagons, and both his wealth and leisure time increased. He read widely, traveled abroad, and regularly attended the ten-cent lectures at McCormick Hall, where he heard some of the great liberal orators of his day, Theodore Tilton, Robert Ingersoll, and Charles Bradlaugh. During this period Fielden's convictions steadily shifted from Methodism, to agnos-ticism, to freethinking, to anarchism while losing none of their missionary zeal. He joined the Liberal League in the fall of 1880, mingling with his future chief legal counsel, Captain William Perkins Black, as well as with numerous other defenders and supporters at his trial. When the International Working People's Association formed in 1883, an organization that rejected the political and incremental meth-ods of its socialist predecessors and instead pledged itself to immediate revolutionary change by any means, Fielden not only joined but emerged as one of its most pop-ular open-air rally speakers. At the time he was arrested, Fielden was a 39-year-old man large enough to be intimidating. He had a full beard, a fiery attitude that had earned him the nickname "Red Sam," and a doting wife then pregnant with their second child.[6]

Police knew where they would likely find other suspects, as the anarchists' publish-ing office was only a block away from the Central Police Station.[7] Near the corner of Fifth avenue (today Wells street) and Washington stood the offices of the Socialistic Publishing Company, a firm that published four anarchist newspapers: the *Arbeiter Zeitung*, the *Fackel*, the *Vorbote*, and the *Alarm*. The office occupied the upper stories of a well-built stone commercial building with a saloon and a Chinese laundry on the ground floor. Detective James Bonfield, brother of the anarchists' most reviled police commander, John Bonfield, arrived at the building the morning after the bombing. Bonfield enlisted the saloon keeper to take him upstairs and to point out August Spies. The bar keep motioned to a dapper man with an immaculately groomed han-dlebar moustache underscoring his angular face sitting at a desk near the tall window overlooking the bustling avenue below. At the desk across from him was his assistant editor, Michael Schwab, who was appropriately bookish in his tiny round spectacles, his full beard, and his unkempt hair.[8]

Bonfield announced to Spies and Schwab that they were under arrest. Bonfield blew through his brass whistle, and Officer Wiley came bounding up the stairs and stood at his side. Spies and Schwab offered no resistance, and for good measure,

Bonfield also took in Spies' brother Chris and Adolph Fischer, who happened to be there.

August Spies was a bit of a dandy, known for his taste in finer clothes. More than most of his scruffier radical comrades, Spies seemed comfortable with his luxuries, justifying himself in his memoirs writing, "My philosophy has always been that the object of life can only consist in the enjoyment of life . . . I held that ascetism, as taught by the Church, was a crime against nature."[9]

Spies was born in Faff, Saxony, and immigrated with his family as an adolescent. Upon arriving in Chicago, he found work with H. Sander Co., makers of umbrellas on West Madison and Halsted streets. Spies worked for the umbrella company for five years, enjoying a steady rise in wages from $3 a week to $14. Seeking their fortunes, Spies and a brother-in-law tried their hands at sales, hitting the roads and rails with their wares, but riches eluded them and they returned home within a few weeks. Spies set up his own umbrella shop near the corner of Lake and Ashland but this too went bust, and he took a job as an upholsterer.[10]

Spies first became involved in Chicago's budding workers' movement when he attended a lecture on socialism delivered by "a young mechanic" that more than made up for in passion what it lacked in sophistication. Unlike most labor leaders of his generation, Spies had the advantage of an elite education—private tutors at home and classical studies at the Cassel Polytechnicum—cut short only by his father's early death and his family's emigration. Once exposed to socialist ideas, Spies had the scholarly skills to explore radical theories deeply and was especially impressed by Karl Marx's *Das Kapital*. Erudite, eloquent in several languages, and socially polished, Spies buoyed to the top of every organization he joined.

Spies' brief political career traced the arc of radicalism from the early 1870s, when socialists debated whether organizing labor unions or waging electoral campaigns was the surer path to a cooperative commonwealth, to the mid-1880s, when a third way was proposed—engaging in dramatic acts of violent resistance against state authorities. Chicago was a particularly fertile place for the growth of all these radical tendencies, and all were well represented at the time of the Haymarket bombing. But Spies and a handful of other radical leaders were distinctive in having traversed all these positions in little more than a decade. Because they had tried, tested, and found wanting first moral suasion, then electoral campaigns, then trade unions, these activists arrived at their militancy with the deep surety that experience brings.

An early activist of the Working-Men's Party and its successor, the Socialistic Labor Party (SLP), Spies emerged as a leader of the SLP's radical tendency, a faction that rejected compromise with mainstream parties. His faction provoked a split in the party by parading through the streets in military uniforms and shouldering muskets. After the English-speaking section of the SLP attempted to combine with the reformist Greenback Labor Party in 1880, Spies helped engineer a takeover of the party's executive committee and ousted the compromising Yankees. When the national leadership of the SLP denounced the Chicago radicals and removed their newspaper the *Arbeiter Zeitung* from its list of party organs, Spies led the formation of a revolutionary alternative to the SLP.

A conference of SLP dissidents in Chicago tapped Spies as the corresponding secretary for a loose network of a handful of the similar minded in 1881. Two years later, Spies was one of the leaders of a "Revolutionary Congress" held in Pittsburgh that formally launched the International Working People's Association, the organizational center of the revolutionary anarchist movement in America. Each of these intra-party battles advanced Spies' standing among the radicals, and he climbed from assistant editor of the *Arbeiter Zeitung* to its editorial chair by 1884. By that time the radicals Spies called "comrades" had begun to refer to themselves as "social revolutionaries," but were dubbed by others as "anarchists."[11]

The men and women popularly called "anarchists" were given that moniker at the time not because of their social philosophies—in terms of political or economic theory they were not that different from other socialists of their age. They understood capitalism not simply as an economic arrangement but as a historical epoch that corrupted and governed all other institutions from family to church to state. They believed that capitalism must be destroyed for an equitable, peaceful, and bountiful world to be born. In this sense, they were "socialists." But they rejected the hopes and plans of other radicals: worker cooperatives were misleading panaceas, labor parties could not win elections that mattered because the capitalists would never voluntarily surrender their power, and even trade unions were doomed to domestication by bosses who cleverly purchased workers' loyalties. Rather, they had arrived at a fundamentally logical but ruthless proposition: all institutions and rulers propping up the existing order, that is, the church, the government, elections, courts, jails, bankers, kings, policemen, and bosses, were legitimate targets in a war of class liberation. Pointing to the contemporary actions of European colonial powers; the English fleet sitting safely beyond the smooth-bore guns of the Egyptians and pummeling Alexandria with its long-range naval cannons; the American cavalry tearing through Indian encampments; and the Russian Cossacks putting to the torch rebellious villages; revolutionary theorists like Mikhail Bakunin, Johann Most, Peter Kropotkin, and Chicago's own Paul Grottkau argued not only for the efficacy of violent actions but for their necessity and even their morality.

For Spies and the other "anarchists" of Chicago, stockpiling, drilling, and occasionally flourishing their rifles and their bombs served multiple purposes. Forming a militia illustrated in the most immediate manner their philosophy of armed resistance, attracted more press and notoriety than their numbers would otherwise warrant, and perhaps gave the authorities pause before breaking up their meetings. Of course, arming also built up the means of their ultimate liberation. Either way, as it happened, the "anarchists" grew more bellicose just at the moment that clashes between a modernizing police force and a unionizing labor force became more frequent. Thus, Chicago's anarchists and police were set to a collision course long before the bombing at the Haymarket.[12]

As one of the usual speakers at protest rallies and public events, Spies had by 1886 a long history of troubles with Chicago police. He was on hand several times when gatherings of workers clashed with police, most notably the day before, May 3, when he addressed a crowd of workers who then stormed the McCormick Reaper Works and skirmished with police. More personally, his own younger brother Wilhelm, a wild youth who ran with a local street gang, had been killed by a police officer just 18 months earlier. "Willy" Spies and his friends were drinking beer on a corner near the Spies' home when Officer Jacob Tamillo ordered them to move along. Later, justifying the shot he fired into Willy's stomach, Tamillo claimed that Willy had tried to reach into his coat.[13]

The moment before Detective Bonfield stepped into Spies' office was the last moment of freedom Spies would enjoy. Spies was well aware of the gravity of his situation for as he was led off to jail, he told the men tromping to jail with him that they were all going to "swing."[14]

Adolph Fischer was a family man, having at the time of his arrest a pregnant wife and three children. Most of what has been documented about his life prior to the May days in Chicago is drawn from the brief "autobiography" published in the *Knights of Labor* journal while his case was being appealed. In it, Fischer says that he was born in Bremen and attended school there until he was 15, when he immigrated to America and "soon after my arrival on these shores" moved to Little Rock, Arkansas, to be apprenticed under his brother William, who published a weekly German newspaper. Apparently, the paper in Little Rock failed, for in 1877 William was to be found in St. Louis, where he emerged as one of the leaders of the socialist movement in the city. When the great wave of railroad strikes rolled westward across the country and finally reached the Gateway city, William was one of the "Ring of Five" who, for a couple days, effectively took over the city establishing what alarmist newspapers referred to as the "St. Louis Commune."[15]

The foreman of the Cincinnati *Freie Presse* remembered Fischer arriving in that city and taking up a job with the paper in the spring of 1878. The foreman remembered firing Fischer for his "anarchical and rampant speeches," after which Fischer found work across the street at the print shop of the *American Israelite*, but was then fired by the proprietor of that journal after a month. The foreman of the *Freie Presse* gave him his old job back, but he was soon shown the door again—when the foreman learned of an insulting letter Fischer had wrote about him and demanded that Fischer apologize, but Fischer refused.[16]

Fischer returned to St. Louis and began to put down roots. He joined the Typographical Union in 1879 and married in 1881. Then, in June 1883, he took his family to Chicago, where he had secured a job as a compositor for the *Arbeiter Zeitung*.[17]

Even his friends thought that Fischer's militancy had hardened him. One, who knew him well, described him as "of hewn granite." Later, in jail, he seemed less interested in the course of his appeals than in the games of pinochle he played with his guards through the bars of his cell.[18]

As was usual procedure, the police searched their captives and found that Fischer was wearing a belt with a sheath holding a sharpened file and a holstered .44 caliber revolver. The belt buckle was engraved with the initials "L. & W.V." short for Lehr und Wehr Verein, an armed militia unit of workers. In his pocket were ten cartridges and a blasting cap. According to the testimony of one of the paper's print-ers, James Aschenbrenner, Fischer was carrying these weapons because Aschenbrenner had found them stashed at his work bench and demanded that Fischer take them away "so as not to get anybody in trouble who does use any arms . . . "[19]

When questioned, Fischer claimed that he knew nothing about the blasting cap. It had been given to him months earlier by a socialist who had visited the office; he didn't know what it was and had forgotten that he had put it in his pocket. Bonfield, however, thought that the cap looked untarnished, "perfectly new and the fulminate was fresh and bright on the inside," when he confiscated it. Later, when questioned by assistant district attorney Edmund Furthmann, Fischer admitted that he knew what the cap was and what it was for, having read about how to use such a thing in a how-to terrorism manual entitled *Revolutionäere Kriegswissenschaft* (The Science of Revolutionary Warfare) published the year before by the most notorious anarchist in America, Johann Most. The subtitle of Most's work was "A Hand-Book for Instructions on the Use and Manufacture of Nitro-Glycerine, Dynamite, Gun-Cotton, Mercury Fulminate, Bombs, Incendiary Devices, Poisons, Etc."[20]

Apparently hesitant about the legality of searching the building without a war-rant, the police sent for chief prosecutor Julius Grinnell. He arrived around noon with assistant district attorney Edmund Furthmann and reportedly told the police to conduct a thorough search of the building and worry about the legal points later. Grinnell's cavalier attitude toward obtaining a warrant was universal in this era. Searches of homes and seizures of evidence without a warrant during criminal inves-tigations were so common in the late nineteenth century that these were considered standard practices in most police departments. An editor of the *Albany Law Journal* noted in 1899, "As a practical matter, it is well known that police officials, sheriffs, marshals, detectives and the like, when they make arrests, quite invariably search their prisoner and seize property upon his person or in his vicinity which they deem to be of probative force as bearing on the charge against him . . . the rule has been until now that [judges] will not inquire in to the legality of the methods of procuring the testi-mony, but will determine its admissibility . . . solely by considerations of its relevancy and materiality, and will not enter into such collateral inquiry."[21]

It wasn't until 1914 that the U.S. Supreme Court made the Exclusionary Rule the national standard of due process. Courts in the 1880s generally held that the remedy for an improper, warrantless search was a private torts action by the party whose rights had been invaded, against the official who had violated them. Tellingly, when the defense raised a protest at the anarchists' trial against evidence obtained without a warrant, the presiding judge hastened to grant that it may have a point, but that such action must take place in another court and in another trial. The prosecutor then volunteered that "I am willing to be tried for that act." Ironically, the standards for obtaining search warrants in Illinois were quite low at this time, requiring not specific evidence of crime but only a "reasonable suspicion." Grinnell and Furthmann could have obtained a search warrant quite readily had they taken the trouble of asking a judge for one, but given the lack of legal sanctions for not having it, they simply didn't bother.[22]

Once the search began, it did not take long to turn up more incriminating evidence. Another "fulminating cap" (though this one was tarnished and didn't look "fresh and bright" according to Detective James Bonfield), a few inches of fuse, and a revolver were discovered in a wooden box a few feet from August Spies' desk. A locksmith jimmied open the drawers of Spies' desk and inside was more fuse, and a box labeled "Quintuple Caps. Manufactured by the Etna Powder Company" that held ten more "fulminating" caps. There were also two paper-wrapped sticks that the officers assumed were dynamite. August Spies later admitted during his trial that these sticks were indeed composed of "Giant Powder" (a brand of dynamite), that these items were his, and that he kept them in his drawer to brandish in front of reporters to gain publicity and for "experimenting" with.[23]

In another room of the building, Lieutenant Shea watched as a patrolman brought out a package from a closet and unwrapped it, exposing what looked to be some sort of oily sawdust, and said, "Look out for that. That is dynamite." Gingerly, it was carried to a safe at the Central Station. Police also confiscated leaflets, newspapers, books, letters, metal type locked in printing frames, and scraps of manuscripts hanging from compositors' hooks. Two black flags and four red ones were seized, as was a banner inscribed "Our capitalistic friends may well thank their Lord we, their victims, have not strangled them."[24]

While police ransacked the building Mayor Carter Harrison arrived, and a short time afterward Oscar Neebe, a "hustler" and "organizer" who succeeded in keeping an *anarchist* business running, climbed the stairs to the editorial offices and asked where Spies was. The mayor took him aside and questioned him. Neebe told the mayor that he simply wished to get out the day's edition of the *Arbeiter Zeitung* and promised that "nothing of an incendiary nature" would appear in the paper. "That there won't I can assure you," was the mayor's reply, and a few minutes later all the compositors, printers, and everyone else employed by the publishing company, a total of 21 people, including the paper's lone female reporter, Lizzie Holmes, and two office boys, were arrested and paraded to the Armory building as the Central Station was not large enough to accommodate them all. In patting them down, one of the printers, Julius Stegemann, was found carrying a pistol and a knife. Judge George Meech hurried down to the fortress-like structure and there arraigned the crowd for murder, ordering them held without bail for one week. Stegemann was also charged with carrying a concealed weapon.[25]

After lunch a "powder man" was sent for, and he with two officers and a reporter in tow took some of the oily sawdust seized from the anarchist offices to the lakefront. The powder man placed a bit of it, about the size of a walnut, on an oak railroad tie, covered it with bricks, set a fuse, and stood off at a distance while it splintered a hole large enough "for a man's two fists" in the wood. The bricks were pulverized to dust. He then molded a second charge into an egg shape and placed this inside a heavy oval of iron from a railroad hitch and covered this with more bricks. After that blast a small piece of the iron remained, while the rest were cast out into Lake Michigan.[26]

Having turned up a cornucopia of evidence in their first day's search of an anarchist office, police began a general raid of known radical haunts. These weren't hard

to identify from the meeting announcements and advertisements published in anarchist newspapers. Before the day was over, five other meeting places were searched.
A large squad of police under the command of Chief of Police Frederick Ebersold
raided Greif's Hall, 54 West Lake street, a place known to be a center of anarchist
activity. Bonfield and 20 heavily armed men scoured Zepf's Hall, the anarchist saloon
just down the block from where the bomb exploded and seized three red flags, four
muskets, one bayonet, and a stack of papers. Further into the heart of the German
district, police searched the saloon and hall at 636 Milwaukee avenue, which, as it
turns out, was one of the armories of the Lehr und Wehr Verein. There, police discovered a secret shooting range in the basement and confiscated two old muskets.
Over the next three days a couple dozen other locations were searched.[27] Some time
later that week police searched Adolph Fischer's house but for their efforts carried
away only a box of .44 caliber cartridges and the blue tunic of the Lehr und Wehr
Verein. Disappointed with that haul, they made much of the three-foot length of gas
pipe found in a shed out back. Fischer's house did not have gas service.[28]

Investigators had gathered some evidence that this group of anarchists had
obtained the components for a bomb, but they had as yet no leads on the bomber.
The legal necessity of identifying and apprehending the bomber in order to make a
successful prosecution was a subject of much discussion in the legal community. The
day after the bombing, a group of business and legal leaders, led by Judge J.O. Glover,
visited the mayor to offer their interpretation of Illinois' statutes. Glover spoke for
the group and told the mayor that in their opinion anyone who had advised the use
of dynamite was as guilty of murder as the person who lit the fuse and threw the
bomb. Glover read a paragraph of the statutes defining "Accessories": "An accessory is
he who stands by, and aids, abets, or who, not being present, aiding or abetting, hath
advised, encouraged, aided or abetted the perpetration of a crime. He who thus aids,
abets, assists, advises, or encourages shall be considered as principal, and punished
accordingly."[29]

According to the self-aggrandizing memoir of Melville Stone, editor of the *Chicago
Daily News*, this question of whether a group of men can be prosecuted as accessories
before the fact when the principal of a crime remains unidentified troubled state
prosecutor Julius Grinnell. Stone was one of several men called into the coroner's
office the morning after the bombing to discuss how best to word the coroner's jury
verdict on the death of patrolman Mathias Degan. According to Stone (who remains
the sole source of information about this meeting), "I joined them in the basement of
the court house . . . Julius S. Grinnell, the prosecuting attorney, and Fred S. Winston,
the city attorney, had been discussing with Mr. Herz, the coroner, various questions
of law concerning the case when I joined them. They were in trouble. No one knew
who had actually thrown the bomb, and they both felt that this was important in
the conduct of the case. I at once took the ground that the identity of the bomb
thrower was of no consequence . . . . I finally . . . wrote out what I considered to be a
proper verdict for the coroner's jury to render . . . After some more discussion my draft
was accepted by Messrs. Grinnel [*sic*] and Winston, and Coroner Herz hurried away
to hold his inquest." Whether Stone was exaggerating his role or not, the coroner's

jury's verdict did attempt to legally separate the throwing of the bomb from the conspiracy that made it possible. "We the jury, find that Mathias J. Degan came to his death from shock and hemorrhage caused by a wound produced by a piece of bomb, thrown by an unknown person, aided, and abetted, and encouraged by August Spies, Christ Spies, Michael Schwab, A.R. Parsons, Samuel Fielden, and other unknown persons . . ."[30]

Nevertheless, prosecutor Grinnell clearly believed from the outset that his best strategy was to tie all the conspirators as closely as possible to the act of throwing the bomb. Grinnell was not satisfied to merely prove that anarchist leaders had written in their newspapers and shouted from their platforms paeans to the power of dynamite to solve the world's problems, even going so far as urging workers to fling bombs at their oppressors. He proceeded on the assumption that the law required that the state show that these men aided, abetted, encouraged, advised, or assisted not just any bombing but the particular bombing that occurred on May 4. To do so required identifying the bomber even if the culprit could not be presented in the courtroom.

Even before the police began to uncover the secret meetings and plans of the anarchists, Grinnell had found a number of witnesses who provided the first links he needed to forge a legal chain connecting conspirators to the bomber. A grocer by the name of Malvern M. Thompson was the first important witness to come forward, claiming at patrolman Degan's inquest on May 5 to have overheard August Spies and Michael Schwab conferring in the mouth of Crane's alley while Parsons was speaking. Thompson said that he caught the word "pistols" and the suspicious phrase "Do you think one will be enough?" A young candy maker by the name of John Bernett also contacted authorities and told them that he saw the man who threw the bomb. Bernett was taken to the jail and shown the prisoners but could not finger any of them as the bomber. This put to rest the investigators' initial theory that either Fischer or one of the Spies brothers was the bomb thrower.[31]

Then, on Thursday, two days after the bombing, a tall rangy man in the vicinity of the city hall boasted to a clutch of men that he had seen the man who threw the bomb and was certain he could identify him. A reporter for the *Chicago Times* overheard this man, Harry Gilmer, and published a short note of the incident in that evening's edition. The reporter quoted Gilmer saying, "I was standing on the corner of the alleyway, alongside Crane's factory, and saw the police come along, and when the crowd was ordered to disperse a young man who stood near me threw the bomb. I am positive of this, because he lit the fuse before he threw the bomb. He was a medium-sized man, with whiskers and mustache, and he wore a slouch hat." That night police summoned Gilmer for questioning.[32]

By a coincidence that turned into an embarrassment, while police gathered a description of the bomber from Gilmer at police headquarters, the likely bomber, a carpenter by the name of Rudolph Schnaubelt, who was also the brother-in-law of Michael Schwab, was questioned at a different station. Had the two crossed paths that day, the whole course of the trial would have gone differently, but just as one set of police officers learned they were looking for a man slightly above average height, the nearly six-foot Schnaubelt was convincingly answering other police officers' questions. Schnaubelt admitted being on the wagon during some of the speeches, but accounted for his movements to the satisfaction of his interrogators and was let go—never to be seen in Chicago again.[33]

Part of the reason that Schnaubelt was let go was that detectives and prosecutors weren't quite sure at first whether to believe Harry Gilmer. They gained confidence in his testimony only after he proved able to pick a man (out of a group of prisoners) who had stood on the speakers' wagon but had not delivered a speech. That Gilmer happened to be at the station at the same time as this suspect was brought into custody was a lucky break for the police that was made possible by a stakeout of the Parsons' home.

Beginning the morning after the bombing, undercover officers kept a constant watch on the Parsons' home. One night, detectives observed a man slipping a note under the Parsons' front door and retrieved it before Lucy Parsons knew it had arrived. The little missive expressed the writer's sympathy with what had happened at the Haymarket and was signed "W.S. 287 Lake Street." Within an hour detectives bundled off four people they found at that address to the Central Station. Among them were William Snyder and Thomas Brown. Both men denied having attended the Haymarket meeting or knowing anything about it. Snyder was asked to write some short statement, and once detectives saw that his handwriting matched that on the note left at Lucy's door, began quoting his note to him. "...you never saw a fellow so surprised and terrified," recalled assistant prosecutor Francis Walker. "He turned seven colors at once, and his hand shook like ague." According to Walker, Snyder and Brown were put in a cell with a couple dozen others and Harry Gilmer was let in and asked if he could identify any of the prisoners. Gilmer pointed out Snyder and Brown and said he remembered seeing them on the speakers' wagon at some point in the evening. Snyder was interviewed privately again, and when confronted with both his note and Gilmer's identification, he broke down and told them more about the progression of events that tragic night and how he walked Parsons to the Desplaines viaduct and gave him 5 dollars to get out of town.[34]

Detectives only began to focus on Schnaubelt as the leading suspect for the bomb thrower when they learned that he had shaved his beard the morning after the riot. Of course, since Schnaubelt was nowhere to be found, police could not ask Gilmer to pick him out of a group of other prisoners as they had in the case of Snyder. Instead, Detective James Bonfield and assistant prosecutor Furthmann returned to Michael Schwab's home on the pretext of searching it for weapons. While Bonfield "made a great fuss looking under beds and into closets," Furthmann pretended to be "aimlessly killing time by glancing over Mrs. Schwab's [photo] album." Furthmann found a picture of her brother Rudolph Schnaubelt and noted the photographer's stamp on the back. It took only a visit to the photographer's studio to have a copy made without alerting the Schwabs and Schnaubelt that they were closing in on his trail. When shown the picture, Gilmer identified Schnaubelt as the man he saw throw the bomb.[35]

Balthazar Rau, a young anarchist who made his living by selling advertising spaces for the *Arbeiter Zeitung* and other publications of the Socialistic Publishing

Company, was picked up by the police the day after the bombing. At first, police did not consider Rau much of a danger or a suspect, perhaps because he had a reputation as a "masher" who was more interested in chasing women than politics, a charge made believable by his neatly trimmed blond mustache and imperial beard setting off his handsome blue eyes, and so they promptly let him go. As the chain of informers sketched in the details for the investigators over the next three weeks, police realized it was Rau who Spies sent to find Parsons once the Haymarket meeting began and his name was added to the dwindling list of bomb throwing suspects. News of the increasing police interest in his actions that night trickled back to him and on May 25 Rau fled and sheltered among a colony of socialists in Omaha, until Detective John Bonfield and assistant state attorney Edmund Furthmann traveled to Nebraska to retrieve him.[36]

Back in Chicago, Rau confirmed much of what investigators had already uncovered. He reportedly told investigators that he had gone with Spies, Schwab, Neebe, Engel, Schnaubelt, and one other man he couldn't identify out to the wilds of Sheffield, Indiana, where they experimented with the round "czar" bombs. Rau said Engel and Schnaubelt were the ones who set off the explosives. He said that he found out what the code word "Ruhe" meant from the socialist militia leader August Belz, and it was Belz who told him that the word applied to a meeting at the Haymarket and "if it appeared in the *Arbeiter-Zeitung* . . . then there would be trouble . . . fighting with the police." When Rau asked Spies about the code word's appearing in the paper, Spies told him that it was all Fischer's doing and that he had tried to send out word to the armed groups that the word was printed in error and they should stand down.

Along with searching the homes, halls, and businesses of the anarchist movement, police detained or arrested dozens of known and suspected anarchists in order to squeeze them for information and leads in the case. In some cases, police lodged charges against the men they pulled in. James Dajnek, a distributor of the *Arbeiter Zeitung* was arrested on the morning of May 8 on suspicion of firing at a police wagon during one of the riots. Police also claimed to have confiscated two pistols found in his pockets. James' brother Henry and a man named Novak, identified as a locksmith, were picked up and jailed as well.[37] In most cases, the police quickly released the suspects they detained. On the evening of Thursday, May 6, Lieutenant Quinn arrested George Engel at his toy shop on Milwaukee avenue. The phlegmatic and doctrinaire Engel was born in Cassel, Germany, in 1836 and was the son of a brickmaker, who died while he was still an infant. Orphaned at age 12, Engel was placed in a foster home until he reached his fourteenth birthday, when the city stopped paying for his care and he was turned out to wander until he found a painter who apprenticed him. In his twenties, Engel followed the customary path of poor young tradesmen and wandered around Central Europe seeking jobs. He married in 1868 in the city of Rehna and five years later emigrated to Philadelphia with his wife and toddler, George, Jr. Work in America seemed plentiful and wages were good at first, but sickness laid him up for a year and threw his family onto the charity of the German Aid Society. As soon as he was well, Engel moved his family to Chicago, where he found a job at a wagon factory and was introduced to socialism. In 1876 the enterprising socialist opened a toy store on Milwaukee avenue, the main artery of the German district, and as he put it, "as a storekeeper I had more time which I could devote to reading." Engel soon earned a reputation as an adroit debater and an uncompromising radical and though his neighbors shunned him, he plowed ahead, preaching the gospel of anarchism to all who would listen and many who didn't wish to.[38]

Somehow, police had been tipped off that Engel had recently purchased dozens of revolvers from a downtown gun dealer. However, a search of Engel's home and shop failed to turn up any firearms and later that night Engel was released.[39]

From interviews with all their captives, the police began to narrow down their list of high-value suspects. One name, Louis Lingg, continually cropped up in interviews, and police resolved to take him in.

On Friday morning, May 7, five policemen arrived at the small two-story frame house on the north side (442 Sedgwick street) where Lingg rented a room from a carpenter, William Seliger. All the doors and windows were locked. Lacking a warrant didn't deter them from forcing the front door with their shoulders and going in. In Lingg's room they collected a few tools: a chisel, a ladle, a porcelain-lined cup with a heavy soldered bottom, and a hammer. In a steamer trunk marked with the initials "L.L." they found a loaded Remington rifle, a stack of pamphlets and letters, a small bit of fuse, and, down toward the bottom in a grey sock, a round lead bomb. Under the bed was a bucket with what looked like sawdust but was later declared to be dynamite. In a tin lunch box were four pipe bombs, two loaded. They also found some long bolts in a wash stand that was missing its basin—bolts that were of the same dimension as one found among the bomb debris in Desplaines street. In the closet they found two more loaded pipe bombs, another loaded spherical bomb, two empty pipes along with some solder, and some unused sheets of lead, what the police described as "babbit metal."[40]

Later that day, detectives found William Seliger at work at a planing mill and took him in for questioning. Investigators confronted him with the extensive explosive cache taken from his house and pressured him by threatening to arrest his wife. Seliger caved and implicated a number of others who had assisted him and Lingg in making bombs. From Seliger, investigators confirmed that Lingg was the bomb maker and in addition to him gathered leads on half a dozen others who Seliger fingered as being at the center of a revolutionary conspiracy.[41]

While Seliger was being detained and questioned, a fellow carpenter and friend of his, John Thielen, arrived at the East Chicago avenue station house and inquired as to why his friend was being held. Rather than giving him an answer, police hauled him to a cell and sent a pair of officers to his home where they questioned his wife and took his 15-year-old son into custody. Later, the son showed detectives where two pipe bombs, two cigar boxes of dynamite, and two boxes of gun cartridges were buried beneath the house. Both the elder and the junior Thielens confirmed key parts of Seliger's story, and Lingg became the most wanted man in Chicago.[42]

It took a week after arresting Seliger for detectives Jacob Lowenstein and Herman Schuettler to finally locate Lingg's hideout in the southwest side of the city. Lowenstein and Schuettler staked out 80 Ambrose street, a cottage that stood just a couple of blocks north from that spot on Blue Island avenue where the McCormick riot had begun on May 3. Undercover and posing as the anarchist Franz Lorenz, Schuettler knocked at the door and a Mrs. Klein answered. He told her his name was Lorenz and he was looking for Lingg. Klein showed Schuettler into the kitchen, where he saw Lingg, but momentarily mistaking him for the owner of the house asked, "How do you do Mr. Klein?" Lingg wheeled and pulled a revolver. Schuettler grabbed the gun before Lingg cocked it and the two tumbled to the floor. Lowenstein was outside when he heard the unmistakable crash and thud of a violent struggle and kicked in the backdoor. When he burst in he saw Lingg on Schuettler's back, Lingg's thumb clamped in the cop's mouth, both men gripping the pistol. Lowenstein smacked Lingg in the ear with his baton, which failed to stun him, and grabbed hold of Lingg's sleeve, which tore away. He then found a grip around Lingg's throat and pinned him against a wall. According to Schuettler, the only thing Lingg said to him while he fastened the "comealongs" onto his wrists was "You can shoot . . . Shoot . . . Kill me."[43]

Two weeks after being arrested Lingg still wore the ragged clothes he had been captured in. A reporter who visited the jail noted that one of Lingg's sleeves was torn away at the elbow. The reporter was fascinated to see that Lingg had decorated his eight-by-eight-foot cell with drawings he smudged on the whitewashed walls with charcoal. Most of his pictures depicted "men armed to the teeth putting to flight other men who may or may not be meant for policemen." Around these scenes Lingg wrote mottoes that this reporter translated from the German as "Long Live the Revolution" and "If the law catches (or has caught) me I shall have to suffer."[44]

Louis Lingg was born in Mannheim and was the son of a lumber shover. His mother wanted him to learn an office trade but Louis insisted on becoming a carpenter and entered the workshop at the age of five. When Louis was ten years old his father fell through the frozen Neckar River while attempting to retrieve an errant log. Although dragged from the icy waters by his fellow workers, Lingg's father never recovered his vigor, prompting his boss of 12 years to lay him off, "cast aside like a worn-out tool" in Louis' words, and driving his family into desperate poverty. The broken man held a government job for a time before declining into dementia and dying as Louis reached the age of 13.

Lingg completed his apprenticeship at the usual age of 18 in 1882 and struck out on his own as a journeyman, wandering through Alsace, southern Germany, and Switzerland. In spite of Germany's strict antisocialist laws, Lingg joined the remnants of Lassalle's General Association of German Workingmen and enjoyed the hospitality of socialist "eating societies." Lingg's first act of political resistance was to dodge the Kaiser's draft, and he suddenly was a hunted man, running from town to town one step ahead of the Swiss police who were eager to deport him. Along the way he helped found a socialist club in Aargau and struck up a friendship with August Reinsdorf, the most uncompromising German revolutionist of his age. Reinsdorf was an apostle of the "propaganda of the deed," the idea that revolutionaries need not wait and patiently build up their forces until they could mount an insurrection, but that individuals could rip the liberal mask from the brutal face of the state and demonstrate to working class people the inherent power they possessed by engaging in spectacular acts of violence.

In the summer of 1885, with money given to him by a stepfather he barely knew, Lingg embarked at Harve, France, for America. Landing in New York but making his way directly to Chicago, a city well known for having the largest German community in America, Lingg had little difficulty finding a job. In the burgeoning city, one of whose biggest industries was the manufacture of wood products, skilled carpenters were in great demand. Working first as a house carpenter, Lingg immediately joined the carpenters' union and through his union contacts secured a succession of factory jobs. When the wood working trade slowed, as it did each year after the lakes and rivers froze, Lingg devoted his time to radicalizing his union. As Lingg confessed in his memoirs, "I had long since [had] ... the opinion that in the present state of society the working classes could make no gain in the direction of improving their condition by means and ways of Trade Union, but, nevertheless, I participated in the organization of the latter, because I knew that the working men from their past and coming experiences and disappointments would become revolutionists... I held the opinion that the forces by which the workers are kept in subjugation must be retaliated by force..."[45]

Lingg's fervor and commitment earned him the trust of his union brethren, who appointed him delegate to the radical Central Labor Union and the union's official organizer. Lingg became an active member of a secret military wing of the union that armed and drilled and prepared for clashes with the police. Soon Lingg's revolutionary organizing extended beyond his own trade. When workers went on strike at the vast McCormick Reaper Works in March 1886 and the throng at the front gates clashed with police, Lingg was one of the men arrested and released. Apparently, by this time, Louis Lingg had emerged as an important radical organizer in the southwest district of the city who focused his attention on both the workers at the McCormick factory and those who labored in the surrounding lumber yards.[46] When Lingg was arrested two months later for his part in the bombing, he had lived in America for less than a year, was just 22 years of age, had no family closer than Germany, and spoke only a few words of English. Yet, in spite of his youth, his loneliness, and his inexperience with the ways of his host country, throughout the long and arduous trial he was the most defiant and unbending of the accused.

Besides the bombs taken from Lingg's apartment and the shells seized from the *Arbeiter Zeitung* office, a dozen bombs were discovered in four locations around the city. Harry Wilkinson, a reporter for the *Chicago Daily News*, came to the police and surrendered a bombshell he said had been given to him as a present by anarchist leader August Spies months earlier. Gustav Lehman, who turned on his friends and became a key witness at the trial, led Officer Michael Hoffman to the corner of Clyde and Clybourne streets and showed him where he had stashed a little arsenal of bombs under a sidewalk: three round "czar" bombs, one of which was loaded, two coils of fuse, a tin can stuffed with dynamite, and a box of blasting caps.[47] More bombs were found under an elevated wooden sidewalk by children playing in front of fireman George Miller's house on Siegel street.[48] After the city repaved Paulina street in front of his house, Frederick Drews was forced to tear up his old sidewalk and install a new one. Under the old timbers he found four oil cans (four inches in diameter and six high, closed at the top with screws and fuses) that he turned over to the police, who determined that they were incendiary devices made according to plans detailed in the anarchist instruction manual, *The Science of Revolutionary Warfare*, by Johann Most.[49] Just a few blocks from Wicker Park, where the anarchist militias were supposed to muster when the revolution began, police discovered a cache of 30 pipe bombs, all loaded and fused, three coils of extra fuse, and two boxes of blasting caps, wrapped in an oil cloth and hidden under an elevated sidewalk.[50] While not all of these bombs could be connected to the anarchists on trial, some were linked to Lingg through the testimony of his friends and associates, though none quite as firmly as the one found in his sock.[51]

Police took a couple of these bombs to the Michigan lakefront and exploded them to document their power. The rest were analyzed in what was a novel attempt to use scientific techniques to link the bomb maker with his bomb. Walter S. Haines, professor of chemistry at the Rush Medical College, and Mark Delafontaine, a chemistry teacher at West Division High School, were called upon by the prosecution to perform a chemical examination of these unexploded bombshells and bomb fragments.

At the time, Haines and Delafontaine were probably the two most renowned and capable chemists in the city. Haines was a graduate of the Chicago Medical College and was such a promising student that he was offered his mentor's chair soon after his graduation. Haines devoted much of his career to finding new ways to apply chemistry to legal proceedings and coauthored the first and leading textbook on forensic toxicology. He developed the standard test for sugar in urine and was late in his life consulted on the drafting of the authoritative reference work *Pharmacopeia*. Delafontaine held the less prestigious post of professor of chemistry at Chicago's West Division High School, but was nonetheless respected as an active researcher and a member of the Chicago Academy of Sciences, his reputation established by his extensive comparisons of the chemical composition of the city's well and lake water.[52]

The "wet" chemical techniques of 1886 were simple but effective in determining the elemental ingredients of these samples. Haines and Delafontaine—using solvents, Bunsen burners, and filter papers—were able to determine the metallic composition of the recovered bomb casings and found them to contain elements not usually found in commercially available products. (This was possible because the bomb maker apparently made his bombs by melting lead and other soft metals together in a home-made furnace and casting his own bomb casings in clay molds.) They were able to determine the percentages of tin in each sample, but not the percentages of the other trace elements they detected. As Haines admitted on the witness stand, "I didn't separate the antimony . . . and didn't make an accurate determination of it. The precise quantity of antimony and tin is very difficult to determine where it is present in a small amount."[53]

The chemists then assayed shrapnel fragments removed from two of the victims of the bombing: Officer Mathias Degan, who died at the scene, and Officer Lawrence

Table 1.1   Prof. Haines and Delafontaine's 1886 chemical analysis of evidence

Source	Tin	Antimony	Zinc	Iron	Copper
Lingg bomb #1	1.9	trace	trace		
Lingg bomb #2	7	trace +	trace +		trace
Lingg bomb #3	2.4	trace	trace		
Lingg bomb #4	2.5	trace	trace		
Murphy fragment	1.6	trace	trace	trace	
Degan fragment	1.6–1.7	trace	trace	trace	
Spies bomb	1.1	trace	trace	trace	
Old lead pipe "wiped" with much solder	0.7	not examined	not examined	not examined	not examined
Commercial lead	0	trace			
Commercial solder	30–50	trace			

Note: Testimony of Mark Delafontaine, HADC, Vol. K, pp. 676–679; Testimony of Walter S. Haines, HADC, Vol. K, pp. 664–674.

Murphy, who recovered from his wounds.[54] These fragments were found to be very similar in composition, both having about 1.7 percent tin and trace amounts of antimony, zinc, and iron (see table 1.1). Though the results did not precisely match those of the unexploded bombs, they were close enough for the prosecution to establish that the bomb thrown on the night of May 4 was made by similar methods and according to a similar recipe as the ones found in Lingg's apartment.

The prosecution's contention that these samples were connected was largely based on the assertion (an assertion that the defense did not challenge) that no commercially available compound of lead contained an amount of tin comparable to that found in the bomb casings or the bomb fragments. Commercially available lead, Dr. Haines observed, contained no tin, while lead solders were a compound of at least 30 percent tin. This claim seems plausible as, even today, raw "pig lead" contains less than two-one thousandths of a percent of tin, antimony, and arsenic combined, a level probably undetectable in 1886.[55] Rather than melting down bars of common lead, the Haymarket bomb maker must have combined pieces of lead, solder, or other lead alloys in his crucible. Moreover, he must have been fairly consistent in his methods and recipe if, with one exception, his proportions of tin varied by less than 1 percent.

There is no reason to doubt the integrity of Haines and Delafontaine's analysis. Indeed, many of these same artifacts were reanalyzed using modern methods in 2003 and the results were in the same range as Haines and Delafontaine's original figures.

The results clearly connected Lingg to the Haymarket bombing. But what was his role? It is possible that Louis Lingg threw a bomb that he himself had made. But several witnesses testified that Lingg was miles away from the Haymarket Square when the bomb exploded, and no one ever alleged that he was present. Therefore, if the bomb maker and the bomb thrower were not the same individual, it must be that the bomb that landed at Mathias Degan's feet was the result of a conspiracy involving at least two men.[56]

Gradually, by a process of detaining or arresting a succession of suspects, detectives pieced together the broad outlines of what appeared to be the conspiracy behind the

Haymarket meeting and bombing. Suspects were coaxed and cajoled into turning informants, and the beatings and tortures that would come to be associated with the "third degree" in the early twentieth century appear not to have been employed in this case. An anarchist, John A. Henry, who was locked up for nearly three days had nothing but warm words for his jailors and interrogators. "I was buried in a 6×9 enclosure of brick and iron, relieved only by an occasional word with the keepers who were very clever men and have my best feelings." Henry complained that reporters had described him as being "hustled" out of the courtroom by police and described the officer who escorted him, Lieutenant George Hubbard, as a "gentleman" (unlike "some of the police force of this city who would be honored by kinship with savages") in whose company there was "no danger of my being hustled." But, Henry's compliments aside, there were two documented cases of police abuse. The first was actually an incident in which a police officer restrained a superior officer from physically abusing a prisoner during interrogation. Detective James Bonfield admitted under oath that Police Chief Ebersold became so angry during his questioning of Spies and Fielden that he had to "get between" him and the prisoners. Though Bonfield's German was sketchy, he knew enough to know that Ebersold was cursing at the anarchists, using words that "compared a man to a dog, or something low." The second came up during the trial when William Seliger denied that he had been hit while in custody but said, "when I was arrested one of the policemen pulled me a little on my beard."[57]

Investigators gave cooperative informants small sums of money, though none as large as what most Chicagoans of that era would have considered a decent bribe. Gottfried Waller, one of the prosecution's star witnesses, had his rent paid by Captain Michael Schaack during the two months that he was unemployed during the trial. Schaack also paid him and his wife 11 dollars as compensation for days of work he lost while being questioned at the stationhouse. All told, Waller admitted to being given a total of 21.50 dollars for his troubles, a significant sum, but only about what a skilled cabinet maker like Waller normally earned in a couple of weeks. William Seliger, a key witness who admitted to helping Lingg make bombs, was likewise given a total of 6.50 dollars by Schaack for sundry expenses.[58]

During his rambling address to the court before being sentenced, anarchist leader August Spies charged that one witness who could have supported his alibi was paid 500 dollars to leave Chicago and "threatened with direful things if he remained here and appeared as a witness for the defense." A year after the trial, Ernst Legner sued the *Arbeiter Zeitung* for libeling him when it repeated Spies' charges that he had accepted a bribe from prosecutors of 500 dollars to leave Chicago during the trial. Legner took the stand and testified that he did not leave Chicago until the end of July and left to find work, going first to Kansas City, then to Aurora, Nebraska, finally finding a job as a bridge builder in Lincoln, Nebraska. He said that before leaving he had asked August Spies' brothers, Henry and Chris, whether he would be needed as a witness and they had told him that his testimony was not that important and he could go.[59]

Certainly, the threat of prosecution was the most effective prod to cooperation, but it also appears that some important informants may have been turned by appeals to their responsibilities to the German-American community. Just a few days prior to the commencement of trial prosecutor Grinnell organized an extraordinary meeting of the most valuable informants at Folz's Hall, a well-known meeting place for socialists nestled in the heart of the Bavarian district at the corner of Larrabee and North streets. Gathered with a dozen of the nervous informants in a little cluster in the large empty hall were the prosecutor and his chief investigator, Edward Furthmann; Captain Schaack with two of his most trusted German police officers; and some "prominent" Germans, including Adolph Schoeninger, owner of the Western Toy Company, and Louis Nettlehorst, president of the Chicago Turners and renowned as the member of the school board who introduced physical education into the Chicago public school curriculum.

Schoeninger, a wealthy and powerful businessman, certainly was in a position to hold out financial inducements for the men to sing. But according to one of the anarchists there, this was not the purpose of the meeting. One of the anarchists—Abraham Hermann—complained that someone had leaked news of his secret grand jury indictment to the newspapers and he had lost his job because of it. Schoeninger invited Hermann to come to his factory and promised to find a place for him. Hermann was the only man who said that he was without work and the only one extended such an offer. Ultimately, Hermann did not testify at the trial.

Rather than to attempt to bribe them, according to the testimony of Gottfried Waller, the officials and "prominent" men tried to appeal to their Germanic heritage and to their consciences. Schoeninger opened the meeting by scolding the anarchists, telling them that the Haymarket bombing had been a disgrace to the German nationality. Lecturing on, the manufacturer insisted that they could have gotten "further without such means, without the shedding of blood" as he and other manufacturers were themselves "in favor of the eight hour day . . . " Schoeninger continued, "it was now time in this free country for the laboring man, if he had any rights, to get them by agitation, legitimate agitation and proper legislation" and not by "bloodshed and riot." Then came his offer: "if you told the truth, the whole truth and nothing but the truth, . . . the police of the town would see that your person was safe, and that you would be fairly dealt by with the State." Grinnell too pointedly reminded the men that they were all indicted for conspiracy and urged them all to "tell the truth . . . " Such appeals must have worked at some level as two of the prosecution's star witnesses, Gottfried Waller and Gustav Lehman, sat through this meeting.[60]

Prosecutors and police were only one tine of the vise squeezing potential witnesses. There are numerous indications that anarchists and even their lawyers worked assiduously to suppress damaging testimony. Gottfried Waller admitted that he was pressured to attend a secret meeting of defense witnesses that was to take place at Lincoln Park to discuss what they would say during the trial "so as not to have the answer wrong." That there was a concerted effort on the part of supporters of the accused anarchists to intimidate and silence witnesses appears to be at least partially confirmed in the pages of the weekly anarchist paper *Der Fackel*. Buried in the last page of the first issue to appear after the bombing, are two lists of names. The first list was described as a list of informers, those who "swore proof against our incarcerated comrades." The second was a list of the names of the members of the grand jury that would investigate the crime.[61]

A couple of days after William Seliger was released from jail, he was called upon by the anarchists' attorney Sigmund Zeisler. It is not known what the two discussed, but soon afterward Seliger left his home and went into hiding for two weeks at a friend's house, later admitting that he did so out of "fear of revenge by the workingmen—the socialists." Seliger feared enough that he wrote a letter claiming that everything he told the police was made up (so that he wouldn't be prosecuted himself) and sent it to Zeisler's office. Later, under cross-examination by the defense, Seliger explained that "I wrote it because I believed that I was not safe at liberty. I had been told at various times that I was a traitor." No copy of this letter exists as defense lawyers who introduced it at the trial as proof of Seliger's duplicity, quickly retrieved it from the evidence hopper and refused to share it with reporters after Seliger's testimony transformed it from evidence of his unreliability into evidence of his intimidation.[62]

Another anarchist captured during the first week of the investigation was so afraid of the reprisals of his former associates that he offered to point out to investigators the homes and haunts of leading anarchists only if he were heavily disguised. According to the account of the lead detective in the case, the informant, a young butcher named Julius Oppenheimer, who went by the alias Julius Frey, was dressed up "as a darkey" before riding sandwiched between detectives Schuettler and Loewenstein through the northwest district neighborhoods. Police plans nearly met with disaster, however, when Oppenheimer's presence, whether as a suspected informer or merely a black man, nearly provoked a riot and the trio were forced to make a galloping retreat.[63]

In the end, pressure from investigators and prosecutors overcame the solidarity among the anarchists or the threats of those in the movement and at least two dozen insiders revealed incriminating details about the plans and activities of anarchists in the days and hours leading up to the throwing of the bomb. In less than a month investigators had uncovered the details of what appeared to be a broad conspiracy.

Only a small fraction of the informants who spilled their secrets to the police were called to the witness stand and made to swear their revelations into the record. Though it seems that detectives took detailed statements from all the suspects they questioned, these vital records have not survived in their original form. Lacking them, historians have relied entirely on the testimony given in open court to piece together the secret activities of the Chicago anarchists during those violent May days.

Astonishingly, it appears that many of these witness statements were preserved, but have long been overlooked by scholars because they were disregarded as police propaganda. In 1889 the best-selling book to appear about the bombing was published. It was written by the lead investigator of the case, police captain Michael J. Schaack, and it carried the typically hefty Victorian age title of *Anarchy and Anarchists: A History of the Red Terror and the Social Revolution in America and Europe: Communism, Socialism, and Nihilism in Doctrine and Deed: The Chicago Haymarket Conspiracy, And the Detection and Trial of the Conspirators.* Schaack's account is at times sensational—much of it is written in the then popular style of dime novel detective thrillers and is filled with secret rendezvous with disguised informants, undercover detectives fearlessly entering the dens of cutthroat assassins, and even a femme fatale luring a spy to his untimely death. On these grounds and for the simple reason that it is the police version of events, historians have ignored it as a serious source. But when examined closely it can be seen that *Anarchy and Anarchists* is really two books: alongside the detective murder mystery is a serious chronicle of the police department's investigation. Schaack indicates this in his prologue: "I have drawn upon the records of the case, made in court, but more especially upon the reports made to me, during the progress of the investigation, by the many detectives who were working under my direction." Throughout his book, Schaack sets off those items that he purports to be letters, notes, shreds of evidence, and witness statements from the rest of the book by printing them in a different typeface. Reproduced in this volume are 24 witness statements and a dozen other pieces of evidence not submitted at trial and not part of the official record.[64]

Of course, it is entirely possible that these statements were forged or altered to shine the most favorable light on the vainglorious Captain Schaack. Beyond the facts that there is no evidence showing that such was the case and that no contemporary critics of the prosecution denounced Schaack's book on these grounds, there are two other characteristics of this book that argue against such suspicions. First, all of the witness statements are worded in the cramped and unadorned prose that one would expect to find in a summary prepared for internal rather than public purposes. Some even contain the sort of legalese that must have been drafted by Grinnell's staff lawyers. If they are forgeries, they are good and carefully composed ones.[65]

Second, Schaack did not author this book alone and his collaborators seem to have been sympathetic to the cause of labor. Schaack's volume was written with the help of two veteran and highly respected Chicago newspaper men. Thomas O. Thompson was a reporter for the *Inter-Ocean* and the *Chicago Times* and also was Mayor Carter Harrison's private secretary up to the time of his assassination.[66] John T. McEnnis learned the reporter's craft under the tutelage of Joseph Pulitzer at the St. Louis *Post-Dispatch*, then moved to Chicago and wrote for the *Daily News*, the *Chicago Times*, and the *Chicago Mail*. McEnnis was remembered by Theodore Dreiser (whom McEnnis "discovered") as "amazingly intelligent and genial . . . a well- and favorably known newspaperman of the Middle West—truly a brilliant writer whose sole fault, in so far as I could make out, was that he drank too much."[67] A prolific writer, McEnnis, in addition to ghostwriting Schaack's volume, wrote a number of other popular books, including one of the first books on the other famous Chicago murder trial, the Cronin murder case, *The Clan-Na-Gael and the Murder of Dr. Cronin* (1889), and an early exposé of "white slavery," *The White Slaves of Free America, Being an Account of the Suffering, Privations, and Hardships of the Weary Toilers in Our Great Cities* (1888). Clearly, McEnnis was the more experienced and felicitous writer of the pair. Beyond staff reporting, Thomas O. Thompson had only one publication to his name—he penned a party pamphlet for the Democrats, "The Tariff, Its Use and Abuse," in 1884.[68]

Judging by his writings around the time of the Haymarket bombing, John T. McEnnis could be described as a progressive and an advocate of labor reform.

McEnnis wrote one of the earliest histories of labor, *The Story of Manual Labor* (1887), a book whose preface and a chapter entitled "The Army of the Discontented" were written by Terence Powderly, leader of the largest labor federation in America, the Knights of Labor. McEnnis wrote:

> After all it is the advancement of the mass of labor which should be the ideal of every person who attacks this subject.... Ninety per cent of the laboring class will remain laborers all their lives. The loop holes of escape to a condition less arduous are growing narrower and narrower every year. We are forming distinct divisions in America. The laborer's son will be a laborer and so will his grandson... The cunning hand will never be wholly displaced by labor saving machinery. It is for the amelioration of this class that the workingmen's organizations have been formed. These combinations gather up all the strength of the scattered units and their impact on society is so strong that they force us to a line of action which the single workman uncombined with his fellows could never command.[69]

The book's chapter on the Knights of Labor concludes: "If the Knights of Labor were to dissolve tomorrow or the next day a new society would be formed to push on their work. No fair man can object to the ends which they propose. Labor must win and the sooner we all come to a realizing sense of this fact the better will it be for America."[70]

To a surprising extent, the informer statements reprinted in *Anarchy and Anarchists* supported the accounts of the state's witnesses delivered in open court without suspiciously echoing their details. Johannes Gruenberg, a 45-year-old carpenter, was arrested on June 17 and according to Schaack told him that he was a member of the Northwest side group, that he distributed Fischer and Engel's newspaper the *Anarchist*, and that he attended the Greif's Hall basement meeting where the Haymarket rally was planned. Gruenberg later testified to a minor point for the defense, but the manner of his cross-examination by assistant prosecutor George Ingham was clearly guided by some sort of earlier interview with police. In the line of Ingham's questioning can be seen the outlines of the statement he supposedly gave to Captain Schaack. Ingham pointedly asked him whether he was a member of the Northwest side group and whether he had delivered the *Anarchist*; Ingham also inquired about his whereabouts on Monday, when the secret meeting was held. None of these topics came up during Gruenberg's direct examination by the defense counsel and so Ingham must have known what to ask from some other source.[71]

Schaack includes statements from several men who allegedly confessed to him that they had helped Louis Lingg fashion his bombs. William Seliger, Lingg's landlord and fellow revolutionary, confessed in court that on the day of the Haymarket bombing he had assisted Lingg to assemble bombs along with at least two other men, Ernst Hubner and Herman Mutzenberg. Neither Hubner nor Mutzenberg appeared in court but in their statements to Schaack both men admitted to having fabricated bombs in Lingg's apartment with the others. Even their estimates of the numbers of bombs finished that day are similar. Seliger thought the group made between 30 and 50 bombs, though he never counted the exact number. Hubner recalled filling

Table 1.2   Bomb makers' statements

	# of Round Bombs	# of Pipe Bombs	Total
Seliger	Not specified	Not specified	30–50
Hubner	20	15–18	35–38
Mutzenberg	10–18	16	26–34

and bolting together about 20 round bombs and 15–18 pipe bombs. Mutzenberg remembered helping to fill six or eight shells and counted another ten round and 16 pipe bombs. While their precise totals differed, both Hubner and Mutzenberg's estimates of the number of bombs produced that day fall in the range given by Seliger in his official testimony (see table 1.2). Except for this variation in their counts of the total number of bombs produced, all three men's statements corroborate each other.[72]

In nearly all cases, the informant statements contained in *Anarchy and Anarchists* tell the same story as that laid out by the state's witnesses in the anarchists' trial. Their value lies not in revealing some new or hidden aspect of the episode, but in filling in the details that a court proceeding necessarily skips over. Taken together, the testimony of witnesses and the results of Schaack's interrogations paint a fairly complete picture of the decisions and the actions taken by anarchists in the weeks and days leading up to the Haymarket bombing.[73]

In 1937, a year after Henry David published his magisterial work on the bombing and trial, *The History of the Haymarket Affair*, he received a letter from a man in Chicago named John F. Kendrick, whose neighbor was none other than Oscar Neebe, the one man the jury spared from the noose and was pardoned by Governor John P. Altgeld in 1893. Kendrick wrote how around the time of the Great War he spent many evenings with Neebe and how Neebe frequently remarked that "Capt. Mike Schaack's book, after making allowance for the romantic bunk, came nearest of all to telling the truth . . . " According to Kendrick, Neebe was "indignant at the 'defense' literature that made the victims bleating lambs. They were emphatically brave soldiers . . . "[74]

Of course, Neebe, then in the last feeble years of his life—losing his sight, no longer active in the city's radical movements, and being the last survivor of the eight radicals tried for the bombing—could describe things as he wished without fear or concern for the consequences. In the weeks and months immediately after the bombing, however, the truth was much more costly.

CHAPTER 2

PREPARING FOR TRIAL

As HUNDREDS OF SUSPECTS, COCONSPIRATORS, AND MATERIAL WITNESSES were being dragged into police cells and a very busy grand jury churned out scores of indictments, two obscure lawyers took charge of the anarchists' defense. Like most of their clients, Moses Salomon and Sigmund Zeisler were both recent immigrants to America. As partners they had handled most of the legal business arising out of the anarchist movement for several years and advertised their services in the anarchist newspapers. Neither had earned much of a reputation or had much experience. Samuel McConnell, a leading Chicago lawyer, later noted that, "one of them had just been admitted to the bar. Neither had ever tried a criminal case before and neither had a decided personality."[1]

Actually, McConnell was wrong, Salomon had conducted a criminal defense but was unsuccessful. Four years earlier he defended a man who had shot and killed a Chicago cop after a botched burglary. Salomon unsuccessfully appealed for a hearing before the Illinois Supreme Court and was noted in the press not for his lawyerly ability but for his pluck: "however unsuccessful Mr. Salomon may be in this his first murder case, it is a certainty that no lawyer ever made a more earnest fight for a client." Salomon's client was hung without delay on the original date set by the trial judge.[2]

Salomon later earned a reputation as a mercurial presence in the courtroom. Following his most famous case, his legal career was punctuated by embarrassing moments. In 1891 while arguing a motion before Judge Collins, Salomon "became excited and struck Norden [the opposing council] with his fist in the mouth." Salomon was levied a fine of $50, Judge Collins telling him that "were I satisfied that he could afford to pay a heavier fine I would impose it." Salomon was an active member of the Cook County Democratic Club and was appointed to its Committee on Registration just three weeks after the Haymarket bombing. In 1892 his loyalty paid off with his election to the State Senate on the Democratic ticket. During his term Salomon championed a single crusade, the prohibition of department stores. He introduced a bill prohibiting the selling of more than one kind of good in a single establishment. Ultimately, the anti–department store bill passed three committee readings and was sent to the floor, where it was defeated in a 76 to 63 vote.[3]

In 1897, Salomon was accused of stealing funds from an estate whose probate case he handled, though Salomon's case was dismissed on a technicality. A couple of years later he was indicted again for stealing from a client, this time for draining the meager estate of a tailor of all it was worth, $2,200. Salomon was disbarred in 1900 for helping himself to the accounts of his probate clients. Salomon spent his last years living in a room in the Auditorium Hotel and speculating in real estate.[4]

Salomon's partner, Sigmund Zeisler, was 26 years old and had arrived from his native Austria just three years earlier. Zeisler had high academic credentials, having graduated from the University of Vienna and studied law at Northwestern University. At the time, Zeisler was known in the city less for his own accomplishments than as the husband of Fannie Bloomfield, a gifted concert pianist from a prominent Chicago family whom he met in Vienna and married in Chicago the previous year. Fannie was eight years old when she survived the Chicago Fire of 1871 and the story of her playing an abandoned and legless grand piano while the flames lit the sky became legendary. (When asked how she could play when the city was burning, Fannie retorted, "I know Chicago's burning, but this is my practice hour . . . ") For all his impressive education, Zeisler was woefully inexperienced, having been admitted to the bar only months before the Haymarket explosion.[5]

Well before the trial began, one of the anarchists' attorneys revealed a serious lack of understanding of the existing statute and case law that governed his case. On Saturday, May 8, Zeisler told reporters a number of newsworthy things—that he claimed to have "startling evidence" of the way police had "fixed the case" against his clients and that he anticipated asking for a change of venue from Chicago— but the most significant comment he made was probably the least noticed of all the things he said. Though his exact words were not quoted, one reporter summarized his comments this way: Zeisler "expressed himself as confident that the prisoners could never be convicted of murder. If they could, then everybody who had ever taught Socialism and the inventor of dynamite were equally responsible." It is possible that Zeisler did not know that prosecutors were at that moment uncovering evidence that would connect his clients to a specific plot to attack the police on the fourth of May. But he should have been aware that the law provided that if such direct connection were proven, his clients could hang.[6]

It has been often alleged that the anarchists had difficulty obtaining legal counsel in a city embittered and biased against them. Support for this assertion comes from two sources, one unattributed and another that is far removed from the event itself. The first is a short history of the case published in 1891 in the *Magazine of Western History* in which the author, Howard Louis Conard, recounts that all "the lawyers of recognized ability . . . declined to face public sentiment, and refused to appear in the case" except for William P. Black, who took on the case out of "his conscientious regard for the duties of his profession . . . " This was a heroic act on the part of Black toward men "with whom he had no acquaintance, and to whom he was under no obligation . . . "[7] On the fiftieth anniversary of the trial, Sigmund Zeisler recalled that he and his partner, Moses Salomon, attempted to retain Luther Laflin Mills and William S. Forrest, who both declined, he believed, because they "feared the consequences to themselves of undertaking the defense of so unpopular a cause . . ." Only after these rejections, claimed Zeisler, did they finally convince William Perkins Black, the junior partner of a prominent Chicago firm, to reluctantly take the case. "Nothing but a high sense of professional duty could have induced him to come into the case," remembered Zeisler, the last surviving participant in the trial.[8]

While Sigmund Zeisler's distant memory of the events of 1886 was fixed on the difficulty of finding a willing attorney to take up the anarchists' case, it does not seem that any of the anarchists' defenders thought this was going to be a serious problem at the time. While the Cook County grand jury was still considering whom to indict, Dr. Ernest Schmidt organized a meeting to establish a defense committee and raise funds for those held in jail. Zeisler was given the floor and he explained to the 50 or so people present that they had to raise a large fund, because "it was necessary to employ at least two good lawyers of reputation who possessed the respect of the court and the public, and had a larger practice than Salomon and Zeisler."[9] Zeisler went on to explain that it was going to be hard to empanel an impartial jury and that the judges were against them, but he never suggested that finding those "two good lawyers of reputation" might be difficult.

On Tuesday, May 25, two days after this first defense committee meeting, Dr. Schmidt announced that the committee had raised nearly 1,000 dollars, a sufficient sum to retain a prominent lawyer. Rather than being the committee's last resort, Capt. William Black was their first choice. Two days later, Schmidt told a reporter that Black had been retained, but would not say who else was being considered; however, the reporter gathered from the chatter from the defense that "he will be some Eastern lawyer, perhaps Robert G. Ingersoll."[10] Apparently, the prominent Chicago criminal attorney William S. Forrest did in fact agree to take up the case but the defense committee balked at his exorbitant fee. Friday morning, the grand jury filed into Judge John Rogers' courtroom and handed down additional indictments; Zeisler officially announced to the court that Black had been retained by Dr. Schmidt's defense committee and that "we hope to secure the assistance of other attorneys" as well.[11] To assist Black, another litigator who had criminal trial experience, William A. Foster, was hired. Foster was not the ideal choice as he had only recently arrived from Davenport, Iowa, and was unfamiliar with Illinois law and precedent.[12]

After the indictments were issued, the main legal battle was the question of when the trial would begin. Prosecuting attorney Grinnell made it clear from the outset that he wished for a speedy trial and planned on asking the court to begin on the first Monday in June, just two weeks after indictment. Zeisler met with Grinnell to discuss the calendar for the trial and afterward told reporters that he planned on petitioning for more time and the reasons he gave for doing so bear on the question of the anarchists' ability to recruit star lawyers. Zeisler explained to the reporters that "We are not prepared for trial. We only know unofficially that our clients have been indicted. I don't like this idea of rushing the cases. The public mind is inflamed just now. We had better wait until public passion shall subside. We want time to prepare our case. We have not been able to get at our witnesses, as many of them have been locked up in the police station."[13] Several times over the next several days, Zeisler was asked about plans for an early trial date and he complained that he and his cocounsels had not seen all of the indictments and could not map out their strategy for the defense until they did.[14]

Grinnell's original plans to begin the trial early floundered as the grand jury took longer than expected to complete and sign all the indictments, as one of his key witnesses, William Seliger, fled and had to be dragged back to Chicago by Detective Bonfield and as the defense successfully appealed for a change of venue out of Judge Rogers' court on the grounds that his charge to the grand jury had been biased. Grinnell relented and petitioned that the trial begin no later than June 21 as this would give the defense enough time to prepare and give the court a chance to conclude its business before the summer's heat became too oppressive. Contrary to conventional accounts of the trial, Judge Joseph E. Gary did not reject Black's concerns out of hand, but took them into account when he noted that the process of jury selection would likely take weeks, thus allowing additional time for the defense to prepare before any testimony would be heard. In any event, just a few days later, when the trial opened, defense counsel Foster told Judge Gary that the defense now wished for a "speedy trial," abandoning its delaying tactics altogether.[15]

It is remarkable that over the course of nearly two weeks when the primary goal of the defense was to delay the beginning of the trial, neither Zeisler or Black ever argued that the trial should be postponed because they were having difficulty securing legal representation for their clients. Never once in that time did they suggest to reporters that the more august members of the Chicago bar were reluctant to represent their clients. Certainly, had they made the case that the preparation of their defense was hampered by their inability to persuade biased or fearful lawyers to take up their case, this would have strengthened their motion and provided further grounds for appeal. The fact that the defense did not pursue this argument indicates that perhaps Zeisler's later and distant memories of these events were colored and shaped by the tragic conclusion of the case.

In fact, the record of the case shows that not all lawyers were so reluctant to take up the case and that the defense did not face so much difficulty in getting prominent attorneys to take up the case as it had difficulty in finding lawyers that it felt were sufficiently sympathetic to the politics of the accused. On May 8, Adolph Fischer, Gerhardt Lizius, and Lizzie Holmes appeared at a habeas corpus hearing before Judge Rogers. Salomon and Zeisler were present to defend their motion but alongside them was the highly regarded Chicago attorney Kate Kane, who had been retained separately by Holmes. Kane was then on her way to a legendary legal career. Educated at the University of Michigan and admitted to the Wisconsin bar at the age of 25, she had established a practice in Milwaukee where she had displayed her ferocity in defending her place in a very chauvinistic profession by dousing a judge who was dismissive of her gender with her water glass and then defending herself on his contempt charge. Kane relocated to Chicago in 1883 and was quickly admitted to the Illinois bar, specializing in criminal law. By 1890 she boasted that she had "prosecuted or

defended every crime known to modern times except treason and piracy." Though
Kane was not asked to assist the defense of the men accused of murder, she took an
interest in the trial and attended some of its sessions. Toward the end of the trial Kane
arrived early to find that a row of choice seats had been roped off and reserved for
female friends of the judge. Kane took one of these seats and was arguing with a bailiff
who was attempting to coax her out of it when Judge Gary entered the courtroom.
She shouted, "This court is free and one woman's as good as another!" and Gary
waved the bailiff off, replying patronizingly, "There, there. That'll do. Of course,
she is."[16]

Another group of men who were arrested on suspicion of involvement in the
Haymarket bombing also had little difficulty securing legal representation. Frank
Schmidt, Christoph Bartell, and Frederick Bendrine were rousted from their beds
over Florus' saloon by Captain Ward and a detachment of over two dozen cops and
then arrested when "papers bearing upon the riots" were found in their pockets.
A short time later their lawyer C.W. Dwight demanded to see them at the Desplaines
street station and then filed a writ of habeas corpus for their release. Another lawyer,
John C. King, successfully argued for the men's release but once they had left the
courtroom they were rearrested. King rushed back to Judge Collin's courtroom and
told his honor what had just happened, and Collins immediately ordered Police Chief
Ebersold and Captain Ward to appear before him. Calling them to a private meeting
in his chambers, reporters could hear the judge giving them a "heated colloquy,"
and then returning to the bench, the judge ordered the men released and reminded
the officers that the fine for arresting someone on a charge they had been acquitted
of was 500 dollars. Judge Collins then told attorney King that if he could establish
exactly who had spitefully ordered the men's second arrest, he would deal with him
harshly.[17]

Early on in the legal proceedings, there was another Chicago lawyer involved with
the case, W.H. Buettner, who over a number of days filed some pleas and motions
regarding bail for some of the accused.[18] On May 12, the *Tribune* reported that
Buettner had been retained as the counsel for both Spies brothers, Samuel Fielden,
and Michael Schwab, and that Buettner was in the process of securing a second attorney from Chicago and another from out of town.[19] Apparently, personal differences
between Buettner and Salomon led to Buettner's ouster from the defense team—the
Tribune reported that "Salomon and Buettner are at outs, each declaring that he will
not try the case if he has the other for assistant," and a short time later, Salomon
remained and no more was heard of Buettner.[20]

William Perkins Black, the chief counsel recruited to the defense, has generally
been portrayed as a reluctant lawyer who accepted the anarchists' brief out of his sense
of duty and professionalism.[21] In fact, Black appears to have been less the reluctant
third choice he is made out to be than a man selected more for his ideological affinity
with the accused.[22]

At the time he received his retainer, Black was a successful 44-year-old partner
in a firm, Dent and Black, that handled many lucrative corporate cases. He was
a charter member of the Chicago Bar Association and a man who by all outward

appearances was a stolid representative of Chicago's elite; in fact, his sprawling Victorian mansion was located in an exclusive upscale development just a few doors down from prosecutor Grinnell's residence.[23]

Black was accustomed to wealth and privilege: though he was born to a Kentucky minister, his mother married well after his father died when he was a young boy. His stepfather, Dr. William Fithian, was a successful physician, judge, Illinois state legislator, and land speculator who, when he died at the age of 91 in 1890, was hailed as the "oldest and richest citizen of the great county of Vermillion."[24] Though interested in pursuing the ministry himself, Black's studies at college were interrupted by the Civil War; he and his older brother John survived heroic tours of duty, William being decorated with the Congressional Medal of Honor. After Appomattox, Black moved to Chicago, took up the study of law, married, voted for Grant, and settled into what promised to be an entirely conventional and conservative legal career.

Such was not to be, as his youthful religious idealism and his open mind combined to lead him in an unconventional direction. By 1872, he had embraced Horace Greeley and the Liberal movement. Soon after, he apparently left his well-heeled congregation and began preaching to the downtrodden at the "Railroad Chapel," located downtown at State and Fourteenth streets. Black's range of humanitarian concerns seemed to expand steadily over time in a typically Yankee reformer fashion: in 1876 he gave a speech at the annual meeting of the Illinois Women's Suffrage Association, in 1877 he became a founder of the Citizen's League for Suppression of the Sale of Liquors to Minors, in 1880 he helped found a "Home for Incurables," and in 1882 he became a director of the Chicago Humane Society, a lifelong vegetarian, and spoke movingly at a meeting commemorating the death of the great Italian republican Giuseppe Garibaldi.[25]

Black turned his back on his old religious associations, quitting his church and the YMCA, began writing for the free-thought newspaper published in Chicago *The Alliance*, and took an interest in class issues. Near Christmas of 1881, he prepared a speech to be given at the Philosophical Society of Chicago entitled "Socialism as a Factor in American Society and Politics." He thought so much of the topic, he reread his speech before the Industrial Reform Club the following spring.[26] Black's next public oration was entitled "Russia and Nihilism" (Nihilism being another name for anarchism at the time), which Benjamin Tucker, editor of the journal of individual anarchism *Liberty*, reprinted as a pamphlet and advertised in the back pages of his magazine along with works by a panoply of anarchist authors, including Pierre-Joseph Proudhon, John Ruskin, William B. Greene, and Stephen Pearl Andrews.[27]

Black's reformism brought him into contact with some of the more radical elements in Chicago. He apparently became a member of the Chicago Liberal League in the summer of 1882 and gave some public lectures on its platform, though he bowed out of his scheduled lecture on Thomas Paine in January 1883 at the last minute for reasons he never disclosed. Chicago's Liberal League was a free-thought organization founded by what the *Chicago Tribune* described as an assemblage of "Socialists, skeptics, and labor agitators." Liberals shared space with anarchists and held their gatherings at No. 54 West Lake street, the meeting place of Chicago's anarchist Central Labor Union.[28] In addition to Black, other leading members of the Chicago Liberal League included anarchists William Holmes and Lizzie Swank (Lizzie Holmes after they married), as well as defendant Samuel Fielden.[29]

How far Black had traveled toward a radical position was revealed in the fall of 1882 when he threw his hat into the political arena for the first time, running for Congress on the ticket of the Anti-Monopoly Party. It was an advantageous time to be an independent political candidate. Reform-minded "sorehead" Mugwump Republicans bolted their party in protest of its corruption, while Democrats, weak in all areas of the city but holding the mayor's office, could not agree on a candidate of their own. After announcing that he would stand for election on the ticket of the miniscule "Anti-Monopoly Party," Black's candidacy was seized upon by a faction of the regular Democrats who saw that he had the potential of widening the breach in Republican ranks. As a result, over the course of the month leading up to the election, Black had the unusual opportunity of delivering acceptance speeches before three different political conventions.

The remarks Black made in the run-up to the November election provide an interesting snapshot of his views and political philosophy just a few years before he led the legal defense of the anarchists. The image that emerges is that of a maturing individualist anarchist with a clear sympathy for socialist proposals.

Black's individualism was foremost. Speaking before the regular Democrats, Black had few good things to say about the Democratic Party, praising only its devotion to individual liberties: "One of the best features of the . . . party was its bold and dignified stand against sumptuary laws [code in those days for prohibition] and against the sacrifice of personal liberty to the caprice of the majority." A few days later, speaking before the "kickers and bolters" of the Republican Party, Black found the same virtue in that party's history, praising the Republican's "old-time doctrine of individual liberty and individual responsibility . . ."[30]

After collecting these nominations, Black appeared before his chosen party, the tiny Anti-Monopoly Party, whose convention was described as consisting of two or three dozen curious boys, an equal number of men, and three or four women, but which was led by a fellow member of the Liberal League, J.K. Maggie. But in spite of its insignificant numbers, this was where Black felt most at home, explaining in his longest speech detailed views of the party's main planks. Here, his socialistic tendencies were clear. He was, he said, "in accord" with "the demand for National control of railroads and telegraphs," though he did not believe this should be achieved through a total nationalization of property, but might be accomplished by nationalizing just enough of the lines to bring down shipping rates and breaking up the monopolistic pooling agreements that kept prices high. Black advocated abolishing all state and national banks and creating in their place one central national bank that would issue all currency, including paper money. He was willing to consider the nationalization of land, but was against its outright confiscation.

On labor issues, Black was solid. He was in favor of federal protective laws to keep women and children from "starvation and shame." In his only emotional appeal, Black said that with "all my heart" he was behind the party's principle that "labor ought to receive a greater proportion of the profits derived from it." While a measure short of a full embrace of the labor theory of value, Black's idea was a large step toward it.[31]

With the conventions behind him, Black began his campaign, but chose an unusual and revealing venue for his first campaign appearance. The day after receiving the Anti-Monopoly Party's nomination, Black traveled to the heart of the immigrant west side, to the Aurora Turner Hall, an institution closely identified with the more radical elements of the German community. Reading through the prejudices of the *Tribune*'s reporter, it is clear that at the Aurora Hall, Black faced a sort of working class audience he had not had much contact with before. The place, according to one biased reporter, was filled with the "unwashed rabble," "air redolent with smoke," and "low-browed loafers...laughing and jeering..." Clearly determined to win his crowd over, and apparently aware that anarchist beliefs ran high among them, Black gave a lengthy speech in which he stressed his free-thought credentials and announced that he had quit all his former associations with Christianity and organized religion.[32]

The reform circles in which Black orbited increasingly intersected with those of the anarchists in Chicago. When anarchist leader John McAuliffe committed suicide in 1882, 250 of his friends filled the West Twelfth street Turner Hall to eulogize him. McAuliffe, who had been a divisive and fiery radical in life, provided an occasion in death for socialists of all varieties to put aside their differences for one night. Arrayed on stage were nearly all the men elected to office under the banner of the now defunct SLP—Ernest Schmidt, Frank Stauber, Leo Meilbeck, Henry Stahl, Timothy O'Meara. Moderate socialist and trade unionist George Schilling sat on the dais alongside the uncompromising Peter Peterson. Against a backdrop of red flags and a red banner inscribed "Liberty, Equality, and Fraternity, In Memory of John McAuliffe. Equal Rights; Equal Duties," the first speaker stepped forward. It was William P. Black who remembered having met McAuliffe just once but was in that moment impressed with his "honesty and manliness." According to one reporter present that night, Black "said many good words for the Socialists, and thought it was fitting to commemorate the virtues of a fellow worker who believed in the brotherhood of man. There were occasions, he said, when the motto, " 'Peaceably if we can, forcibly if we must,' should be followed out, and it would be one day unless certain evils were remedied..."[33]

In March 1884, a protest meeting was organized at the Aurora Turner Hall to denounce the city's chronic underfunding of its public schools. This event featured not only Spies and Grottkau as the evening's principal speakers, but the crowd also heard from William A. Salter from the Society for Ethical Culture and H.H. Vickers of the Liberal League, organizations Black was affiliated with in these years.[34] Apparently, Black's fame as a radical orator had spread sufficiently that he was invited to speak before the anarchist International Working People's Association in 1885, though it is not clear whether he actually did so. By early 1886 the *Arbeiter Zeitung* referred to Black as "a local professional politician, friend of the workingman, and former plug-hat Socialist who has also been a member of the Socialistic Labor Party..."

Anarchist William Holmes described Black similarly, saying, "The captain is a natural orator, is a deep student of Socialism, and, best of all, had his whole heart in his work."[35,36]

Just a few months before the Haymarket explosion, in January 1886, Black's wife, Hortensia, contributed a lengthy article to Joseph Buchanan's *Labor Enquirer*, a journal that declared itself an organ of the anarchist International Working People's Association. Entitled "Pension Children," Mrs. Black's piece argued for the establishment of a universal system of child and mother pensions modeled on those granted to soldiers. In the course of advocating her modest proposal, Black revealed a deeper streak of radicalism running through her thinking. She observed, "...a government that recognizes the just claim of everything living within its limits to protection...such a government the people demand. Such a government the people will have. Every other form of government the people will overthrow."[37]

Less than one month before the bombing, William P. Black was firmly associated with the city's labor movement. Reporters on the local political beat noted that Black was the leading choice of the woeful Democrats for nomination in the county's upcoming judicial election. In this solidly Republican area—of the six judges whose terms were due to expire, only one was a Democrat—the Democrats had very long odds of winning a seat, their best hope being that the Republicans would fracture and the usually apolitical trade unions would wade into the race. Toward this end it was reported that "a scheme is now being worked to drag in the Knights of Labor in the interest of a certain judicial candidate," a thinly veiled reference to Black and his apparent popularity with the unions.[38]

JOINDER AND SEVERANCE

Even before the trial opened the tactics of the defense lawyers defied the expectations of legal observers. It was widely anticipated that one of the first defense tactics would be to move for separate trials of the seven defendants. The legal reporter for the *Inter-Ocean* wrote a week before the trial opened, "the counsel for the defense will undoubtedly move for separate trials for every one of those indicted..." Feeding this prediction was the different ways in which the defendants were being treated by the prosecution. Though all seven accused men were indicted on similar counts, State's Attorney Grinnell agreed on June 3 to allow Oscar Neebe alone to post bail. Grinnell's exception in Neebe's case cannot be explained by his own circumstances as he was not the only family man—Engel, Fischer, Schwab, and Fielden also had wives and children. Arguably all these family men were less likely to flee than was a single man like Lingg. By granting Neebe his freedom while holding the others in cells, Grinnell conceded that either Neebe was less culpable or the case against him was different from that of the others. Clearly, if Neebe was treated so differently in the issue of his bail, a request to separate his trial from that of the others had a good chance of success.[39]

The start of the trial was three days away when the pundit's predictions were startlingly disproved. Reporters happened to be milling about outside of the state's attorney's offices when a copy of a defense motion for severance was delivered. According to reporters on the scene, State's Attorney Grinnell was puzzled and surprised, one even described him as looking "panicked" when he opened the papers, but within moments, as the full importance of what he was reading dawned on him, Grinnell became jubilant. He wasted no time in passing it around the circle of reporters, clearly feeling this was a terrible concession on the part of the defense that he was glad to splash in the daily papers. The reason was plain. Rather than asking for a separate trial for each of the defendants, the lawyers for the accused had petitioned to divide the seven into two groups. The motion for severance asked only for a separate trial for the group of four: Spies, Schwab, Fielden, and Neebe.[40]

Defense attorneys had numerous options before them. They could have moved for separate trials for all defendants, for groups of defendants, or for any combination of the seven. There was no legal reason why they could not have requested severance into two groups, as they did, and at the same time requested separate trials for individuals as well. Given the different treatment already accorded to Neebe by Grinnell, who allowed him to post bail, it was more likely that a petition to separate his trial from that of the rest would have succeeded. Why was only one severance petition submitted? Why did defense lawyers lump Spies, Schwab, Fielden, and Neebe into the same group?

In dividing the accused into two groups, the defense lawyers conceded an important point. They admitted that there might be evidence that Lingg, Fischer, and Engel were members of a conspiracy hatched at a meeting held on Monday, May 3, the night before the Haymarket bombing. In their petition for severance, they wrote, "Certain evidence of an alleged conspiracy, it is claimed, will be introduced upon the trial of this cause, with which these defendants are in no way connected, and which . . . may be competent as against other defendants, jointly herein indicted . . ." Such evidence, they argued, when presented would "be prejudicial and greatly damaging" to Spies, Fielden, Schwab, and Neebe, who they apparently believed could not be shown to have attended the meeting, and therefore had a right to separate trials.[41]

But why separate them on the basis of who attended the Monday night conspiracy meeting? Wouldn't it have made just as much sense to divide the trial into those who were present at the Haymarket around the time of the riot and those who could be shown to never have attended the Haymarket meeting? Were this done, Spies, Fielden, Fischer, and Schwab would have been in one group, and Neebe, Lingg, and Engel, all of whom had witnesses to prove they were elsewhere in the city at the time of the bombing, in another. Or the defendants could have been divided between those against whom there was evidence that they procured explosives or made bombs, namely, Spies, Lingg, and Engel, and those against whom the state had no such evidence.

The defense tactic of separating the defendants into two groups was portrayed by the daily press as a betrayal—a ploy to sacrifice three men in order to save four others. One reporter caught George Schilling, the Chicago labor leader who had long been closest to the anarchists without joining their ranks and was an organizer of the defense support committee, and drew from him a comment that suggested that there was in fact more culpability in one group than the other:

> *Reporter*: "Don't you think that Spies, Fielden, Schwab, and Neebe are virtually attempting to save themselves by sacrificing the others?"
>
> *Schilling*: "Look here, now, you are probably charging the four men with the deeds of their attorneys. At any rate you can rely upon it that the petition is no mistake, nor a cowardly resort. What if it were true that among those seven men there are two classes? Aye, what of it?" [42]

Why the defense chose to plead for the severance into only two groups remains a mystery. Why did Captain Black tell the state's attorney that he presented the severance petition only as a "matter of form?" Why did Zeisler tell a reporter that he was not inclined to make a "hard push" for a separate trial for any of his clients?

When Foster finished reading his petition for the severance of Spies, Fielden, Schwab, and Neebe, he concluded by saying that the defense was anxious to have a speedy trial. Judge Gary seemed puzzled by this remark—after all, to severe the trial would require rescheduling not only the present proceedings, but potentially scheduling several new trials at later dates. Gary responded to this comment, "Gentleman, that seems to imply that you expect me to overrule this motion." Foster retorted, "That is our expectation, Your Honor." Gary fired back, "Well, I won't disappoint you then." [43]

Legally, at the time he ruled, Judge Gary was on firm ground in denying this motion for severance. The last Illinois Supreme Court case to adjudicate the issue, *Johnson, Backus, Morse v. The People* (1859), dispensed with a plea to grant a new trial on the grounds that a just motion for severance was brusquely denied: "We are aware of no reported case of any court, which has ever held that it is an error to refuse a severance in the trial of a criminal case. The right is discretionary with the court, to be exercised as all other matters of discretion." [44] Such was the long-standing precedent at common law as was the standing U.S. Supreme Court ruling on the issue, *U.S. v. Marchant & Colson*, a capital case from 1827 in which the justices likewise held that questions of severance are discretionary with the court and "not a right in the parties." [45] As the *Albany Law Journal* summed up the issue the year after the Illinois Supreme Court had weighed in, "As to the refusal of separate trials, we suppose that at common law, although the government may sever, the defense may not. The court of review says so, and we have no doubt they are right." [46]

No one was more affected than Oscar Neebe by the defense's decision to allow all seven cases to be joined as one. Leonard Swett, the experienced criminal attorney later hired to organize the anarchists' appeal to the Illinois Supreme Court, was quite certain of this: "The evidence mounted against him amounted to almost nothing. Had he been tried separately there is no doubt he would have been acquitted." [47]

It was an odd thing for an attorney to seemingly go out of his way to antagonize a judge at the very outset of an important trial. Zeisler later recalled that when Foster told Judge Gary that he expected him to deny their motion, "a shock went through me and I noticed a pained expression on the faces of Captain Black and Mr. Salomon and several of our clients. According to Zeisler, Spies then slipped him a note reading, "What in hell does Foster mean? I thought our motion was meant seriously. What was the sense of making it appear perfunctory?" Foster's remark must have made quite an impression that day for it seemed so gratuitous to at least one observer of the trial that he commented upon it 40 years later in a private letter to Sigmund Zeisler, "I cannot understand why a lawyer making a plea to a judge should say that he does not expect it to be granted, as Foster did."[48]

Spies' puzzlement at the cavalier manner in which Foster handled the severance petition was likely due to the fact that he had not been told of a major change in defense strategy since the original severance petition had been drawn up the previous week. Defense attorneys had debated the issue and resolved to urge Albert Parsons to leave his hideaway in Wisconsin and turn himself in. Of course, Parsons could do this at any time, and if he waited until the trial was under way, he would have automatically been severed from those proceedings and tried separately. But attorneys Salomon and Black, over the objections of the more "cool-headed" and experienced trial lawyer Foster and the unsure Zeisler, decided to have Parsons surrender before the trial began and thereby join all the defendants into one grand group. Obviously, if the defense had decided to have Parsons surrender on the first day of the proceedings rather than on the second so as to ensure that he did not have a separate trial, then they no longer meant their previously drafted motion for severance, which was introduced merely as a pro forma matter.

Attorney Salomon tipped his hand on his thinking in these matters a few days before the trial began when he told the *Tribune* that he wished Parsons was among the defendants as that would "save him some trouble." Apparently, some of the men most active in the affairs of the city anticipated Parsons' surrender. Melville Stone, publisher of the *Chicago Daily News*, reportedly contacted Lucy Parsons and offered her a sizeable sum of money if he could accompany Albert into court.

In the early afternoon of June 21, the day scheduled for the examination of the jurors and for the trial to officially begin, a man hurried out of a house on Morgan street, holding a handkerchief to his face, and into a waiting hansom cab whose curtains had been drawn closed. The cab pulled up to the front of the courthouse where Captain Black waited, pacing along the sidewalk. Black and Parsons hurried into the building, followed by Lucy and Gerhard Lizius, a reporter for the *Arbeiter Zeitung*. Black's plan was to march up to the judge's bench and have Parsons formally surrender himself, perhaps with a little speech. But as he and Parsons entered the courtroom, attorney Grinnell spotted them and jumped up (interrupting Judge Gary as he was reading something), called the court's attention to Parsons, and demanded that a bailiff take him into custody. Black shouted that Parsons was surrendering himself voluntarily and ushered the eighth defendant to his seat, where he was greeted warmly by his fellow prisoners.[49]

According to Ziesler's memory of these events, Salomon and Black believed that the lack of evidence against Parsons and his noble surrender would help save those more deeply implicated: "Captain Black was enthusiastically in favor of it . . . He expressed his conviction that the presumption of guilt which had taken possession of the public mind would instantly change to a presumption of innocence, the benefit of which would extend to the other defendants." More experienced legal minds did not agree. Fellow Cook county judge Samuel McConnell commented later, "Of course it was a great blunder on Captain Black's part to advise Parsons to return when he did, for if he had waited until the jury had been impaneled and then had had Parsons return, Parsons could have secured a separate trial..."[50] Years later, Black himself admitted his foolish mistake, telling a reporter on the day of Parsons' execution, "...I had made a fearful mistake in permitting Parsons to give himself up..."[51]

Of course, legal precedents aside, it is clear that as an issue of fairness the trying of these seven men in one joint trial had unjust consequences. This point was made in an editorial in the free-thinking journal of ethical commentary *Open Court* (and reprinted in *The Albany Law Journal*), where it was pointed out that even though it was the fault of the defense in allowing the eight to be tried together, the prosecution should not have taken advantage of it. "Whether designed or not the effect of such a number of defendants was to throw confusion into the jury box.... By trying all the men together the peril of each one of them was multiplied, for each had to defend himself against his own words and actions and those of the other seven."[52] Clearly, Neebe, Schwab, and Fielden were not as fully implicated in either the alleged Monday night conspiracy or the actual violence at the Haymarket as were Engel, Fischer, Spies, and Lingg, with Parsons somewhere between these extremes. Had the defense lawyers pursued a vigorous motion for separation, rather than, as all evidence seems to suggest, offering an insincere and perfunctory motion while gambling that a joint trial had strategic benefits, the outcome of this historic trial might have been different.

None of the accused men dared criticize their own lawyers publicly until their last hope for appeal had been extinguished. Minutes after his comrades had met their fate at the end of the hangman's noose, Michael Schwab unburdened himself to a friendly reporter who asked him if he was "satisfied with the work of your counsel..." Schwab responded, "I believe that had the proper method been pursued we would have had separate trials, and no seven juries ever impaneled would have found us all, even under the evidence conjured up, guilty of the crimes alleged." Schwab praised the "eminent counsel" who worked on their behalf, but by this he did not mean Black, Zeisler, Salomon, or Foster. "Yes, we had eminent counsel, true; but the damage wrought could not be repaired at the late hour they took hold of the case. If we had the money which later poured in, and could have used it at the outset, not a man of us would have been held under any indictments filed."[54]

THE SPECIAL VENIRE

Most criticism of the case has focused on the manner in which the jury was selected, yet here too, the most basic facts of the trial's proceedings have been consistently misrepresented by its leading historians. There are two main lines of attack that historians have used in their attempts to show that the jury selection process was tainted by bias from the start. First, it is generally written that the usual procedure for selecting jurors was bypassed. That the judge allowed the appointment of a special bailiff to hand-select a pool of prospective jurors ("veniremen"), and this bailiff consciously picked people he hoped would convict. Second, it is alleged that Judge Gary refused to dismiss jurors who confessed to being biased or having minds already made up, forcing the defense to waste their precious preemptive challenges. As a result, the jury that was seated was an elite assemblage of men, none of whom was a worker or an immigrant, not the jury of peers guaranteed under the rule of law.[55]

To our contemporary sensibilities the manner in which the jury was drawn does seem unusual and biased.[56] The facts are as follows. After examining the two hundred and forty ninth candidate for the jury box, the standard jury pool was exhausted, and prosecutor Grinnell noted that there would soon be a need to recruit potential jurors on a daily basis. Grinnell thought that the sheriff's office would be charged with the task of dragooning 50 men a day into the courtroom, but defense attorney Black, pointing to Illinois statutes, demanded his right to have one special bailiff appointed instead. From the defense point of view, it was far better to entrust this task to one man, who could later be held accountable for his actions (and possibly provide the basis for appeal), rather than have it done by an agency that had among its own lawful powers the ability to deputize private citizens and charge them with the duty. Judge Gary, scrutinizing the statute books from the bench, ruled in favor of each of Black's motions—to call a special bailiff, to appoint a man unaffiliated with the sheriff's department, and to instruct him to do the work himself and not farm it out to others. Gary even asked the defense to suggest a man to fill the post and readily agreed to the names Black provided. When both men declined the dubious honor, Grinnell suggested another, Henry L. Ryce, an employee of the clerk's office, and Black immediately endorsed him, saying, "I am entirely willing that Mr. Ryce should act; I know him."[57] Ryce then procured the remaining 600 odd members of the jury pool.

In the nineteenth century the drawing of a special venire was done routinely for a variety of reasons. Special juries were called to fill the gaps between the terms of regular grand juries. They were summoned when members of a sitting grand jury could be shown to have conflicts of interest in the case. The Illinois criminal codes passed in 1874 (Rev. Stat. 1874, Sec. 13, p. 633) gave judges broad authority to call special venires, and superior courts were reluctant to question their discretion in such matters.[58] When Peter Davison of Lake County appealed his murder conviction to the Illinois Supreme Court, he claimed his grand jury indictment was improper because some of the jurors were over the age of 60 and another was a resident of Wisconsin, but he did not object to the fact that four of the jurors had been selected specially by the county sheriff.[59] Not only were special venire accounted for in the law, court precedent, and common procedure, but the law governing this method of procuring jurors was hailed as being among the more clear and forthright in the statute books. In 1877 Justice Scott of the Illinois Supreme Court wrote of the statute that provided for the appointment of special venire, "Construction can not make this clause of the statute plainer than it is." In 1885 the U.S. Supreme Court upheld a Utah court's drawing of a special venire by a marshal even though Congress had not provided a mechanism for doing so in its laws governing the territory. Without dissent the court reasoned that because federal law "does not forbid the ordinary and well known resort to an open venire" it was legal for the court to do so when the names in its jury box ran out.[60]

Empanelling juries by drawing names randomly from voter or tax lists was actually a rather recent innovation in the mid-nineteenth century. Prior to then common law practice was for sheriffs to use their discretion to summon "good and lawful men" from among the freeholders of the county.[61] It was not until the 1850s that states began establishing more regular procedures for procuring juries.

But just because a name is pulled from a box does not mean that it represents a random or bias-free sample of the citizenry. Illinois law required each county board to make up a list of names to be dropped in the box each September. The law did not specify how each board would compile its list or who should be included or excluded. Leading Chicago lawyers complained bitterly at the lack of care with which county commissioners fulfilled their duties. S.S. Gregory, the Chicago attorney who along with Clarence Darrow represented Eugene Debs after the Pullman Railway Strike, before being tapped to be president of the American Bar Association, complained in a speech in 1888 that "too little responsibility has attached to those charged with the exercise of this duty, and so through their neglect it has been in the power of unscrupulous men to secure venal and corrupt jurors." Gregory understated the problem. Less than a year earlier, eight members of the Cook County Board and seven ex-commissioners were indicted for bribery and conspiracy. Even Sigmund Zeisler (the lawyer for the anarchists) complained in 1890, "The method of making up jury lists and supplying the different courts with jurors, though it has recently been somewhat reformed in our State, is far from satisfactory; the material of men we usually get on juries is far below that standard of intelligence which the nature of many of the cases submitted to them seems to require..."[62]

In Chicago it proved difficult to make a list of names that did not waste the court's time sifting out many unqualified men. There were many more restrictions on who could be a juror than who could be a voter. Jurors could not be younger than 21 or older than 60. They could not be disabled, infirm, or "decrepit." They had to speak and understand English. They could not have served on a jury in the past year. Additionally, many categories of citizens—lawyers, doctors, ministers, members of the state militia, firemen, policemen, teachers, and all public office holders—were exempt from jury duty. Consequently, admitted Judge Robert Jenkins before the Illinois Bar Association in 1896, the Cook County Board regularly fell behind in meeting the needs of the courts and only made up small lists of names from time to time as needed. "These lists have contained at most, only a few thousand names, and it has often happened that when the names were written upon cards, and put into a box, the larger part thereof would be almost immediately drawn out to provide jurors for a single term of court."[63]

While Chicago lagged far behind most of the nation's large cities in establishing a jury commission system to compile jury lists, the problem of drawing juries vexed many big cities and caused the empanelling of special venires on a regular basis.

According to a reporter for a popular magazine in the 1880s, the summoning of special venires happened so frequently in one big city that the practice supported a few "professional jurors." The magazine profiled one drunk who hung around court-houses waiting for his chance to be picked by a lazy sheriff and thereby earn a small per diem.[64]

The Haymarket trial was not the first time the issue of empanelling a jury was one of concern to working people. In 1881 Judge Murray Tuley reportedly dis-missed an entire panel of jurors because most of them were unemployed or "ignorant" workingmen. Tuley ordered the bailiff to go down in the warehouse district and get a jury of quality men. Chicago's Trade and Labor Assembly protested Judge Tuley's clear class bias at the time.[65]

The man given the enormous job of dragooning hundreds of men to court was Henry L. Ryce, a native of Indiana who enlisted at the very beginning of the Civil War and served as quartermaster for the Eleventh Indiana Zouaves.[66] Ryce's method of enlisting men into his service is not documented, but it can be roughly gauged by his results. For example, if the composition of the jury pool shifted dramatically, in class or ethnic structure, after Ryce began his work, this would tend to support allegations of bias. Moreover, in order for Ryce's alleged jury-packing scheme to work he would have to have worked in coordination with a biased judge who refused to discharge biased jurors for cause. (Jurors excused for cause did not count against the 270 peremptory challenges the defense had to work with.) The record should reveal the proportion of challenges for cause granted compared with challenges denied and whether these proportions changed over time.

One way to measure the effects of the switch in jury selection procedures is to distinguish the veniremen by their class and ethnic backgrounds and compare their proportional numbers before and after the appointment of Bailiff Ryce. A total of 27.7 percent of the jurors were selected by having their names drawn from a jury box compared with the 72.3 percent that were summoned by Ryce. Categorizing prospective jurors' stated occupation as industrial wage worker, service sector wage worker, manager, businessman, and financier (investor or banker) reveals that Ryce's appointment had a significant impact on the numbers of industrial wage workers and independent businessmen included in the venire, though comparatively little on the rates of recruitment of managers or their white-collar employees. The rate of selection of industrial workers declined from 26 percent to 7 percent, while that for businessmen shot up from 41 percent to 59 percent. However, the rates for the two other groups, service sector wage workers (salesmen, clerks, etc.) and managers, hardly changed at all. White-collar wage workers nudged up from 18 percent to 19 percent, while managers moved from 9 percent to 11 percent. Bailiff Ryce seemed uninterested in stuffing the venire with capitalists as their rate vis-à-vis the luck of the jury box draw remained steady, just moving from 5 percent to 4 percent. (Note: among those classed as "businessmen" are a large number of grocers, saloonkeepers, and drug store owners.)

Ethnically, the deputizing of Bailiff Ryce had a measurable impact, slightly depressing the numbers of jurors of German ancestry and increasing those of English heritage. On balance, Ryce's activities increased the number of English jurors by nearly 6 percent (leading to 41 additional Anglo jurors) and slightly depressed the rate of selection of Germans by 3 percent (keeping, at most, 22 Germans out of the pool). Interestingly, the rates for selection of veniremen with Irish or Scottish surnames hardly budged, increasing by 1 percent (leading to an additional 6-7 Irish veniremen).

Such numbers both support and contradict the defense allegation against Ryce (that he selected jurors from the commercial districts with the intention of provoking additional peremptory challenges). Certainly, it seems evident from the decreasing numbers of industrial wage workers and the increasing numbers of businessmen that Ryce did selectively draw from the commercial districts of the city rather than from the working class neighborhoods ringing the downtown. But this fact does not shed any light on Ryce's motivations—after all, the task he was given was daunting, summoning 50 men a day (five or six an hour or one every ten to 12 minutes) to court all by himself. It is just as likely that Ryce chose to work in the densest part of the city and in the area closest to the courthouse because that was most efficacious and convenient. Certainly, had he wanted to refine the jury pool to aid the prosecution, he would have packed in more capitalists and Irishmen (most of the policemen murdered at the Haymarket were Irish), and avoided Germans. In fact, Ryce selected just as many Irishmen and capitalists and insignificantly fewer Germans as would have been summoned had he pulled the names out of a box.[67]

On July 14, upon examination of juror number 920, the architect W.J. Edbrooke, lead defense counsel William Black rose to raise an objection to the manner in which the venire was assembled. When Judge Gary refused his motion on the grounds that it was in conflict with a standing Illinois Supreme Court interpretation as well as with Illinois statute law, the defense appeared to switch its tactics. At this point, the jury box had only one empty seat and at the rate at which the defense was using peremptory challenges and the judge was granting challenges for cause, it looked like the process could drag on for another week at least. Suddenly, the defense began expending its remaining challenges at an accelerated pace and did so without first requesting the removal of prospective jurors for cause. After juror 920, the defense looked at only 53 more jurors to use its remaining 25 peremptory challenges, all but two employed without first asking the court to excuse objectionable jurors for cause. The defense used its last challenge on juror 972, W.H. Wait, a former deputy sheriff of Cook County, a solid move, no doubt, leaving it without challenge for juror 973, Harry T. Sandford, a 24-year-old clerk in the freight auditor's office of the Northwestern railroad, who completed the panel.[68]

Why the haste in expending challenges after venireman 920? One possibility is that after Gary denied its motion for changing methods of selecting the venire, the defense believed that it had a strong legal case with which to appeal but such appeal required that at least one member of the jury be imposed upon it in order for it to properly argue that a flawed selection process denied it an impartial panel. Courts in this era were generally reluctant to order new trials on the basis of a judge's erroneous overruling of a challenge for cause of a juror as long as the biased juror was or could have been removed by the defense's remaining peremptory challenges.[69] Wasting its challenges was the quickest way to establish such grounds for its appeal. If it were the case that so many challenges were actually wasted so as to better its chances for a successful appeal, then the jury selection process was tilted by the defense's own gamesmanship of the proceedings as much as it was by the actions of Bailiff Ryce.

Samuel McConnell, a fellow sitting judge in the Cook County courts at the time, whose recollections of the case are among the most frequently cited by historians, made some pointed comments on the jury selection process. McConnell observed, "It has been charged that the jury was selected for conviction by the bailiffs, but I doubt that because it certainly was unnecessary. Any jury, considering the state of public opinion and Judge Gary's rulings and instructions would have convicted the defendants."[70]

Even had Bailiff Ryce attempted to pack the jury by exhausting the defense's 160 peremptory motions, such a scheme would have depended on the willingness of the judge to turn a blind eye to indications of juror bias and to not discharge jurors for cause. As there was no limit on the number of jurors who could be excused by the court, if the judge excused the biased jurors who Bailiff Ryce allegedly dragged to court, all that Ryce would have accomplished by selecting biased jurors would have been to draw out and complicate his own job.

On this point all historians have agreed: Judge Gary misused his authority and ignored the law and overruled objections to men who freely admitted their prejudice and bias against the anarchists.[71] But historians have overlooked the legal context of Gary's rulings. The process of voir dire, the questioning of prospective jurors, was circumscribed and governed by a very specific set of standards established by both state statute and consistent high court rulings. The law of the day tended to err on the side of qualification rather than disqualification in an era when a higher value was placed on judicial order and form than on substantive outcomes. Gary's rulings were governed by a legal code passed by the Illinois legislature in 1874 that established the positive grounds upon which veniremen must be removed (one's age, citizenship, residency, language skills, physical ability, prior jury service, suits pending in court, office-holding, and even working in some occupations were all grounds for removal) and specified other attributes that could not. In a clause that had far-reaching implications for highly publicized trials, the law prohibited the disqualification of jurors for having formed an opinion as to the guilt or the innocence of the accused on the basis of press accounts. " . . . it shall not be a cause of challenge that a juror has read in the newspapers an account of the commission of the crime with which the prisoner is charged, if such juror shall state, on oath, that he believes he can render an impartial verdict . . . " Legislators went even further in protecting newspaper readers and denied grounds to disqualify them even if they tended to believe the accounts they read. " . . . the fact that a person . . . has formed an opinion or impression, based upon rumor or upon newspaper statements (about the truth of which he has expressed no opinion), shall not disqualify him to serve as a juror . . . "[72]

This sort of juror qualification statute became common in America with the rise of the kind of sensational newspaper publishing that flourished after the mid-1850s.

The coverage of trials shifted from being brief notices of appearances in court to full-blown narratives of police investigations, grand jury testimonies, and courtroom dramas. As more and more people eagerly consumed daily papers, it became harder to find jurors who had not been exposed to detailed accounts of the crimes they were being called upon to judge.[73] Such juror qualification laws as Illinois passed in 1874 had already passed judicial muster in other leading states. Ohio amended its legal code in 1860 to provide that a juror whose opinion was gathered from press accounts "and not upon conversation with witnesses of the transaction, or hearing them testify" could be certified as long as he swore that he could deliver an impartial verdict on the evidence. Similar provisions were upheld by the Ohio Supreme Court twice— in 1865 and again 1873—and by the Illinois Supreme Court numerous times prior to the Haymarket trial. The U.S. Supreme Court approved the same sort of juror qualification statute in a Utah territory murder case in 1887.[74]

Illinois' statute of 1874 permitting the empanelling of jurors who had read about a crime and formed a general opinion about it was based on a common law distinction between having a "general" opinion and having a "decided," "positive," or "fixed" one. The case of *Smith v. Eames*, decided in 1841, laid down the fundamental rule followed by Illinois judges throughout the nineteenth century:

> *We then lay down this rule, that if a juror has made up a decided opinion on the merits of the case, either from a personal knowledge of the facts, from the statements of witnesses, from the relations of the parties, or either of them, or from rumor, and that opinion is positive, and not hypothetical, and such as will probably prevent him from giving an impartial verdict, the challenge should be allowed.*

The critical nuances in this judge's ruling can easily be missed if the distinction drawn by the qualifying words used in this rule—"decided" and "positive"—is not properly understood. A "decided" or "positive" opinion is here distinguished from a "general opinion" in that the holder of a decided or positive opinion has not only formed a belief, but firmly trusts the grounds upon which that opinion is based. Elaborating this distinction, *Smith v. Eames* continued:

> *If the opinion be merely of a light and transient character, such as is usually formed by persons in every community, upon hearing a current report, and which may be changed by the relation of the next person met with, and which does not show a conviction of the mind, and a fixed conclusion thereon, or if it be hypothetical, the challenge ought not to be allowed; and to ascertain the state of mind of a juror, a full examination, if deemed necessary, may be allowed.*[75]

The distinction drawn between positive, decided, or fixed opinions and the ones that are more general, impressionistic, and hypothetical was not merely an exercise of judicial hairsplitting. Such a distinction was needed because often in high-profile crimes virtually all members of a community had heard some reports of the case and individuals, if they were candid and honest in their juror's examination, would admit that they harbored some idea, some "prejudice" (in the literal sense of having "pre-judged") about it. As early as 1822, in an age before the rise of mass-circulation newspapers, the Illinois Supreme Court worried about the effect of barring all venire-men from the jury box simply because they had heard news of the case and had some impression of it prior to the commencement of the trial. " . . . as the mind of man is organized, it is almost impossible for a jury to be perfectly impartial. Slight impressions will appear on the mind of any person who will at all think of any subject. This is unavoidable . . . " That court arrived at a practical and objective rule: as long as individuals had not expressed their opinion in the case and had kept their opinions to themselves, then objections to their service on such grounds of bias should be overruled. Later courts chose not to solely rely on such a clear but severe rule and allowed judges to probe and determine if a person had a fixed and definite belief or just a provisional one.[76]

Given these legal precedents, a juror could be disqualified only if he sprung any of a number of legal triggers, and the lawyers' questioning was aimed at leading a witness they were suspicious of into these traps. A venireman could not be excused just for saying that he had an opinion about the case, but (in keeping with the old common law litmus test) he would more likely be dismissed if he had expressed his opinion to someone else, which the courts held, staked his reputation for veracity on the outcome. It wasn't enough to say that one believed that socialism or anarchism or communism was wrong or immoral, though a man being examined might be removed for cause if he said he was biased against the specific men on trial because they were socialists, communists, or anarchists. A prospective juror usually wouldn't be excluded just because he said he had a firm opinion about the guilt or the innocence of the accused, but he would be bounced if he stated that he did not think he could set aside his opinions and prejudices and weigh only the evidence presented in the courtroom.

Defense lawyers made a great show of protesting Judge Gary's refusal to excuse many of the prospective jurors who admitted that they had "formed opinions" about the guilt of the accused. These objections formed one of the footings of their later appeal but were not as sincerely drawn as historians give them credit for. Years later, defense lawyer Zeisler published an article entitled "Defects of the Jury System" that advocated that judges interpret the law just as Gary had done: "In these times of rapid dissemination of news the rule which disqualifies persons who have formed or expressed an opinion based upon other than original evidence is an anachronism. In cases exciting wide public attention it tends practically to exclude all intelligent newspaper readers. It furnishes an easy method to escape jury service for the man willing to swear that his mind is made up."[77]

Judge Gary followed the long established guidelines in both the 1874 Illinois revised legal code and numerous precedents in examining the veniremen and in ruling upon motions to reject them based upon their opinions. His line of questioning was aimed at uncovering the degree to which admitted opinions about the case were decided or positive. Opinions derived merely from media reports or general conversation were not disqualifying as long as the prospective juror was not convinced of their truth and he persuasively testified as to his own ability to act impartially.

In fact, the court transcript shows that Judge Gary frequently and consistently excused jurors for cause. While 160 jurors were disqualified peremptorily by the defense, 589 more were excused by Judge Gary on the motion of the defense. Fewer than 10 percent (9.5 percent) of defense objections to jurors were denied by Judge Gary. This amounted to a total of 56 objectionable men qualified as potential jurors, about a third of the 160 challenges the defense had available. Defense lawyers used a larger number of peremptory challenges to eliminate 107 veniremen without first asking the judge to do so for cause.

In the end, neither was the jury as unrepresentative as historians have heretofore alleged, nor was it representative of the city as a whole, which was entirely typical for this historical era.[78] Allegations that the jury was devoid of members of the working class are patently false. There were two, and there would have been more had not the defense itself challenged so many industrial workers. Indeed, 40 of the 66 industrial wage workers excluded from the jury were removed at the instigation of the defense. Over and over the wage workers who were on the jury are mischaracterized as being "middle class" in the existing literature.

One of these supposed unsympathetic middle-class professionals was Scott G. Randall, who has often been described as "a salesman." But looking at the record of Randall's testimony, it does not seem that this is an appropriate way to describe him. Randall himself rejected the word "salesman" as a description of his occupation when he was asked about his occupation by the prosecutor:[79]

Randall: I am in the field and garden seeds department.

Grinnell: A salesman?

Randall: No, I pack the orders and help ship them and send them down to the shipping clerk.

Randall revealed many things about himself during his questioning that place him well beneath the comfortable middle class and several rungs beneath the enterprising life of a salesman. Rather, Randall was one of Horatio Alger's typical poor boys who had left their farms and struck out west to find their fortune. Randall left the family farm in Erie County, Pennsylvania, when he was 20 and went straight to Chicago. He worked as common laborer for a while before getting a job as a waiter in a hotel. He saved enough money to purchase a team and wagon and for a time tried to make a go of purchasing milk from farmers and peddling it in the mornings and afternoons. But this business didn't pan out and Randall's older brother got him a job filling and weighing seed sacks in a downtown wholesaling house. Randall didn't make enough money to rent his own place, so he lived in a room above the warehouse.[80]

Another juror, 27-year-old Theodore Denker, a young man descended from an old line of Minnesota Germans, had a job similar to Randall's and worked as a shipping clerk for a wholesale clothing company. Denker, like Randall, was the low guy on the totem pole, having worked there just a couple of years, and made it clear on the stand that "there is no men under me." Prior to getting his job at Henry W. King & Co., Denker worked as a conductor on a United States Express Company wagon. Denker lived at home with his mother.[81]

With but three jurors left to select, reporters leaked news of an attempt to fix the jury. Reporters caught wind of the fact that a manager of the Park Theatre, John Long, had been offered 2,000 dollars to find a juror who would promise to acquit. Apparently approached because of his extensive contacts and influence, Long was given a confidential list of names of prospective veniremen to identify and target. Long went along with the scheme for a week or so before getting nervous and exposing the project to prosecutor Grinnell. When a reporter following up on the story asked to see John Long at the Park Theatre, he was told that Long had suddenly left for a trip to the Dakotas, his return uncertain. Nothing ever became of the matter, Grinnell charging that the leak of the story had made it impossible to investigate further. Defense attorney Zeisler told reporters that he did not doubt that John Long had been enlisted in a jury-tampering scheme, but believed it was a conspiracy "instigated in the police department for future use against us."[82]

Finally, with the selection of Harry T. Sandford the jury was complete and the trial commenced. All the legal experts who had struggled for six weeks—probing, arguing over, and winnowing nearly 1,000 potential jurors—were relieved that this phase of the trial was at last complete.

CHAPTER 3

THE PROSECUTION

On July 14, 1886, a confusion of lawyers, jurors, bailiffs, defendants, and spectators took their seats as the most anticipated trial in the city's history began in a courthouse that was a perfect monument to the corrupt character of its age. Originally conceived as an important symbol of the city's rebirth out of the ashes of the Great Fire of 1871, the Cook County Court Building was to have been the architectural centerpiece of the reconstructed city. Naïvely a 5,000 dollars prize was offered to fire the creativity of the leading architects of the age, but art was immediately slain by politics as county commissioners split and chose two winners, each side holding the design hostage until the third place entrant was agreed upon to end the stalemate. At least one architect later admitted to having bribed the judges.

Ground was broken in 1873 but the court building was not completed for a decade as county bosses used their influence to bulk up the contracts of their cronies and every element of the structure grew steadily larger, heavier, and more costly. A domed cupola was begun but before its last copper was hammered in place it was torn down in favor of an open rotunda. Fortress-like granite and limestone walls rose up from the pilings thicker and higher as construction plans were revised repeatedly to meet the appetites of contractors who split their profits with the county bosses. Eventually the structure had more polished Maine granite adorning its façade than any other building in America and the blocks were cut so thick that the structure began to slowly settle back into the Chicago marsh.

Plasterers, known then as "calicimators," found plenty of work keeping up with the cracks feathering across the interior. In spite of being one of the most expensive public buildings in America, when the *American Architect* polled architects to determine the "Ten Best Buildings in America" it received only one vote. Later this vote was revealed to have been cast from among architects in Chicago, implying either an excess of boosteristic pride or, more likely, that this lone ballot belonged to none other than Mr. J.J. Egan, the courthouse's own architect.[1]

At the time the courthouse was not only imposing in its ornate almost baroque excess, it was regarded as a most up-to-date facility. Each courtroom had not only its own jury rooms and judge's chamber, but each judge was afforded his own private water closet and lavatory lined with marble wainscoting. A law library occupied part of the fourth floor beneath stained glass skylights and frescoed walls. All the building's rooms were brightened by electric lights, among the first installed in the city. Judge Gary's courtroom was one of the largest in the nation, taller, wider, and with its two balconies that ran the full length of the 50-by-130-foot room. It had more public seating than the great hall designed by Cass Gilbert for the U.S. Supreme Court in 1932.[2]

As was the American practice of that day, the space within the courtroom was not as clearly or functionally divided as it would evolve to become in the Twentieth century when permanent structures demarcating distinct spaces for jurors, witnesses, judge, and sometimes legal clerks and bailiffs became the norm. Commonly courtrooms in this age had only three divisions: the space afforded to the public, that occupied by the legal parties and professionals, and that which elevated the judge above all the other legal actors. In Judge Gary's courtroom an elaborately ornamented baluster marked the boundary between the judicial participants and observers while Judge Gary's raised bench was not only supremely high, but it ran the full width of the bar. Jurors, witnesses, the defendants, lawyers, stenographers, reporters, and even a few friends and family members sat closely together in the crowed "forum" behind the bar. Jurors sat apart but occupied what seems today like an unusual position, seated in front of the judge's bench facing the defense and prosecution tables. This meant that when lawyers made their motions and objections, they directly faced both the judge and the jurors simultaneously and the judge could not see the juror's faces.[3]

Just as unusual from a contemporary viewpoint was the seating arrangement of the accused. The men on trial sat in a row that ran along the side of the bar, from the edge of the common lawyers table to the judge's bench. Thus the accused were physically apart from their counselors and closer to the nine men who would decide their fates. Reporters for various daily papers sat nearly at the elbows of the legal teams. So cramped was the space shared within the bar that when the trial opened one of the first things Judge Gary did was to ask the lawyers to scoot their tables back away from the jurors who he worried might overhear their whispered strategizing.[4]

The courtroom had one last unusual feature. When architect J.J. Eagan designed it he allowed for a large space, 15 feet in width, behind the bench so that a judge, stiff from sitting through long arguments, could take a break and "exercise." It is not clear if Eagan envisioned a black robed figure performing jumping jacks or running in place, but Judge Gary used this commodious extravagance of space for additional seating for favored spectators, which often included his own wife, the wife of the prosecutor, and other "elderly ladies."[5]

While the large crowd, the lack of clear separation between spectators and court officials, and the jumbled arrangement of jurors, defendants, and lawyers compared with modern trials seems chaotic, even carnivalesque, at the time Judge Gary's courtroom was considered orderly and disciplined. A reporter for the *Chicago Tribune* declared at the end of the trial's first week, "The trial, in fact, is being conducted with a church like decorum that is rare in famous trials."[6] Though physical space was not segregated by function or tightly controlled, the individual conduct of spectators was. On the trial's first day Judge Gary paused the proceedings and ordered the bailiff to remove a man in the gallery who had laughed at an attorney's joke. The *Chicago Legal News*, a journal of and for local lawyers, observed of Judge Gary's conduct of the trial that "He allows no nonsense in his court.... He governs his court in a quiet way with a strong hand and a clear head, never descending to wrangling with counsel."[7]

Such was in keeping with the character of the judge, a prototypical self-made westerner who, once established on the bench, settled into a life of punctilious routine. Raised with the staid moral injunctions of his Puritan heritage and apprenticed as a carpenter, Gary followed Greeley's call to "Go West Young Man," and tramped through to St. Louis where he read the law. Continuing west he first practiced in Santa Fe, where the locals called him "no save andar el cavallo" (the lawyer who doesn't know how to ride a horse), then Las Vegas, and finally on to San Francisco a little too late to profit from the gold rush. Failing to have struck his fortune in California he settled in Chicago where his old partner from Santa Fe, Murray F. Tuley, had begun to practice.

That was enough wandering for Gary. Within a year of landing in Chicago he married a girl from Berlin, Wisconsin, Elizabeth Sweeting, and moved into a townhouse on Ontario street. From that point on his life was one of pendulous regularity. One tradesman who passed his house each morning commented, "The curtains in the Garys' house are the best timepiece I know, they rise at 5 to a minute. I could set my watch by them." He walked back and forth to the courthouse. He played billiards with his old partner Tuley on Saturday afternoons. He sat on his elected bench for 47 years and held court the day before his heart failed.[8]

From the start of the proceedings, the panel of defense lawyers, half of whom had never tried a serious criminal case before, were jumpy and suspicious. When a bailiff prepared for the first day's session by laying an inflatable rubber ring on each juror's wooden chair, the defense sprung to object, saying it was an obvious attempt by the prosecution to purchase the sympathy of the jurors. When Judge Gary suggested that the court provide its transcripts of testimony to the jurors after each day's proceedings, the defense objected again on the grounds that it would be too much work for them to verify their accuracy.[9]

All three of the foremost lawyers in this trial, William Foster, Julius Grinnell, and Captain William P. Black, happened to be the same age—43. Foster was a rotund man with a shock of red hair and flourishing moustache of the same color. His manner was that of a man reaching above his upbringing—like the Iowa farmers who raised him he spoke with a pointed economy of words but he dressed to impress with upright starched collars, a diamond pin in his necktie, and a gold chain draped across the pocket of his vest. Foster's habit of playing with a pocketknife while interrogating witnesses revealed his humble roots.[10]

Moses Salomon and Sigmund Zeisler were notable for their youth and inexperience. Salomon was 28 and lived with his parents and Zeisler was a year younger. Neither man was well suited to the spotlight glare of a show-trial, both being scholarly and bookish. Salomon, a graduate of the Union College of Law, and Zeisler a graduate of the University of Vienna, were both known as "a good book lawyers," a backhanded compliment in a world where the quick turn of a clever phrase, brashness, even arrogance, counted most highly.[11]

Once the jurors were sworn and took their places, the tables that had been used by reporters were pulled aside and in their place a wooden chair positioned for the witnesses. After Judge Gary ordered everyone in the room to find a seat and warned those who could not that they would have to leave, Grinnell strode before the jury and opened his case.

Grinnell began by telling the jurors that he did not want them to judge the defendants for their beliefs. Rather, they were all there not because of what the defendants believed but because of their actions, actions that culminated in the bombing at Haymarket Square, an attack that Grinnell hyperbolically described as "the most fearful massacre ever witnessed or heard of in this country."[12]

The beginnings of this tragedy were with the men who advocated that "the only way to adjust the wrongs of any man was by bloodshed, by dynamite, by the pistol, by the Winchester rifle." Though no one took them seriously at the time, the State would prove that "they have meant what they said, and proposed to do what they threatened."[13]

Among the things Grinnell promised to prove over the course of the trial were that Spies and others laid plans to hijack the eight-hour movement to spark a general revolution. Reliable witnesses would testify that Spies had revealed his military plans to throw bombs into a police phalanx and even flourished a homemade bomb that he claimed were being distributing from his editorial offices. He would show that Spies provoked the riot at the McCormick works and then spread the false news that a dozen workmen had been murdered by the police, by writing and publishing a circular calling for "revenge." The same day a secret word was published in Spies' newspaper calling the armed men "those of the Anarchists who are willing to throw bombs and fire pistols" to meet. Down into Greif's basement went Fischer, Engel, Lingg, and Schnaubelt where they agreed that if conditions were right the word "ruhe" would be printed and this would mean war. Lingg was detailed to provide the bombs and he and others worked feverishly the next day to assemble them. Lingg then brought his bombs to Neff's Hall to distribute to the others. The meeting at the Haymarket was moved north onto the narrow Desplaines street by plan where alleys afforded escape and concealment. Fischer saw to the printing of the flyer advertising the meeting, a flyer that contained the incriminating line "Workingmen, come armed." Spies saw an opportunity to establish his own alibi and ordered the line stricken and the flyers reprinted.[14]

For two hours Grinnell painted a dark scene of conspiracy. Spies published broadsides calling for the protest meeting at the Haymarket that demanded "Workingmen Arm Yourselves and Appear in Full Force!" A cipher, known by the paramilitary forces as the signal for them to secretly assemble at their prearranged place, was published in the *Arbeiter Zeitung* on Monday afternoon. All that day Lingg labored away in his rooms, filling 16 half-hemispheres with dynamite and screwing them together. Three of the defendants were present at the conspiracy meeting—Lingg, Engel, and Fischer.

The location for the attack, a narrow block of Desplaines street intersected by blind alleys, was chosen and the plans laid.[15]

When the police approached, the prearranged signal was given and the bomb was thrown. Grinnell thought the anarchists' plan a sound one, but was thwarted by the bravery and resoluteness of the police who did not scatter but held their ground. Only Fielden, thought Grinnell, showed manly courage by standing and shooting at the police after all his comrades had turned tail.

Grinnell wasn't above name-calling, referring to Spies, Parsons, Schwab, and Neebe as "the biggest cowards that I have ever seen in the course of my life" and the *Arbeiter Zeitung* newspaper office as "a nest of snakes" and a "nest of treason and Anarchy." Nor did he shy from depicting the trial as more than a criminal matter but as a test of the rule of law, of democracy, and of the patriotism of the jurors. " . . . the strength of our institutions may depend upon this case, because there is only one step beyond republicanism—that is Anarchy. See that we never take that step . . . "[16]

When he was done, it was the defense's turn to make its opening remarks, but surprisingly, the lawyers seated amid the eight men on trial for their lives chose to waive their introduction. Instead they waited until the state had rested their case two weeks later to summarize their defense.[17]

The prosecution then called its first witness, a surveyor who drew the large maps adorning one side of the courtroom. Next Inspector John Bonfield recounted both the night of the bombing and the outlines of his investigation that followed. It wasn't until late in the day when the third witness was called that a hush fell over the room as the first anarchist informant was called to testify.

Gottfried Waller, the prosecution's star informant, was a Swiss-born cabinetmaker who immigrated to America in 1883 and worked at a billiard table factory. Waller, a man in his mid-thirties, married with one son, was a member of the Northwest Side Group and the Lehr und Wehr Verein.[18] Though the most damaging parts of his testimony related directly to his exposure of the plans laid for the Haymarket meeting, Waller painted a rich picture of a militant underground that had long been preparing for revolution. He revealed the existence of a secret code, "Y-Komme Montage Abend," published in the *Arbeiter Zeitung* that summoned the armed men to their meetings.

Waller described preparations made in 1885 for an open-air meeting to be held at Market Square to protest the idea of giving thanks on Thanksgiving Day. A planning meeting was held at Thalia Hall, and at some point Adolph Fischer handed out bombs made from capped sections of lead pipe telling his comrades to "use it if we would be attacked by the policemen . . . " Fischer's bombs were apparently no bluff as a couple of weeks later the one that he had given to Waller was taken out to the prairie and exploded in the crook of a tree.[19]

Waller had attended both the Emma street meeting and chaired the even more secretive gathering in the basement room of Greif's Hall the night before the bombing. He fingered Engel and Fischer as being the leaders of the Greif's Hall meeting. Engel as the man who suggested meeting places for the troops, and advised that bombs "would be the easiest mode—throwing a bomb in the station." Fischer was the one who objected to holding a downtown rally at Market Square, "as Fischer said this was a mouse trap; it should be on the Haymarket, because in the evening there would be more workingmen there, because people were at work late . . . " Fischer was also tagged as the man who proposed that the word "Ruhe" be published in the paper as a signal to set the plan in motion and volunteered to print the hand bills announcing the Haymarket meeting. Waller also unintentionally weakened Engel's alibi that he was home the night of the bombing playing cards by mentioning that on his way to the Haymarket he stopped by Engel's house and he wasn't home.[20]

Every legally trained ear in the room listened to hear one particular thing from Waller, one type of testimony that was critical to the prosecution. They strained to hear Waller say that those who planned the Haymarket meeting anticipated that it would lead to a violent confrontation with the police. Legally, the prosecution did not have to show that the throwing of a bomb was specifically part of the plan if, as part of the general preparations for the meeting, bombs were in fact readied for use. Prosecutor Grinnell knew he had witnesses who would testify that Lingg and others hurried to complete an arsenal of bombs just hours before the Haymarket meeting and physical evidence that one of these bombs was in fact the bomb thrown that night. However, whether a violent attack was part of the plan for the Haymarket meeting was a crucial link in the chain of evidence needed for a conspiracy conviction. Waller's testimony weakly reached this connection, but did not definitively prove it.

Waller's revelation that Fischer objected to the Market Square location because it was a "mousetrap" implied that at least Fischer foresaw this meeting as culminating in violence. While Waller revealed much more detailed plans for bombing police stations and shooting police in outlying areas, he was clearly reluctant to talk too much about the plans for Haymarket meeting. This line of questioning also made the defense lawyers nervous as twice one of them jumped to object when Ingham tried to ask Waller if anything was said about what to do if the police interfered with the meeting. Ingham continued hammering away on this point and finally pulled an incriminating answer from Waller:

Q: Was anything said as to why the police station should be attacked as to that particular time?
A: Yes, It was the plan to attack the police station to prevent the police from coming to aid.
Q: Coming to aid what?
A: If they should be a fight in the city.
Q: Was there anything said bout there being a fight in the city?
A: There was nothing said about it but we supposed so; we thought so.
Q: Who thought so?
A: All of us.[21]

Defense counsel again leaped to object. Judge Gary agreed and ordered the jury to disregard Waller's speculation about other men's state of mind. But Waller had tipped his hand. After all, how could he have known that "all of us," everyone at the meeting, "supposed" that there would be a fight in the city that night unless it had been discussed in some way? From other points in Waller's testimony it was clear that when he alluded to a "fight in the city" there was only one location where he and the others huddled in Greif's basement thought this fight was to occur on May 4: near the corner of Desplaines and Randolph. Earlier in his testimony Waller described how a "committee" was charged to "watch the movement in the city . . . and if something happened they should report" to the armed groups mustered on the city's outskirts. He then clarified the role of this committee: "It was said that we ourselves should not participate at the meeting of the Haymarket; we should meet at the respective places; only a committee should be present at the Haymarket, and if they should report that something had happened then we should come down upon them—attack them." Here it was; the clearest point of connection between the Haymarket meeting and the armed groups with their rifles and bombs lurking among the trees in Wicker Park. It wasn't the iron-clad revelation the prosecution had hoped for but it met the needs of the law. The men who made their secret plans in their dark basement had conspired to meet the police violently at the Haymarket meeting.[22]

Waller's testimony consumed the rest of the day and continued the next morning. When the court reconvened, Assistant Prosecutor Ingham pushed Waller to strengthen this link between the armed groups waiting to attack and the Haymarket meeting itself from a new angle. Ingham pursued the missing defendant, the ninth man listed in the indictment but not present in the courtroom—Rudolph Schnaubelt, the presumed bomb thrower. First he asked Waller if Schnaubelt was present with the others on those rough benches in Greif's basement. Then he went fishing and asked if Schnaubelt had said anything at the meeting and Waller answered:

Q: Did Schnaubelt say anything at that meeting?
A: Yes.
Q: What did he say?
A: He said that we should inform our members in other places of the resolutions.
Q: Did he say anything else?
A: He said that the thing should commence in other places also.
Q: What thing?
A: "It." He said that "it" should also commence at other places.
Q: Ask him what he means by "it" ?
A: The revolution.[23]

"Revolution," of course, was not a defensive or reactive posture but a program of action. By his second day of testimony, Waller had shifted from his initial insistence that the Greif's Hall conspiracy was just a matter of preparing to defend the strikers if assaulted by the police and exposed the more aggressive purpose behind the conspiracy.

This was enough for Ingham and with an overly dramatic "Take the witness!" sat down. The bookish and inexperienced Sigmund Zeisler stepped forward and attempted to break the chain of testimony the prosecution had drawn out of Waller. First he attempted to get Waller to retreat from the notion that the conspirators' goal was "revolution" and asked, "Now, is it not the fact that Mr. Engel both at the meeting on Sunday and at the meeting on Monday night stated that this plan was to be followed in case the police should interfere with your right of free speech and free assembling only?" Waller refused to agree, saying the plan was to commence "If the police should attack us." Zeisler hammered at this point, asking the same question four different ways and each time Waller indicated there were fewer conditions on what would set the revolutionary wheels in motion. Zeisler again: "Did he not say that that plan was to be followed only in case the police should interfere with your rights that I have mentioned, and by brutal force?" and Waller responded, "It was said that any time whenever we should be attacked by the police we should defend ourselves." Zeisler pushed harder: "Did he [Engel] not say that this plan was to be followed only when the police would by brutal force interfere with your right of free assembly and free speech?" And Waller backed further away from the response Zeisler looked for: "It was said that we should use—we should resort to this plan, or to the execution of it whenever it would suit us, or whenever the police would attack us." Finally the fourth time Zeisler asked if Engel said they should defend themselves if the police interfered with their rights Waller stood his ground and answered, "No—he did not say that."[24]

Zeisler had not helped his cause by eliciting these answers from the witness so he switched to another tactic and tried to disconnect the overall plan of the Greif's Hall conspiracy from the Haymarket meeting. This tack seemed to catch the wind Zeisler was seeking for a time until he suddenly crashed into some hidden rocks:

> Q: And you say that nothing was said at the Monday night meeting with reference to any action to be taken by you on the Haymarket?
> A: We should not do anything; we were not to do anything at the Haymarket Square.
> Q: Wasn't the plan that you should not be present there at all?
> A: Yes.
> Q: And you also say that you did not anticipate that the police would come to the Haymarket?

THE INTERPRETER—He said simply, no.

> Q: What do you mean by no—it was not anticipated?
> A: We did not think that the police would come to Haymarket.
> Q: And for this reason no preparations were made for meeting any police attack on the Haymarket Square?
> A: No; not by us.[25]

When Waller added the little phrase, "not by us" he sowed a seed of doubt over what he had just said. He could have just said, "No," but he chose to add, perhaps a little puckishly, "not by us," as if he had knowledge of some other group who was making such preparations. Zeisler changed direction again and tried to attack Waller's story from other angles but Waller remained consistent in his answers and Zeisler gave up.

The importance of Waller's testimony to the case cannot be overemphasized. One juror who spoke anonymously to reporters at the conclusion of the trial indicated the paramount importance that he and his colleagues placed on Waller's account: "We had made up our minds if Waller's testimony was corroborated by independent testimony to convict every one of the prisoners."[26]

As if Gottfried Waller's testimony had not been damaging enough by both implicating many of the defendants directly, establishing the existence of a specific conspiracy and opening many avenues for further probing and questioning, it also served as the occasion for a ruling on a critical point of law and allowed the prosecution to essentially repeat its opening remarks. From a tactical standpoint this was a disaster for the defense on every level.

It began with a defense objection—a point that led to a debate over a point of law that would have better been made without the jury present. After Waller had reached the end of his account of the night of May 4, Ingham abruptly turned the line of questioning in a new direction, asking, "Mr. Waller, did you ever receive any bombs from anybody?" Foster sprang to object and opened a lengthy discourse on the admissibility of evidence of a conspiracy that boiled down to the contention that even if the prosecution could prove that there was a conspiracy, unless they could also prove that the man who threw the bomb was a member of that conspiracy and was carrying out the specific prearranged plan of that conspiracy, they must acquit the defendants of the specific crime of murdering Officer Mathias Degan.[27]

Foster's point was clearly of great importance to the defense and one that reads as though much thought had gone into preparing it in anticipation of just such a moment. After all, were Gary to rule in favor of Foster's exception, the state would have had to prove who the bomb thrower was before testimony as to a general conspiracy would be allowed. Potentially a point of law that could kick the props out from the state's case, this objection was irresistible to the defense.

Even more harmfully, Foster at one point in the debate seemed to lose his way and conceded a point to the prosecution's interpretation of the law that sounded very much like he had accepted their argument altogether.[28] That moment came after Judge Gary stated that he believed that there were situations in which time and occasion of the unlawful action were not established and therefore the identity of the bomb thrower need not be preliminary to testimony indicating that such a conspiracy existed. Gary presented one example:

[Suppose] there was a general combination and agreement that weapons of death should be prepared to use against the police if they came in conflict with the workingmen's or striker's meetings . . . but the time and occasion at which the assault was to be were not foreseen, but were to be determined by the parties who were to use force when, in their judgment, the time and occasion had come . . . are not all who entered into the combination and agreement equally liable?[29]

At this point, Foster could have deflected the argument by stating that such individuals would be guilty of conspiracy and not murder, or simply stating that this is not what the state has alleged in this case, or some such response to hold the line clearly and consistently at the insistence of having the bomb thrower's identity and role in the conspiracy established first. But Foster, out of some misplaced deference, in front of a jury that according to the reporters in the room now all "seemed electrified and intensely attentive to every word," accepted Gary's logic and thereby tightened the nooses around his client's necks. After the meaning of Judge Gary's ruling had sunk in, one reporter observed a change in the demeanor of the defendants. "Their disappointment was clearly visible and for the first time their faces showed an expression of great concern."[30]

"I can imagine a case where they would be, if that was the arrangement—," stated Foster plainly, "that whenever we or any of us, according to our judgment or opinion believe that the time has come for an attack, it shall be made, and in pursuance of that agreement it is made by one of the conspirators, then I will admit that your Honor's reasoning will be good; but it has no more application to the facts of this case as they are developed now than day has application to night."[31] The problem, of course, was that to most jurors and perhaps most people in the room, the case as previewed by Ingham sounded exactly like that. Ingham had already stated that he was going to prove that there was not only a general conspiracy, but that the defendants had conspired to kill police specifically on May 4 at the Haymarket square for the specific reason of revenge and revolution. In the end, Foster's objection sounded very much like a distinction without a difference at best and an endorsement of the prosecution's legal theories at worst.

Not everything went as the prosecutors had planned. One of the informers they placed on the witness stand decided at the last moment to keep his secrets to himself. Prosecutor Grinnell later rued that one of his "squealers" went back on him.[32]

Bernhard Schrade, a fellow member of Lingg's carpenter's union and a commander of the Lehr und Wehr Verein, was pushed onto the witness stand by prosecutors who hoped he would be a star witness but when placed on the witness chair before the hundreds of eyes in the gallery and the hard glare of his anarchist friends just a few feet in front of him, Schrade quailed into an uncooperative witness. A *Tribune* reporter thought that Schrade appeared to be in a "fearful or doubtful half-decided state of mind" about testifying. This was evident in the way Schrade evaded the assistant prosecutor's questions and that "whatever was got from his lips was wrung from him by from two to three persistent, driving questions." Finally, an exasperated Ingham resorted to asking Schrade about statements he had made weeks earlier to police, prompting the defense to object that the State was impeaching its own witness, which it was. Judge Gary agreed and ordered Ingham to drop this line of questioning.[33]

Nevertheless, Schrade unwittingly revealed more than he meant to. When asked what the presiding officer spoke about in the basement of Greif's Hall, Schrade inexplicably remembered only the Haymarket meeting being discussed and replied that everyone was told to come and "be prepared" in case the police "went beyond their bounds." He remembered seeing Engel and Fischer at the Haymarket about an hour before the speaking began, becoming the first witness to place Engel anywhere near the Haymarket on the night of the riot. More oddly Schrade remembered meeting both men right at the spot where the meeting would later be gathered, "the corner of Randolph and Desplaines streets." Haymarket square extends across the intersection of three different streets (Halsted, Union, and Desplaines) and the fact that Engel and Fischer happened to wait on the one corner where the rally later took place along the block that contained the greatest number of crisscrossing alleyways probably lent weight to the prosecution's contention that this block was chosen for its tactical advantages by those in attendance at the meeting in the basement of Greif's saloon.[34]

In the end Schrade provided the prosecution with far less than they had hoped, but his brief time on the stand did allow the State to lay the groundwork to later introduce into evidence Johann Most's manual of bomb making, *Revolutionaere Kriegswissenschaft* (*Science of Revolutionary Warfare*). Ingham handed Schrade a number of newspapers and asked him if he had seen various articles and after getting him used to such questions produced Most's innocuous-looking slim volume. Ingham asked Schrade if he had ever seen this book before and Schrade said that he had seen it being sold at workingmen's meetings. At this point both Foster and Black objected to a question being asked about a piece of evidence that had not yet been shown to be connected in any way to the defendants. Ingham explained to the judge, "I simply wanted it marked so that when it was offered we could identify it, as having been seen by this witness." Gary allowed it. "Let it come in. They have to go a step at a time. If the book was sold in meetings then how far the persons connected with the meetings adopted the sentiments of the book may become a question for the jury." Captain Black took the book and put a mark in it and Albert Parsons reportedly asked to have a look at it. Black was was overheard whispering to him as he passed it over, "You had better put a mark on it. They might hang you on that book."[35]

Having gotten all they could from the resistant Schrade, Grinnell and his prosecution team switched gears and placed on the stand half a dozen police officers who vividly recounted the seconds leading up to and following the bombing. These officials testified to important details indicating a broader conspiracy. All of them were positive that men in the crowd began shooting at them almost immediately after the bomb exploded. Five officers testified that Samuel Fielden was one of these, though they disagreed where he was when he began shooting; two policemen thought he opened up as he was stepping off the wagon, two others thought he ducked behind the speakers' wagon and used it for cover (one other wasn't asked to specify Fielden's location). Three cops caught a glimpse of the bomb in the air and had opinions about where it originated. Five officers said that they heard someone yell something along the lines of "Here come the bloodhounds; do your duty and I'll do mine" as the police marched up the street. All of the policemen who were asked, testified that as they marched up the street they had their clubs sheathed and their guns in their pockets. All of the officers were given the opportunity to name the dead and wounded. Most pitiable among them were two officers whose debilitating wounds required no explanation: Lieutenant James Stanton who leaned heavily on a cane and shuffled to the witness chair and Officer Jack Doyle who limped up with the help of crutch.[36]

During this parade of uniformed witnesses two of the jurors asked questions of the witnesses, highlighting again the significantly different trial practices of the late nineteenth century. When Lieutenant Edward Steele was on the stand, juror J.H. Brayton interrupted and asked the witness if he knew how many men in his company had been struck by shell and how many by shot. It was an excellent question and somewhat embarrassing to defense attorney Foster that he had not offered it. Steele replied that he did not. When Lieutenant Quinn was being examined Juror John B. Greiner asked him to clarify exactly when it was that he heard Fielden exclaim to Officer Ward. He said, "We are peaceable," Quinn clarified, just as Fielden was stepping off the wagon. Juror James Cole then got in on the action and asked in what direction it was, exactly, that Fielden fired. All of these questions fortunately stayed within the bounds of the rules of procedure for the trouble with juror participation in the quizzing of witnesses is that it makes it very hard for counsel on either bench to object without risking offense.[37]

In the midst of their examination of the string of policemen, a key witness for the prosecution arrived from out of state and was immediately put on the stand. Luther Moulton was an official of the Knights of Labor from Grand Rapids, Michigan who happened to have hosted August Spies during a speaking tour of the Midwest the year before. Spies and a travelling companion paid a visit to Moulton's house and in the course of their conversation revealed what Moulton took to be his master plan for revolution in Chicago and the nation.

Moulton was the first of many witnesses that the state called for the purpose of establishing that anarchist leaders had planned for more than a year prior to the bombing to inflame the impending eight-hour general strike into a proletarian insurrection by attacking the police with explosives. As it was permissible within the rules of evidence to introduce both testimony and documents that revealed any aspect of the preconceived plan that motivated the criminal act, Judge Gary had no choice but to allow Prosecutor Grinnell to call witnesses like Moulton who had no connection to the events of May 1886 and only a passing acquaintance with one of the accused a year earlier. It was also through this legal window that the prosecution smuggled into the trial reams of articles that had been written, edited, or published by some of the men on trial that seemed to indicate their foreknowledge of police attacks that would commence in coordination with the eight-hour strikes.

Spies and a friend had sought out Moulton to request that he officiate at their coming mass meeting and introduce Spies to the gathering, as it was clearly to his advantage to have a local labor leader do so. Moulton did not readily agree but probed Spies about his beliefs and after Spies said that his aim was socialism, Moulton asked him how he planned on bringing it about, through the ballot box perhaps? Moulton recalled Spies expressing "no confidence in such methods and [Spies] expressed the opinion that force and arms was the only way in which the results could be accomplished directly; that they were prepared for such a demonstration." Pressing further Moulton asked for more details of his plans and related their conversation in this way:

> [He said] that they had a sufficient force already organized in Chicago to take the city, number about 3000; I objected that 3000 would not be sufficient. He said they had superior means of warfare. I then conceded that if they might take the city how would they keep it; he said that they would rapidly gain accessions to their ranks if they were successful. I said where would it come from. He said from the laboring men. I said how could they get the laboring men to join them? He said hold out inducements. I said what inducements. He said they would embrace the opportunity to make the demonstration when laboring men were idle in large numbers; out on strikes and lock-outs and would hold out to them inducements in the shape of means to reduce their wants and employments, which would add to their numbers great strength quite rapidly so they would be able to hold the city . . . I inquired how they would carry out these results without bloodshed, if there was no danger of killing some one. He thought there might be. That that happened frequently in the case of revolutions. I then inquired if this would not amount to a criminal action which would be actionable and in substance he thought it might be if it failed, but if it was a success it would be revolution, and George Washington would have been punished had he failed, and therefore all such things were considered crimes if failures and heroism if successful and thereby they would be able to escape the consequences of punishment if they were successful; they would have to take their chances.[38]

Under further questioning Moulton thought Spies had mentioned that explosives were among the "means of warfare" he meant. When Moulton asked when this uprising might begin, he remembered Spies saying "it would probably come at a time when the working men attempted to introduce the 8 hour system of labor." A machinist who boarded with Moulton, George Shook, and happened to be around that day confirmed most of Moulton's recollections, though he didn't remember Spies specifically referring to an eight-hour strike only that the revolutionary action should commence "when there would be the most men idle—the most confusion."[39]

A number of witnesses were called by the prosecution to firm up their contention that the Haymarket bombing was the culmination of more than a year's planning and preparation. A liberal republican politician, James K. Maggie, who attended some of the anarchists' mass meetings was seated to recall the mass meeting in October of 1885 when Spies proposed a resolution calling upon workers to arm themselves and prepare to fight for their rights on the first of the coming May. Another witness, the reporter, Henry O. Heinemann, was quizzed about this meeting and confirmed that Spies' resolution proclaimed that force was the only way that workers could hope to gain their rights and called on them to arm and prepare for the May Day strikes. Like Maggie, Heinemann could not remember Spies' exact words verbatim, though Heineman did clearly recall the last phrase Spies used to conclude his resolution: "Death to the Enemies of the Human Race, our Despoilers."[40]

Having established to their satisfaction the existence of a plan to use the eight-hour movement as the occasion for a revolutionary insurgency, a conspiratorial meeting at which a specific plan of action involving the stationing of armed units and pickets, the calling of the Haymarket meeting itself, the discovery of bombs at the offices of the *Arbeiter Zeitung* and bomb making material at Lingg's apartment, the prosecution moved to add yet one more link to this chain of evidence by introducing witnesses who could show that the McCormick riot that precipitated the whole affair was instigated by the anarchists for this purpose. Officer James West told how he and another policeman stood their ground against the roaring mob until reinforcements arrived. Wisely, the defense declined to cross-examine West, whose understated testimony and apparent heroism combined to make him a witness who evoked much sympathy. Other observers and participants in the rally of union lumber yard workers followed, including Frank Haraster, the president of the Lumber Shovers' Union, who accused Spies and his fellows of usurping his union's meeting and then egging on the mob and several newspaper reporters, one of whom was chased away by the crowd under a hail of stones.[41]

The McCormick's riot was then connected by a string of witnesses to the Greif's Saloon basement meeting and the Haymarket bombing. Typesetters and other employees of the *Arbeiter Zeitung* revealed that August Spies penned the first inflammatory circular printed that weekend, the so-called Revenge Circular. This single-paged call to arms printed in both English and German hit the streets within hours of the McCormick riot.

In addition to being an important piece of physical evidence pointing toward the existence of a conspiracy to murder policemen prior to the Haymarket meeting, the Revenge Circular contained clues implicating Spies in the conscious manipulation of facts. Prosecutor Grinnell pointed out a curious discrepancy between the text of the Revenge Circular which claimed that the police "killed six of your brothers at McCormicks this afternoon" and the fact that at the time news reports indicated that one and at most two men had been fatally wounded. (In the end one man, Joseph Srauiek, Jr., died of his wounds the following day.)[42]

Another key witness was Theodore Fricke, the mustachioed bookkeeper for the *Arbeiter Zeitung* who had come to America from Germany just three years earlier. Assistant prosecutor Ingham handed Fricke wads of yellowing paper and asked him to identify the handwriting scrawled across it. Fricke examined the announcement published in the "Letterbox" column of the newspaper that consisted of the single word "Ruhe," and said it was the handwriting of August Spies. Godfried Waller had already testified that he and the other leaders of the armed sections had agreed in Greif's basement that the codeword "Ruhe" would be the signal for the anarchist militias to muster at their prearranged locations. Though the code was only supposed to appear if "downright revolution" had broken out, the typos testified that Spies passed it on to the printing room on the afternoon of May 4, even though nothing of any consequence had yet occurred that day. By establishing the timing of this code the prosecution indicated that there were those in the movement and in the editorial offices of the Socialistic Publishing Company who expected trouble the evening of the bombing because they were themselves orchestrating it.[43]

Eager to widen the crack through which they could force Johann Most's militant bomb making manual, *Revolutionaere Kriegswissenschaft* (*Science of Revolutionary Warfare*), into evidence, Ingham asked the bookkeeper if Most's book was part of the *Arbeiter Zeitung's* library. Captain Black objected to the contents of an entire library being open to examination, but Judge Gary allowed this line of questioning on the grounds that "If there is evidence tending to show whether the men had any views on overthrowing by force of society, then the possession of such a book would be admissible with other evidence." Such evidence, Gary pointed out, had already come in through the testimony of Luther Moulton and others. The assistant prosecutor continued fishing, getting the accountant to admit having seen the book being sold at anarchist picnics. Black jumped to object again and this time Gary took his side and required the prosecutor to first establish the date and location of these picnics before asking about the book itself.[44]

Under cross-examination, Captain Black steered the witness to admit that he never saw any of the defendants themselves sell the book, but the point was lost nevertheless. A German scholar was called to provide full and accurate translations to a stack of articles churned out from the editorial offices of the Socialistic Publishing Company and of Most's manual of revolutionary warfare. It was at this point that the state formally submitted *Revolutionaere Kriegswissenschaft* into evidence and the defense made their last ditch effort to keep it out.

Prosecutors capitalized on the anarchists' eagerness to boast of their military prowess to reporters. Reporter Harry Wilkinson of the *Daily News* was called as a witness to recount how he interviewed Spies in his editorial office and how Spies showed off his "czar bomb." Wilkinson also described the lunch he had with Spies and Joseph Gruenhut where Spies used matches laid out on the clean white tablecloth to illustrate how anarchists armed with bombs could shred a phalanx of police in the tight streets of Chicago. Another *News* reporter, Marshall Williamson, covered what was probably the largest march and rally the anarchists held prior to the May Day weekend, a protest on the occasion of the dedication of the new Board of Trade building. Williamson's account was supported by undercover police officer, Thomas Treharn, who Williamson recognized on the sidewalk outside the *Arbeiter Zeitung* building and brought upstairs.

As the trial moved into its second week, the first of a train of witnesses with accounts that tied the Monday Night Conspirators to the Haymarket bombing took the stand. The first was William Seliger, a pale 31-year-old whose gnarled hands missing the thumb of his left hand told the story of his life as a factory carpenter. Seliger rented the middle floor of a backlot tenement on the Northwest side and subleased a room to his fellow carpenter Louis Lingg. Seliger had immigrated three years earlier from Silesia and quickly rose to be recording secretary of the same Carpenter's Union that Lingg belonged to. Seliger's examination proved so rich and revealing he was kept on the stand for nearly five hours. Over the course of this time Seliger provided many condemning details of Lingg's bomb making and most importantly revealed convincing evidence that Lingg and others of the Northwest Side Group anticipated that the evening of the Haymarket meeting would be their moment of truth and they hurriedly prepared their bombs and arms in anticipation.[45]

Seliger said that he rose early on the morning of the Haymarket meeting and told Lingg that he wanted "those things removed from my dwelling," referring to Lingg's collection of bombs. Lingg, who apparently was accustomed to ordering Seliger around, told him instead "to work diligently at these bombs and they would be taken away that day." He also told Seliger that they didn't have enough connecting bolts and he needed to go out and purchase some more. Seliger obeyed and brought back 50 more and then set about drilling holes in the cast lead hemispheres. Seliger worked for half an hour drilling the holes through which the connecting bolt threaded until Lingg left for some meeting and then quit. When Lingg returned later that afternoon he scolded Seliger for having done so little and told him that "we have to work very diligently this afternoon . . . "

Assistant prosecutor Ingham held up one of the globular bombs seized from Lingg's rooms and Seliger identified it as one just like the ones he worked on. Judge Gary asked if the bomb was loaded and Prosecutor Grinnell indicated it was. Peeved, Judge Gary scolded the prosecutors during a recess when the jurors were out of earshot. "We don't know what might . . . happen if one of these machines fell on the floor and though [Inspector] Bonfield handles them as if they were so much wood or iron, I don't propose to run the smallest fraction of risk, especially when there's no need for it." The judge ordered the prosecutors and the police to empty all explosives out of their specimens before bringing them to court.[46]

Seliger and Lingg's work apparently had special urgency that particular day, for six other members of the "armed section" arrived at various times to assist them. By that evening, the industrious group had assembled, according to Seliger's estimate, somewhere between 30 and 50 bombs, some of the round "czar" bomb variety and some pipe bombs. When the prosecutor asked Seliger why they were in such a rush to complete their work, Seliger at first said that it was because he had asked Lingg to remove the bombs from his room but then quickly added that Lingg made a remark that "they should be used that evening—that they were to be used that evening." When Seliger was asked if Lingg had said anything about what they were to be used for, Seliger answered, "he said that was going to be good fodder for the capitalists and the police when they came to protect the capitalists."

When they finished a little after eight that evening, Seliger and Lingg put the loaded bombs in a trunk which proved too heavy for one of them to carry alone, so Lingg broke a stick and snaked it through the trunk's handle and the two of them carried the potent parcel to Neff's Saloon, on Clybourn street, about a mile away. They passed through the saloon to the back hall that was so often used by anarchist groups it was known as "the shanty of the communists" and there they left the open trunk. Seliger said that he saw "three or four" men help themselves to bombs and he took two for himself before leaving with Lingg and two other burly Lehr and Wehr men.[47]

The four of them walked to Larrabie street and Lingg and Seliger took up a position within sight of the Larrabie police station. When asked why they went there,

Seliger explained, "... there were disturbances to be made on the West and North Side to prevent the police to go over to the West Side." Seliger went on to claim that if not for his clever diversion of Lingg, his companion would have tossed the bomb in his pocket into a passing police wagon. Later that night, after eleven, Seliger said that he returned with Lingg to Neff's saloon and there ran into men who had come from the Haymarket with news of the bombing. One of them scolded Lingg, yelling across the bar, "You are the fault of all of it." [48]

Seliger's testimony closed one of the links of the chain of evidence between the plans laid in Greif's basement on Monday night and the bombing the following day. Lingg did not just make bombs, he and his comrades in arms redoubled their efforts the day of the Haymarket meeting to fashion as many bombs as they could before that night. According to Seliger, Lingg knew of important elements of the Monday night cabal's plans: he knew that the main action was to be a "disturbance" on the West Side and he spotted the code printed in Tuesday morning's *Arbeiter Zeitung*—"Ruhe"—that was the signal for the mustering of the armed groups. Seliger testified that Lingg told him that "Ruhe" meant that "everything was to go upside down—topsy turvy—that there was to be trouble."[49]

Seliger's testimony was backed up by his wife, Bertha, a small woman "with a shade of asperity in the tone of her voice...," and by the bartender at Neff's saloon where he said he and Lingg dropped off their satchel of bombs. Through an interpreter Bertha told how she spied on Lingg and his friends making bombs that day and how she had scolded Lingg for melting lead on her cooking stove four times in the previous weeks. The day after the bombing she caught him hollowing out a hiding place inside his closet and covering it with fresh wallpaper. Defense attorney Foster got Bertha to admit she had been locked up twice by the police and then given money by Inspector Schaack to pay her rent, though she earnestly denied that she was shading her testimony to please the police.[50]

Moritz Neff was tending his saloon that fateful Tuesday evening when he recalled seeing Seliger and Lingg and another companion carry a "satchel" into the bar. They stayed a short time and went out through the back hall. Later, after eleven o'clock that night, a number of radicals arrived including Lingg and Neff, just as Seliger had testified, overheard one of them shout at Lingg, "Its all your fault."[51]

Neff, the anarchist barkeep, later hinted to a reporter that he knew more about the circumstances of the Haymarket bombing than he revealed from the witness chair. A few months later when the prospect of a second trial loomed, Neff made arrangements to immigrate to an anarchist colony in the Republic of San Domingo (the present day Dominican Republic) rather than be called again as a witness. "If Spies and the other convicted Anarchists really get a second trial the State will make it warm for some people in Chicago who believe that nobody knows of their close connection with the bomb throwing." Neff believed that a second trial would only serve to implicate more people and further incriminate those already convicted. "I honestly believe Spies should avoid a second trial under all circumstances. As things are now he may be pardoned; a second trial will bring out such additional evidence as will send him and his accomplices now in jail to the gallows sure and add perhaps a dozen more to the list." Neff and the other organizers peddled stock certificates in their St. Domingo Colonization Society for 50 dollars each. The scheme must not have panned out as by 1900, Neff was living alone in a crowded boarding house on Broome street in New York city, ironically listing his occupation as a broker.[52]

The testimony of Gustave Lehman, yet another anarchist carpenter and colleague of both Lingg and Seliger, connected Lingg to the Greif's Hall conspiracy meeting and the Haymarket bombing. When Lehman arrived for the basement meeting he was told to stand outside on the sidewalk to make sure no one lingered around the water closets and eavesdropped through the door on their meeting. Lehman only ducked into the room a few times and caught bits of the proceedings. He did not remember seeing Lingg there but he did distinctly remember walking home with him and Seliger and a couple of other radicals from the meeting. Lingg baited his companions and said, "You are all oxen—fools," and told them that if they wanted to know what was going on they should all be at Neff's the following night.

The next day, Tuesday, the morning of the bombing, Lehman and a friend went to Lingg's house around five in the evening to buy a revolver. They found a number of men hard at work, Lingg and another man had kerchiefs tied around their faces and were busily working on something he couldn't see in the back room. In the front room another man was cutting fuses and pushing them into blasting caps. It doesn't seem that Lehman got the gun he was hoping to buy, but Lingg gave him a small leather-covered case that contained three round bombs, two coils of fuse, blasting caps, and a tin can filled with a substance he assumed was dynamite. None of these activities surprised Lehman at the time as his anarchist carpenters union had held a benefit dance at Florus Hall weeks earlier that raised over 10 dollars from the sale of beer. The militant carpenters unanimously voted to dedicate this tidy sum to purchase explosives for their "armed wing" and it was duly entrusted to brother Lingg to fulfill the union's charge.[53]

Two men swore to have seen things that, if true, confirmed that the Haymarket bombing was the culmination of the anarchists' plans. Malvern Thompson was an ambitious young man who had opened his own grocery store at 108 South Desplaines Ave., three blocks south of Haymarket Square when he was just 23. But by the time he appeared as a witness, Thompson had lost his store to the sheriff for unpaid debts and had taken a job as a hosiery clerk for Marshall Field, the same firm he had worked for before going into business for himself. His fortunes seemed to continue to decline once the trial was over. In 1910 he was working as a janitor and living on Butler street, an occupation he maintained over the next decade.[54]

Thompson, claimed to have shadowed Spies and Schwab as they walked around the Haymarket making preparations for the meeting. He didn't know either Schwab or Spies but claimed Schwab was pointed out to him by a reporter he knew. Purely out of curiosity, Thompson walked near to where Schwab stood and observed Spies climb onto the wagon and ask if anyone had seen Parsons. Spies climbed off the wagon and Thompson hovered near the mouth of Crane's alley that Spies had ducked into with Schwab. Thompson claimed he caught bits of their conversation, overhearing Spies ask his companion, "Do you think one is enough or hadn't we better go and get more?" and a reference to "pistols" and "police." Following the pair as they left the alley and walked up the two blocks to Halsted street and back, Thompson said that he eavesdropped on more of their conversation, though some was in English and some in German. He did catch Schwab remark, "Now, if they come, we will give it to them." Back near the speaker's wagon ten minutes later, Thompson watched as the pair were joined by a third party that Thompson later identified as Schnaubelt who was handed something by Spies that he stuffed into his pocket. Spies then began his speech and Schwab disappeared.

It was firmly established, indeed later not even disputed by the defense, that Schwab arrived at the Haymarket from a meeting at the *Arbeiter Zeitung* office. Thus, through the young grocer, the prosecution had not only linked two of the supposed conspirators with the bomber, but through Schwab connected the bomber to the *Arbeiter Zeitung* office on Fifth avenue, a building the prosecutors called the "headquarters of anarchy," and a place where bombs had been discovered by the police and where Spies and others had handled and brandished bombs to reporters.[55]

Defense lawyers did find one opening to exploit. They ridiculed Thompson's claim that he overheard the pair speaking in English, a language they claimed Schwab spoke only "brokenly." "Don't you know," asked defense attorney Foster, "that Mr. Schwab can speak with but very little English, and he and Mr. Spies always talk German when they speak together?" Prosecutors didn't rebut this statement, but Schwab, in his own autobiography, noted that he began studying English in Germany before emigrating to the US; that once in the US "With all my energy, I commenced to study the English language. When I was so far advanced that I could under-stand books written in that language, I studied the history of the United States. Bancroft's was the best work among those I read." Schwab documented how he traveled throughout the west in non-German communities and even had long con-versations with a Morman elder in Cheyenne. Most importantly, his English was good enough that Spies first hired him to translate the potboiler English romance *Wanda Kryloff* into German.[56]

The day following Thompson's appearance proved even more dramatic. In what the *Tribune* reporter described as the "sensational climax" of the trial, prosecutor Grinnell called Harry L. Gilmer to the witness chair. Gilmer strode forward and as he did everyone in the courtroom could see what an odd and eccentric being he was. He was 45 years old, thin and tall, six foot three with a long neck, dangly limbs, and awkward size 14 feet. His hair was long and curly, his moustache poorly trimmed and his black suit seedy. One reporter thought he looked like a Methodist circuit rider or like he belonged in Barnum's circus. Of course, what most made him the most "sensational" witness was not his strange and eccentric appearance but the story he told. Gilmer claimed to have seen the faces of the bomber and his accomplices.[57]

Gilmer was a pathetic loner. His family was from Virginia but he spent most of his years in Iowa. He moved to Chicago in 1879 after his wife died and since then had worked odd jobs by the day or week, usually as a painter, but sometimes as a hand on a lake freighter, or a night watchman. Likely an alcoholic, he lived in a succession of flop houses, boarding houses, and apartments. His itinerant lifestyle allowed him to avoid being found by the census enumerator and Gilmer left few records besides his appearance in court, though there are a few scraps: about the same time as he arrived in the city, Gilmer was hauled up on charges of larceny but he was acquitted. The weekend of the eight-hour strikes Gilmer managed to find work as a watchman for a private security company under contract with the railroads. He was given a little tin star to pin on his lapel and assigned to look over the Wabash freight houses that had long been the target of radicals.[58]

By his background and rootless, some would have said shiftless, existence, Gilmer was far from being an ideal witness. But what he lacked in status and character he seemed to make up for in his performance as a witness. Gilmer told his story emphatically, carefully, and could not be shaken into contradicting himself through an afternoon of intense cross-examination.[59]

He said that he arrived at the meeting about a quarter to ten and heard Fielden speaking from the back of the wagon. Listening for a minute, he moved around the crowd looking for a man he knew and stepped into Crane's alley when he heard a man out on the street yell, "here comes the police." Most of those in the alley rushed forward to get a look. Gilmer saw a man come from the wagon and approach some men huddled together in the alleyway. According to Gilmer, the man "lit a match and he touched it off . . . the fuse commenced to fizzle, and he gave it a couple of steps and tossed it over into the street." Grinnell asked him to describe the man who threw the bomb and Gilmer said that he was "a man about five feet, perhaps ten inches high, somewhat full chested, and he had a light or sandy beard, not very long." Grinnell then showed him a photograph, and Gilmer said, "that is the man that threw the bomb out of the alley." Then Grinnell asked if he knew who the man was that came from the wagon and lit the bomb and Gilmer extended a bony finger and pointed it at August Spies and said, "That is the man right there." Gilmer then identified Fischer as the third man who huddled with the bomber and Spies.[60]

Gilmer's testimony influenced the jurors. After the trial was over one of the jurors, the clerk C.B. Todd, was asked whether he had been "impressed" with Gilmer's testimony and he replied, "Well, it was corroborated, you know. The testimony impressed me as strong, and, I think, it had effect with the other jurors."[61]

Following Gilmer the remainder of the prosecution's witness list comprised legal housekeeping, mostly witnesses whose purpose was to establish the chain of physical evidence in the case. Police officers and detectives who searched the offices of the *Arbeiter Zeitung* and the houses of the defendants detailed where they found their bombs, banners, flags, letters, and fuses. Physicians who treated wounded cops described their wounds and what they did with some of the bits of metal they cut out of their flesh. Chemists described how they scratched samples from the inside of the bomb shells seized from the paper office and Lingg's apartment and found them to have a unique and similar mixture of elements to the Haymarket bomb's shrapnel. One poor citizen was called to swear before the court that the square steel nut exhibited was in fact the same one that had been extracted from where it lodged in his butt. The nut was of the same bore as the bolts found in Lingg's room.[62]

In a final tug on the heartstrings of the jury, Grinnell called officer John Stift, the policeman who lifted the bloody body of Mathias Degan into a patrol wagon and rushed to the hospital, and then called John Degan, Mathias' brother. John Degan told the court that his brother was born in Germany and was 34 years old and lost his wife some years back leaving him alone with his 14-year-old son. John Degan was asked when was the last time he saw his brother and he answered, "In the morgue ... Dead."[63]

William Holmes, a member of Parsons' American section and husband of the equally radical Lizzie, wrote several reports of the trial for *The Commonweal*, the official journal of the English Socialist League. In his dispatches Holmes scathingly criticized the conduct of the trial, the bias of Judge Gary, the viciousness of prosecutor Grinnell, and the transparency of the perjured testimony and manufactured evidence he heard. None of Holmes' criticisms were unusual among those of the anarchists' defenders and nearly all could later be found in Dyer Lum's *Trial of the Chicago Anarchists*. But what is notable about Holmes' letters to London are the points raised by the prosecution that he did not condemn.

At the time of writing his first article the prosecution had not yet rested though it was nearly finished presenting its evidence and Holmes seemed sure that what he thought was perjured testimony and false evidence would be easily refuted when the defense took its turn. Flush with such confidence, Holmes was willing to concede a few points that he thought the prosecution had proven but which he didn't think amounted to much: " ... the State has proved nothing except that Socialists in Chicago were actively preparing for the social revolution, that a few of the boldest and most enthusiastic had manufactured and stored explosives, that some of them were armed with rifles and revolvers, and a very few wished to inaugurate the revolution on or about the first of May." In his next dispatch sent a week later after the state rested and the anarchist lawyers began calling witnesses, Holmes again accepted these allegations as facts: "It is true the defense have not disproved what the prosecution apparently showed, that there was movement on foot to precipitate the social revolution ... " Holmes evidently did not at this point think that admitting that there were some in the Chicago movement who seriously plotted and even took actions to "inaugurate" an armed revolution, conceded much. But as the trial dragged on and the defense took its turn in the ring but stumbled about like a blind fighter, swinging hard but landing few blows, Holmes' tone changed and he never again glibly mentioned that anarchists prepared for social revolution, armed themselves, and stockpiled explosives.[64]

CHAPTER 4

THE DEFENSE

IT WAS ONLY AFTER THE STATE RESTED ITS CASE and the youthful defense attorney Moses Salomon stepped forward to deliver his opening statements that the defense's strategy became clear. For two weeks the mystery had thickened. How would the lawyers for the accused anarchists attempt to extricate their clients from the nooses dangling ever closer to them with each successive witness? Usually in cases of such magnitude some hints would have emerged at the beginning of the trial when the defense offered its rebuttal to the prosecutor's opening statements. But the defense had waived this right at the outset and so the first inkling of the defense's strategy came at this late date when Salomon outlined his case before calling his first witness.

Predictably, Salomon indicated that the defense would lean heavily on alibis. After all, State witnesses placed only five of the eight men on trial near the Haymarket square that night: Spies, Parsons and Fielden, who all delivered speeches, Fischer who was spotted ambling around the area, and Schwab who was seen having a conversation with Spies just before the rally began. Salomon told the jurors that the defense would prove that Parsons and Fischer were "quietly seated at Zepf's Hall, drinking, perhaps, a glass of beer at the time the bomb exploded," while Engel was at home, Lingg was miles away roaming around the Northside, Schwab was delivering a speech near the Deering factory and Neebe didn't even know the meeting was happening.

Salomon's speech was a routine summary of his defendant's alibis until he turned his attention to the most problematic of his clients, Louis Lingg, whose case in many ways was the weakest point of the defense and one that probably should have been left alone:

> With the whereabouts of Lingg you are already familiar. It may seem strange why he was manufacturing bombs. The answer to that is, he had a right to have his house full of dynamite. He had a right to have weapons of all descriptions upon his premises, and until he used them, or advised their use, and they were used in pursuance of his advice, he is not liable any more than the man who commits numerous burglaries, the man who commits numerous thefts, who walks the streets, is liable to arrest and punishment only when he commits an act which makes him amenable to law.[1]

It is not recorded whether Lingg thought it helpful to his defense to have his lawyer admit he made bombs and had "his house full of dynamite" or to be compared to a common thief.

Few legal observers could have been surprised to hear that the defense would rally witnesses who would refute the testimony of several key prosecution "squealers." Salomon promised to show that Harry Gilmer, the keystone of the prosecution's case who claimed to have seen Spies light the fuse, would be exposed as a "professional and constitutional liar." Malvern Thompson, that nosey grocer who claimed to have followed Spies and Schwab around Haymarket Square and overheard snippets of their conversation, was simply mistaken.

Salomon announced his attention to disprove the theory that there was any plot to murder policemen at the Haymarket: "We expect to show you, further, that these defendants never conspired, nor any one of them, to take the life of any single individual at any time or place..." Any lawyer worth his salt would have attempted to punch holes in this crucial element of the prosecution's theory and there were numerous ways to go about it, such as stressing the weak points of connection between some of the supposed conspirators or arguing that the rhetoric of "revolution" was metaphorical, a moral and inspirational tale but nothing meant to cause immediate action. But Salomon took a different and eyebrow-raising approach. Rather he chose to argue that there was no conspiracy to commit murder because the conspiracy these men entered into was only to act in self-defense of their constitutional rights. Incredibly, Salomon told the court the accused "...never conspired or plotted to take, at this time or at any other time, the life of Mathias Degan or any number of policemen, except in self-defense while carrying out their original purpose...." At one stroke Salomon confirmed that his clients were indeed conspirators and that part of their conspiracy included violence under certain previously agreed upon conditions. Salomon asked rhetorically, "what have these defendants done?"

> Have they murdered any people? What was their plan when they counseled dynamite? They intended to use dynamite in furtherance of the general revolution; never, never against any individual. We will show you that it was their purpose, as the proof, I think, partly shows already, that when a general revolution or a general strike was inaugurated, when they were attacked, that then, in fact, while carrying out the purposes of that strike or that revolution, that then they should use dynamite, and not until then. If it is unlawful to conspire to carry out that thing, these men must be held for that thing..."[2]

While Salomon may have tried to seize the high and patriotic ground of American traditions of resistance to tyranny and the popular defense of inalienable rights, did he really think throwing such considerations onto his half of the balance would tip the scales when there were eight police corpses heaped on the other pan? Was he oblivious to the fact that he had just conceded the State's most vital point, that his clients did conspire together to use force?

There is some evidence that this tactic may have actually originated not with the anarchists' lawyers but from one of their clients. In the early days of the trial Albert

Parsons watched the proceedings attentively and wrote notes to himself. A few of these scraps have survived and expose a bit of his thinking about how he thought his defense should be structured. Parsons jotted down what he heard Judge Gary say to the newly empanelled jurors: "The task before this jury will be to weigh the evidence and ascertain if these 8 men or any one of them is guilty of killing Officer Durgan." (*sic*) Parsons then wrote to himself:

> Note. Aside from this, the question of *justification* will arise. There was no *overt act* by any man in the Haymarket audience, there was merely an expression of opinion to which all are entitled. Yet without any overt act, the Police, in menacing, armed array, ordered the peaceable assemblage to disperse. This was unlawful force, and provoked resistance, which is justified by the higher law of self-preservation, etc." & of God resistance to tyrants, etc.[3]

Parsons added that his older brother, William H. Parsons, was counseling that he should claim self-defense. "W.H.P. says make a defense of your constitutional right of resistance. *Prove* the base and awful conspiracy of Monopoly to suppress Labor organizations by the use of Hand Grenades, . . . police clubs, rifle diet, & which they have used repeatedly since 1878."[4]

The danger of this defense was that it conceded many material points at issue to the prosecution. It was, after all, less a denial of the charges than a justification of them. By claiming that the police were the aggressors and the assembled citizens on Desplaines Avenue were merely defending their inherent Constitutional rights, the defense opened the door further to putting their clients' beliefs on trial. Salomon seemed eager to parade his clients' ideology before the jury and confident that if their socialism were properly understood he would garner sympathy for the noble and self-sacrificing impulses of the men the prosecution had characterized as fiends and murderers.

> Now, these defendants claim that Socialism is a progressive social science, and it will be a part of the proof which you will have to determine. Must the world stand as we found it when we were born, or have we a right to show our fellow-men a better way, a nobler life, a better condition? That is what these defendants claim, if they are forced beyond the issue in this case. . . . [5]

Salomon revealed that the defense was going to pursue an affirmative defense and show that not only did the police lack justification for breaking up a peaceful meeting, but that they were themselves plotting to attack and destroy the anarchists once and for all. The police, Salomon charged, had a "devilish design" and "came down upon that body with their revolvers in their hands and pockets, ready for immediate use, intending to destroy the life of every man that stood upon that market square." In the face of such provocation, the crowd acted with laudable restraint and "not a single person fired a single shot at the police officers." The fact that so many policemen appeared to have been wounded by gunfire was to be explained by showing that these men fell victim to the errant and excited shots of their own fellow cops.[6]

The task that Salomon laid out for himself and his fellow lawyers was unnec-
essarily complicated. It required not only distancing his clients from the claims of
the state by highlighting their alibis, but to succeed had to show also that dozens of
police officers perjured themselves in their sworn testimony. Salomon's only hope was
to construct an alternative narrative of events that hinged on proving two elements:
that the police rushed to destroy the anarchists gathered that night and in their frenzy
succumbed to their own friendly fire and that the bomb thrower launched his missile
from a location that was entirely inconsistent with the allegations of Harry Gilmer
(that Spies lit the bomb in Crane's alley and the bomber took a few steps to the alley's
mouth to throw it).

Keen legal minds who heard Salomon's speech thought it a disaster for the defense.
Chicago's city attorney, who had no part in the trial but was simply observing that
day, was caught by a reporter and asked what he thought of Salomon's opening. He
replied, "I think it was a splendid speech for the state; I think it was sufficient in itself
to hang every man on trial."[7]

Judging from the lineup of witnesses they called as they took their turn at the bar,
the defense strategy was to begin by justifying the throwing the bomb as a necessary
response to a police attempt to trample on their rights. The first defense witness called
to the stand was the mayor of Chicago, Carter Harrison. In spite of having come
under intense criticism for having coddled the anarchists out of fear of damaging
his support in the vast immigrant wards that kept his Democratic machine in office,
Harrison was a popular and charismatic figure and his presence that day overfilled
the courtroom. Judge Gary disapproved of the packed crowd and ordered his bailiffs
to remove anyone who did not have a proper seat and among those ejected were a
"prominent lawyer and his three lady friends."[8]

Captain Black led the questioning himself and seemed to be steering the mayor
in a positive direction as he asked him to characterize the tenor of the meeting and
Harrison replied that he feared the direction it was going until he resolved to make
his presence known:

> Mr. Spies, a part of his speech was of the character that I thought was leading up to
> it, and it was just after I lit my match, I say—my cigar goes out a great deal, and I use
> more matches than I do cigars a good deal—I struck it, and the first one went out.
> I put two together, and the flame was wide and it made quite a blaze in my face. Almost
> immediately afterwards I noticed this change in the tone of his speech, and as I say,
> I turned to my son and said, "Spies has seen me."[9]

From that point on the mayor described the speeches he heard as "tame." Having
established that the meeting was a peaceful one (though perhaps reluctantly so in
respect to the presence of the mayor), Black pushed on to his punchline. What he
most desired was to get Harrison to repeat a comment he had made to the papers in
the days after the bombing that he had given the order to Bonfield to send his reserve
troops home. To do so Black had to employ the utmost finesse as such testimony
not involving any of the defendants or their actions was not normally admissible
under the rules of evidence. Black probed the margins of this subject gingerly by

asking a permissible question about Harrison's movements that night: "How long was the interview you had with Inspector Bonfield...?" It was about five minutes long Harrison replied and Black pressed on and asked him what that conversation was. Prosecutor Grinnell leaped to object. Captain Black argued the point:

> It is admissible upon our theory of the defense. We propose to show by this witness that in the course of that interview, he had a talk with Capt. Bonfield, submitted to him his views as to the nature of the audience, and communicated to him the fact that he did not think there would be any trouble; that the meeting was a quiet and orderly meeting as such meetings went; and that he was about to go home and also directed that the police patrolmen which had been held under his direction at the other stations should be directed to go home; and having given these directions to Capt. Bonfield, he himself went home.... We propose to follow that up by other testimony which will show that the attack made by the police that night upon the meeting was a deliberate attack planned and carried out after Mr. Harrison's departure.[10]

Judge Gary ruled Black's line of questioning out of order and just when Black's strategy seemed sunk, Grinnell revealed a suspiciously generous heart and withdrew his objection, saying "The conversation may be irrelevant to this issue but if any orders were given by Harrison to Bonfield that night with reference to that meeting, let it come in." Black should have been sensed that something foul was afoot when Grinnell asked if he was sure he wanted to walk down that road: "What you want is in regard to this matter that night?" but Black did not scent the trap and emphatically responded, "That is what I want." Harrison who had been patiently watching this legal joust unfold then proceeded:

> I went back to the station and stated to Bonfield that I thought the speeches were about to be over; that nothing had occurred yet, or looked likely to occur to require interference, and I thought he had better issue orders to his reserves at that other stations to go home. He replied to me that he had learned the same and reached that conclusion from persons coming and going—he had men out all the time—and had already issued the order; that he thought it would be best to retain the men that were in the station until the meeting broke up, and then referred to a rumor that he had heard that night that would make it necessary for him, he thought, to keep his men there, which I concurred in. Do you want that rumor?

Cocounsel Zeisler sensed their jeopardy and interjected, "That was not in reference to the Haymarket..." Grinnell reeled in his catch: "Yes, it is a part of that conversation and it should all go in." Judge Gary then ruled that Grinnell could probe this "rumor" in his cross-examination of the witness. Black hastily backtracked and unsuccessfully tried to argue that the same conversation he had just wedged into the record should be kept out. Grinnell asked the mayor what rumor he had heard:

> ...Capt. Bonfield told me that he had just received information that this meeting would...adjourn or go over to the Milwaukee & St. Paul freight houses that were

then filled up with what they call scabs, and blow it up; and then there was also an intimation that this meeting might be merely a ruse to attract the attention of the police to the Haymarket while the real attack if any should be made that night would be on McCormick's. Now, it was with regard to those two possible, if not probable contingencies that I was listening to those speeches. . . .

Harrison then clarified what he told Bonfield that night while the speeches were still in progress:

. . . [I thought] the reserves held at the other stations might be sent home, because I learned that all was quiet down in the second district in which McCormick's was; and that I thought there was no design for anything that night. Bonfield replied that he had reached the same conclusion from reports brought in to him, and he had already ordered the reserves elsewhere sent home . . . but that if something might occur yet before this meeting was over or after it, that he would hold the men that were in the station until everything was over. I acquiesced in his suggestion . . . [11]

The reserves that Harrison referred to were not the 200 or so officers sprawled around the interior of the Desplaines station, but the 50 extra men held in readiness at each of the other outlying stations of the city.[12]

In a gut-wrenching turn of events for the defense team, their lead witness was now not only arguing against their theory of self-defense, he concluded by implying that the violence two days earlier at the McCormick factory that set all these events into motion was a calculated provocation on the part of the anarchists. "I was determined," said the mayor, "that there should be no reoccurrence of the violence at McCormick's hall; that if there was an overt act, it would be caught in its incipiency and not wait until it took absolute form."[13]

Black had better luck with his next witness, a traveling wholesale clothing salesman named Barton Simonson whom Judge Gary permitted to recall a conversation he had with Captain Bonfield over the objections of the prosecutor. Simonson had chatted with Bonfield at the police station before the riot and remembered Bonfield taking a threatening tone: " 'The trouble there is that these'—whether he used the word socialists or strikers I don't know which—'Get their women and children mixed up with them and around them and in front of them, and we can't get at them.' . . . After he said that he would like to have and get a crowd of three thousand of them without their women and children, then to the best of my recollection he said: 'And I will make short work of them,' or something to that effect. That is the way it impressed me at the time." Simonson's testimony further clouded the reputation of the already controversial Bonfield and proved the strongest evidence that Black was able to produce in support of a necessity defense. But however hot was Bonfield's hatred of the anarchists, Black still faced the difficult prospect of proving that the police attack was unprovoked and that the bomb was thrown in self-defense in order to win this legal point.[14]

Like Simonson, the next witness, John Ferguson, a cloakmaker, promised to be particularly valuable to the defense because unlike most of the witnesses the defense called to testify, Ferguson appeared to not have any connection to the anarchists. He swore he was not a socialist, or an anarchist, and had only come to the Haymarket at the suggestion of a friend. Judging by the questions Black put to him, Ferguson's purpose was to establish that the police had rushed out of their station with unnecessary haste to disperse the meeting and that they had done all the shooting that night. At the time the bomb exploded, Ferguson was on the far side of Randolph street and heading south with his friend William Gleason. He watched as the police double-timed up the street, one of their commanders yelling for the ranks to "hurry up." There was a sharp sound, like that of a board breaking and Gleason commented that he thought it was a shot and they looked back at the protest in time to see the bomb explode and the flash of muzzles from the center of the street where the police were massed.

Ferguson appeared to have been a very persuasive witness until the following day Captain Black called to the stand Ferguson's companion at Haymarket that night, William Gleason, a shoemaker who was also cruelly known as "club foot Gleason." Though Ferguson had claimed that he and Gleason were never separated that night, indeed they stood most of the night "arm in arm," from the moment he began talking, Gleason's account veered sharply away from that of his friend. Ferguson said that Spies was talking when they arrived but Gleason remembered Parsons as the first speaker he heard. Ferguson remembered hearing a sound like the breaking of a board before the bomb exploded and even remembered Gleason remarking that the sound was a "shot." But Gleason was quite sure he heard no noise prior to the thunder of the bomb. Like his friend, Gleason testified that he saw muzzle flashes from the midst of the police and none emanating from the crowd but when pressed on this point he admitted that from where he was standing near the police station "I was too far away to see."[15]

Having forced Gleason to retract some of his testimony, Grinnell then pressed him, and by implication Ferguson, on their credibility. Both men had denied having any association with the anarchists but as Grinnell poked and scratched at his background and activities a different portrait emerged. Gleason admitted he belonged to an Irish "revolutionary society" before he immigrated to America though he denied being one of O'Donovan Rossa's "dynamiters," a gang with strong connections to revolutionary anarchists in New York city. At first Gleason denied serving on a labor committee charged with petitioning the mayor to fire Captain Bonfield but Grinnell hammered away at the witness and he relented, admitting that he had advocated this course of action as a member of the Trades and Labor Assembly.[16]

Grinnell displayed a talent for pressing the weak points in the testimonies of defense witnesses until they found themselves trapped by their own statements. Many a witness under Grinnell's persistent cross-examination twisted themselves into knots or revealed more than they intended. Friedrich Liebel presented himself as a disinterested worker who had no connection to the anarchists when he answered Zeisler's questions. But Grinnell maneuvered him around to admitting that he subscribed to the *Arbeiter Zeitung*, was a member of Lingg's carpenter's union, lived in the same building with a member of Lingg and Schwab's group, Abraham Hermann, and on the same block as Neff's Hall, had visited Lingg, Schwab, and Spies in jail, had attended a fundraiser for the defense at Ogden's Grove, and had attended more anarchist meetings than he could count or remember. Grinnell asked him a series of rapid fire questions about the addresses and building numbers of various meeting halls and then abruptly tacked in another direction catching Liebel unguarded:[17]

> Q: Do you belong to any group?
> A: No sir.
> Q: Never did?
> A: No sir. Do you mean armed group?
> Q: Did I say anything about armed?[18]

Grinnell hadn't mentioned anything about groups, armed or not until that point.

Such discrepancies could not have escaped the attention of the attentive jurors who in this era were allowed to take notes and confer about each day's testimony over dinner and in their hotel rooms. Defense lawyer Sigmund Zeisler observed that most of the jurors "were almost incessantly writing in little note books, while evidence was introduced, most of them in long-hand, one juror...in short-hand." Such discrepancies were only compounded by the fact that the prosecution's witnesses were much more consistent in their accounts of how the bomb was thrown, the sequence of gunfire, and the general terrain of the street.[19]

Nearly all the rest of the witnesses that the defense called to testify were selected in reaction to the testimony of the state's eyewitnesses to the bomb throwing, Gilmer and Thompson. A dozen witnesses were summoned to show that Michael Schwab could not have huddled with Spies and Schnaubelt before the meeting as the grocer Melvern Thompson alleged, including Michael Schwab himself. Just as many witnesses were paraded through the court to swear that the bomb was thrown from a point far away from the alleyway where Gilmer claimed to have seen the bomber. Another group of witnesses attempted to show why Samuel Fielden could not have fired on the police while yet another clutch of witnesses firmed up alibis for Parsons and Fischer, placing them quaffing beers at a nearby bar when the bomb exploded. A final string of ten witnesses were called simply to state that they believed Gilmer was a man of bad reputation and they wouldn't believe something he said was the truth.

THE CURIOUS MOVEMENTS OF MICHAEL SCHWAB

Of all the defendants, Michael Schwab's alibi was the most dependent on a careful accounting of his movements and the time he spent at various locations that night. Schwab admitted that just prior to the start of the meeting he had walked to the Haymarket Square but by the time the meeting was in full swing he was four miles north addressing a rally of striking workers. About the time of the blast, he was climbing aboard a streetcar to go home. But regardless of where he was when the bomb exploded, the most crucial timeframe of his alibi was his claim to have paused only a few moments in the Haymarket Square, just long enough to look around for Spies, talk briefly to his brother-in-law Schnaubelt, and then jump on a streetcar going back downtown. For Schwab's accounting of his movements contradicted the testimony of Malvern Thompson, the young grocer who claimed to have shadowed Schwab and Spies as they wandered around the square conspiring about pistols, police, and remarking about "Do you think one is enough . . . ?"

Schwab was the first of the defendants to take the stand in his own defense. Meticulously, Foster, the most competent defense litigator, led Schwab step by step through all of his many movements that night in order to show that he could not have been in the Haymarket Square as long as Thompson (and Officer Timothy McKeough) claimed he had been. Schwab detailed every minute of an evening in which he took a horsecar downtown to attend a meeting on Fifth Avenue, walked to the Haymarket, rode a horsecar back the way he had just come to catch a second horsecar heading north, stopped at a saloon, addressed an outdoor rally, stopped at another saloon, took another horsecar south, and walked the last mile to his home. When Foster asked him how long he lingered about the vicinity of the Haymarket, Schwab answered with certainty, "it could not have been more than five minutes."[20]

Grocer Thompson claimed to have first seen Schwab at the Haymarket around 7:45. He estimated that it was about 8:15 when Schwab and Spies stepped into Crane's Alley and that it was around 8:25 or 8:30 when Spies climbed onto the wagon to resume speaking and Schwab disappeared. His recollection of the sequence and timing of events was in harmony with those of other witnesses. *Chicago Times* reporter Edgar Owen was on time for the Haymarket meeting, 7:30, and remembered the meeting beginning shortly after 8:30. Owen remembered seeing Schwab in the area sometime before that. The star witness for the defense, Mayor Carter Harrison, recalled that he arrived in the area around 7:50 and that the Spies began his speech around 8:30.[21]

Schwab testified that he left his home on the North side at 7:40 and rode a horsecar down to the *Arbeiter Zeitung* building arriving a little past 8 P.M. At 8:10 he left the office and walked over to the Haymarket. He lingered there for no more than five minutes, then jumped on a horsecar going downtown, transferring to the Clybourne avenue car at "about half past eight" or "maybe 8:40." By his own estimate, at most there was 30 minutes between the time he left the office and the time he caught the northbound horsecar. This all checks out as the distance from the office to the Haymarket was a walk of eight-tenths of a mile, a distance covered by an average man at an average gait in roughly 15 minutes; he spent five minutes in the Haymarket; and the streetcar from the Haymarket to Clark street took ten minutes, assuming he caught it without waiting: for a total of 30 minutes. Lending credence to his account, the defense called a local butcher who lived on Randolph street and swore he was looking out his window when he saw Schwab step onto an eastbound streetcar "a few minutes" after eight.[22]

However, through all the details of his travels, Schwab must have lost track of the amount of time he had to account for on the other end of his trip. Three days earlier Edward Preusser, a deliveryman for the *Arbeiter Zeitung* who lived up near the

Deering factory and claimed to have been the man who called down to the newspaper office seeking a speaker for a meeting of Deering workers, testified that he met Schwab as he was arriving on the Clybourne avenue streetcar at "Half past nine or twenty minutes to ten."[23] Schwab said that he boarded that streetcar around 8:40 leaving a margin between when Schwab said he boarded the northbound horsecar and when Preusser saw him step off between 50 minutes and one hour. But Schwab testified that this leg of the horsecar trip only took between 40 and 45 minutes, leaving a gap of between 10 and 20 minutes that Schwab hadn't accounted for. Thus, if Edward Preusser was accurate in his judgment of time, Schwab could have waited till between 8:35 and 8:50 to leave the area of the Haymarket (about the time Thompson said he lost sight of him) and still arrived in Deering when Preusser thought he did. Ten or twenty minutes was more than enough time for Schwab to have done all the things Malvern Thompson claimed to have seen him do in the vicinity of the Haymarket.[24]

Schwab's own inventory of his travels was contradicted by his fellow party members. Schwab claimed he walked from the newspaper office to Randolph and Desplaines in the company of Balthazar Rau, the man who carried the message that speakers were needed at the Haymarket. Parsons testified that he walked with Fielden. Fielden said that he walked with Parsons, Rau, and Snyder but that Schwab had left the meeting earlier and alone. Snyder said that he walked with Parsons, Fielden, Brown, Thomas, and one other man, but did not see Schwab that night. Brown said that he walked to the Haymarket alone. Lizzie Holmes was most insistent that she didn't see Schwab that night either but saw Parsons and Fielden leave together and left soon after with Lucy Parsons and everyone else who had been at the meeting. All of these statements could not be true.[25]

Complicating the record of who left with who is a curious discrepancy of timing. Albert and Lucy Parsons rode a streetcar from the corner of Randolph and Halsted to Fifth Avenue with their close friend Lizzie Holmes. Parsons testified he left his home at 8 P.M. and did not arrive at the *Arbeiter Zeitung* office until "after eight, possible half past eight . . ." If he left home at eight he could not have arrived much earlier than 8:30. It was one half mile from his apartment at 77 W. Indiana Avenue to the streetcar stop on Randolph (which should have taken ten minutes or longer with two children either in tow or in their arms), then a ten minute car ride to Fifth Avenue and another two-tenths of a mile to the office. But Holmes claimed they arrived at 8 P.M. William Snyder remembered the Parsons arriving about 8:30. Henry Heinemann, a reporter who ran into the Parsons waiting for their streetcar, saw them trundle off toward the loop between "half past seven and eight o'clock" a time incompatible with any of the others' testimony.[26]

Two defense witnesses who attended the IWPA meeting at the *Arbeiter Zeitung* office, including William Snyder who chaired it, stated categorically that they did not see Schwab that night. There were only a dozen or so people at this meeting so it should not have been hard to remember the bespectacled former bookbinder. Four other defense witnesses remembered spotting him there. Those who saw Schwab had a variety of memories about when he left the meeting. Fielden thought he left between 8:10 and 8:15. Joseph Bach thought Schwab left at 8:30. William Patterson put it at "a little after eight."[27]

Deepening the mystery surrounding the comings and goings of Michael Schwab was the nature of the meeting they had all been summoned to. The morning of the meeting Albert Parsons wrote a short announcement and rushed it to the advertising desk of the *Evening News* for publication that same day.[28] It was a brief but curious announcement:

> "American Group Meets To-Night, Tuesday, 107 Fifth Avenue. Important Business. Every Member Should Attend. 7:30 O'Clock Sharp. Agitation Committee."[29]

Not only was the purpose of the meeting not stated, but the location was switched from their usual meeting spot. This club, the American Group of the International Working People's Association, usually met on Thursday evenings at 106 E. Randolph street. The "Armed Section" of the American Group held its musters on Monday nights at Neff's saloon and the American Group of the Central Labor Union met at Zepf's Hall on Wednesdays. Parsons and other Yankee anarchists who attended this meeting claimed that the business that was so important that the "agitation committee" demanded attendance of every member. Its purpose, according to Parsons, was to plan how to organize the sewing girls, but there is scant evidence that this was indeed the case. Earlier that day a strike of factory sewing girls expanded and a reporter on the scene interviewed several of those active in the movement and they expressed their intention to affiliate with the Knights of Labor. No mention was made of a meeting to be held later that evening. Lizzie Holmes who had once worked as a sewing girl and organized sewing girls years before admitted under cross-examination that sewing girls actually attended their meeting. Holmes hurried to explain the suspicious absence of any bona fide sewing girls from a meeting supposedly about them, adding "it was nothing but a business meeting of the Group." But would an ordinary business meeting warrant such urgent efforts to call the membership together? Thickening the mystery of this "sewing girls meeting" was the fact that at the very time the American Group was converging on the editorial offices of the *Arbeiter Zeitung*, actual sewing girls were holding a meeting nearer to the Haymarket at Foltz Hall.[30]

Though the American group members were instructed to appear at "7:30 O'Clock Sharp" not one of the half dozen or so radicals who came to the meeting and later testified were even close to being on time. Parsons who placed the advertisement claimed to have arrived about an hour late. Samuel Fielden was 20 minutes late. Michael Schwab, Lizzie Holmes, Joseph Bach, William Patterson, and Henry Waldo all claimed to have arrived around eight o'clock. William Snyder who presided over the meeting claimed it wasn't called to order until eight-thirty.[31]

There is a simple way to clear away this cloud of confusing recollections. If the urgent meeting actually started when it was supposed to, and the time frame for the actions of everyone involved in it are wound back 30 minutes, the whole sequence then makes sense.

ENGEL'S ALIBI

Prosecutors had presented a strong case that George Engel was the mastermind of the original conspiratorial plan, but they had not attempted to connect him to the Haymarket meeting. Gottfried Waller, one of the state's most important squealers, testified that he stopped by Engel's house on the way to the Haymarket but Engel was not at home. Waller stopped by Engel's store again after the bombing and found a number of men (Bretenfeldt, little Krueger, Kreamer and a few others) gathered in a back room "around a jovial glass of beer." Waller told them that a bomb had been thrown at Haymarket, that about a hundred people had been killed, and that they should all go home. Engel, remembered Waller, agreed and said "yes, they should go home."[32]

August Krueger, or "Little" Krueger as he was known, testified that he left the Haymarket meeting before the bomb exploded and went to Engel's house at about a quarter past ten. Waller burst in and told them the news about the bombing. Krueger remembered Engel's response to the news differently from Waller. Krueger claimed that Engel replied that "it was a foolish act, and the revolution ought to grow out of the people, and this was nonsense, butchery, and he didn't sympathize with it . . ." Engel, according to Little Krueger, scolded Waller for urging them all to "go down there" and do something about it. Policemen, Engel purportedly lectured, "are just as well people [too] . . . that is nonsense at the Hay Market, whoever did so done a foolish thing to throw that bomb shell."[33]

Krueger's version of what was said that night in the back room of Engel's store was repeated by another member of the little group drinking beers that night, August Kreamer, who boarded in Engel's home. For reasons not known, Kreamer was never called the stand to confirm Krueger's story. But according to chief investigator Captain Schaack, Kreamer told police that Engel said that night that it was wrong to kill police in that way. That "he did not believe in killing a few people," rather "all revolutions . . . ought to come about by themselves, and then the police and soldiers would be with them."[34]

Little Krueger's credibility, already low with his admission of being an active anarchist and partner with most of the defendants, fell to pieces when Grinnell pointed out that Krueger had denied he was ever at the Haymarket meeting when he was first questioned by investigators and he snapped back, "I told Mr. Furthman [Grinnell's assistant] that I was not at the Haymarket—that is what I told Furthman; and Mr. Furthman told me a lie too, and I think I have the same right."[35]

At one point testimony was introduced placing Engel at the Haymarket at some point that evening, though this information was only secondhand. Captain Schaack, the chief detective in the case, testified that he had investigated and found that Engel was at the Haymarket at some point. In another case of mishandled questioning, this information was not offered by Schaack or elicited by the prosecutors during their questioning of him, but was drawn out by defense lawyer Foster who ineptly pursued a line of questioning that gave Schaack the opportunity to place Engel on the scene.

Q: And he [Engel] told you that he was at home also the night of the Haymarket meeting when you questioned him as to his whereabouts?

A: He did.

Q: You have also discovered from inquiry, have you not, that that was so.?

A: We have found out also that he was at the Haymarket.

Q: But early in the evening he was at the Haymarket?

A: Yes sir. The latest I traced Engle [sic] at the Haymarket was nine o'clock.

Q: And at the time of the explosion of the bomb and from before that and after he was at home?

A: I could not learn where he was except what he told me himself.[36]

PARSONS' ALIBI

An important and oft-repeated reason why the prosecutions' theory that the accused planned to ambush the police at the Haymarket must be wrong, was that Albert Parsons brought his family with him to the meeting. What sort of a man would bring his family to a place were a deadly battle was about to begin? Parsons, by all accounts, was a devoted family man and a loving father and the idea that he would callously put his children in harm's way seems beyond belief. This objection to the prosecution's conspiracy theory has been repeated by all historians who have seriously studied the event.[37]

Parsons, in a brief autobiography written soon after the trial concluded, made the same claim. Parsons wrote: "When I had finished speaking and Mr. Fielden began, I got down from the wagon we were using as a speaker's stand, and stepping over to another wagon nearby on which sat the ladies (among them my wife and children), and it soon appearing as though it would rain . . . I assisted the ladies down from the wagon and accompanied them to Zepf's hall, one block away . . ."[38]

A few witnesses mentioned in their testimony that Parsons' children were with him earlier that evening. Henry E. O. Heinemann, a reporter for the Chicago *Tribune*, remembered seeing the Parsons and their two children on the corner of Halstead and Randolph speaking with Mr. Owen of the Chicago *Times* before any of the speaking had begun between 7:30 and 8 P.M. He saw Parsons (though it is unclear if he meant the whole family) then take a streetcar eastbound.[39] This was confirmed by Lizzie Holmes who testified that she rode that streetcar with the Parson family to the meeting of the American group at 107 Fifth Avenue.[40]

A number of witnesses also noted that Parsons' children were with him at the American Group meeting. William A. Patterson, a member of the American Group, recalled that Mrs. Parsons often brought her children with her to the group meetings.[41]

Joseph Bach, a tailor and a witness for the defense saw "Mrs. Parsons and Mrs. Holmes, I believe, several ladies, were there with their children, and some others . . ." at the meeting of the American group.[42] Samuel Fielden, too, remembered that the children were present. He remembered leaving to walk to the Haymarket but waiting on the corner while Parsons "brought his two children down stairs and gave them a drink of water in the saloon . . ." But then, when Fielden described how he and

Parsons walked together to the Haymarket he failed to mention any children tagging along. Certainly, this would have been as noteworthy as having given them a drink of water as the distance is nearly a mile and a four- and a six-year-old would likely have had to have been carried for some portion of the trip.[43]

When Parsons had his turn on the stand, he confirmed that his children were with him up to the point where he left the anarchist headquarters. He said that he left his house with "Mrs. Holmes, my wife and two children" about eight o'clock to for the meeting at 107 Fifth Ave which he did by way of a streetcar he picked up at Randolph and Halsted streets. Before catching his ride he recalled having had a short conversation with two reporters. He estimated his arrival at the meeting at 8:30. But after this point, Parsons no longer mentions the presence of his children. Under direct questioning the way he described his walk with Fielden to the Haymarket seemed to indicate that neither Lucy or his children were with him:

> Q: Who of the party walked with you going to the Haymarket?
> A: Well, sir, we didn't all go together. They strung themselves along, and possibly all didn't go the same way . . . myself and Mr. Fielden I distinctly remember crossed the river through the tunnel . . . he was in company with me, and there were three or four others, but I don't remember their names."[44]

Now, the possibility remains that Lucy brought the children with her apart from Albert. But no one who noted Lucy's presence at the Haymarket meeting mentioned that she had her young children with her. Lizzie Holmes stated that she walked to the Haymarket meeting with Lucy from the 107 Fifth Avenue, but did not mention the presence of any children. She was asked where she was during the speeches and stated that she was in the wagon to the north of the speakers. "Who was with you in that wagon . . . ?" asked defense counsel Foster. Holmes replied, "Mrs. Parsons."[45] Snyder, the president of their organization and the man who had presided over the meeting of the American group just a few hours prior to the Haymarket, was asked directly "Who was in the wagon to the north, if you remember?" Snyder answered, "Mr. Parsons and Mrs. Holmes and Mrs. Parsons."[46] Snyder made no mention of any children being present in that carriage. Whiting Allen, a reporter for the Chicago *Times*, also remarked that "Mrs. Parsons was sitting, behind the speaker's wagon," but Allan also made no mention of seeing any children.[47]

William Sahl, a blacksmith and self-described "sympathize[r] with the socialists," did not see Lucy or her children where they were supposed to have been. Sahl was questioned by defense counsel Zeisler who asked him, "Do you remember a wagon standing a little north of the truck on which the speakers stood?" Sahl replied, "Yes."

> Q: Did you see ladies on that wagon?
> A: I did not see any ladies, but I saw men on those wagons.

Zeisler quickly changed the subject.[48]

From the witness chair, Parsons recalled what he did upon concluding his speech: "I went to the wagon North of the one from which I had spoken, about 15 or 20 feet.

There was a spring seat upon this wagon, and my wife and Mrs. Holmes were seated upon this listening to us." Again, Parsons makes no mention of any children present at the time.

According to Parsons, it was at this point that the weather turned and he and others left for a nearby saloon. Parsons explained that he decided to leave "because the ladies were there and I didn't want them to get wet . . ."[49] But wouldn't a man who had two infant children, certainly two children who by this late at night would have been making themselves noticed, explain that he was concerned that his children not get wet?

Lizzie Holmes also said that she went to Zepf's saloon. Defense counsel Foster asked, "Who went over there with you, if any one?" Again Holmes failed to mention any young children, "Mrs. Parsons went with me."[50] Thomas Brown, who later when the shooting was over reputedly loaned Albert 5 dollars, remembered walking from the speakers' wagon to Zepf's with Parsons and then later seeing Lucy Parsons and Holmes in the saloon and later on the street. But Brown at no point mentions any children in tow.[51]

A number of the defense's witnesses testified that they saw Albert or Lucy or Lizzie Holmes in Zepf's saloon, but not one witness remembered seeing children there. M.D. Malkoff, an Russian anarchist who occasionally wrote for the *Arbeiter Zeitung*, saw Lizzie Holmes and Mr. and Mrs. Parsons in Zepf's saloon just "five to ten minutes" before the bomb went off down the street. He did not mention there being any children with them even though he was able to remember that "Mrs. Holmes was standing and Mrs. Parsons was sitting on the window, sitting right on the side of Mr. Parsons."[52] Sleeper T. Ingram, a young worker at the nearby Crane Brothers factory, also saw Parsons "with a couple of ladies" but didn't mention seeing children with them in the saloon.[53]

The only witness whose testimony could in any way support the idea that Parson brought his family to the Haymarket meeting was Henry Schultz, who remembered that "when that cloud came up the people all wanted to adjourn and the women and children pretty much all left. Then there wasn't many left any more of the audience . . ."[54] Of course Schultz was not asked about or referring to any particular women and children, certainly not specifically to the Parsons family, just women and children who were there in the crowd, in general.

From the evidence presented at the trial, it would seem that the Parsons brought their children with them to the IWPA meeting but arranged for someone to look after them while they went off to the Haymarket meeting. Such an arrangement would not by itself indicate that the Parsons were aware of a plan to attack the police in the Haymarket area, only that they reasonably understood what everyone else in the city seemed to know well, that large gatherings of workers anywhere in the city at this extremely tense time were dangerous. Prosecutor Grinnell did not make an issue of the absent children at the trial, though he did mention this to a reporter once all the judicial appeals had run their course. "It's a little strange, but Parsons and his friends have always tried to make out that Mrs. Parsons and her children were at the haymarket. I know all about that, and as a matter of fact they were not there."[55]

Another critical element of Parsons' alibi was his claim to have left the meeting and gone to Zepf's hall with his wife and Lizzie Holmes and was there when the bomb went off. All witnesses do agree that Parsons suggested that the meeting adjourn to Zepf's once the skies grew threatening and that Fielden said that he had just a little more to go and finished his speech. This sequence of events frames the problem nicely, for how much time was there from the moment Parsons suggested the meeting adjourn and the police arrived?

Most observers estimated the time was somewhere between five and ten minutes (see table 4.1). However one reporter, G. P. English, took down a verbatim transcription of Fielden's remarks in shorthand. English noted the point at which Parsons suggested they adjourn so it is possible to see the length of Fielden's remarks from that point to the time when the police arrived. After Parsons interrupted, Fielden concluded his speech as follows:

> Is it not a fact that we have no choice as to our existence, for we can't dictate what our labor is worth. He that has to obey the will of any is a slave. Can we do anything except by a conciliatory armed resistance . . . Socialists are not going to declare war; but I tell you war has been declared upon us; and I ask you to get hold of anything that will help to resist the onslaught of the enemy and the usurper. The skirmish lines have met. People have been shot. Men, women and children have not been spared by the capitalists, and minions of private capital. It had no mercy; so ought you. You are called upon to defend yourselves, your lives, your future. What matters it whether you kill yourselves with work to get a little relief, or die on the battle field resisting the enemy. What is the difference? Any animal, however loathsome, will resist when stepped upon. Are men less than snails or worms? I have some resistance in me? I know that you have too. You have been robbed and you will be starved into a worse condition.[56]

This is a total of 194 words. Assuming a slow pace of speech to be about one word per second, this speech could not have gone on much longer than three to four minutes. English said that someone in the crowd spotted the police as Fielden reached the end of this passage. It then took some more time for the ranks to make their way up the street. Thus, the amount of time that Parsons had to complete all the things he said he did after getting off the wagon was not much more than the time it took Fielden to

Table 4.1   Estimates of time from proposed adjournment to arrival of police

Witness	Witness's Estimate of Time	Source
Freeman	". . . perhaps five or ten minutes."	K, 65
Heinemann	". . . it might have been five minutes, it might have been ten."	K, 255
Ferguson	"It could not have been longer than 5 minutes"	L, 135
Charles Heiderkrueger	". . . could not have been longer than 5 or 10 minutes."	L, 555
Max Mitlacher	"About 5 or 8 minutes before the police came . . . five or ten minutes, not longer"	M, 435–6
Joseph Bach	"about five to ten minutes, I guess"	M, 420

deliver these lines and then for the police to march 50 yards. In that interval Parsons claimed that he helped the ladies step down from their wagon, stopped to talk to a friend, walked the half-block to Zepf's hall, introduced his wife to a friend, went to the rail and enjoyed a schooner of beer with a Russian journalist, smoked a cigar, went and sat with Fischer, then moved over to where Lucy and Lizzie sat, only then to see the flash of the bomb through the window.[57]

Michael D. Malkoff, a Russian who was exiled in 1879 for his student activism and for a time lived in New York City where he had his mail delivered to Justus Schwab's saloon, the headquarters of the revolutionaries in the city, before eventually landing a job as a reporter for the *Arbeiter Zeitung*, placed Parsons in Zepf's saloon, sitting by the nearest window to the door "five or ten minutes" before the explosion. Malkoff was a roommate of Balthazar Rau, one of the inner circle of leaders of the *Arbeiter Zeitung* and before that Malkoff lived with Michael Schwab.[58]

Lizzie Holmes testified that she and Lucy and Albert Parsons arrived at Zepf's five minutes before the bomb exploded. She and Lucy took seats at a table near the door and Albert went and had a glass of beer at the bar. Assistant prosecutor Ingham again lured her into a trap, asking her if she ever got up from her seat. No, Lizzie answered. Then how is it, he asked, with a barroom as tightly packed as Zepf's was that night, that she could see Albert across the room:

Q: How far could you see across the room from where you were sitting?
A: I could see all over it.
Q: Now, Mrs. Holmes, wasn't that saloon crowded with people standing up?
A: Well, I don't know.—
Q: So that the people sitting down at one table could see but a very short distance?
A: The room wasn't really crowded.
Q: Wasn't the room really crowded so that a person sitting down could only see a very short distance in it?
A: No, the room was not so crowded as that.
Q: It was not so crowded as that?
A: No sir.[59]

Ingham knew very well that every witness who claimed to have been in Zepf's Hall that night had remarked on how crowded it was.

Whiting Allen was a reporter for the *Chicago Times* who happened to be inside Zepf's Hall when the bomb exploded. At the trial Allen testified that he did not see Parsons in the bar that evening. However, the *Times* the next morning featured a report from one of its reporters inside Zepf's entitled "The Anarchists' Den." "A moment before the explosion of the bomb, Parsons and his negro wife entered the room. The woman took a seat near the door, and was soon surrounded by a crowd of admirers of her bloodthirsty eloquence. Parsons stood near by . . ."[60]

One last tantalizing detail dropped from the testimony of *Chicago News* reporter W.M. Knox. Knox was one of the first to interview Spies after his arrest and he was given the opportunity to recount what Spies told him in his jail cell. Spies explained to Knox that after the bombing he ran to Zepf's hall and there ran into Mrs. Parsons. Knox reported that Spies said that "he found Mrs. Parsons waiting for her husband."[61]

SPIES' ALIBI

It will ever remain a mystery why the defense lawyers thought there was some advantage in calling August Spies to testify on his own behalf. It didn't take hindsight to understand the danger inherent in opening up lines of inquiry about his activities in the days and months leading up to the bombing. As it turned out, giving Spies, a vain leader who relished attention and a man averse to short answers, the opportunity to expound upon why he collected bombs and dynamite was the worst tactical blunder of the trial.

Captain Black conducted Spies' direct examination himself and walked him through his actions over the May Day weekend. Spies recounted being called by the CLU to give a speech on the Black Road where he did his best to calm the crowd and restrain those peeling off to attack McCormick's factory. He described how in a rage he returned to his newspaper office and composed the infamous "Revenge Circular."

Captain Black and his fellow defense lawyers were often slow to grasp the damaging course of their own witness' testimony. Nowhere is this better illustrated than during this examination. At one point, when pressed as to whether he was "laboring under the excitement of the hour" when he composed the "Revenge Circular," Spies blurted out, "I was very indignant. I was excited. I knew positively by the experiences that I have had in the past that this butchery of the people out there was done for the purpose of defeating the eight hour movement in this city, that all large strikes, wherever they have taken place—" Whereupon he was suddenly cut off by Judge Gary who interjected, "That is not admissible, but however if it is not objected to, I suppose it may go in."

It is not recorded whether Gary looked toward the defense bench at that moment, but one can imagine him doing so as his cutting Spies off mid-sentence was a prompt for the defense to object to this line of inquiry. For if Spies had been allowed to continue and denounce the actions of the police in various strikes and protests, the prosecution would then be permitted to press their questioning into those areas and probe what role Spies and his associates had taken in these strikes, thus entering into the record potentially even more evidence of the anarchists' efforts to fan strikes into violence. There was nothing to be gained by this line of testimony for it would allow the prosecution to put even more stoic police officers on the stand to recall how they defended citizens and property from the alien menace.

Black was apparently slow to catch on, for there was enough time after Gary gave the defense his prompting for Spies to ask, "May I proceed?" before Black rose to say, "As the court has interposed an objection, we will stop there." Black must have perceived that Spies' day in court was not going well for his side as he seemed to be trying to use Gary's interruption as an excuse to end the questioning, but this is not what Gary was trying to help Black to do. Rather, Black needed to object to this line of questioning and Gary, in apparent exasperation, then lectured him on what he should have known already: "If you go on with the history of former transactions, of course it opens the door to a large class of testimony...Up to this time there has been but two occasions put in evidence—the McCormick and the Haymarket; but if this witness goes into the history of any former transactions, then it opens the door to a very large number." Black finally understood and said, "We don't care to do that." Gary then ordered Spies' earlier testimony on police conduct stricken from the record. The prosecution then moved on to questioning Spies about his activities on the day of the bombing. This episode reveals not only the poor quality of the anarchists' legal counsel, but shows a judge going beyond his role to assist the defense in raising an objection.[62]

Besides Lingg and Fischer, Spies was the only other defendant specifically implicated with possessing bombs by the state's witnesses. It seems that part of Captain Black's thinking in inviting Spies to take the stand was to give him the opportunity to explain that the shells he brandished for the benefit of a few newsmen were just for show, just a method of grabbing headlines and attention, a dangerous bit of braggadocio no doubt, but hardly the arsenal of a serious terrorist. Black asked Spies if he kept any dynamite at the *Arbeiter Zeitung* office. Spies answered that he kept "two giant powder cartridges in my desk for two years." ("Giant powder" was a brand of dynamite at the time.) Why did he possess them? "...I used them to show...to reporters. The reporters used to bother me a good deal, and they were always up for a sensation and when they came to the office I would show them these giant cartridges...they would go away and write up some big sensational article."[63]

Black may have succeeded in getting into the record a benign explanation for Spies possessing bombs, but only at the cost of opening the door to greater mischief. When assistant prosecutor Ingham cross-examined him, Spies could not help but implicate himself and by implication his codefendants. As he had before Spies admitted keeping dynamite in his desk and Ingham pried further, getting Spies to admit he ordered the explosives from the Aetna Powder Company. Then Ingham popped the obvious question that Black should have known was going to come:

Q: Why did you get that dynamite?
A: I got that dynamite to experiment with in the first place—that was my intention.
Q: Did you ever experiment with it?
A: I did not.
Q: Why did you want to experiment with it?
A: Oh, I thought—
Q: What object did you have in experimenting with the dynamite?
A: I had read a good deal about dynamite? I thought it would be a good thing to get acquainted with the use of it.
Q: Why would it be a good thing to get acquainted with the use of it?
A: Well, for general reasons.
Q: Could not you get acquainted with it enough for the use of your purposes by reading?

A: I wanted to experiment with dynamite just the same as I would take a revolver and go out and practice with a revolver.

Q: Was that the only reason you had?

A: Yes sir.

Q: Just merely from curiosity?

A: No, I cannot say it was merely curiosity. I don't want to say that exactly.

Q: Then what was it, if it was not merely curiosity?

A: I think I have explained sufficiently.

Q: Can you give any further explanation than you have given?

A: No, I don't see as I could.[64]

Ingham then dropped his own bomb and handed Spies a letter and asked him if he remembered receiving it. Spies reluctantly admitted that since it had his name on it, "I suppose I did receive that letter." The letter dated sometime in 1884 was sent to Spies from Johann Most, the author of the notorious *Revolutionaere Kriegswissenschaft* (*Science of Revolutionary Warfare*) and it contained references to dynamite and to its uses that went far beyond curious experiments and frightening reporters:[65]

> Dear Spies: Are you sure that the letter from the Hocking Valley was not written by a detective? In a week I will go to Pittsburgh, and I have an inclination to go also to the Hocking Valley . . . On the other hand I am in a condition to furnish "medicine", and the "genuine" article at that. Directions for use are perhaps not needed with these people. Moreover, they were recently published in the "Fr." The appliances I can also send. Now if you consider the address of Buchtell thoroughly reliable I will ship twenty or twenty-five pounds. But how? Is there an express line to the place, or is there another way possible? . . . Greeting to Schwab, Rau and to you. Your Johann Most.[66]

The letters' allusion to the "Hocking Valley" was particularly incriminating as it was a reference to the rebellious coal district in Ohio where a miner's strike had led to violent clashes with Pinkertons, militia, and the frequent dynamiting of mine heads and railroads in the area. Twenty or twenty-five pounds of "medicine" also seemed a quantity in excess of what was needed to scare the press or to play with out on the prairie.

Adding to the disaster that was Spies' day on the witness chair, he ruined his brother Henry's attempt to provide him with an alibi. Henry (Heinrich) testified two days earlier that he walked with his brother to the Haymarket meeting, stuck by him the whole evening, and once the shooting began saved his life by grabbing the pistol of an assassin aimed at his brothers' back, only to have the assailant fire into his groin, tearing away one of his testicles. From the most trivial details to the most important ones, August couldn't seem to line his testimony up with his brothers. Henry testified that "We were at Zepf's hall before the meeting began, and walked down Desplaines out to Randolph looking for Parsons and Fielden." August recalled: "I left home about after half past seven o'clock I think and walked down with my brother Henry arriving at the Haymarket about twenty or twenty-five minutes after eight."[67]

Henry told how he saw a man jump behind his brother with a gun placing it "right by his back, and I grabbed it and received my shot." But August was oblivious to his brother's heroics, even though it all transpired within his arms' reach. "I jumped down, and as I reached I think it was the sidewalk or may have been the street, I don't know exactly—I think it was the sidewalk, the explosion took place. I heard the detonation. And he said "What is that" I said "That must be a cannon" or I may have said "That is a Gatling gun" or "It must be a Gatling gun." And then I lost sight of him. There was a throng and I was carried away and I didn't see him any more." August said that he didn't see his brother again until nearly an hour later at his brother's house. Black asked him if that was "the first you knew of the wound he had received was when you met him there?" Spies, replied that it was. "I heard it when I went home—I heard it and went right up to his house."[68] August's testimony was all the more damaging to his brother's credibility as Henry admitted under cross-examination that he told a completely different story to the police after the riot:[69]

Q: Did you tell them the story you now have told?
A: I did not.
Q: You told them that when the bomb exploded that you were in Zepf's hall and walked out and were shot in the door—that is true, is it?
A: Yes, that is what I told them.[70]
... Q: You also said at that time that you did not see your brother that evening until he called at the house and asked you if you had a good physician—is that true?
A: That is true.[71]

The legal team for the defense had tried their best to provide an alibi for August Spies. It was not for lack of trying that in the end their effort was unsuccessful. Individually neither Spies brother was a very persuasive witness but they were even less convincing as a pair as together their testimony clashed and contradicted each other. As neither Spies, or Fielden, for that matter, could possibly argue they weren't present when the bomb exploded, there remained only one route to saving them from the hangman. The defense had to show that the recollections of most of the prosecution's eyewitnesses to the bombing were faulty. Their hopes now hinged on their ability to sell a completely different story of the moments leading up to the blast to the jury.

CHAPTER 5

THE ELEMENTS OF A RIOT

THERE CAN BE NO DOUBT THAT BULLETS FLEW THICKLY THAT NIGHT, but the question of whether anyone in the anarchist crowd joined in the gunplay was one of the keys to the whole case. Dozens of police officers testified that they were shot at by members of the mob. Some police officers claimed that the crowd shot first and some even claimed to have seen Samuel Fielden, one of the defendants, crouch down behind the speakers' wagon and fire off a few shots himself. Police recovered a pistol from the area with several spent rounds. Nearly unanimously, defense witnesses claimed that no one but the police fired shots that night.

For prosecutor Julius Grinnell proving that members of the crowd began firing immediately when the bomb exploded was central to proving that the attack had been coordinated beforehand, that a wider conspiracy existed, and that the accused were its leaders. The prosecution's theory of the case was that the bomb had been a signal for the members of the armed sections of the International to open fire upon the police. Grinnell had no difficulty in finding police officers willing to testify that they saw members of the crowd shooting at them and others who said they had recovered weapons at the scene. With dozens of police officers lined up to testify to the fact that they were fired upon, Grinnell did not probe deeply into the details and evidence surrounding the shooting. Only the defense, burdened with having to discredit the testimony of scores of credible, uniformed witnesses, cared to pursue the question, but in doing so, it unwittingly uncovered evidence that supported the prosecution's case.

Lead defense counsel William Black called numerous witnesses including Samuel Fielden himself in an attempt to refute the allegation that Fielden had snapped off several rounds. Removing the gun from Fielden's hand was an essential step toward countering the claim that he was part of a wider conspiracy. However, by concentrating on Fielden, Black let in other testimony that lent credence to the assertion that some members of the crowd did indeed fire at the police.

Black's most promising witness was a German machinist, Frank Stenner, who was apprehended at the scene and accused of firing at the police from behind the speakers' wagon. Stenner was a unique witness in that Officer John Wessler who testified that he saw Fielden shooting from behind the wagon also testified at Stenner's initial hearing and, according to Stenner, told the judge, "I seen this man on the steps of Crane Bros., and from this place there was a shot, but I don't know whether that is the man or he is not. I guess that is the man who shot." Stenner's account, if true, shows Wessler was less sure about who shot where at first and his recollections firmed later.[1]

Frank Stenner's testimony was deemed so damaging by the prosecution that the first two witnesses Grinnell called in his final rebuttal were the judge who presided over Stenner's original hearing and the lawyer who represented him. Daniel Scully had served as a justice of the peace operating out of the Desplaines street station for 16 years before young Stenner was brought before him along with a crowd of other detained rioters. Judge Scully did not remember Officer Wessler saying to him that Stenner was the man who fired a shot from behind the wagon. Rather, he recalled Wessler describing the man who did as a stout man with a full beard whom he could identify if he saw him again and that he released Stenner on the recommendation of assistant prosecutor Furthmann. John B. Ryan, Stenner's attorney, remembered things differently but no favorably to the defense. According to Ryan, it wasn't Officer Wessler who said he could point out the heavily whiskered man who did the shooting, it was his own client, Frank Stenner.[2]

Under cross-examination Stenner admitted a number of things that boosted the prosecution's case. Stenner stated that when the bomb was thrown there was nobody on the wagon, Fielden being the last to climb off. But just before the police came up, Stenner noted that "there were very many," closely paralleling Gilmer's own account.[3]

Samuel Fielden was the first defendant Captain Black called to the witness stand. Black's purpose was clearly to rebut the policemen who had claimed that Fielden drew a pistol and shot at them. According to Fielden he was just stepping off the speakers' wagon when the explosion occurred. He saw the flash and joined the stampede of the crowd up the street away from the cops. "I had possibly gone three or four steps— I was struck with a ball. It felt, as near as I can estimate the feeling, now, as though a small hammer had struck me very quickly there with a strong powerful blow. I didn't feel much pain at the time in the excitement, but as I dropped into a walk down there on Randolph street I felt the pain and put my finger in the hole in my pants and felt my knee was wet."[4]

According to this story, Fielden was shot while fleeing and managed to run more than a full block before noticing he had been wounded. Later that night Fielden found a young doctor on Canal street who dressed his wounds. That physician, Dr. E. G. Epler, testified that Fielden told him a very different version of events while he stitched him up:

Q: Did you have any conversation with him as to how he received the wound?
A: I asked him what position he was in when he received the wound.
Q: What did he say?
A: He said he was crawling on the pavement, trying to get away from the crowd, and the bullet glanced off from the pavement and struck him in that position.
Mr. FOSTER: That is all.[5]

Though it may not have mattered much whether Fielden was in fact running or crawling away, such a discrepancy in testimony, if it was caught by astute jurors, might have given them reason to doubt other elements of Fielden's testimony.

Many of the defense's own witnesses were not sure that other people in the crowd had not opened fire. Frank Stenner when asked, "Are you sure that any one else except the police fired?" replied, "I can't tell you. It may be they shot."[6] Friedrich Liebel, wasn't sure either whether the shots came "from the police and from the crowd—I can't say from whom exactly.[7] Even those who could conclusively say that the crowd had not shot back, testified that the shooting began "the instant" the bomb exploded.

Ludwig Zeller, the secretary of the Central Labor Union who lived in a room above the anarchist headquarters at Greif's Hall, when put on the stand by the defense was asked by Black:

Q: Was the shooting before or after the explosion of the bomb?
A: I guess it commenced exactly by the explosion of the bomb.[8]

Likewise, Frederick Liebel said that the shots and the bomb's explosion "came so near together that I can't tell which came first."[9] William Gleason agreed, replying to the question: "Did you hear the bomb explode first or did you hear the pistol shot first?" by saying: "It was so instantaneous, the whole affair, that I can't say."[10] Cornice maker Robert Lindinger had the same impression:

Q: When did you hear the shooting with reference to the explosion of the bomb, before or after that?
A: Pretty near after, immediately afterwards.[11]

The uncertainty of these witnesses as to the sequence of events—whether the gunfire followed the blast or vice versa—was common. A total of 17 defense witnesses described both the bombing and the shooting. Four of them thought they heard shots before the bomb exploded. Seven others testified that the bomb blast and the shooting coincided. Four were sure that the shots followed the explosion but they did so almost immediately. Only two men thought there was a pause of a second or two between the explosion and the shooting. Such striking variation in the recollection of witnesses over a basic material fact strongly supports the allegation that the gunfire occurred so soon after the bombing because only in that event would it have been so hard to distinguish one from the other.

Such a short interval between the blast and the shooting is significant because all witnesses not directly associated with the anarchists swore that the police did not have their pistols in their hands prior to the explosion. In those days, police did not wear their guns in holsters, but simply carried them loose into their overcoat pockets. Nearly unanimous testimony at the trial indicated that none of the police approached with their guns drawn. Only some of the six officers had their guns more available, on sockets set on their outer belts.[12]

Retrieving a gun from a coat pocket is a more cumbersome and time-consuming action than drawing it from a holster not only because the coat is loose and the pocket deep, but also because a pocket does not hold a gun oriented so that the grip is facing the hand the same way that a holster does. Even in a situation where there was no shock or confusion, as there certainly was amidst the smoke, screams, and concussion of the blast, it would have taken a few seconds to draw their weapons, aim, and shoot. For the police to have shot first, there would have had to have been a significant pause, a several second interval between the explosion and the shooting. Given that many defense witnesses claimed that the shots preceded the bomb (a mistake that could be attributed to the proximity of the events) while others testified that the bomb and the shots were "instantaneous," lends support to the prosecution's claim that some members of the crowd not only fired upon the police, but were standing ready to do so as soon as the bomb exploded.

Beyond the testimony of witnesses present at the rally that night, the bullets that whizzed around Desplaines street left many traces whose patterns tell more of the story. Though hundreds of bullets were fired that night, there was no ballistic science available to investigators back in 1886. Neither the police or defense lawyers thought of making a survey of the crime scene or to retrieve slugs embedded in the wooden streets and brick walls. Once defense witness did claim to have noted the following day that the south-facing surface of a telegraph pole was pocked with bullets while its north face was smooth. However, this information was of little use not only because the pole had since been removed (the defense insinuated that the city removed it to obliterate this evidence) but because a pole standing on the sidewalk would not have been hit by shooters standing next to it. By the time of the trial there was only one source of physical evidence available—namely, the torn bodies of the policemen themselves.[13]

Newspaper accounts of the nature of the policemen's wounds varied not only from reporter to reporter but from day to day. The most reliable information came from three surgeons who listed their patient's wounds in gory detail from the witness stand. Surgeons were far more careful to distinguish those wounds caused by bullets and those caused by shell fragments than were medically untrained reporters who often simply fudged the issue by referring to a victim's injuries as being the result of being "shot." Much confusion has subsequently crept into the literature on the Haymarket bombing because of the ambiguity of the word "shot," which in the nineteenth century made no distinction between bullets and shrapnel.

Though it is not always a simple matter to distinguish bomb and bullet wounds, especially when the missile passes completely through the body, the doctors who cared for the fallen policemen had no doubt about the nature of wounds they examined.

Doctor Andrew J. Baxter was one of the first surgeons called to the Desplaines street station that night. He remembered a number of his patients and of these he was quite certain what struck them. He remembered Officer Thomas Redden whose right leg was shattered. "That was a bomb wound," he said confidently, "I removed the piece of bomb myself." When asked how he knew that another policeman, Timothy

Sullivan, had been hit by bomb fragments and not bullets, Baxter gave a brief lesson on what distinguished these wounds:

> He had a large ragged wound in the upper part of the thigh so that you could put your hand in; and I supposed from the character of the wound that I would find some large missile embedded in the tissues of the thigh; but after considerable search I could not find anything and was somewhat annoyed to think I could not find it, but ultimately I found it on the inside of the thigh. It was one of these pieces of zinc. Then he had another wound on the outside of the leg, and the piece I removed from the inside passed between the bones, and I removed it from the inside. Then he had a wound on the opposite leg which looked like a scratch, but on further investigation, I found it was also made with one of these pieces of zinc, but it had hit the surface edgewise, and consequently it did not make a large external wound. The external wound depended on the manner in which the missile hit the surface. These bomb pieces were undoubtedly cut from pieces of zinc, and they were oblique, of course, after leaving the bomb. They would be revolving on their axes- and if they happened to hit the surface edgewise, they would make a linear incision, but if they hit it flat, they made a very large ragged wound, which made part of the wound have this torn ragged appearance.[14]

Baxter's keen observations reveal how such a seemingly small bomb could cause so many scores of serious injuries among the policemen. When it exploded the bomb fragmented into many small jagged pieces, each of which moved with great speed and spun wildly as they moved. Though small, these irregular and erratically spinning shards could tear horrifying wounds into flesh. Combined with the fact that the policemen moved up the street in closely packed ranks standing shoulder to shoulder, this resulted in a high casualty count.

In the end, the three physicians agreed that seven police officers that they had personally examined had been hit by bullets while an eighth, Officer H.F. Krueger, brought the bullet that shattered his knee into the court with him. Two of these, George F. Miller and Michael Sheehan, died of their wounds and were officially declared to have perished as a result of being "shot by pistol during riot" by the county coroner. Another police officer, Officer Krueger brought the bullet that shattered his knee into the court with him. Another police officer, Henry W. Weinecke, testified that his physician also concluded that his head wound was caused by a bullet rather than a piece of the bomb. A closer look at these eight confirmed cases of gunshot injuries among the police reveal a telling pattern.

Of these eight shooting victims, at least six were hit by bullets moving in a downward trajectory. (The trajectory of Lieutenant Stanton's wound cannot be determined as it passed through his arm and he did not pay particular attention to it given the fact that he also sustained numerous shrapnel injuries.) Four of the men were shot in the legs. The bullet that killed George Miller entered his left side below the armpit, slicing downward across his intestines to lodge in his right hip. Michael Sheehan was struck in his back, below his ninth rib, cutting through his kidney and following a downward line before exiting above his belly button. Officer Weinecke carried a bullet that entered behind his right ear and bored into his brain.

The preponderance of bullets either striking the officers on the lower parts of their bodies, or moving in a downward trajectory, suggests the possibility that the shooters were at a higher elevation than their victims. Had the gunmen and those shot been on the same elevation, more of the wounds should have been inflicted on the torso, arms, or heads of the officers as the natural firing position of a pistol is chest-high. Of the three confirmed wounds suffered above the waist two traced a downward slope: one of them struck at an extremely steep angle (from armpit to hip) and one from a moderate angle (from middle back to belly button). Only Weinecke's bullet trajectory was on a level plain or took an upward course. Had the shooters and their targets been on the same elevation, it is just as likely that the bullets would have been struck above the waist as below and the distribution of injuries should have reflected this element of chance.

The sidewalks along that block of Desplaines street were ten inches or more above the grade of the street. Anyone firing from the elevated sidewalks into the ranks of the police would have done so at a downward angle. As a result, if shots were fired by the crowd, injuries should follow a pattern where those officers closest to the sidewalk should tend toward wounds higher on their bodies while those further away should tend toward wounds in their lower extremities. Officers Miller and Sheehan, both of whom were shot above the waist, were part of Lieutenant James Bowler's company that occupied the east end of the street. The other man shot above the waist, Weinecke, stood in the very first rank, nose to nose with the crowd. Of the two policemen shot who were most distant to the speakers' stand, Thomas Hennesey was struck in the thigh and Lieutenant Stanton in the arm, though Stanton may have been on the ground when he was hit, having just been knocked over by the bomb's blast.

According to the policemen themselves, the gunfire that they claim poured in upon them as soon as the bomb exploded came from all "sides", but particularly from the east side of the street near the speakers' stand. If this was true, then a higher number of gunshot wounds should have been suffered by those companies that occupied the right hand or east side of the street, those in Lieutenant Steele's and Lieutenant Bowler's ranks (see table 5.1).

Three-quarters of the confirmed gunshot wounds were sustained by the two companies standing along the east sidewalk. The two companies occupying the eastern end of the street sustained the highest proportion of wounds caused by bullets,

Table 5.1   Distribution and cause of police injuries

Commander	Steele	Quinn	Bowler	Stanton	Hubbard	Total
Position	1st East	1st West	2nd East	2nd West	3rd (Rear)	
# Men	24	24	26–27	19	28	121–122
# Wounded	7	14	18	16	7	62
% Wounded	29	58	67–69	84	25	50–51
# Bullet Wounds	2	0	4	2	0	8
% Wounded by Bullet	8	0	15	11	0	7
% Wounds Caused by Bullet	29	0	26	14	0	15

29 and 26 percent respectively. The companies positioned in the front of the phalanx of police sustained fewer gunshot wounds than those behind them. Most of the
gunshot wounds were sustained by men in the third and fourth files of police. Had
most of the gunshots been the result of wild police shooting as the defense and their
supportive historians have claimed, then a greater percentage of the injuries would
likely have been inflicted upon the policemen caught between those officers behind
them and their targets in front of them.

One of the men injured by a bullet was officer H.F. Krueger who stood in the
front rank of police, furthest east and closest to the sidewalk. Krueger testified that
he saw Fielden duck behind the wagon and blaze away with his revolver. Krueger
returned fire and at the same moment was struck in his right leg. For his part, Krueger
claimed to see Fielden stagger and then run off with the crowd. Krueger's testimony
was probably persuasive with the jury, especially when he held up the 38 caliber bullet
that his doctor had dug out from behind his kneecap, but his injury provides clues
that were not appreciated at the time.

The bullet that Krueger exhibited could not have been fired by Fielden in the way
he described. The bullet entered his right leg from the right and slightly from the
rear. Krueger swears he was facing forward at this point placing the shooter somewhat behind him and to his right. From where Krueger was standing, this means the
shot came from near the mouth of Crane's alley. If, as Krueger claimed, he was hit
just as soon as he had time to draw his revolver and begin shooting, his wound must
have come from someone on the sidewalk or in the alleyway rather than from the
ranks of the police.[15]

Of course none of this precludes the possibility that some policemen were victims
of friendly fire. Just days before the trial was due to open a disgruntled police officer gave an interview to a *Chicago Tribune* reporter on the condition of anonymity.
This "well-known officer" alleged that many rank and file cops blamed Bonfield for
the massacre. Bonfield, this secretive source charged, acted rashly in his eagerness
to "break-up" the anarchists' meeting. Worse, Bonfield didn't anticipate the danger
and ignored the advice of "old officers" who advised the street be cleared by deploy-
ing a single file to clear both the street and sidewalk from wall to wall instead of
Bonfield's favored massed formation that merely pushed the crowd onto both adjoining sidewalks thereby contributing to their own encirclement. After the bombing and
shooting began utter confusion reigned and according to this inside informant at least
five officers were "wounded by each other's revolvers." Bonfield's claim that the command was given to "close-up" and "fall-in" in the wake of the bombing "is laughed
at by everyman on the force who has any idea of the facts in the matter." Rather,
"It was every man for himself, and while some got two or three squares away the rest
emptied their revolvers, mainly into each other."[16]

Anarchist defenders (and most later historians) gleefully seized on this unknown
officers' account as proof of both police misconduct, the suppression of important
evidence, and the falsity of allegations that any anarchists supplemented the bombing
with their own firearms. But to accomplish this purpose it is necessary to ignore other
things that this anonymous officer told the *Tribune*. This cop was quite certain that

men in the crowd opened fire first. "The firing began from both sides of the street, as well as from in front . . ." It was this that made this policeman so angry at Bonfield—had Bonfield taken proper precautions and listened to his "old officers" the police would not have been enfiladed from both sides.[17]

More confirmation that the shooting erupted from the crowd almost immediately after the bomb blew came from the pen of one person who, though present through most of the Haymarket speeches, was claimed by a number of defense witnesses to have left and retired to Zepf's saloon just before the police marched. In a column written for the *Labor Enquirer* dated May 10, Lucy Parsons described what had happened the previous Tuesday which she called a "demonstration of the new method of scientific warfare." She described how the 300 "minions of the oppressing class" marched toward the peaceful assembly, sweeping up the street from curbstone to curbstone. The police captain gave the command to disperse and "the reply was given in thunder tones, which shook the great massive buildings for blocks around." Parsons then described the moments after the blast:

> A great swath had been cut in the ranks of the police. But before their groans, mingled with the succeeding echoes, of the great explosion, could rise, as it were, from the place where they originated, there came a fusilade (sic) of pistol shots. The bomb had been flung with such sudden and deadly effect that it had thoroughly disorganized and demoralized the police, and they became an easy prey for an enemy to attack and completely annihilate, if there had been any conspiracy or concocted understanding, as has been howled and shouted by the capitalistic press.

Lucy Parsons constructs her account of these events in a way that she seems to think undercuts the threatening charge that the anarchist meeting was planned to lure police into an ambush. To do so she emphasizes the power of the bomb and the moment of tremendous opportunity when had there been a true and proper coordination most, if not all the police, would have been shot down. But in stressing the effectiveness of the bombing in momentarily stunning and paralyzing the police, she clearly implies that the "fusilade of pistol shots" was fired by the crowd. According to her, these shots rang out before the echo of the explosion had died away. Interestingly, nowhere in this account does she discuss any shots fired by the police toward protesters but instead suggests that there weren't significant numbers of civilian casualties:

> It was the shortest, sharpest, and most decisive battle, I believe on record. In less than three minutes, the most horrible explosion ever known, of its kind, had taken place; over 200 shots had been fired, and over fifty police lay writhing in their blood upon the ground. The 3,000 and more persons who had assembled on the spot less than five minutes previous—where were they? For now nothing was to be heard or seen but the writhing, groaning police and the coming and going of the patrol, each loaded with them, and conveying them to the hospitals.[18]

Similarly, Lizzie Holmes who was spotted that night sitting in a carriage with Lucy Parsons a few feet north of the speakers' wagon, mixed some of her own observations of that night into an article defending free speech that was also published in Denver's *Labor Enquirer*. Though far more cautious than Lucy Parsons' rash letter a week earlier, Holmes does vaguely imply that gunfire was as much a part of the attack on police as the bomb was. "No one knows how the battle began... No one will ever know the exact truth... It is terrible that such things must occur, in the evolution of the human race... I shudder to think of bloodshed....[but] A bullet speeding from a legal revolver is no less "fiendish" to me than a bullet from some desperate, unorganized hungry workingman's gun."[19]

In the dark of a moonless night, on a street lit by a single hissing gas lamp and the distant electric glow of theater lights, amidst the shock and concussion of a bomb blast, ears ringing, pulses racing, acrid smoke swirling, it is not inconceivable that some police officers may have fired errant shots that struck their fellow cops. But this possibility does not negate the evidence showing that some men in the crowd seized on this opportunity to even the score with Bonfield and his bullies in blue. Given the number of policemen felled by bullets there was room enough for both scenarios to have played out. Unfortunately for the defense, their theory of the case did not tolerate dividing the injuries in this way and the testimony they assembled in support of the claim that police did all the shooting was not strong enough to carry the point.

GILMER AND THE MEN ON THE WAGON

There was no prosecution witness the defense fought harder to discredit than Harry Gilmer. Gilmer's testimony provided the prosecution with a damning link between the act of the throwing the bomb and the wider anarchist conspiracy by placing both Spies and Fischer in the alley with the bomber. Defense lawyers set about to discredit Gilmer's story in two ways: by providing witnesses who claimed to have stood in Crane's alley and did not see a bomb thrower at all, and witnesses who claimed that August Spies did not step off the wagon until just a moment before the blast. Either claim, if true, proved Gilmer a liar.

Ironworker Adolph Temmes, denied being an anarchist or socialist and only heard of the meeting from seeing an announcement for it in a copy of the *Arbeiter Zeitung* he was reading in the public library. Temmes testified that he stood just four or five feet away from the wagon when the police marched up and ordered the crowd to disperse. Temmes ran up the street when the shooting began and dodged down another alley north of the fracas but swore that Spies was standing on the wagon when he fled. While accomplishing its purpose of contradicting Gilmer's account, Temmes recollection also sat awkwardly alongside that of other defense witnesses who remembered seeing Spies either off or in the act of stepping off the wagon when the bomb exploded.[20]

Sleeper Ingram, an 18-year-old apprentice machinist who had gone on strike the Friday before the Haymarket meeting, somehow managed to be in the right place at the right time throughout the entire evening to contest the prosecution's version of events. He was near the wagon when Spies first called the meeting to order and Ingram saw him walk south but not in the company of Schwab. Ingram listened to the speakers and then walked up to Zepf's Hall where he happened to see Parsons enter and take a seat with his wife. He then walked back to the protest just in time to see that Fielden and Spies stood on the wagon just before the bomb was thrown, but recalled seeing Spies climbing off the wagon just as Officer Ward gave his order to disperse. The young mechanic didn't see anyone shooting but the cops and survived by pressing flat against the wall of Crane's factory. Ingram claimed that after a few minutes the street emptied, all was quiet and he simply walked down toward the Lyceum theatre.

Ingram's story frayed quickly under cross-examination. An assistant prosecutor simply asked Ingram to point out Spies, Parsons, and Fielden from the eight defendants and Ingram mixed them all up and then admitted that he didn't know which one was Parsons. Asked about the order in which these three men spoke, Ingram recalled Spies speaking first, who then introduced Fielden, and was followed by Parsons (Parsons actually spoke in between the others).[21]

Strangely, defense witness Carl Richter, who swore he and his friend stood at the same spot in the middle of Crane's alley near the wagon from before the time Spies called the meeting to order to the moment Ward read the riot act, testified that Spies was not in the wagon when the police arrived. Richter knew what Spies looked like, having been part of an acting troup, "The Eisenstein Dramatio Company" who had been employed to perform for one of the IWPA's festivals. Other defense witnesses had differing opinions. Konrad Messer was sure Spies was on the wagon until just before the bomb exploded while another defense witness, Frank Raab, was not able to say for sure whether Spies was on or off. August Krumm who like Richter claimed to have stood in Crane's alley the whole meeting, when pressed in cross-examination was not sure he ever saw Spies that night at all.[22]

In the end, defense witnesses couldn't provide a consistent and convincing account of Spies' actions just before the bombing. Spies himself sensing this weakness in his own case, used a portion of his opportunity to address the court before his sentencing to accuse State's Attorney Grinnell of suppressing a witness who could have proved that he remained on the wagon and didn't duck into the Crane's alley to light Schnaubelt's bomb. In his opening salvo, Spies charged that Ernst Legner, a young man who spent much of the evening of May 4th with him on the wagon, had been spirited out of town before he could testify. [23]

I will state a little incident which may throw light upon this charge. On the evening… [of May 4] about 8 o'clock I met a young man, Legner by name, who is a member of the Aurora Turn-Verein. He accompanied me, and never left me on that evening until I jumped from the wagon, a few seconds before the explosion occurred. He knew that I had not seen Schwab on that evening. He knew that I had no such conversation with anybody as Mr. Marshal Field's protege, Thompson, testified to. He knew that I did not jump from the wagon to strike the match and hand it to the man who threw the bomb. He is not a Socialist. Why did we not bring him on the stand? Because the honorable representatives of the State, Grinnell and Bonfield, spirited him away. These honorable gentlemen knew everything about Legner. They knew that his testimony would prove the perjury of Thompson and Gilmer beyond any reasonable doubt. Legner's name was on the list of witnesses for the State- He was not called, however, for obvious reasons. Aye, he stated to a number of friends that he had been offered $500 if he would leave the city, and threatened with direful things if he remained here and appeared as a witness for the defense. He replied that he could neither be bought nor bulldozed to serve such a damnable and dastardly plot. When we wanted Legner, he could not be found; Mr. Grinnell said—and Mr. Grinnell is an honorable man!—that he had himself been searching for the young man, but had not been able to find him. About three weeks later I learned that the very same young man had been kidnapped and taken to Buffalo, N. Y., by two of the illustrious guardians of "Law and Order," two Chicago detectives. Let Mr. Grinnell, let the Citizens' Association, his employer, let them answer for this![24]

As Legner did not testify it is hard to assess the accuracy of Spies' charges. Prosecutor Grinnell insisted to reporters after Spies' speech that he had nothing to do with Legner's disappearance and pointed out that he had no interest in making him unavailable as he had told him that Spies left the speakers' wagon well before the bomb was thrown.[25] Legner did testify to the Grand Jury but his testimony according to leaked sources was vague and evasive. Reportedly Legner replied to nearly every probing question with "I could not say positive" or "Well that is something I don't know certain."[26]

Fortunately for history, a year after the trial, Legner reappeared in Chicago and sued the *Arbeiter Zeitung* for libel. Legner accused the paper of libeling him when it alleged that he had accepted a bribe from prosecutors of 500 dollars to leave Chicago during the trial. Zeisler appeared in court representing the Socialistic Publishing Company. When Legner took the stand, he testified that he did not leave Chicago until the end of July and left to find work, going first to Kansas City, then to Aurora, Nebraska, finally finding a job as bridge builder in Lincoln, Nebraska. Before he left he asked the August Spies' brothers, Henry and Chris, if he would be needed as a witness and they told him his testimony was not that important and he could go. In his cross-examination, Zeisler asked Legner about the Haymarket events, perhaps hoping to finally get Legner's testimony on the record. Legner admitted having written an affidavit in Zeisler's office but denied telling anyone he had received payment for leaving town. While the full transcript of this case, and with it Legner's exact words, no longer exists, the summary of his reply to Zeisler's questioning published in the newspapers seemed to be contrary to the version of events the defense crafted a year earlier:

> . . . Legner said he was at the haymarket with Spies before the riot occurred. He saw Spies on the wagon, and heard him call out for Parsons. He saw the police coming, and told Spies to get down off the wagon. Capt. Ward came up and ordered the crowd to disperse. After Spies got down off the wagon Legner said he did not see him, and he himself left before the bomb was thrown.[27]

At this point the judge cut off this line of questioning, saying he did not want to try the anarchist case over again. The *Tribune* reporter who covered the trial simply reported this exchange and made no comment about its significance.

In fact, Legner's chronology of events contradicts Spies' and other accounts by witnesses for the defense. Legner recalls telling Spies to get off the wagon when he saw the police coming. Spies himself and other anarchist witnesses claim that Spies did not get off the wagon until Captain Ward gave the order to disperse which did not allow enough time for Spies to have gotten off the wagon, slip into the alley, and light the bomb as Gilmer alleged. But if Legner saw Spies get off the wagon when the police were first spotted a block away assembling under the bright lights of the Lyceum theatre, Spies certainly had enough time to take a few steps into a nearby alley. After this hearing the editors of the *Arbeiter Zeitung* agreed to print a retraction in exchange for Legner withdrawing his suit.[28]

THE BOMBER'S LOCATION

The question of where the bomb thrower stood directly weighed on the question of whether there was in fact a conspiracy and, unsurprisingly, defense lawyers went to great lengths to attempt to move the bomber as far from the speakers' wagon, where the men on trial were gathered, as possible. Witnesses for the state all placed the bomber within a step or two of Crane's alley. Harry Gilmer, the one witness who claimed to have actually seen the bomb lit and thrown, stated that Spies lit the fuse in the alley and the bomber took several steps onto the sidewalk before hurling it. Defense lawyers were certainly aware that the further they could place bomber from the speakers' wagon the less believable was Gilmer's story.[29]

Ten witnesses for the defense all testified that they saw the bomb in flight and could locate the spot where the bomber must have stood. But while all these witnesses placed the bomber far away from the speakers' wagon and from Crane's alley, they couldn't seem to agree on how distant he actually was. Two witnesses, Zeller and Urban, placed the bomber less than 20 feet from the alley. Two others, Simonson and Krumm, located him exactly 20 feet south. Three men (Taylor, Gutscher, and Lehnert) thought the bomber stood somewhere between 20 and 40 feet away, while three others (Koehler, Bernett, and Liebel) had him 40 feet or more down toward Randolph street, making for a throw of well over 60 feet, an Olympic shot-put distance.[30]

Nor could these ten agree on a few basic details of their surroundings. Five of these men remembered the street lamp that burned near Crane's alley, but Simonson didn't think there was a light post there. Two witnesses (Simonson and Taylor) remembered a row of fish crates lined up along the curb while two others (Zeller and Liebel) weren't sure and one (Krumm) denied there were boxes there at all.

Krumm proved an especially embarrassing witness for the defense. Capt. Black put him on the stand to swear he stood with his back against bricks of the factory wall in Crane's alley for from that position no person could have entered or left the alleyway without Krumm seeing him. But from this position Krumm's vision of both the speakers' wagon and the alleged position of the bomber down the sidewalk toward Randolph street would have been obscured by the walls of the alley. Under the gentle examination of defense attorney Foster, Krumm claimed he saw the bomb rise up ten feet over the sidewalk 20 feet south of the alley, "something like a burnt out match that was lit yet, and kind of dropped down that way," arc west toward the middle of the street, and explode. Grinnell probed Krumm relentlessly about where he saw the bomb in flight and what it looked like until Krumm realized he had twisted himself into an impossible position: "I didn't know where it come from . . . I couldn't tell where it come from. I seen it up in the air ten foot." Exploiting this opening Grinnell picked at Krumm's recollection of where the bomb landed and Krumm got tangled up even worse than before and he ended up flatly contradicting himself:

Q: In reference to the alley where did it fall—it fell on the street you say?
A: Yes sir.
Q: Was it in the middle of the street?
A: I don't know exactly whether it was in the middle.
Q: Was it about the middle?
A: Somewheres around the middle.
Q: About the middle it fell?
A: Yes.
Q: Did it fall at that time so you could see it when it fell?
A: No sir.
Q: Why?
A: I never noticed it no more.
Q: You saw the explosion?
A: Yes sir.
Q: Where was that explosion?
A: Right in the street.
Q: Did you see it?
A: No sir, I didn't see the explosion.
Q: It was too far south?
S: Yes sir.
Q: How far south was it from the line of the alley—supposing you took that alley and projected it across the street, how far south of that was it the bomb exploded?
A: Twenty feet.
Q: Twenty feet south of there?
A: From the alley, yes sir.
Q: Exploded twenty feet south of the alley?
A: I think so.
Q: That is right?
A: I guess so.
Q: You were there, you saw it?
A: I didn't see it explode.
Q: It was too far south?
A: Yes sir.[31]

Grinnell then asked Krumm if he'd seen the stack of boxes that nearly every other witness had recollected and that the defense had been struggling to suggest that the bomber hid behind. Krumm had no recollection of any boxes or crates on the sidewalk. Grinnell asked him how that could be if he had spent the whole evening with his back to the alley wall facing south and Krumm indicated he had stood in this position but kept his eyes toward the speakers' wagon the whole time, an impossibly neck-craning feat.[32]

Another witness, John Bernett, a candy maker, at first seemed to be the defense's best answer to Harry Gilmer. Bernett testified that he stood on the sidewalk just south of Crane's alley and saw the man who threw the bomb, though this man did not fit the description that Gilmer gave police and he threw his hissing weapon from a point well south of where Gilmer claimed the bomber was.

Apparently, the prosecutors had dealt with Bernett before and had some inkling of what he was brought to court to say, because soon after Bernett took the witness chair the rhetorical stakes were raised. Defense litigator Foster had only begun to question Bernett when Grinnell leapt out of his chair to object to Bernett having stepped off the witness chair to demonstrate the motions of the bomber. Immediately all the lawyers were on their feet shouting with such venom that one reporter worried (or hoped) that "the whole matter was about to be decided in the twenty-four-foot ring style." Among the things purportedly said in this heated exchange that the court reporter chose not to include in the official transcript was defense counsel Zeisler yelling at prosecutor Grinnell, "He has told you all this long ago!" and Judge Gary scolding the youngest lawyer in the group, "Mr. Zeisler should not interpose any such remark as that." Zeisler sat back into his chair and promised to control himself and Judge Gary overruled Grinnell's original objection and allowed Bernett to finish his story.[33]

Even more curious was the account of James D. Taylor, a 76-year-old "eclectic" physician who proudly proclaimed his membership in the American section of the IWPA and boasted that "I first learned Socialism from Father Owen, the father of Robert Dale Owen . . . in England."[34] Unlike many other witnesses who hedged their statements by saying "they guessed" or "they thought" or "as best they could remember," Taylor boldly phrased every detail as a solid fact and then stubbornly refused to modify his statements even when they later ran into conflict with each other. Taylor provided two crucial alibis for the defense: he saw the bomber pitch the bomb from a point well south of Crane's alley and he kept Fielden in his view through the whole melee and never saw a gun in his hand. Taylor claimed he stood south of Crane's alley when the bomb was thrown and watched as he could see a man "twenty or forty feet" south of Crane's alley throw a bomb that arced over a row of boxes and crash into the police. He also swore his eyes never left Fielden, not even for a moment, from the moment the police arrived till well after the shooting began and most of the crowd, including Fielden, had run away. But Taylor refused to recognize that from where he stood Fielden would have been north of him and the bomber due south, another improbably contorted position from which to witness both things.

Taylor was just as definite about the improbable circumstances of his arriving in that favorable spot. Seemingly unaware that nearly every other person who sat in that witness chair had confirmed that the meeting started after eight-thirty, Taylor was certain that he had arrived at the Haymarket around seven that evening and waited for 20 or 30 minutes before the meeting started. He was just as certain that he went directly to the spot near Crane's alley where he was when the bomb exploded, because he was "hard of hearing" and wanted to be close to the speaking. But at seven or even seven-thirty there was no gathering near Crane's alley until Spies walked over, climbed up on the wagon and asked for Parsons half an hour later. Either Taylor was mistaken or he somehow knew that the meeting wasn't going to take place in the "Haymarket" as advertised, but a half block north on Desplaines street.[35]

For all the effort the defense team put into pushing the bomber as far away from Crane's alley as possible, it is remarkable how little they had to show for it when all was said and done. In focusing most of their witnesses' testimony toward this one salient fact the defense lawyers played a high stakes game. Had they been able to provide convincing evidence that the bomber was more than a couple of steps from the alley, they would have undercut the state's most damaging witness. But in making this wager they risked undermining their credibility with the jury over a matter that even had they been able to carry their point only impaired and did not destroy the state's case. Prosecutors had backfilled against Gilmer's credibility by calling a parade of witnesses whose testimony piled up evidence that the Haymarket meeting was designed to attack the police. As long as the state could prove that material steps were taken to prepare for bombing or shooting police at the Haymarket meeting as part of the conspirators' plans, they could bypass Gilmer's eyewitness testimony and establish a chain of events from conception to execution without having to identify the bomber. But because few defense witnesses could convincingly claim they were not partisans or supporters of the men on trial and those that were able to establish that they were some distance from the anarchists could not get their stories straight, this strategy proved a loser.

From a strictly historical perspective, the most convincing material evidence placed the bomber near the mouth of Crane's alley.

W.C. Metzner, a merchant whose stove store stood across from Crane's alley, went out early the morning after the bombing and inspected the street where the explosion occurred. Metzner was as neutral an observer as one could hope to find. He had no connection to the anarchists, no obvious connection to the police, and he was not there that fateful night. He just happened to own the store fronting the street where the tragedy occurred. Before the rush of the day's traffic had had time to rumble over the area, Metzner crouched down and inspected the pavement until he found the spot. There, "somewhat on the west side of Desplaines street" and "slightly north" from the "south line" of Crane's alley, he found a hole. "It was an opening into the pavement about four to four and half or five inches across at the top, and kind of diamond shaped downwards to a depth of about three and half to four and a half inches."[36] As the defense offered no witnesses to dispute Metzner's veracity, as they did with other more prominent witnesses, and his placement of the location of the hole is consistent with most other witnesses' accounts, there is no reason not to believe that his description of what he found was as close to a factual record of the physical scene of the crime as history has bequeathed to us. So Metzner's hole, for the purpose of this study, will be assumed to be a fixed point of reference in establishing the location of other relevant clues.

W.C. Metzner seemed to have a keen eye, for not only did he notice the obvious hole that was blasted into the cedar paving blocks of Desplaines street, he also noticed another crucial clue. Nearby the hole he noticed a dent in one of the wooden blocks. About a foot away there was "another hole about an inch and a half to two inches, sort of egg shaped . . ."[37] This smaller hole or indentation could have been caused by the blast itself, though had it been so it seems unusual that it was singular, rather than being one in a blast pattern surrounding the main hole. Metzner was specifically asked if there was any other damage to the wooden paving blocks in the area and he decisively stated that there were no other holes or indentations in the area and the general condition of the road in front of his store was good.

The other, more interesting, possibility was that this second minor hole was actually a deep dent from where the bomb struck before rolling on to its detonation. Cedar is a softwood, being softer than pine, and is particularly weak in measurements of hardness having to do with denting (the "Jenka" scale). In fact, it is nearly impossible for an object as hard, as heavy, and falling from the height that the bomb did for it *not* to have made a substantial dent in the street. That the bomb fell and then rolled on was consistent with the observation of Lieutenant George Hubbard, who commanded the third company and watched the bomb plunk down in front of the company directly ahead of him. Hubbard testified that the bomb "appeared to roll a little" after landing.[38]

Moreover, Metzner testified that the large hole had a "jagged appearance" while the other was "egg-shaped" a description that implies that its edges were smoother. If the second hole was made by a piece of the shell flying off the bomb, it would have had a ragged outline because the shrapnel that flew off the bomb was haphazardly and roughly shaped. Metzner's description of this hole being "egg-shaped" fits perfectly with the sort of impression a heavy object would make striking the block from an acute angle.

If this minor dent was, in fact, a mark upon the spot where the bomb fell before rolling, the two holes, that "jagged" main hole and the more smooth "egg-shaped" one, would be arrayed along the axis of the bomb's path. If a line were drawn from the jagged hole through the minor one it should point to directly to the hiding place of the bomb thrower. Significantly, Metzner estimated that the small egg-shaped hole was "about one foot to the east." A line drawn between these two points would have placed the bomber in the mouth of Crane's alley.

Lieutenant James P. Stanton inadvertently corroborated Metzner's testimony. Stanton commanded the third company of the police, who comprised the left half of rows three and four of the police. Stanton stood well in front and on the right of his leading line. When he barked the order to "halt" to his men, he estimated that he stood "about the alley" by which he seems to have meant that he was nearly to its southern line. He couldn't have been beyond the south line of the alley because the company on his right had not yet reached the alley according to the testimony of John Wessler. Wessler stood in the first rank and to the far right of Lieutenant Bowler's company. When he came to a halt he was even with the lamppost which stood on the south corner of the alley.[39] Stanton's lines were close behind Bowler's lines, not even with them as was true of the companies in front of them because Stanton had more men and their line was wider than the street would allow, so they marched just in back of Bowler's men, lapping the first four men on Bowler's left. Just before the blast, Stanton had moved forward: "I heard the talking and I kind of stepped up a few steps to try to hear what was going on, and I then came to a front; with that I saw the bomb."[40] Stanton's odd phrasing here, "came to a front", indicates that he drew even with the front rank of Bowler's men, or, as he himself put it, "about" or nearly to the alley.

Stanton seemed eager to place the bomb thrower next to the speakers' wagon and testified that he thought the bomb must have come from north of the alley.[41] But his testimony actually provides a series of fixed references that trace a trajectory directly east to west. Stanton testified that he first noticed the bomb when it was "right overhead." Later, under defense probing, he was pushed to be more specific and thought it may have been overhead but "probably a foot or two north" of him. He seemed quite certain that it landed six feet to his left and added, "it first went away from me, and then in some way rolled back towards me."[42]

According to Metzner's estimation, the bomb actually came to a rest "slightly north" from the "south line" of Crane's alley. In order for Stanton to have seen the bomb overhead, it must have come from a point directly east of his position. Had it come from any point further south on Desplaines street, closer to where the defense tried to place it, he could not have seen it because it would flown behind him. None of the police officers in the ranks in front of Stanton, including Officer Wessler who was on the extreme right by the curb, saw the bomb in the air, though nearly all observers south of him did.

Other defense witnesses also inadvertently corroborated that the bomb came from a point near the alley. John Holloway, a 54-year-old teamster, father of nine children, and recent immigrant from England, was one of the first defense witnesses to testify about what he saw that night. Holloway listened to the speeches from the mouth of Crane's alley. Just before the police marched up he stepped up onto the sidewalk on the south side of the alley next to the lamppost. Then he heard a police officer give the command to disperse, and he recalled hearing a man on the wagon say "you can't do it. We are peaceable." Then Holloway describes what he saw at the moment of the blast:

A: The next that took place, before the words were out of his mouth, they were smothered in smoke from the explosion of what I suppose was the bomb. I didn't know it was the bomb until the next morning. I thought it was a volley of rifles from the smoke.

Q: Where was the smoke in reference to where you stood, in front or behind you?

A: The smoke come from out in the middle of the street and go up like a cloud up to the officers, come up from amongst the officers, come like a cloud.[43]

If Holloway was facing north-northwest, as he later testified, it is significant that he did not notice the arcing trail of the fuse as so many other witnesses did before the bomb exploded. Had the bomb come from a point yards to the south, as other defense witnesses claimed, Holloway should have clearly seen the bomb entering his field of vision from the left and cross to the right before hitting the street. However, if the bomb had been thrown from behind him and high over his head, it would have fallen nearly straight down from above, a trajectory that would have been more difficult to notice from his perspective. Thus Holloway's lack of observation of the bomb's flight actually supports prosecution assertions that the bomber stood in the alley.

At this point defense attorney Salomon seemed to sense the box he had put himself into and tried to move Holloway's testimony of the bomb toward the south:

> Q: According to your best judgment, about how far from the south was it this smoke came from?
> A: I can't answer that question.
> Mr. Grinnell: He has not said it came from the south, he said it came from the front of him, and the question is objected to as leading.
> Mr. Salomon: Where did this come from?
> A: The smoke swam away from the south going north.[44]

Though Holloway seemed to slowly have picked up on Salomon's cues and belatedly tried to comply and imply a southern origin as best he could, the refinement of his testimony was clumsy, obvious and certainly not as impressive as his original statements.

Likewise, Joseph Schwindt, a young shoemaker who would not celebrate the second anniversary of his coming to America until November, said that he stood just south of Crane's alley between the lamp post and the fish boxes. Schwindt was facing the street looking at the columns of police when the lit bomb fell directly in front of him. As he put it, it fell "square from me . . ." Had the bomb been thrown from a position a few yards north or south of Schwindt, he might have seen the fiery arc of the fuse angling in from the left or the right of his vision. For Schwindt to have only seen the bomb fall "square" in front of him meant that the bomber likely stood behind him not far to his left or right, a position closer to what Gilmer thought he saw than most of those called to the stand with Schwindt.[45]

* * *

Understandably, as they neared the end of their witness list, the defense lawyers were not confident that they had successfully discredited Gilmer's story. Had Black, Zeisler, Salomon, and Foster believed their witnesses had convincingly undermined Gilmer's account they would not have resorted to calling a dozen additional witnesses merely for the purpose of stating that they believed Gilmer to be a generally disreputable man and a liar. Such a line of questioning was both difficult and of limited usefulness.

Codes of criminal procedure and legal precedents narrowly restricted the sorts of statements that could be made about a person's character. Because of the danger that hearsay evidence might slip in, character witnesses were only allowed to say whether they had knowledge about a person's general reputation for truth and whether that reputation was good or bad. They were not permitted to repeat the stories and gossip that their neighbors and associates told about a person, only that when you added all such comments they amounted to a good or bad reputation. For this reason such testimony usually carried little weight against the otherwise compelling testimony of a witness and was considered something of a legal last resort.

Defense lawyers called ten men and women to testify about Gilmer's general reputation. Most had difficulty establishing even the simple proposition they were brought to swear to. Lucius Moses, a 64-year-old grocer, was the first to state under oath that he thought Gilmer's reputation was "rather bad" and he wouldn't trust him. But under cross-examination Moses admitted he had known Gilmer for only a few months, had no mutual friends with Gilmer, traveled in different social circles, and he actually knew little about Gilmer. The next witness, Austin Mitchell, was a fellow painter and knew Gilmer better, but when asked if he knew Gilmer's general reputation surprised everyone by answering, "No sir." Moses Salomon attempted to lead his witness toward the proper answer but the way he tried to reframe his question violated the code of criminal procedure and prompted Judge Gary to interrupt saying "That is not competent." Each time Salomon asked him the proper question, "Do you know his general reputation for truth and veracity ..." Mitchell answered, "no." Apparently exasperated, Salomon sat down and allowed his colleague Foster to finish the examination with the same result.[46]

Attorneys for the defense had more luck with B.P. Lee who had known Gilmer for about a year and said that he knew Gilmer's reputation to be bad, so bad that "I have heard people say that they would not believe him under oath." A printer named John Brixley seemed in the best position to weigh Gilmer's reputation, having known Gilmer since 1880 when they shared a house together. Brixley began by saying he knew his reputation to be bad but when questioned by assistant state's attorney Walker, Brixley backed away from his first statement and said he had never had any trouble of his own with Gilmer, "never had any trouble at all," just that he had heard rumors to the contrary. John Garrick, a former deputy sheriff for Cook county, thought Gilmer's reputation was "very bad, as far as I heard" and that he had "seen him associate with very questionable characters." But again, prosecution lawyers got Garrick to admit that he only had known Gilmer personally for one month when Gilmer rented a room from him and that this relationship was five years in the past.[47]

Mary Grubb, another of Gilmer's landlords, had known him since May and thought his reputation was "very bad" but she, herself, had "never had any trouble with him." Phineas Adams, a machinist, who lived on the same block with Gilmer two years earlier knew him to be of "very bad" character, but admitted he didn't associate with Gilmer and or know any of Gilmer's friends or associates. An elderly retired railroad contractor, Edward Castle, who also rented to Gilmer for a few months swore his reputation was bad and said he wouldn't believe him even if he swore an oath. H.S. Howe, an undertaker who was "slightly acquainted" with Gilmer agreed. J.W. Gage who owned a painting company and lived next door to Gilmer for four months stated that Gilmer's reputation was "not very good" but wouldn't go so far as to say he wouldn't believe him under oath. [48]

Against the ten witnesses the defense called to condemn Gilmer's character, few of whom knew him closely or for long, two of whom could not be brought to state that they would not believe him, the prosecution responded with 18 witnesses of their own. As a group the prosecution's character witnesses were a far more impressive crowd. They included the former city attorney of Chicago, a former Iowa Supreme Court justice, a governor of Iowa, three lawmen, two lawyers, and a number of men who knew Gilmer as a fellow militia member, a fellow member of the Chicago Union Veterans Club, and as a coworker. Richard Tuthill was probably the only person who had reason to formally investigate Gilmer's character, a duty he was charged with when he was a member of the employment committee of the Veteran's Association to which Gilmer belonged. Gilmer applied for help finding work and Tuthill's committee was charged with judging whether he was worthy of their charity (a detail only brought out by inept cross-examination). [49]

The defense tried every trick they knew to smear Gilmer on cross-examination. At one point Foster fired a succession of impermissibly "how-often-do-you-beat-your wife" type questions to one witness: "Did you ever hear of his [Gilmer's] being in the Cook county jail?" or "Did you ever hear of his being arrested in Cedar Rapids, Iowa?" or "Did you ever hear of his having a wife in Wisconsin and one in Chicago?" and "You don't remember seeing anything [in the paper] about his attempt to seduce a young girl . . . ?" [50]

When the last witness swore to Harry Gilmer's good character, the state rested and both panels of attorneys readied for their chance to sum up the meaning of the six weeks of testimony the jury had heard. Every one of the attorneys were allowed a summation and over the next two days they delivered a succession of impassioned and eloquent addresses.

The state's attorneys went first, assistant prosecutor Francis Walker, aiming first at an easy target, namely, Moses Salomon's inept opening speech, pointed out that it amounted to a plea of guilty to the charge of conspiracy, which, Salomon mistakenly argued was not the same as a charge of murder. Walker carefully dissected the legal definition of a conspiracy and the meaning of being an accessory before the fact. Carried away by the apparent clarity of the law on this point, Walker admitted that the eight defendants had been singled out because of their prominence in the anarchist movement. "The statute of conspiracy is ample to hold every one of these defendants—even if they number 3,000—guilty of the murder of Mathias Degan on May 4. The men who are on trial are only the leaders." [51]

Walker mocked the postured neutrality of defense witnesses, many of whom claimed not to be socialists but admitted otherwise on cross. Walker exaggerated when he charged that "Every witness who testified for the defense was a reader of the 'Arbeiter Zeitung' and a tool of August Spies . . ." Such hyperbole was unnecessary to secure Walker's general point that many of the defense witnesses not only had a stake in the outcome, but many were unindicted coconspirators: "Wouldn't a man who would kill for the social revolution lie for the same cause? Was it a hard thing for a man to take the stand and say he was not a Socialist when he knew that it could not be proved that he was?" Worse, Walker descended to exploiting exploit ethnic prejudices saying that not one of the witnesses who appeared for the defense was "an American citizen or a naturalized citizen, none of them in this country but two or three years." (Grinnell followed suit and railed, ". . . we Americans who adopt this country as our own—have the right to criticize the nationality of the defendants; because, if a man come here in this, our country . . . [and] seeks these shores only for anarchy, only for communism, only for selfish ends and desires, he is no part nor parcel of this country.")[52]

This gave defense lawyer Foster a rich opportunity to tear into Walker's obvious nativism: "The statement that they are foreigners and Germans is made to wring from you a verdict founded on prejudice." Foster parried Walker's charge that all the defendants but Parsons were foreigners by pointing out that Neebe had been born in Pennsylvania, Fielden had lived in the United States for more than 20 years, Spies came to this country while still an infant, and both Fischer and Engel had been residents of Chicago for more than a decade.

Of all the anarchists' lawyers, only William A. Foster seems to have understood that the key to defending against the mountain of murderous excerpts from his client's newspapers and speeches was to argue that the state had failed to forge one final critical link in the chain of evidence: Grinnell had not proven that the defendants' advocacy of murder had reached the ears or the eyes of the bomber. But before this line of defense could be fully developed, the anarchists themselves, according to one observer, "some of whom seemed not unanxious to pose as martyrs for the 'cause,' hotly resented Mr. Foster's plea, which resulted in his withdrawal from the case, and they practically dictated the policy of their other counsel." This was to be Foster's last speech as a council for the defense.[53]

Having scored some good points, Foster unfortunately plunged on and ruined the progress he had made. For some inexplicable reason, Foster reminded the jurors that Lingg was in fact a bomb maker and added an entirely new concession: "There is nothing in the case, so far as Lingg is concerned, except that he was a bomb-maker, and that he walked into Larrabee street on the 4th of May with two bombs in his pockets." As if that was not enough damage for one speech, during the course of his remarks, Foster made other disastrous admissions, telling the jurors that the unusual metal-melting furnace that George Engel had in his possession "might have been for making bombs," that he was prepared "to admit that Spies had tons of dynamite in the *Arbeiter Zeitung* building," and that though he wasn't prepared to admit Fielden pulled out a revolver and shot at the police, if he "did so, he was justified in shooting."[54]

Foster was not the only member of his team to gratuitously grant factual points to the prosecution. Captain Black's rambling speech contained its share of gifts. Black conceded that the bomb that killed Officer Degan had been made by Lingg, apparently thinking that it was some sort of defense to say that Lingg didn't know what his bomb would be used for. "The State must show not that a bomb of certain manufacture did a certain work, but that the man charged with murder exploded it . . . Did Lingg know on Monday night that one of his bombs was to be used? He could not have known it . . . And yet the State asks you to say that Lingg shall be hanged because he manufactured bombs." Though he had earlier called two witnesses to refute the claim that Lingg's Carpenter's Union had made plans to take violent action during the May strikes, Black admitted that the Carpenter's Union armed itself in anticipation of May Day: "The Carpenter's Union at one of its meetings resolved to devote a certain amount of money for the purpose of experimenting with dynamite. You may say that was not right, but [Lingg] was not responsible for it." Black even conceded the heart of the prosecution's contention, that these men were part of a conspiracy to violently oppose the police, but again seemed to think that by picturing this as a "defensive" plan he would help save the necks of his clients:

> What was the purport of that resolution? I think I state it fairly to the State and fairly to the defendants themselves, when I say that the action then and there resolved upon was this, no more, no less: That if in the event of a struggle the police should attempt by brute force to overpower the strikers unlawfully and unjustly, those men would lend their help to their fellow wageworkers as against the police. A plan of action was suggested by one of the group which contemplated the blowing up of police stations, cutting telegraph wires and disabling the fire department . . . Nothing was to be inaugurated by the so-called conspirators, there was to be no resort to force by them in the first instance. It was solely defensive, and had reference alone to meeting force by force . . . [55]

Such a statement was but a hairsbreadth away from one that could have been delivered by prosecutor Grinnell.

Zeisler based his remarks to the jury on the erroneous legal claim that Illinois law required the identification of the principal to an act before anyone could be punished as an accessory. Zeisler's apparent strategy was to deny that the defendants ever meant what they said rather than to deny they said it and to deny their actions, whatever nefarious or illegal preparations they were making, ever involved the particular meeting at the Haymarket. All the talk about arming and building bombs or looting downtown department stores was just a way of reaching the rude workers who "could not in the nature of things be very intelligent and highly cultivated and educated." One couldn't expect Parsons and Spies to "talk to those men by stating to them abstract principles of social science . . ." When Spies showed off his bombs to reporters it was merely "braggadocio"; a way of getting attention and scarring the capitalists into making concessions.[56]

Zeisler only half-heartedly disputed the evidence brought against his clients. He didn't dispute the evidence of a "special conspiracy entered into by a number of persons at No. 54 West Lake Street [Greif's Hall] . . ." only that none of the defendants besides Engel and Fischer were involved and the plan that they agreed to wasn't carried out.[57] He raised the testimony of plasterer Henry Lindemeyer who swore there were no suspicious objects or parcels at the *Arbeiter-Zeitung* on the day of the bombing and claimed to have stored his hat, coat, and tools in the closet where police found a sack of dynamite. But in the next breath Zeisler volunteered that Spies kept "bombs" in the same office, "As to the bombs there was no secrecy, and Spies admitted that he had one more bomb than the police discovered."[58]

Much of the rest of Zeisler's summation was an attempt to reinterpret the anarchists' ideology in a way that made it incompatible with the prosecution's conspiracy theory. This was accomplished by denying that any of the men on trial ever seriously believed a proletarian revolution was near or even possible. Rather, they believed in "evolutionary revolution." They flung violent rhetoric merely to highlight the wrongs done to the working class. "What do you take these men for? Are they fools? Are they children? Don't you see what their ideal is, and the last aim and end of theirs? It is the social revolution, yes, but not the social revolution brought about by the throwing of dynamite." But, Zeisler couldn't resist the pull of his own soapbox: "And I tell you, gentlemen of the jury, this social revolution is coming . . ."[59]

For their part the prosecutors could be just as emotional. Ingham used his moment of soliloquy to stress the uniqueness and vital importance of the case, not only to the eight men on trial, to the city of Chicago, but also to the full sweep of human history. "Gentlemen, I think I exaggerate nothing when I say to you that never since the jury system was instituted, hundreds and hundreds of years ago, has there been elevated and placed upon the shoulders of any twelve men the responsibility that rests upon you today . . . for . . . the very question itself is whether organized government among men shall perish from the face of the earth; whether the day of civilization shall go down into the night of barbarism; whether the wheels of history shall be rolled back, and all that has been gained by thousands of years of progress be lost." Prosecutor Grinnell though opening his speech with self-deprecation, "I bring to your attention no genius; I have nothing in me of that . . . I can stir no pulse . . . ," and saying that "the facts in this case . . . are more eloquent and forceful for conviction than any words . . . ," pitched the jurors' duty as a choice between democracy and anarchism. "Gentlemen, the red flag has passed in our streets enough . . . Ah, gentlemen, there is but one flag of liberty in this land, and that is the stars and stripes. That flag is planted on our soil, and planted to stay, if you have the courage to carry out the law."[60]

After tightly wrapping himself in the flag, Grinnell got down to the business of explaining once again how the accessory law worked and why it was that those men who had been peripheral to the act of the throwing the bomb were guilty of murder when the bomb thrower himself was not on trial. "Whether the deceased fell by the hands of the accused in particular or otherwise is immaterial; all are responsible for the acts of each if done in pursuance and furtherance of a common design." Grinnell described the legal basis of the case as plainly as it could be told:

> We have not got the bomb thrower here. We have got the accessories, the conspirators, the individuals who framed the plan, who got it up, who advised and encouraged it, and if we never knew who did it, if there was not a syllable of proof in this case designating the name of a single individual who perpetrated that offence, who threw that bomb, still the defendants are guilty.[61]

There were other famous moments when Grinnell's temper and language rose to an operatic pitch: "...if you have now prejudice against the defendants under the law...you have a right to have it. Prejudice! Men, organized assassins, can preach murder in our city for years; you deliberately under your oaths hear the proof, and then say that you have no prejudice!" (Captain Black leapt to object to the use of the term "assassins.") Later Grinnell struck the same notes in excoriating the anarchists' lawyers maneuver of arguing that there could not have been a conspiracy to provoke a revolution because such an idea was sheer folly. "There is no way that any criminal can excuse his act by the declaration that it has been foolish... Black says they are humanitarians... Don't try, gentlemen, to shirk the issue. Law is on trial. Anarchy is on trial; the defendants are on trial for treason and murder." (Black again is on his feet: "The indictment does not charge treason; do it, Mr. Grinnell?")[62]

As he neared the end of his remarks and one of the longest trials in the history of the state up to that time, Grinnell softened and gave permission to the jurors to be merciful. "My duty is performed, and yours begins, and in this connection, gentlemen, let me suggest to you another reason why it is important that you should be careful. You can acquit them all, one or none; you can parcel the penalties out as you please; to some you can administer the extreme penalty of the law; to others less than that, if you desire..." Grinnell then singled out Neebe for their clemency and asked the jurors to not to take his life. As for the others, Grinnell admitted in his eyes each of the prisoners had varying degrees of responsibility and listed their culpability for the panel: "Some of these people we sincerely and honestly believe should receive at your hands the extreme penalty of the law. Spies, Fischer, Lingg, Engel, Fielden, Parsons, Schwab, Neebe, in my opinion, based upon the proof, is the order of punishment."[63]

Grinnell's effort was effective. Juror Andrew Hamilton thought of all the speeches the jury listened to over the eight weeks of the trial, "none affected the jury like Mr. Grinnell's closing arguments, and fairly aroused our sympathy. Black and Foster had no such effect... The most tiresome and weary task I ever had was to listen to Mr. Zeisler. Perhaps it was his way of looking at things, but it was very tiresome."[64]

Letting down their guard, two of the defense lawyers spoke to reporters after Grinnell concluded his closing remarks. One of them as much as admitted that they had not been up to their task. "If we save the necks of our clients we will be satisfied. The evidence surprised us. The manner of its presentation took us unawares all through the case." Another defense counsel who spoke anonymously hinted that they had little chance all along: "Our case has been desperate from the beginning. Our only hope lies in a disagreement."[65]

CHAPTER 6

THE VERDICT

ALL THAT REMAINED FOR JUDGE GARY was to give the jury its charge. Judges were responsible for specifying to the jurors what laws applied to the case at hand and what their options were in considering the case. Both the prosecution and the defense were permitted to suggest to the judge those instructions and legal interpretations they believed necessary to clarify key issues. State's Attorney Grinnell handed the judge 14 points of law, while the anarchists' defense team asked the judge to read 74 instructions to the jury on its behalf, two-thirds of which (46) he delivered, the rest Gary marked "refused."[1]

Most of the state's instructions dealt with mundane and general aspects of criminal procedure. Judge Gary provided a detailed and technical definition of the charge of murder and told the jurors that if they found any of the defendants guilty, Illinois law required a sentence no fewer than 14 years in the penitentiary or any term beyond that including death. He defined the meaning of "reasonable doubt" and told the men in the jury box that circumstantial evidence was just as valid as any other type of evidence but warned them not to go beyond the testimony and evidence presented to "hunt up doubts" as the presumption of innocence was not intended to aid the guilty to escape. The four defendants who testified on their own behalf should be viewed as any other witnesses, the judge lectured, although their conduct and demeanor and their personal stake in the outcome could be considered along with their words. Should any part of their testimony be persuasively contradicted by other evidence, the jury was permitted to disregard it as a material fact. When deliberating, the jury was not permitted to allow concern over the fates of the eight accused men to influence its decision as to their guilt. Judge Gary reminded the jurors that any or all of the accused could be found guilty or innocent as the jury wished, and the jurors had the right to not only consider the facts of the case but, if they felt competent to do so, even to interpret the laws of the state for themselves.

From the remainder of the prosecution's recommended instructions it is clear that Grinnell and his colleagues were most concerned about two elements of their case: the question of freedom of speech and the absent bomber. There was a fine line between punishing men for the beliefs they expressed publicly and convicting them for plotting together to achieve a certain end, especially when their purpose was political. At what point does advocacy of an abstract revolution cross over into planning an armed attack? Judge Gary told the jurors that the general right to "freedom of speech" was no defense in this case because this right did not allow a man to advise another man to commit a crime. In this case the state alleged that there was a conspiracy to "excite the people . . . to sedition, tumult and riot, and to use deadly weapons against, and take the lives of other persons . . ." a matter well beyond the liberties granted by the First Amendment.

Lacking the bomber, the prosecution from the beginning of the trial labored to overcome its feared reluctance of a jury to condemn a group of confederates while the murderer ran free. Most of its instructions were aimed at ensuring that the jurors were well plied with the legal basis for the charge of conspiracy. Gary began by reading the definition of an "accessory" from the Illinois statutes: "[one who] aids, abets or assists, or who, not being present, aiding abetting or assisting, hath advised, encouraged, aided, abetted the perpetration of the crime." Such a definition, by itself, seemed to cast a broad and open-ended net, capturing not only the assistant but also anyone who merely "encouraged" a crime from a distance. Gary appeared to widen this definition even further by observing that accessories could be considered just as culpable as the principal offender and need not be prosecuted at the same time as the person they aided. An accessory could be found guilty of a crime even when the main actor was not caught, charged, or convicted.

However, Gary's other instructions made clear that the legal requirements for condemning any of the conspirators lined up before his bench were higher than this. To find the defendants guilty the person who threw the bomb must have been shown to have acted as a "member of their conspiracy" and in "pursuance of such conspiracy." Then each of the defendants also had to be shown to have been a part of this conspiracy, meaning at least that they had "knowledge of the conspiracy." To be a conspiracy the plan hatched by the defendants did not have to specify when or where the "use of deadly weapons" was to take place. It was enough to merely show that those involved had agreed to leave it up to the individual initiative of each conspirator to do so.

Most of the instructions that Judge Gary accepted from the defense and read out to the court hammered home the responsibility of the jurors to scrutinize the evidence skeptically and to acquit if a reasonable doubt lingered in their minds. Unlike a civil trial, a "preponderance of the evidence" was not enough to tip the scale toward conviction. Reasonable doubt, Judge Gary explained, is equivalent to a moral certainty and unless the jurors had arrived at "an abiding faith amounting to a moral certainty" that the accused were guilty, they must be released. Rather, "they must be proved to be guilty so clearly and conclusively that there is no reasonable theory upon which they can be innocent . . ." Indeed, if there was even a single fact that was proved to the jury's satisfaction and was inconsistent with a guilty verdict, this sole fact alone was sufficient to acquit a defendant and the jury should do so. Circumstantial evidence was to be accorded extra suspicion and was to be disregarded if there was any "reasonable" explanation for it that contradicted the theory of the defendants' guilt.

Of course, jurors were to exclude, as best they could, their personal opinions, beliefs, and biases, but even beyond that they did not have the right to speculate or to consider facts they were aware of but that were not brought forward in the trial. If they pronounced the defendants "not guilty" they were not saying that they were innocent, but only that the evidence brought against them was not convincing. Most importantly, all the burden of proof rested with the prosecution and every juror was to presume that the person who threw the bomb was not connected to the others unless that too was proven beyond a reasonable doubt.

Witnesses were a special matter. Jurors were instructed to use the testimony of accomplices, such as Gottfried Waller and William Seliger, with "great care and caution," as they should take into consideration when weighing their statements, the possibility that they were "induced or influenced" by promises of immunity or a lighter punishment. Likewise, jurors were specifically allowed to take into consideration what they may have perceived to be witnesses' "prejudices, motives or feelings of revenge" and asked to disregard the testimony of any witness who they believed had knowingly lied. Defendants who testified on their own behalf should not be disregarded merely because they stood in jeopardy of being convicted for a serious crime, and the fact that any defendant chose not to testify should not be taken as evidence either for or against his guilt. Judge Gary even allowed an instruction that almost seemed as though it was a reluctant admission from the defense counsels: that in weighing the testimony of witnesses for the defense the jury should proceed with the "belief that all the witnesses have endeavored to tell the truth...and if reasonably possible, attribute any differences or contradictions in their testimony, if any exists, to mistake or misrecollection rather than to a willful intention to swear falsely."

Judge Gary warned jurors to be wary of any statements of the prosecutors that were not based on evidence, especially any "allusions or references...to the supposed dangerous character of any views" the defendants expressed. Likewise, he cautioned that those men on trial could only be found guilty of the particular crimes they were charged with and even persuasive evidence that any of them committed other offenses was not relevant.

One series of instructions supported an affirmative defense, and Gary read these instructions as well. They began by observing that individuals and groups have the right to arm themselves for their mutual protection and to publicly advocate arming in such a manner was not a crime. Nor is it a crime for groups of people to make a pact to resist violently an unlawful attack, even to agree among themselves "that in the event of the workingmen or strikers being attacked that they would assist the strikers to resist..." Whether such an agreement was an illegal conspiracy pivoted on the question of whether the force to be resisted was unlawful and whether the resistance to it was not excessive.

Finally, the judge accepted a clutch of instructions that together made it perfectly clear that whatever any of the defendants publicly advocated or privately conspired to do, to arrive at a guilty verdict the jury had to be convinced that the bomber had acted as part of their plan. In Gary's words:

> It will not do to guess away the lives or liberties of our citizens nor is it proper that the jury should guess that the person who threw the bomb which killed Degan was instigated to do the act by the procurement of the defendants or any of them. That fact must be established beyond all reasonable doubt in the minds of the jury, and it will not do to say that because defendants may have advised violence, that therefore when violence came, that it was the result of such advice. *There must be a direct connection established by credible testimony between the advice and the consummation of the crime, to the satisfaction of the jury beyond all reasonable doubt* (italics added).

To make this point as forcefully as possible, the last instruction composed by the defense and accepted by the judge walked the jurors through a hypothetical scenario. Even assuming that the defendants hatched a plan on the evening of May 3 in the basement of Greif's Hall to position armed units throughout the city and agreed to destroy police stations in the event of a clash between workers and police, if it could not be proven that the Haymarket bomber hurled his bomb as part of this plan, then none of the defendants could be held responsible for the murder of Mathias Degan:

> Although the defendants or some of them may have spoken and also published their views to the effect that a social revolution should be brought about by force, and that the officers of the law should be resisted, and to this end dynamite should be used, to the extent of taking human life, that persons should arm to resist the law, that the law should be throttled and killed; and although such language might cause persons to desire to carry out the advice given as a foresaid, and do the act which caused officer Degan's death yet the bomb may have been thrown and Degan killed by some one unfamiliar with, and unprompted by the teachings of defendants or of any of them . . . Therefore the jury must be satisfied beyond all reasonable doubt that the person throwing said bomb was acting as the result of the teaching or encouragement of defendants or some of them before defendants can be held liable . . .[2]

Of the two dozen or so instructions written by the defense team that Judge Gary refused to read to the jurors, some simply confused or confounded settled legal principles. No judge would have allowed the defense's proposed instruction number four that attempted to alter the definition of "reasonable doubt" by calling on jurors to acquit if testimony "awakens an apprehension in your mind." Or instruction number three that stated that for the conspiracy to be an illegal conspiracy, the Haymarket meeting had to be an unlawful gathering. Or number twelve that claimed that as a matter of law the guilt of a principal must first be established before the guilt of an accessory can be determined. Even number five that told jurors that unless every "material allegation" in the indictments against the men was proven beyond a reasonable doubt they must be acquitted, went well beyond the standards of criminal procedure of that day.

Judge Gary rejected other instructions proposed by the defense on the grounds that they were based on theories for which no evidence had been presented at the trial. One of these asked the jurors to consider whether some of the defendants that tragic night "declared to their fellow conspirators that nothing be done in furtherance of the common design, beyond the making of speeches ..." Another painted a picture of the Haymarket meeting in which the police "sanctioned and conceded its lawfulness," and one police officer "of his own volition" went to the meeting "for the pretended purpose of dispersing it but in fact for the purpose of destroying the lives of all persons there assembled ..."

Most of the other defense instructions that Judge Gary refused were substantially the same as those that he did accept and read to the court. Fourteen of the interpretations of law that Gary rejected dealt with the definition and standards of proof of a conspiracy. The defense vainly attempted to argue that the bomber's intentions and state of mind had to be proved beyond a reasonable doubt in order for the principal to be connected to the conspiracy. After all, what if the bomber acted out of "his own passion, fear, hatred, malice, or ill will ..." and not according to a common plan? But Gary had already instructed the jury that the identity of the bomber need not be proven beyond a reasonable doubt as long as other evidence convincingly proved that the bomber, whoever he was, acted as part of the prearranged plan.

Later, when Gary's handling of these instructions was reviewed by the Illinois Supreme Court, the justices found one prosecutorial instruction that they thought Gary should have rejected:

> If these defendants ... conspired together ... to excite the people ... to sedition, tumult and riot, and to use deadly weapons against, and take the lives of other persons, as a means to carry their designs and purposes into effect, and in pursuance of such conspiracy ... by print or speech advised or encouraged the commissions of murder without designating time, place or occasion at which it should be done and in pursuance of and induced by such advice or encouragement, murder was committed then all of such conspirators are guilty of such murder whether the person who perpetrated such murder can be identified or not ...[3]

In its appeal the defense pointed out that this instruction implied that mere "general advice" to the public to commit violent acts warranted a charge of murder. Reluctantly, the appellate judges conceded the point, writing, "if we construed the instruction to mean what counsel claim it to mean, we would be forced to agree with them, that it was erroneous." But this error was not significant, the justices decided, as it was superseded by numerous other instructions that correctly interpreted the law to require that the state prove that the conspirators laid particular plans and engaged in specific actions to accomplish those plans.

Tellingly, on the day the verdict was handed down this error was not mentioned by defense lawyers when they were asked by reporters about their plans for appealing the verdict. Instead, Captain Black complained that Judge Gary had refused their instruction that "the jury must disregard their prejudice, and not take into account the fact that the defendants were Anarchists. I think there is a fatal error in that alone..."[4] Black was incensed that Gary rejected an instruction that read:

> No person can be legally convicted...on account of any opinion or principles entertained by them. It cannot be material in this case that some of them are or may be socialists, communists or anarchists, and no prejudice ought to be born against them on account thereof by the jury, although the jury may believe their doctrines are false and pernicious.[5]

Why Black was so exercised by the exclusion of this instruction is a mystery, as this instruction was substantially the same as the one Gary did approve:

> The court further instructs the jury that the allusions and references of the prosecuting attorneys to the supposed dangerous character of any views entertained or principles contended for by the defendants or any of them, should in no way influence or prejudice your minds against the defendants in this case; your duty is discharged when you have determined their guilt or innocence of the charge contained in this indictment, and there is no other question involved in this case.[6]

Such instructions seem to have been taken to heart by at least some jurors. Juror Reed said later that "the jury all along tried to keep in view that they should not condemn anybody for mere opinions, but that their business was to pass judgment on the evidence before the court in connection with the law laid down in the instructions."[7]

After all the instructions had been read, the bailiff led the jurors from the courtroom to begin their deliberations. Once they had filed out, Judge Gary called all the lawyers to his bench and discussed with them one additional instruction. It is not clear whether Gary suggested this instruction or whether it was a sudden afterthought on the part of the defense, but at the end of their short meeting the judge told the bailiff to retrieve the jury. At the very least this haphazard moment revealed that the defense had come close to making another grave error. Somehow, through their blizzard of suggested instructions, they overlooked requesting that the jurors be informed of the legal definition of the charge of manslaughter and be told of their right to find the defendants guilty of that lesser charge.

* * *

It was about 3 P.M. when the jurors were led up the marble stairs of the city hall to the inner sanctum of the grand jury room on the top floor. Bailiffs shut the jury in the inner rooms, cleared the outer area, and locked and barred that door as well. Apparently conscious of the prying eyes and ears of reporters straining for any tidbit of information, the jurors drew the blinds over the large windows fronting Michigan street and stuffed the keyholes full with wads of paper. Among the crush of onlookers craning for some sign from the shaded upper windows were two with a particular stake in the outcome—Salomon and Zeisler, lawyers for the defense.

At about half past seven, after a little more than four hours of deliberation, a cordon of police rushed to secure a path through a crowd milling about outside the building, shouts of "Way, there, for the jury!" carrying above the din of the street. Twelve men silently passed through the cordon from the city hall to the Revere House across the street to take their supper in a private room on the upper floor. Reporters who caught a glimpse of the panel dining noted that the jurors seemed relaxed, "resting in easy positions, smoking and apparently enjoying themselves."[8]

When the court reconvened at ten the next morning, the crowd gathered at the building's entrance had grown to more than a thousand. This day, however, few of the gawkers were satisfied as Judge Gary allowed only the immediate family of the defendants, police, reporters, and a "few favored members of the bar" into the gallery. As a further precaution bailiffs directed visitors to sit together at one far end of the large and now nearly empty room behind a double row of police, while the defendants were led to seats on the opposite side of the room. Parsons happened to take a seat adjacent to an open window and leaned out and waved his red handkerchief to the crowd below. Schwab was overheard saying to him, "I wish I could go down and make those fellows a speech." From where they were seated, none of the defendants could see their loved ones.

The jurors filed in and faced the front of the judge's bench. The defendants and their lawyers rose, and Gary asked Frank S. Osborne, the foreman, if he had a verdict. Osborne handed two slips of paper to the clerk, who exclaimed, "there are two verdicts here," causing a moment of confusion until the judge examined the papers and corrected him: "There is only one verdict but it is written on two sheets of paper. Read it." The clerk read:

> We, the jury, find the defendants . . . guilty of murder in manner and form as charged in the indictment, and fix the penalty at death. We find the defendant Oscar W. Neebe guilty of murder in the manner and form as charged in the indictment, and fix the penalty at imprisonment for fifteen years.

There was a rush for the exit as reporters dashed to file their reports. Schwab was overheard exclaiming in German, "My god, we die, and Neebe gets but fifteen years." Parsons took a nearby curtain cord, fashioned it into a noose, and dangled it outside the window for the benefit of the crowd below, who cheered in response. One sympathetic observer of the trial claimed that Lingg was overheard saying, "there is no reason to complain. Had I been in the judge's place and he in mine, I would have sent him to the gallows inside of twenty-four hours."[9]

Captain Black demanded that the jurors be individually polled and then moved for a new trial. Judge Gary placed the motion on his docket to be argued the next month and then thanked the jurors for their long service. The trial was finally gaveled to an end.[10]

Jurors retired from the courtroom to the grand jury room where they had made their fateful decision. Grinnell made a brief appearance to thank the jurors in person for their service, though he didn't reveal to them that he was exhausted and had come close to a nervous breakdown the night before while waiting for their verdict. A clerk appeared and handed to each juror a voucher promising payment calculated at 2 dollars per day for between 51 and 61 days of service, depending on the date of admission to the jury. However, because the county had expended all its funds for the calendar year, these certificates could only be cashed at a substantial discount or held until the next year's budget was approved. Some businessmen floated the idea of raising a fund to compensate the jurors for their service, but all the jurors spoken to by reporters about the idea condemned it "in very severe terms."[11]

Judge Gary granted a defense request for a postponement of the sentencing so that it could gather the materials it needed to move for a new trial. A month later, on the first day of October, both legal teams were back in court and Captain Black entered a plea for a new trial. In support of his motion, Black argued that the jury had been packed and partial, that Judge Gary made biased rulings regarding evidence, testimony, and jury instructions, that the state's attorney had been allowed to make "appeals to the prejudices and passions of the jury," and, most importantly, that the trial had produced "no evidence . . . supporting or justifying said verdict." In another sign of the lack of expertise on the defense bench, Black's motion for a new trial did not list several of the key issues upon which a federal appeal would be made a year later—among them that Spies had been forced to incriminate himself and his papers had been seized without warrant.[12]

For the most part this motion was just a formality, another step in laying the groundwork for an appeal. After all, all the issues the defense now raised were all ones that Judge Gary had already considered and ruled upon and there could be little hope that he would suddenly reverse himself. The defense's only slender hope was contained in the part of their plea where they claimed there was "newly discovered evidence" that would cast new light on central issues in the case. This mysterious new evidence came in the form of an affidavit from one man, E.A. Stevens, who claimed to have heard another man repeat what a third man, Henry L. Ryce, had told him.

The allegations of bias against Bailiff Ryce were the centerpiece of the defense's motion for a new trial. Stevens claimed that his good friend Otis S. Favor told him that Bailiff Ryce had boasted of picking men whom he expected to be challenged by the defense so as to exhaust its peremptory challenges. Stevens swore that Favor told him that Ryce said: "I am managing this case, and know what I am about; those fellows are going to be hanged as certain as death. I am calling such men as the defense will have to peremptorily challenge and waste their time and challenges; then they will have to take such men as the prosecution wants."[13]

Stevens' allegation was potentially damning but, as with all affidavits, its strength rested largely on the reputation and neutrality of those who were willing to swear to it. On this score neither E.A. Stevens nor Otis S. Favor was the neutral bystander the defense made them out to be. Stevens was a longtime associate of both the lead defense lawyer, Captain Black, and some of the anarchists. His path had crossed that of many of the defendants when he had served as an organizer for the SLP in the 1870s. He was the treasurer of the Society for Ethical Culture in Chicago, where he worked closely with William Salter, a leader of the anarchists' amnesty committee and the honored speaker at one of the anarchist American group's weekly meetings in 1885. Stevens was also the founding secretary and later president of the Chicago Liberal League, the free-thought organization that shared a meeting hall with the anarchists and to which Black, the defendant Samuel Fielden, and other anarchists, such as William and Lizzie Holmes, belonged. Stevens later told a reporter that he had in fact known some of the defendants but "was not on friendly terms with the Communists, and did not believe in their theories," but he felt sympathy for them nonetheless. "Parsons and Spies frequently pitched into me, but as they were to be tried for what they had said I felt it my duty to help them all I could."[14] Favor too was but one degree removed from anarchist circles. Favor was also an officer of Chicago's Society for Ethical Culture.[15]

Further complicating matters was the fact that the man in the middle, Otis S. Favor, refused to swear to what Ryce allegedly told him. Black asked Judge Gary to issue a subpoena and haul Favor into court and force him to go on the record. Gary asked skeptically if Black knew of any precedent for "calling a man in" at that point in the proceedings. Black admitted that he knew of none but thought that the judge could issue such an order simply in "furtherance of justice." It is not recorded what Judge Gary's expression was as he listened to Black urge him to take an unprecedented action without an established legal basis, but something of his demeanor is evident in his reply that left little doubt about his feelings as he refused Black's plea:

> If there was any such authority, the occasions for its exercise must have been so frequent that it would be easy to find precedents of the exercise of authority. It cannot be that this is the first instance. Hundreds, thousands, of such incidents have occurred. This cannot be the first instance. I have never known the thing to be done in upwards of forty years.[16]

Without Otis S. Favor, Stevens' sworn statement was even more worthless than the usual affidavit, a class of evidence that the defense lawyer Zeisler later in life described as "meaningless" and "wholesale perjury." In its place the defense threw other affidavits at the court, but none came close to sticking.[17]

Another man swore that he knew the juror T.E. Denker and a few days after the bombing heard Denker remark that the "whole damn crowd ought to be hung." This affidavit may have been more persuasive if it didn't belong to Thomas J. Morgan, a leader of Chicago's nonrevolutionary socialists and a prominent member of the committee raising funds for the defense. Similarly, a man by the name of Michael Cull swore that he heard the juror G.W. Adams say that "the police ought to have shot them all down, that they had no right in this country, and that if I was on the jury I'd hang all the damned buggers." In reply, the prosecutor's office produced affidavits from Adams denying that the conversation ever took place and from the chief of police of Cull's town who swore that Cull was a worthless bum who spent whatever money he made on booze rather than the support of his five children.[18]

Two other men, Albert P. Love and Orrin S. Blossom, swore out affidavits detailing how on the night of the Haymarket bombing they sat with the key prosecution witness Harry L. Gilmer drinking beer until after 10:30. If what Love and Blossom alleged was true, then Gilmer could not have stood in Crane's alley and seen Spies light the fatal bomb. Grinnell countered with more affidavits from Love and Blossom, both men swearing that their statements were false. Love and Blossom explained that they lied for the defense attorneys in exchange for a check for 91 dollars: 30 for Love, 30 for Blossom, 30 for the notary, and the last dollar for cigars all around. Speaking to reporters outside the courtroom, Zeisler admitted paying the notary 91 dollars but explained this was for his work as a detective charged with tracing Harry Gilmer's movements the night of the bombing. Zeisler and his partner said that they knew nothing about this money going to Love and Blossom and never had any suspicion that these affidavits were not all that they were claimed to be.[19]

A few years later defense attorney Sigmund Zeisler wrote an article for a law journal entitled "The Prevalence of Perjury," detailing how easy it was to find a notary who would sign any paper: "... a so-called Notary Public, who is he? ... Any loafer, be he ever so worthless, finds no difficulty in getting 50 signatures to a petition addressed to the Governor for his appointment to the position of notary ... Whether the signers are reputable citizens or whether they are lunatics, criminals, or boys without discretion, nobody cares ..."[20]

Grasping at straws, Captain Black introduced another affidavit and a number of receipts from the owner of a livery showing that he had been paid 140 dollars by the county clerk for the provision of carriages to the jurors during the trial. Judge Gary was puzzled by this as he recalled that he had specifically asked both sides if they objected to the jurors being provided with carriages and Black had accepted the proposal along with Grinnell. What objection could he have to a practice he himself had approved of? Black and Zeisler explained that in endorsing the idea of providing carriages to the jurors they hadn't specifically approved payment out of county funds. Judge Gary wondered whom they expected to pick up the tab, and Ziesler answered that the jurors should have paid. Gary was close to losing his patience: "That is absurd. Nobody ever supposed that the jurors were to pay for their carriages."[21]

Captain Black and his fellow lawyers then filled another day with oratory and additional legal arguments in favor of a new trial. Black spoke for more than three hours, quoting liberally from the dozens of legal tomes piled on his table, his speech only interrupted by a cat that had somehow gotten stuck between a bookcase and a wall and screeched until a bailiff rushed over and pulled it out by its tail. When Salomon stepped forward, one reporter was reminded of the disaster that was his opening statement and remarked, "Mr. Salomon in his speech knew too much about anarchy and socialism and things in general, and too little about what he wanted to say. It should be stated, however, that his speech was a great improvement on his former famous effort ..."[22]

At the end of these lengthy arguments, Judge Gary anticlimactically overruled the motion for a new trial and asked if the defendants had anything they wished to say before he pronounced their sentence. They certainly did, and it took the next three days to hear them out.

After weeks of flagging interest in the trial, evident by the thinning of the gallery through successive days of dreary legal motions, there was a palpable excitement the day the prisoners were to make their personal appeals to the court before their sentencing. The crowd clamoring outside the courthouse doors was estimated to be five times larger than the capacity of the courtroom.

Judge Gary gaveled the packed courtroom to order, seeming nervous and in an "ill-humor." He sternly ordered everyone beyond the bar to be absolutely silent during the proceedings. Looking up, he saw two men sitting on a table against a wall and ordered them to sit on the floor. Now that the defendants were convicted prisoners, their friends and family were not allowed to sit directly behind them and whisper in their ears. This row was now filled by a line of eight burly officers. Gary's precautions were unnecessary as the drama of the men's speeches gripped every ear. As one reporter observed, "Never in any land were prisoners treated with more courtesy. When it became necessary for a moment to interrupt the speaker the court apologized. When his throat became dry a bailiff handed him a glass of water . . . No men ever had a more attentive audience; no men ever had a more powerful incentive to do their best."

All eight prisoners addressed the court but their styles differed according to their personalities—Parsons and Spies lectured for hours on anarchism and socialism, Fielden, Neebe, and Schwab focused on rebutting the evidence against them, while Engel, Fischer, and Lingg expressed their disdain for these proceedings and for the law in general. None of the condemned used this last unrestricted opportunity to speak before a crowd to defiantly confess as their hero Reinsdorf had done in Germany. Beyond the theatricality of the situation, there were few genuinely dramatic moments.

Many of the condemned were eager to correct the falsehoods spread by the prosecutors. The worst of these slanders was the idea that anarchy was all about violence and murder when, in fact, it was a conception of a world free of exploitation and coercion. It was an easy and consistent shift to make: moving attention from anarchist means to anarchist ends. Parsons largely avoided mentioning deeds, force, and actions. (There was but one digression, where he waxed rhapsodically about dynamite: "The Pinkertons, the police, the militia, are absolutely worthless in the presence of dynamite . . . It is the equilibrium. It is the annihilator. It is the disseminator of power. It is the downfall of oppression.") Instead, he restricted his long rambling speech to an analysis of the wages system and capitalism and the specific evidence against him. Parsons asked, "What is Socialism, or Anarchism? Briefly stated, it is the right of the toiler to the free and equal use of the tools of production, and the right of the producers to their product." Toward the conclusion of his speech, Parsons categorically denied the central tenet of the anarchists' revolutionary creed: "You accuse Anarchists of using or advising the use of force; it is false."[23]

Schwab also lectured the court on his political ideals but remained silent about the means he thought would best achieve them: "Socialism as we understand it means that the land and machinery shall be held in common by the people.... According to our vocabulary anarchy is a state of society in which the only government is reason..." Spies, likewise, focused on redefining his anarchism as a philosophical proposition rather than a tactical one. He rhetorically positioned himself in the company of great liberals: "...I am an Anarchist. I believe with Buckle, with Paine, Jefferson, with Emerson, with Spencer, and many other great thinkers of this century that the state of caste and classes... should be abolished."

In pursuing this theme Spies went so far as to deny that he ever had any hopes that the Eight Hour May strikes could inaugurate the great transformation he had long advocated. "To charge us with an attempt to overthrow the present system on or about May 4, by force, and then establish Anarchy, is too an absurd a statement, I think, even for a political office-holder to make. If Grinnell believed that we had attempted such a thing, why did he not have Dr. Buthardt make an inquiry as to our sanity? Only a mad men could have planned such a brilliant scheme..." But Spies couldn't end on such a borderline duplicitous note and in his peroration struck the more active chord again: "It is true that we have told people time and again that the great day of a change was coming...It is true that we have called upon the people to arm and prepare for the stormy times before us. This seems to be the ground upon which the verdict is to be sustained. But 'when a long train of abuses and usurpations pursuing unvaryingly the same objects evinces the design to reduce the people under absolute despotism it is their right and duty to throw off such Government and provide new guards for their future safety.' This is a quotation from the Declaration of Independence...And if you think that you can crush out these ideas that are gaining ground more and more every day...[then] Call your hangman!"[24]

Next to Parsons, Fielden was the most experienced orator, having once been a Methodist minister. Fielden spoke for three hours, interspersing poetry with his philosophical observations and criticisms of the trial. Like Spies, Fielden focused on the political economy of socialism, the miseries of the working class, and the rights of workers to organize against their exploitation. He only spoke of the Haymarket meeting to refute the allegation that his remarks were "inflammatory," insisting that he had simply recounted the difficulties of workers in Chicago. "I am to be convicted—hanged for telling the truth..."[25]

Not all the prisoners were interested in polishing the sullied reputation of philosophical anarchism or portraying themselves as theoretical anarchists. Unlike Spies and Parsons, Engel did not deny that the hallmark of anarchism was its advocacy of action and "force." "Anarchism and Socialism are, according to my opinion, as like one egg is to another. Only the tactics are different. Anarchism has abandoned the ways pointed out by Socialism to free mankind..." Hanging us, Engel told the court, would do nothing to destroy anarchism. "No power in the world will tear from the workingman his knowledge and his skill or opportunity in making bombs." Engel was proud of having advocated this course of action: "I do not intend to deny that I spoke at those meetings, that I also declared that if every workingman had a bomb in his pocket there would soon be an end of capitalistic rule with terror. . . . my greatest desire is that the working classes will at last recognize who are their friends and who are their enemies."[26]

Fischer began by saying that he would not talk much, but before he had completed his first five sentences he had provoked the only tense moment of the day. Just as Fischer said, ". . . I do not deny that I was one of the parties who called at the Haymarket meeting, but that meeting. . ." Salomon jumped up and crossed to him and urgently whispered something. Fischer pushed him back exclaiming, "Will you let me alone? I know what I am doing." Fischer then recounted that he did attend the Monday night meeting, that (as the informant Waller had said) the meeting was first proposed to be at Market Square but it was agreed instead to hold it at the Haymarket, and that he was delegated to print up handbills and arrange for speakers. Fischer admitted authoring the line "Workingmen Appear Armed," but he did nothing more and saw the flash of the bomb through the window of Zepf's saloon where he was enjoying a glass of beer with Parsons. ". . . I will be sentenced to death because of being an anarchist, and not because I am murderer . . . if the ruling class thinks that by hanging us . . . they can crush out anarchy, they will be badly mistaken, because the anarchist loves his principles more than his life."[27]

Lingg, too, chose not to conceal the fact that the meat of anarchism was its tactics. "What is anarchy? Speakers before me have indicated that clearly. They have shown what we are driving at . . . Our tactics have been referred to, the way in which we intend to reach what we aim at, but it has not been shown that we have been forced to the course we took by the brutal attack of the police." In alluding to the course "that we have been forced to . . ." Lingg skirted close to some sort of admission. He approached this point a second time: ". . . I have stated before that I have been forced to my course by the present state of things; that I have been forced to fight force the way I did."

In his turn before the court, Lingg did not contest that he made bombs or, as his friend Seliger claimed, that he took them to Neff's Hall on Clybourn avenue. Lingg's point of defense was that "it has not been shown that one of these bombs was taken to the haymarket." Of all the defendants who spoke, Lingg concluded the most vehemently, ending his speech with defiance and militant vows:

Anarchy is called disorder. Anarchy (is) in opposition against the order of things which does not allow a man to live a life that is worth living. I declare here once more openly, with all my powers, with all my mind, I must combat such disorder . . . Even if this praiseworthy object should be defeated with cannon, I shall use dynamite. You smile. You perhaps think I will not use bombs any more; but I tell you I die gladly upon the gallows in the sure hope that hundreds and thousands of people to whom I have spoken will now recognize and make use of dynamite. In this hope I despise you and despise your laws. Hang me for it.

Neebe spoke without notes and throughout his speech kept his left hand in his trousers pocket. He reviewed the thin evidence against him, concluding, "there is no evidence to show that I was connected with the bomb throwing," but recognized that since he was a labor leader there was no hope for a fair hearing. Neebe told the judge that he'd rather be hung with the others than be sent to Joliet prison. "I think it is more honor to die certainly than to be killed by inches." Neebe told the judge, "hang me too."[28]

*   *   *

After Judge Gary pronounced the men's sentences, condemning seven men to the gallows and Neebe to Joliet State Prison for a term of 15 years, some radicals redoubled their efforts to campaign for a new trial or clemency, while others reflected on the hard lessons of the episode. Though bitterly denouncing the trial's outcome, many of those who attempted to draw meaning from the tragedy seemed now to accept that the condemned men had actually done, at least in part, what the prosecution alleged they had, namely, attempted to provoke a violent uprising in Chicago the previous May. John F. Kelly in a column entitled "The Lesson of Chicago," published in the libertarian anarchist weekly *Liberty: Not the Daughter but the Mother of Order*, praised the seven condemned men saying that they had "risked all in an attempt to set things right. They failed, and by the laws of war they are to die." The lesson Kelly drew from their sacrifice was that "a revolution, to be effective, must be popular. A social revolution can not be accomplished by a man or clique."[29]

William Liebknecht, leader of the Sozialdemokratische Partei Deutschlands (SPD), arrived for a lecture tour of the United States as the Haymarket verdict was handed down. Speaking before a capacity crowd at one of the largest public halls in Brooklyn, the Labor Lyceum on Myrtle street, Liebknecht detailed the lessons of the Haymarket without mentioning it by name, denouncing "certain demagogues" who had come to America to "foment lawlessness and disorder." "Those who thought that anything could be accomplished for the amelioration of society by brute force made a great mistake," Liebknecht lectured. "This was shown by the conduct of the commune during the last revolution in France and by other proofs in history . . . Many persons wanted immediate revolution in society, but such a consummation could not be effected."[30]

The most influential histories of the Haymarket trial all imply that the chorus of cheers for the guilty verdict emanated from the capitalist press and the business community, while the working class quietly dissented.[31] However, William Holmes, writing his third report on the trial to *The Commonweal* in London, had a very different impression of how the public responded. Like modern historians, Holmes was disgusted with the gloating satisfaction of the leading papers with the "splendid result." But Holmes did not think the wave of approval ended there:

> And how does the proletariat, the disinherited workers, regard it? Alas! centuries of oppression have made them stupid and dumb. The average working-man knows nor cares for little else beside hurrahing for this or that candidate at election-time, and

an occasional strike for a few cents' increase in wages. To their eternal shame be it recorded, that led—as calves are led, by the nose—by notorious political . . . workers, the trade's unions of Chicago have either openly endorsed the verdict or refused to condemn it. Only the Socialists have thus far openly and indignantly protested against it. Conservative (hateful word!) working-men are either too cowardly or too ignorant and self-glorified to raise their voices in public protest against this damnable decree of their masters.[32]

Trade union leaders had little sympathy for the condemned men as they blamed the anarchists for strangling the eight-hour baby in its crib. Trades and Labor Assembly president Mark Crawford was certain that the eight-hour movement was succeeding until the Haymarket bombing. "The Anarchists of Chicago have done more harm to the labor movement than the capitalists have. They killed the eight-hour movement as dead as a doornail. Why, the wholesale men and large merchants were tumbling over each other in their haste to fall into line until the bomb was thrown, and then the work of years was neutralized and the movement killed."[33]

The trial took its toll on all those associated with it. It appeared to have damaged Gilmer's ability to earn his livelihood. Soon after the trial ended the Painters' Union blacklisted him. Police Chief Ebersold reportedly found a position for him in the paint shop of the construction department of the city. A few months later someone took a shot at his back as he was unlocking the door to his apartment that went low and splintered the wood between his legs. When a reporter visited Harry Gilmer a year later, he found him living in a cramped ground-floor apartment whose only decorations seemed to be illustrations of the scenes of the Haymarket case clipped from newspapers. In contrast to his choice of decorations, Gilmer told the reporter, " . . . I'd give ten years of my life if I'd never seen the Haymarket, the Judge, or the jury. I'm notorious now, and I'll never be able to shake off the notoriety. If I eat it's a matter of public interest, and reporters come and wake me up to ask if I've digested the meal. I tell you the blamed business is driving me to my grave . . ."[34]

Gottfried Waller, one of the state's star informers, claimed that he moved three times out of fear of reprisals. Foolishly, soon after Gary sentenced the anarchists and the trial was finally over, Waller stopped by one of his old haunts, the Garden City House saloon on North Wells street. The 20 or so men in the place at the time spotted him immediately and chased him out into the street, shouting "traitor," "spy," "coward." The crowd grew as Waller ran toward Central avenue. At one point the mob nearly had Waller in its grasp, but Waller pulled a revolver and fired several shots and escaped to a nearby police station.[35] The day following Waller's narrow escape, police arrested 40 people in connection with the assault. Each was taken before Waller to identify and when finished Waller had fingered just four men, including the man he had shot and wounded.[36]

Jurors too suffered intimidation and threats. After James Cole returned to his suburban home, a group of men came around his house and shouted threats. Cole claimed that one night when coming home from the theatre, he was confronted in a dark spot near his home and a pistol was pressed to his head. But just then a carriage clattered nearby and his assailants fled.[37]

For anarchists there remained a glimmer of hope. They had documented grounds on which to base an appeal and a small but influential corps of defenders who were doing their best to spread the story that eight men had been convicted and seven faced the gallows for advocating unpopular and threatening ideas. The battle would continue in two kinds of courts: the courts of law and the court of public opinion.

CHAPTER 7

ROAD TO THE SUPREME COURT

IT TOOK UNTIL MID-MARCH 1887 FOR THE ANARCHISTS' appeal to finally make its way onto the state supreme court's docket. In the months between their sentencing and their appeal hearing, the defense legal team was reshuffled. Salomon and Zeisler, the anarchists' original law partners, went their separate ways, apparently because they could not agree on how to divvy up the steady work provided by their most important client, the Central Labor Union (CLU). When the CLU washed its hands of the problem and freed individual unions to choose for themselves who they wished to retain, the rivalry between the two radical lawyers doomed their partnership.[1]

William A. Foster, the experienced criminal attorney who had been brought onto the anarchists' defense team from Iowa, was quietly fired. No record remains of why the defendants were displeased with Foster, who seemed to be their most able litigator; his summary to the jury of the case, in which he denounced anarchism, probably sealed his fate. "I do not stand here to defend Communism; I do not stand here to defend Socialism or Anarchism, because I believe in its inception and in its principles it is wrong. Assuming then that Socialism is wrong, assuming that Communism is pernicious, assuming that Anarchy is outrageous, still I say to you, concede it all, and it brings us back to . . . only the one question: Are these men responsible for murder?" It certainly didn't help that after the trial Foster could not disguise his skepticism that an appeal could be successful.[2]

In Foster's place the defense retained Leonard Swett, Abraham Lincoln's closest friend in Illinois and a celebrity lawyer whose name was batted around before the original trial. Salomon and Zeisler remained with the case, though Salomon was muzzled and delegated to a backroom role. Apparently, the convicted anarchists feared a repeat of the embarrassing opening statement that Salomon had made early in the trial.[3]

A glimpse of Swett's regard for his fellow attorneys was afforded by an eavesdropping reporter who was close to the lawyers' table as Swett was signing a stack of papers. Filling in some form, he was overheard to ask Salomon, who was at his elbow, "What is Zeisler's first name?" Swett and Zeisler had by then been partners in the case for four months.[4]

While there was little that could be done legally pending the hearing of the anarchists' appeal, Swett did what he could to control the media. Increasingly worried about the possibility of damaging jailhouse leaks, attorney Swett (now officially "chief counsel" for the defense) sent a letter to Sheriff Canute Matson demanding that he bar all reporters from visiting his clients in jail. "The cases of these men, in my judgment, are being prejudiced partly by the indiscretion of some of them ... I do not want in the end to get my clients clear of murder and have them hung for foolishness."[5]

If Swett was discomforted by the stories leaking out from the jail, he could not have been very pleased with the publicity kicked up by his cocounsel. Nearly as soon as the trial was over, Black helped found a new socialist political party, the "National Industrial Emancipation Society." An awkward name but probably the least clumsy among those proposed at its founding meeting, among the alternatives being the "Socialist Missionary Society," the "Society for the Propagation of Scientific Socialism," and the "Society for the Abolition of Wage Slavery." Its founding manifesto proclaimed the party's purpose as "to help on the work of emancipating labor from the subjection of capital ..." Its first principles were that the "bountiful gifts of nature ... the water, mines of coal and metal, the quarries, forests, and all motive powers and mechanical principles ... are the rightful and equal heritage of all mankind," that all wealth "is the product of labor," and "that the wealth so created by labor belongs of natural right to the laborer." Capt. W.P. Black was elected the society's first and founding president. As Black was already converted to a radical's creed long before he came to represent his anarchist clients, it couldn't in fairness be said that his close work with these articulate and earnest revolutionaries had been a radicalizing experience for him. More plausibly, having already exposed his own radical views in the manner in which he conducted their defense, Black lost some of his professional caution that might have inhibited his political activities up to that point.[6]

In an interview after the Illinois Supreme Court agreed to hear the anarchists' appeal and the slim possibility of a new trial slightly widened, Albert Parsons spoke to reporters and presented himself as a changed man. When asked if he would advocate the same policies if he were released, Parsons revealed some regret about his past actions. "I can't say whether I would write the same things and preach the same doctrines. For my part, I am willing to say that the rascalities, outrages, and robberies to which the working classes have been subjected sometimes get the better of a man who feels for them, and leads him to say things he wouldn't say when in his calmer moments ..." Spies followed suit and admitted, "My course in the past may not have been wise, but I never willingly harmed anybody in my life." Engel and Lingg refused to speak to the "capitalistic press," Engel having stretched a calico curtain across the bars of his cell and Lingg sitting with his back to the door. Neither man supported appealing their cases, Engel because he believed it was a useless waste of time and disliked how it gave his family false hopes, and Lingg on principle.[7]

Swett and Black made their arguments for a new trial before six justices, so stoic and unflappable that they were compared to "six wax dummies." An uncharitable reporter referred to Swett's presentation as "Mr. Swett's $3,000 speech" and noted that "it was conceded on all sides [that it] was of no help to the Anarchists . . ." Black's speech was considered one of his best, even if at times he appeared to beg with tears in his eyes for "justice tempered with mercy."[8]

The court's decision was penned by Benjamin D. Magruder, the son of a college professor from Nachez, Mississippi. Magruder graduated from Yale with two class-mates who would later serve on the U.S. Supreme Court, David J. Brewer and Henry Billings Brown. Earning his law degree in New Orleans, he moved North for good and settled in Chicago just before war broke out. Magruder was elected to the Illinois Supreme Court as a Republican but the Democrats chose to endorse his candidacy by not nominating anyone to oppose him.[9]

Magruder began by noting that the law of Illinois made no distinction between accessories before the fact and principal perpetrators. These eight men were not charged with the crime of conspiracy, but with murder, though their role in that crime was proven indirectly by means of showing each individual's part in the con-spiracy to murder the police. Magruder listed three important questions that had to be answered affirmatively for the charge of murder to stick:

1. Did the defendants have a common purpose to "advise, encourage, aid, or abet" the murder of the police?
2. Did they combine together to carry this purpose into effect?
3. Did they undertake actions or make such declarations in support of this com-mon purpose "as did actually have the effect of encouraging, aiding or abetting the crime in question?"

Magruder began to answer these questions by asking, who made the bomb that mur-dered Degan? After reviewing the voluminous evidence linking Lingg to the bomb, he concluded that "we think the jury were warranted in believing from the evidence that the bomb, which killed Degan, was one of the bombs made by the defendant Lingg."[10]

Having satisfied himself that Lingg was the bomb maker, Magruder then asked the natural next question, "why did the defendant Lingg make the bomb, which killed Degan?" This, Magruder believed, required an investigation into the beliefs and principles of the society to which Lingg and all the other defendants belonged, the International Working People's Association (IWPA), an organization that expressed its views through both its official platform and its German and English newspa-pers in Chicago. Sections of the IWPA existed throughout the city, and some of them drilled with rifles. Every two weeks a general committee of these groups (except for the Northwest side group, which had declared itself "autonomous") met in the library at the *Arbeiter Zeitung* office. Occasionally, there were meet-ings of just the "armed groups" at Greif's Hall, and these were summoned by a code "Y-Komme Montag Abend" inserted in the paper. Taken altogether, Magruder concluded, "there can be no doubt that the organization here described was an unlawful conspiracy."[11]

It was an unlawful conspiracy because it had an unlawful purpose: social revolution. This was unlawful not because it aimed to destroy capitalism and private ownership of the means of production—Magruder made clear that "as a court, we are not concerned with the question, whether it is right or wrong to adopt and advocate an abstract theory in regard to the ownership of property . . ."—rather because this end was conceived as being achievable only through war upon the police and militia. "The destruction by force of the police and militia in the city of Chicago was the practical object which this organization proposed to accomplish . . ." Second, this organization employed illegal methods to attain its goals. Arming and drilling private militias was in violation of the Militia law of the state.[12]

All the defendants were leaders of this organization, and they endeavored to bring about the "social revolution" by attracting recruits and advocating that members arm themselves, especially with dynamite bombs. Spies, Fielden, Schwab, Parsons, and Engel frequently spoke at meetings and urged their listeners to arm themselves. Spies, Parsons, and Schwab wrote numerous articles in their newspapers along the same lines.

Magruder noted that a conception of the coming revolution began to take definite shape among the defendants in 1885 with the growing momentum of the eight-hour movement. By then the idea of the "revolution" ceased being an abstract one and that "The time, when the war against the police was to be inaugurated, was not an indefinite period in the future. The evidence shows, that the date, fixed for the inauguration of the social revolution, was the 1st of May, 1886."[13]

Most importantly, the trial record showed that these radical leaders began to take "practical measures" in preparation for this date. Engel inquired with a gun dealer about placing a large order for pistols and had a tinsmith fashion a device whose purpose seemed to be for manufacturing bombshells. Parsons too sought out a large lot of revolvers and his newly founded "armed group," the "International Rifles," began drilling in earnest in the late summer of 1885. Spies, Schwab, Fielden, Parsons, and Fischer were all shown to have handled bombs or experimented with dynamite— Spies by his own admission, Fischer by giving a pipe bomb to Waller during a protest at Market Square, and the others by testimony about their brandishing of bombs the night of the Board of Trade protest. Magruder thought the evidence was convincing that Lingg made his bombs under the auspices of the larger organization and not on his own. Therefore, Magruder wrote, "We think the jury were warranted in believing from the evidence, that the bomb, which exploded at the Haymarket, was made by the defendant Lingg in furtherance of the conspiracy already described."[14]

All this raises a further important question, the last that would complete the chain of legal logic and put the noose around the anarchists' necks: was the bomb that exploded at the Haymarket thrown by a member of this conspiracy or someone acting under its direction? Magruder here rehearsed the conspiracy in the basement of Greif's saloon on May 3, Engels' plan of attack on police stations, Fischer's codeword "Ruhe" and his handbill with its call for workers to come armed, the selection of the Haymarket over Market Square because the latter was a "mouse trap," the discussion of whether it was better to fight amongst the crowd or from a distance, and Schnaubelt's suggestion that this plan be communicated to comrades in other cities so that the revolution could commence elsewhere at once. Magruder observed that the block of Desplaines street where Spies gathered the meeting together was a "strategical point, no better position could have been selected for the occurrences, which actually took place on Tuesday night, than the spot, where the speakers' wagon was located."[15]

To the defense's objection that even if there had been a conspiracy, the bomb could have been thrown by a person unknown to the conspirators as a personal act of revenge, Magruder listed three pieces of evidence that linked the bomb thrower to the conspiracy:

1. The bomb was made by Lingg.
2. Lingg and other members of the group hurried to finish assembling their bombs in time for the Haymarket meeting, and these bombs were distributed in a known headquarters of members of the group. These bombs were finished such a short time before one was thrown that it was very unlikely that anyone not associated with the group could have obtained one.
3. As both prosecution and defense witnesses testified, the bomb's explosion was followed so quickly by shots from the crowd that it was reasonable to see the two as part of one joint attack.

Magruder took seriously Captain Black's defense that the police acted illegally by dispersing a peaceful meeting but concluded that the anarchists had other means of redress to this infraction of their rights than just tossing a bomb. Moreover, given the experiences of the previous days in the city that were filled with violent outbursts and tumults, the specific rumors that had reached the ears of both the mayor and the police chief that the meeting was a prelude to an attack on the railroad warehouses, the call to arms on the meeting's advertisement, and the increasingly provocative language employed by Fielden as the night wore on, the police were within the bounds of their duty and the law to read the riot act. "We think the weight of evidence is in favor of the State upon this subject. If it be conceded, that the witnesses for the prosecution, who are, for the most part, policemen, are interested on one side of the question, and that the witnesses for the defense, who are, for the most part, partisans of or sympathizers with the prisoners, are interested on the other side of the question, there is yet other evidence which seems to us to be decisive of the matter."[16]

Magruder listed the accounts of the surgeons who pulled bullets along with bomb fragments from the policemen's bodies; the accounts of some reporters at the scene who saw firing from the crowd; the revolver found on the scene, three of whose caps were fired; and the apparent fact that the shooting began almost immediately after the bombing. "This was the order, in which the onset with the two different kinds of weapons was to be made, according to the terms of the conspiracy. The mode of attack, as made, corresponded with the mode of attack, as planned."[17]

The Illinois justice showed great insight in uncorking the avalanche of facts contained in the trial transcript. Magruder observed that the Haymarket meeting began late, a delay that may have been caused by Lingg's delay in delivering his bombs to Neff's Hall. "From the fact that Seliger and Lingg were met on the way to Neff's Hall by Muenzenberger, the blacksmith, it would appear that the latter had been sent forward to hasten their movements." Magruder found a welter of such details that all pointed to foreknowledge of an attack that Tuesday night. In the end, the justice boiled down all the evidence bearing on Lingg:

> Here is a man connected with a certain organization, engaged in arming and drilling for a conflict with the police. He is experimenting with dynamite and in the construction of bombs under the direction of armed members of that organization. He makes bomb-shells, fills them with dynamite, takes them to the meeting place of armed members of that organization, puts them where access to them can be easily had ... At once, certain of these armed members ... come forward and take bombs and go their several ways. In a little more than an hour afterwards one of these bombs is thrown into a crowd of policemen ... It is a fair conclusion from the evidence that Lingg knew that the bombs he was making would be thrown among the police.... Even if he did not know the name of the particular individual who was to throw the bomb, he knew that it would be thrown by some one belonging to the sections or groups ... and this was sufficient to affect him with the guilt of advising, encouraging, aiding or abetting the crime charged in the indictment.

In any event, "notwithstanding the fact, that the Monday night conspiracy may have been varied somewhat to suit the new conditions, we think the jury were warranted in believing, that the bomb was thrown and the shots fired as part of the execution of that conspiracy."[18]

Wading into the morass of testimony that rose up around the recollections of Thompson, who claimed to have seen Spies, Schwab, and Schnaubelt huddled together before the meeting, and Gilmer, who testified that he saw Spies light the bomb thrown by Schnaubelt, Magruder admitted that he found their testimony "conflicting" but also that no particular witness or evidence was such as to so impeach their statements that the jury was not right in considering them. Moreover, Magruder thought that neither Gilmer's nor Thompson's testimony was even essential to the prosecution as there was plenty of other evidence to both reveal the outlines of the larger conspiracy and link it to the act of throwing the bomb.

Magruder and the other justices were keenly aware of the charges being aired by supporters of amnesty that the anarchists were on trial for murder because they had made speeches and written articles advocating arming, bombing, and force. In other words, free speech was on trial. This, Magruder made plain, was not the case: "We do not wish to be understood as deciding that the influence of these publications in bringing about the crime at the Haymarket could be considered by the jury if they were the only evidence of encouragement of that crime ... We only hold that the jury were at liberty to consider the publications in question in connection with all the other facts . . . with a view of determining whether the defendants . . . did or did not belong to the conspiracy now under consideration." Had there been no larger conspiracy aimed at bombing police on the night of Tuesday, May 4, the anarchists could not have been tried just for extolling the virtues of dynamite, even if those words had inspired the bomber.[19]

A large part of the opinion was a review of the evidence individually connecting each defendant to the conspiracy. Lingg's role as the bomb maker was the most certain, as were the roles of Engel and Fischer as the architects of the May 4 plans. Spies, Schwab, Fielden, and Parsons were all shown to have been connected to the conspiracy after its conception at the infamous basement meeting. As for Neebe, the evidence was thin but uncontradicted that he scattered "Revenge Circulars" around the Fourteenth Ward that night before the Haymarket riot, telling one group of drinkers, "It is a shame that the police act that way, but maybe the time comes that it goes the other way . . ." This the court believed was evidence of his knowledge of the plans and material aid to the plot itself.[20]

The last third of the appellate court's decision dealt with the issues raised by the admission of some evidence, the empanelling of the jury, and the decisions that Judge Gary made about what instructions to give the jury. The justices thought no error was made in allowing a thick pile of newspaper clippings to be admitted as evidence, as these revealed the scope, purpose, and form of the anarchist conspiracy that led to the bombing.

There was, however, one scrap of evidence that seemed to have been of dire concern to the robed old men. The so-called Most Letter was a letter sent from Johann Most to August Spies that contained Most's highly incriminating offer: ". . . I am in a condition to furnish '*medicine*,' and the 'genuine' article at that . . ." Justice Magruder indicated that if this important letter had been seized from Spies' own desk without a warrant, as Swett and Black now argued it was, there would be serious constitutional issues to consider. But Magruder found no legal grounds to explore this possibility in this case because none of the defense lawyers objected to this letter's admission on these vital grounds during the trial.

Apparently, Captain Black and his cocounsels didn't foresee that they might later have reason to object to this letter on the grounds that it had been illegally seized. The whole episode was sadly bungled. When assistant prosecutor Ingham first asked Spies about the letter, Foster objected, but on the narrow legal basis that this line of cross-examination departed from the scope of Spies' primary testimony. Judge Gary overruled this objection and Ingham continued pressing Spies to admit that he received this letter, which he reluctantly did. Later, toward the end of his cross-examination, Ingham formally moved to have the letter admitted as evidence and Foster objected again, this time on the grounds that the state had not proven that Spies ever received the letter. Judge Gary consulted a legal treatise and quoted "Letters which have never been in the possession of the defendant cannot be admissible in evidence against him." Black jumped up and seized this point: "There is no evidence in this case that the letter was found in his possession." Had Spies not earlier admitted to receiving the letter this may have been a sharp move, but Black should have recognized that the price of taking this path was to ruin his chances of objecting to the manner in which the police had obtained it. For, if the letter had never been in Spies' possession, it was never in his desk, and if it were never in his desk then the police couldn't be condemned for finding it there.[21]

Gary overruled Black again, this time on the obvious grounds that Spies had just admitted to receiving the letter. Black could have performed a lawyerly about-face at this point and put the police officers who discovered the letter on the stand to establish that it had been taken without a warrant, but somehow this idea never crossed his mind until Justice Magruder rubbed his nose in it.

In reviewing Gary's instructions to the jury, the justices found that those Gary delivered were appropriate and those Gary rejected were excluded for good reason. All the issues concerning the selection of jurors boiled down to a single point: was the last juror selected, Harry Sandford, biased or not? Sandford admitted that he had an opinion about the guilt of the defendants that he had drawn from press accounts of the trial. When asked if he could set aside his views and weigh the evidence presented in the trial fairly, Sandford swore he could. When asked if he had a prejudice against socialists, communists, or anarchists, Sandford replied that he had a "decided" one, but "I know so little about it in reality at present..." Sandford said that he was not opposed to labor organizations in general, knew no police officers personally, and had not spoken with anyone who had firsthand knowledge of the bombing. Magruder concluded that "the examination of the juror shows a state of facts, which brings his case exactly within the scope and meaning of... our revised statutes." As it later turned out, so clearly was Sandford's selection within the rule of Illinois law that the only avenue for appeal left to the defense was to argue that the state code itself was in violation of the U.S. Constitution.

After over 200 pages of opinion, Magruder concluded in the plain and austere manner such appeals always are: "The judgment of the Criminal Court of Cook County is affirmed." Only Justice John H. Mulkey, who had just converted from the Campbellite church to Catholicism in his sixtieth year, filed a short separate concurring opinion. Mulkey felt compelled to add to the record that "while I concur in the conclusion reached, and also in the general view presented in the opinion filed, I do not wish to be understood as holding that the record is free from error, for I do not think it is. I am nevertheless of opinion that none of the errors complained of are of so serious a character as to require a reversal of the judgment." Mulkey hastened to add that "In view of the number of defendants on trial, the great length of time it was in progress, the vast amount of testimony offered and passed upon by the court, and the almost numberless rulings the court was required to make, the wonder with me is, that the errors were not more numerous and more serious than they are."[22]

Magruder's decision was hailed by most legal observers as sound and just. The editors of *The Albany Law Journal* were ecstatic: "We recommend to every lawyer to read Judge Magruder's opinion. A more masterly and convincing one was never uttered. It should always stand as a monument to his intellectual powers. It is marked by perfect calmness and impartiality, stating the *pros* and *cons* of the voluminous and sometimes conflicting evidence with admirable clearness and absence of bias."[23] *The Central Law Journal* observed that "the presumption is almost, if not quite conclusive, that... [the trial was] fair and just... these defendants had the full benefit of every safeguard of life and liberty enjoyed by the people among whom they had elected to dwell..."[24]

Captain Black was surprised and shaken by the decision. His first comments to the press were emotional and rash: "If that decision is correct there is nothing to prevent the arrest, trial, conviction and execution of any man who can be proved an Anarchist. It is infamous."[25]

Even after the appeals court's opinion had knocked out every footing from under his case, defense counsel Captain Black continued to exude confidence that he would win at the next level of appeal. Seemingly oblivious to the consistency of the prosecution's legal theories and the weakness of his own interpretation, Black wrote to a friend as the case moved onto the U.S. Supreme Court docket, "... I have no fears [of a losing on appeal]... the errors are, in my judgment, too glaring to admit of any sanction whatever. The precedent would be altogether too dangerous to establish." Black's letter, besides entirely lacking in lawyerly caution, was self-contradictory. Black wrote that the Supreme Court may "under the pressure of public opinion, affirm this most unjust and unrighteous verdict..." but a few lines later he noted that public opinion had shifted away from the prosecution: "there has been a most remarked revulsion in public sentiment, and it does seem to me that the current has set our way."[26]

On the eve of the hearing of the anarchists' case before the U.S. Supreme Court, General Matthew M. Trumbull, a close friend of Samuel Fielden, spoke to reporters after a visit with his old countryman. Trumbull revealed what many had rumored but the prisoners had kept to themselves—that they had little confidence in Captain Black's legal talents. "It is not that they have lost faith in Capt. Black, for they have not. They believe he is a true friend, but they doubt his abilities. Fielden says he seems to take a moral and not a legal view of the question..."[27]

Lingg and Engel were adamantly opposed to "a continuation of the judicial farce." With Engel's endorsement, Lingg wrote a public letter to the *Freiheit* saying that he was "disgusted" by those who believed that once the "judicial bandits" of the highest court affirmed their condemnation, the eyes of the working class would be opened to the true nature of American capitalist justice. "Should any one harbor the notion that I expect the American people to be thoroughly aroused the day fixed for my judicial murder let him remove that illusion at once." Lingg was also concerned that some of his comrades thought it their duty to "to plan our release by force." Lingg wasn't opposed to the idea, but felt it was impractical, as to be successful it would have to be part of a "general uprising," an event that cannot be "made to order." Nevertheless, Lingg had faith that his death would not be in vain. "I am fully convinced that the sacrifice of my life... if made at the present moment, will hurry on the collapse of the capitalistic order..." Lingg added one piece of advice to his comrades and to "organized labor: Be men!" With a "cheer for Anarchism," he and Engel affixed their signatures.[28]

THE U.S. SUPREME COURT

The next stop for the defense team was the U.S. Supreme Court. While anxiously waiting for word from the justices as to whether they would accept the case, even the pollyanish Captain Black seemed to grow cynical. "If this were a case where some niggers had been tried in a Southern State, I would bet on the result; but since the defendants are some Anarchists who were tried in Illinois I am not so sure." Black's skepticism was misplaced, and the high court agreed to hear the case in October.[29]

With but five weeks left until the remaining five condemned anarchists were scheduled to die, a wagon clattered to a stop outside the Cook County Courthouse. Deliverymen trudged inside, carrying the first of their load of 15 heavy typewriters. These machines had been leased by the defense and for the next ten days hired typists clanked away, churning out a single copy of the 8,000-page trial transcript to send to Washington. In order to appeal their case to the U.S. Supreme Court the defense committee had to file a certified copy of the trial's proceedings, an undertaking that cost 2,800 dollars.[30]

Alongside this expense, the amnesty committee paid for the services of three additional top shelf lawyers. Curiously in this age when southern politicians could still be tarred with the charge of treason and rebellion, when the waving of the bloody shirt in stump speeches was still commonplace, the anarchists' lawyers chose to hire two former high-ranking Confederates to lead their charge to the Supreme Court. General Roger A. Pryor was formerly editor of the *Richmond Enquirer* and U.S. congressman before the war. He was present at the firing on Fort Sumter and led the rebellion, first as a Confederate congressman and then as a brigadier general. He was captured and spent the last year of the war in a federal prison in New York harbor. Upon his release, Pryor stayed in New York and built up a substantial legal practice, specializing in railroad and probate cases until he was retained by Theodore Tilton to sue the nation's most famous minister, Reverend Henry Ward Beecher, for adultery with Tilton's wife. Pryor's retainer was a whopping 2,500 dollars.[31]

Assisting General Pryor was John Randolph Tucker, scion of the powerful Virginia Tuckers, whose middle name indicated his line of descent from his famous grandfather, John Randolph of Roanoke, whom the poet John Greenleaf Whittier immortalized in verse as the very symbol of the "slave power." His father being president of the Virginia Court of Appeals, Tucker naturally pursued a career in law and was elected attorney general of Virginia at the age of 34 and kept that position throughout the war. Like Pryor, after the war, Tucker found lucrative work for the Baltimore and Ohio railroad. Also like his partner he became for a time something of a household name when he prepared to defend his most notorious client, the former president of the Confederacy, Jefferson Davis, on charges of treason. At the time he was retained to assist General Pryor, Tucker was a member of Congress and chairman of its Judiciary Committee.[32]

Perhaps to balance the southward tilt of this panel of lawyers, the amnesty committee also hired General Benjamin Butler, a perennial politician from Massachusetts, a hero to the Union and a hated war criminal in the eyes of the Confederacy. Butler's politics was more similar to that of Captain Black, having long championed various reform panaceas and running for president on the Greenback Party ticket in 1884. Butler came a bit cheaper than the others, demanding a retainer of 1,500 dollars and a fee of 250 dollars per day.[33]

Standard historical accounts devote a scant paragraph or two to the high court's role in the anarchist drama. These accounts portray the Supreme Court as having taken little interest in the anarchists' case and rejecting their appeal on the narrow grounds that it lacked jurisdiction. In fact, the justices granted the case an extraordinary hearing and handed down a careful and detailed decision that went far beyond questions of the scope of federal judicial review to consider many of the detailed charges raised by the anarchists' lawyers. There can be no question that the justices considered this case an important one. One of their robed fraternity, Justice Samuel T. Miller, was caught by a reporter while he was boarding a train; the reporter told Miller that he thought that the anarchist case was attracting "wonderful attention." The stern jurist took umbrage at this remark, scolding the reporter, "Not at all wonderful, not at all wonderful, sir. I consider this case the most important tried in this country for years."[34]

Given the primitive and unsettled state of federal jurisdiction in the wake of the sweeping amendments added to the Constitution after Appomattox, Tucker devoted most of his brief and his oral argument in urging the court to accept the case for review. Using an interpretation of the Fourteenth Amendment that would not be common until well into the twentieth century, Tucker argued that this amendment made the federal bill of rights applicable to the states and empowered the court to ensure for every citizen the due process and civil protections it afforded. By this view both the general criminal procedures of Illinois and the allegations that the anarchists were denied a fair trial were issues that the highest court could and should review.

Tucker focused upon just a few of the many due process claims the defense made in its appeal to the Illinois Supreme Court, presumably those that he felt were the most clear-cut. He charged that the jury was packed and biased, though he didn't allege that this was the fault of Judge Gary but rather that of the flawed criminal code passed in the state in 1874 that permitted Judge Gary to empanel jurors who had admitted their belief that the defendants were guilty. Also, the Fifth Amendment protection against self-incrimination was violated when police officers seized evidence from the homes and businesses of the defendants without a warrant and when Judge Gary allowed the prosecutor on cross-examination to improperly pose questions to those defendants who testified in their own defense that ranged beyond the narrow scope of the topics of their direct testimony.

General Benjamin Butler rose on behalf of August Spies and Samuel Fielden and argued that they, because neither of them was a citizen of the United States, were governed by the treaties in force with their home countries. Treaties, Butler observed, are supreme law, just as is the Constitution, and cannot be changed by simple legislation. Butler then stretched this uncontroversial point past the breaking point, arguing that this means that states must try foreign nationals according to the criminal procedures current at the time that these treaties were agreed upon: 1794 in the case of Fielden's

Great Britain and 1828 in the case of Spies' Germany. He probably sensed the absurdity of the point but made it because it was a question that could only be resolved by the Supreme Court, establishing the firm jurisdiction that would then allow him to smuggle the more convincing issues through the backdoor.

In one last desperate grasping at legal straws, Butler also complained that the anarchists condemned to death were not brought before the Illinois Supreme Court when it reaffirmed their conviction and set a new execution date of November 11, 1887. Overlooking the simple fact that all the defendants stood before Judge Gary when he pronounced their sentences, Butler contended that this was a violation of the unambiguous right of the accused to be present when a sentence is passed upon him.

Julius Grinnell, recently elected to a superior court judgeship with the unwanted help of "every gambler, thief, and boodler in Chicago [who] gladly helped in his election to remove him from the prosecutor's office," and his associate George Hunt, limited their rebuttal to the question of jurisdiction alone and cited scores of cases that denied that the Fourteenth Amendment had the sweeping effect of granting to the court the power to guard the individual civil rights of all citizens against the actions of their own states. Sadly, at this time, all the judicial wind was at their backs and all the precedents supported their stand. As to the jury procedure of Illinois, Grinnell noted that a number of states as well as a federal territory all had laws with wording similar to that of Illinois laws and the court had on several occasions upheld them.[35]

Court chambers were crowded when the court convened, the curious expecting a decision in the anarchist case. They were disappointed as the session dragged on with routine business until the chief justice made the curt announcement that a decision in the case of *Spies et al.* would not be rendered until Wednesday or Thursday. Clearly, the court needed more time to construct an opinion that was not going to be a cursory dismissal of the weighty issues raised before it.[36]

Justice Morrison Waite of Toledo delivered the unanimous opinion of the court. Waite could have avoided wading into the swampy questions of jury selection, search and seizure, self-incrimination, proper cross-examination, rights granted by treaties, and the defendants' right to be present on appeal had he ruled, as he and the majority already had in several cases, that the Fourteenth Amendment did not grant federal jurisdiction over all matters of civil rights against the states. Actually, Waite reiterated this very point but instead of quietly and neatly concluding his opinion there (as nothing else needed to be said once he had denied his own right to rule on the merits of the questions raised in the brief), he approached the case from the opposite direction. He wrote, "Before considering whether the Constitution of the United States has the effect which is claimed, it is proper to inquire whether the Federal questions relied on in fact do arise on the face of the record." Waite could have more easily reversed this sentence.

Why Waite was eager to rule on the merits of the particular issues raised by the plaintiffs will never be known as he left no record of his reasoning. But, given the increasing strength of the amnesty movement (now embraced by the literary luminary William D. Howells and the famed reformer Henry George), Waite may have wanted to use the finality of a Supreme Court decision to put such protests to rest. For, he meticulously picked apart each of the defense's arguments in turn, leaving none of its charges unanswered.

He dismissed first its claims of jury bias, observing that in *Hopt v. Utah* the court upheld a nearly identical Utah jury statute as that of Illinois. "No one at that time suggested a doubt of the constitutionality of the statute, and it was regarded, both in the territorial courts and here, as furnishing the proper rule to be observed . . . in empanelling an impartial jury in a criminal case." Waite dug further and endeavored "to see if in the actual administration of the rule of the statute by the court, the rights of the defendants under the Constitution of the United States were in any way impaired or violated," a charge the plaintiffs had not even made in their brief. Repeating pages and pages of the trial transcript documenting the questioning of jurors Denker and Sandford, Waite concluded "unhesitatingly" that no errors that could be basis of an appeal were evident in the record.

As for Spies being forced to incriminate himself by being asked about the letter from Johann Most that was seized in a warrantless search of his desk, Waite said he couldn't find any indication in the court record that the introduction of this letter was objected to by the defense. By citing this technicality Waite sidestepped major issues of the rights of criminal defendants and of the remedies for illegal search and seizures—issues that would not be properly taken up by the Supreme Court for another quarter century. Waite's conclusion that "the question whether the letter, if obtained in the manner alleged, would have been competent evidence, is not before us . . ." is but a legal sigh of relief.

Waite dispensed with the matters of Spies and Fielden not being tried under the proper procedures as outlined in foreign treaties with little effort, noting that these issues were not raised in the lower courts, nor had General Butler bothered to cite the actual treaties that he alleged to have been violated in his complaint. Just as easily Waite dismissed the allegation that the anarchists were not present at their sentencing, observing dryly that the record of the trial court "on its face shows that they were present." Case dismissed.

After the Supreme Court's decision there was only one hope remaining for the condemned men: the governor of Illinois had the power to commute their sentences. Again, Captain Black remained confident that Governor Richard Oglesby could be persuaded to stop the executions. "I do not believe there would be any execution of the sentence, for I believe there could readily be secured to-day in the City of Chicago 200,000 signatures, including many of our most influential men, and many members of the capitalistic class, for a commutation of the sentence . . . but I do not anticipate that we will be driven to this expedient." Apparently, Black was not aware that in the grand tradition of the American jeremiad, practical politics dictated that a governor could only grant such pleas to those who admitted their crimes, pronounced their reformation, and asked forgiveness. Black either did not understand these practical circumstances or did not really understand his clients very well.[37]

CHAPTER 8

EXECUTIONS AND AMNESTY

ALONGSIDE THE TITANIC LEGAL STRUGGLE PLAYING OUT IN COURTROOMS from Illinois to Washington, D.C., anarchist defenders battled to reverse the public's approval of their heroes conviction. Soon after the verdicts were rendered, one of Chicago's leading labor papers, the *Knights of Labor*, serialized autobiographies of all the convicted men. While their lawyers prepared their arguments for the state supreme court in the spring of 1887, a slim volume with the ponderous title, *A Concise History of the Great Trial of the Chicago Anarchists in 1886* was published by the Socialistic Publishing Company, the house of the *Arbeiter Zeitung* and Parson's *Alarm*. No other single work proved as powerful in shifting perceptions of this event and even influencing the way it would be chronicled by generations of historians.

A Concise History was written by a man who lived in Chicago in May 1886 and had events taken a slightly different turn may well have sat in the dock with the other prisoners. Dyer Lum had all the makings of a typical Yankee radical. He was born in western New York, the so-called burned-over district, just after the evangelical fires of the Second Great Awakening had conjured prophets, saints, messiahs, soothsayers, and reformers of many varieties. The branches of Lum's family tree were heavy with pilgrims, Minutemen, and abolitionists. He apprenticed to the bookbinding trade but at 23 idealistically marched off to put down the rebellion and fought in a number of battles and starved in a Confederate prison. After the war he returned to Western Massachusetts and his paper and his glue in the daytimes and séances and spirit readings at night. His first forays at writing were published in the progressive spiritualist journal *The Banner of Light* though he soon saw through the chicanery and began publishing denunciations of spiritualism for the leading skeptics' newspaper, *The Index*.

Lum was enthralled by the early stirrings of Marxism in the First International and its culmination in the socialist-feminist presidential campaign of Victoria Woodhull. As a skilled artisan he naturally gravitated to the labor reform campaigns of Wendell Phillips, the Greenback Labor Party, and the eight-hour movement. Like other Yankee reformers of his generation, Lum believed in the universality of reform and the unity of all progressive initiatives. His reformers' heart was never big enough and he worked for every cause that begged his time: women's rights, liberation of Ireland from English tyranny, the Single Tax, land reform, paper money, free love, Chinese exclusion, and the religious rights of Mormons.

Lum's career became a perfect bridge spanning several racing cataracts of revolutionary thought. Under the pen name "Gurth" he wrote for Patrick Ford's *Irish World* when that journal embraced the tactics of the Fenian dynamiters. Lum contributed articles to Benjamin Tucker's *Radical Review* and *Liberty* during the early period of Tucker's ideological development when he was influenced by Edward Nathan Ganz and toyed with Bakuninist ideas of direct action. At the same time Lum also wrote for the English language organs of the Black International: Albert Parsons' *Alarm*, Joseph Buchanan's *Labor Enquirer*. Lum was always more inspired by John Brown than William Lloyd Garrison and advocated actions over platforms. His first published reaction to the bombing was an expression of unreserved praise: "My only present condemnation of the one bomb is that there was but one. . . . I hope that I am understood, and for greater clearness will add that to the Chicago bomb throwers I reverently raise my hat."[1] Lum subsequently moved from Port Jervis, New York, to Chicago to take leadership of the *Alarm* and the amnesty movement and he divided his time between visiting the prisoners at the county jail and his editorial office.

A Concise History was a masterwork of movement propaganda. It purported to be "condensed from the official record." It was, claimed Lum, a compilation of facts taken from official records rather than from the biased newspaper accounts. "In the following pages an attempt is made to condense the testimony, omitting nothing essential to the case. The testimony is taken from the official record prepared by counsel for the Supreme Court, not from the newspaper reports." The "official record" Lum referred to was an abstract of the case prepared by the defense for submission to the Illinois Supreme Court. Lum's compilation was actually a condensation of a summary, a distillation sufficiently removed from what was actually said to allow him to shade and spin the testimony according to his whim. A typical example of how what Lum purported to be a direct quotation was actually descended from its original source via the intermediary of defense lawyers can be seen in Lum's handling of the critical testimony of Gottfried Waller summarized in table 8.1.

Table 8.1   Comparison of Lum's sources

OFFICIAL TRIAL RECORD

   THE WITNESS. Several posters about revenge were distributed . . . First it was talked about that at McCormick's six men had been killed; then we had a discussion as to what should be done in the next few days.

   Q: What else, if anything, did Engle say? Give what was said there just as fully as you can.
   A: . . . a committee was appointed to watch the movement in the city. They should observe the movement and if something happened they should report, and if a riot should occur we should first storm the police station and should cut the telegraph wires.
   Q: Who should cut the telegraph wires?
   A: That was not provided for, and then after we had stormed the police station we should shoot down everything that should come out, and by that we thought to gain accessions from the workingmen, and then if that police station was stormed we should do the same in regard to the second, and whatever would come in our way we should strike down, and that is about all.[2]

ABSTRACT AND BRIEF FOR DEFENSE
The Witness: "First there was some talk about the six men who had been killed at McCormick's . . . a committee should observe the movement in the city and if a conflict should occur the committee should report and we should first storm the police stations by throwing a bomb and should shoot down everything that would come out and whatever would come in our way we should strike down."[3]

DYER LUM, *A CONCISE HISTORY* . . .
"There was talk about the men said to have been killed at McCormick's . . . A committee were to observe the city, and in case of conflict occurring bombs were to be thrown into the police stations."[4]

After rehearsing the evidence in this fashion, Lum arrived at his foregone conclusion, ". . . it will be seen, as is sufficiently shown in the testimony, that the defendants were condemned less for the murder of Degan than because they were Anarchists . . ."[5]

Lum's *Concise History* strongly influenced novelist and influential editor William Dean Howells, who after reading it became convinced that seven men had been condemned to death simply for stating their opinions. Howells mistakenly believed that Lum's book was in fact based on the trial record and Lum's work, he told a fellow editor, he found deeply persuasive: "I have had my original feeling that the trial of the anarchists was hysterical and unjust strengthened by reading a condensed history of it, based upon the original record . . ." Howells sent along a copy of Lum's book with passages marked out for special note.[6]

Lum's history of the trial was followed that fall by a number of articles and pamphlets condemning the trial. The most influential of these publications, General Matthew Trumbull's *Was It A Fair Trial?* and William Salter's *What Shall Be Done With the Chicago Anarchists*, both arose from the ranks of Chicago's progressive free-thought community. Trumbull and Salter were both leaders of Chicago's Ethical Culture Society and published in its periodicals, *Open Court* and *The Monist*. William Salter was himself a bridge between the anarchists and the Yankee progressives of Chicago. Just before the May bombing Salter had begun working more closely with Albert Parsons and contributed articles to *The Alarm*.

A combination of factors was now at work transforming the anarchist movement in Chicago and the nation as a whole. Police repression drove the most militant elements underground while the overarching priority of defending men who stood in jeopardy of execution forced radicals to temper their rhetoric and cooperate with liberals like Salter and Trumbull. Out of this mix of circumstances the revolutionary anarchist movement was driven to deny its own existence; to laugh off the suggestion that it ever believed the moment of crisis, the uprising of the working class, was near; to pretend that its advocacy of action and deeds was never anything but attention-seeking rhetoric.

Leaders of the Amnesty movement were given permits by Mayor John Roche to circulate petitions on public thoroughfares. One Sunday before the looming day of execution seven volunteers set up overturned crates and folding tables along heavily trafficked streets imploring passers to sign their petitions for clemency. Petition gatherers were kicked out of the Illinois Central station and in front of several downtown stores, but others reported their work as easy. The man who set up a table in front of the West Side Dime Museum had a steady line of people waiting to sign and by the end of the day reported 2,000 signatures and no incidents other than the occasional drunk and a pickpocket who snatched the pocketbook of a woman who had bent to write her name. Another volunteer did surprisingly well by stopping by Moody's Church during the morning service though the church goers in another part of the city reacted harshly to the canvasser, the church ladies reportedly "especially bitter in their remarks..." Many petition signers reportedly affixed the letters "G.A.R." after their names to indicate their distinction as having fought to save the union.

Others were not so fortunate and reported being harassed by police and strangers. A man collecting signatures on a small board he carried for the purpose down Third avenue told a reporter he had been arrested three times, and once the arresting officer seized his petitions and tore them up. Henry W. Koehn set up a table outside the county building on Clark street and collected 1,500 signatures. But around 5:30 in the evening when the throng along the sidewalk was particularly thick Koehn was accosted by an angry man who whipped up the crowd yelling "I don't propose that any Dutch Anarchist shall defend their doctrines or use the streets of Chicago to save a lot of murderers." Tempers rose and the angry man cuffed Koehn in the back of the head sending him sprawling to the ground. The on-looking crowd was evenly divided between clemency supporters and anarchist haters. A riot seemed certain to break out, so Koehn thought caution the better side of his valor and thought his escape with his papers under his arm to the Amnesty office.[7]

As the remaining days until their death dwindled, the movement in favor of clemency gained momentum. Ministers began preaching in favor of it in their sermons. The often bloodthirsty tone of the city's newspapers softened. A few of the city's "leading men" stepped forward and publicly supported commuting the prisoners' sentences. One legal observer referred to it as "a general stampede of sentiment in favor of mercy..."[8]

In spite of the turning of this tide and the strenuous efforts of the anarchists' friends, the CLU, and a few notables such as William Dean Howells, William Salter, and Henry Demarest Lloyd, a majority of Chicagoans remained resentful of what they viewed as the out-of-state do-gooders who campaigned for amnesty. A local reporter took the city's temperature at this moment: "Chicago people still bear it somewhat hard against Novelist Howells and other humane but inconsiderate persons in the East that they should have tried so hard to get Gov. Oglesby to save the Anarchists' lives... The average Chicagoan does not doubt that if the Governor had done what Mr. Howells wanted him to do the Haymarket riot would have been repeated on a vastly greater scale long before this."[9]

Demonstrating this fact (and complicating the political equation for Governor Oglesby) was that just three days prior to the scheduled execution Chicago's voters would choose between two candidates each representing a different side in the anarchist case. In a contest for the county judgeship held by Judge Gary the only challenger was none other than Captain William Perkins Black. The nomination of Captain Black for Judge Gary's bench was widely recognized as a test of support for the cause of amnesty for the condemned men. Informed observers of Illinois politics thought the governor would read the results of this election as a proxy referendum on the case and make his decisions about clemency accordingly. The *Chicago Tribune* previewed the election with the observation that "the Radicals, Socialists, and Anarchists . . . expect to show how many sympathize with them by voting for Black as against brave old Judge Gary." In doing so Black and the leaders of the amnesty movement gravely miscalculated.[10]

Gary carried all 18 wards of the city over Black by a wide margin, for a total of 39,397 to 5,259. Out of Chicago's 341 precincts, Black won but two: he carried the Second Precinct of the Fifth Ward by one vote and the Seventeenth Precinct of the Sixth Ward by a margin of three. Black's highest total was in the anarchist stronghold of the Fourteenth Ward where he polled 973 votes, but even this did little to threaten Gary's 3,648. Suburban voters and farmers were solid for the old judge, giving him 17,823 to Black's 1,142.[11]

The Republican *Chicago Tribune* crowed over the crushing results: "Without doubt Judge Gary's sweeping majority over Capt. Black, the candidate of the Socialists, is the most significant feature of yesterday's election. The apostles of disorder and anarchy in nominating Capt. Black and in the resolutions of their platform made a distinct issue against Judge Gary's action in the Anarchist trial and in favor of a pardon . . . It is to be hoped that the Socialists are satisfied by the result."[12]

Black and his fellow amnesty advocates had few reasons to expect any different outcome. Just a few months earlier, close to the first anniversary of the trial, the candidacy of Julius Grinnell for a spot on the county bench was also widely seen as a referendum on the anarchists' conviction. Just as would be the case in Capt. Black's bid against Judge Gary, politicos observed that the "Democratic gang and the socialistic organizations" were planning on throwing their weight against Grinnell. Grinnell it was said, "will never receive forgiveness from those who sympathize with the Haymarket rioters . . ." The coming election was to test their strength. "The election of Grinnell by a large majority will be a marked triumph for the lovers of law and order." The United Labor Party (ULP), a recently incarnated coalition of labor and socialist groups, placed the defeat of Grinnell as its top priority in that summer's election. ULP activists distributed thousands of copies of articles reprinted from the *Arbeiter Zeitung* and the *Alarm* "containing nothing but abuse of Mr. Grinnell."[13]

Come election day the strength of the anti-Grinnell forces was exposed to have had little effect on the outcome. Out of eight candidates for judge, Grinnell polled the most votes. His ticket outpolled the opposing slate by more than two to one. Even the Fourteenth Ward, where labor and anarchist support was historically highest in the city, was carried comfortably by Grinnell. The election's obvious postmortem conclusion that "the working people failed to vote the ticket indorsed by their political assembly," seems to have been willfully ignored when Black stood for office that November.[14]

With but a week remaining before the trap was to fall a series of events occurred that convinced many observers that the anarchists on death row were indeed guilty. During those last days certainly two, and possibly as many as four of those on death row attempted to take their own lives. Louis Lingg succeeded while Frederick Engel tried but failed. It was not so much the fact that the condemned tried to cheat their hangman that erased the doubt many had as to their guilt, it was the bizarre method that was chosen that seemed tantamount to a confession.

On November 3, word arrived that the United State Supreme Court had turned down the defense's last appeal, leaving only Governor Oglesby standing between the seven convicted men and the gallows. Immediately rumors swirled around the jailhouse that August Spies would attempt suicide by taking poison that night. Undisclosed precautions were taken and the danger seemed to pass.

However, as the week trudged on towards its awful conclusion, the tensions between different groups of the condemned that had existed from the beginning of the trial but had been kept out of the public eye dramatically erupted into view. On Friday, November 5, an odd clutch of men were admitted onto the corridor of death row. Immediately identifiable to the reporters spending long shifts watching the jail door was lead attorney William Black, Henry Demearest Lloyd, and the current editor of the *Arbeiter Zeitung* Edward Bergmann. A third man, who in initial reports was referred to as "the mystery man" was later revealed to be William Salter. The trio first stopped at Lingg's cell passed him a paper through the bars and struck up a conversation that ended with one of the men slamming his hand repeatedly against the bars of Lingg's cell and shouted while Lingg laughed in his face.[15]

The paper passed to Lingg was a petition to the governor asking for clemency that had been signed by Schwab, Fielden, and Spies. It was a document that reads as something written for the three radicals rather than by them. In it the three do not admit their complicity in the crime, but they do clearly renounce their principles. "We believe it to be our duty as friends of labor and liberty to oppose other use of force than that which is necessary in the defense of sacred rights against unlawful attacks...We may have erred at times in our judgment...If, in the excitement of propagating our views, we were led into expressions which caused workingmen to think that aggressive force was a proper instrument of reform, we regret it." Lingg was not alone in rejecting such a statement; Engel, Fischer, and Parsons also refused.[16]

Irritated by the efforts of the amnesty committee to persuade Governor Oglesby to commute their sentences, Fischer, Lingg, and Engel not only refused to sign the pleading letters composed for them by their lawyers, but composed ones of their own demanding unconditional liberty or a martyr's death.

Fischer's letter begins by rejecting the governor's mercy on the ground that "as a man of principle" he could not apologize for an action he was not guilty of. But then Fischer shifted gears and added that nor could he ask for mercy without compromising his principles: "I am no hypocrite, and have, therefore, no excuses to offer with regard to being an Anarchist..." The verdict he suffered was nothing but the result of "class hatred" inflamed by the "malicious newspaper fraternity" and an effort to stamp out the labor movement. But, Fischer warned, quoting Benjamin Franklin, "the blood of the martyrs will work miracles in favor of your purpose—i.e. your own ruin."

Lingg, true to form, was more direct. "I demand either liberty or death." He admitted his crime: "I have called upon the disinherited and oppressed masses to oppose the force of their oppressors...with force...This—and only this—is the "crime" which was proven against me..." Engel protested "emphatically" against the petition campaign undertaken in his name because he too felt he had violated no laws. "The 'powers that be' may *murder* me, but they cannot *legally punish* me...I renounce any kind of mercy."[17]

Apparently relieved from the burden of pretending to be a philosophical rather than an active anarchist, Parsons revived the passionate rhetoric he was famous for before he surrendered himself. Writing to the eccentric George Francis Train, Parsons excoriated the machinery of laws and the government that undertook his "judicial murder." Warming up to his subject as the letter drew to its peroration, Parsons exclaimed, "Damned be the State, say I! and for this 'the State' says I must die! So be it. For if I live I am duty bound to kill the State."[18]

Dr. Ernst Schmidt, head of the defense committee, decided to take a different tack and apply pressure where it would have greatest effect. He summoned the men's families to his office and explained to them that their loved ones' last hope was signing the petition and sent them all off to the jail to persuade them to agree. Mrs. Engel, Mrs. Parsons, and Mrs. Fischer with her new baby in her arms, crowded into the cellblock and pleaded and cajoled with their husbands to put their names on the paper. Lingg's sweetheart Eda Mueller arrived but her begging was offset by the letter Lingg coincidentally received from his poor single mother and his sister in Germany who urged him not to sign away his manhood and become a coward just to save his life. It was reported that some of the men seemed to be waivering, particularly Parsons and Fischer, but Engel didn't budge.[19]

So as the situation stood at the time, death row was divided between three men willing to bargain for their lives and four men who weren't. Three who had hope that the governor might deliver a reprieve and four resigned to their fate. For those whose fate seemed to them sealed with their refusal to sign the petition there remained only the terms of their exit.

The next night the late watchman heard strange noises and found Engel insensible in his cell. There happened to be a physician, a Dr. Gray, working in an adjacent building where the city's insane were confined, who came quickly and determined from Engel's dilated and spasmodic eyes that he had been poisoned. Dr. Gray forced emetics down his throat and had guards stand Engel upright and walk him around for the better part of an hour. When Engel was out of danger he was confronted with the small bottle still containing a few drops of laudanum guards had found in his cell. Engel admitted he tried to kill himself saying he preferred to die by his own hand rather than let the law have its way.[20]

Engel's suicide attempt prompted jailers to search the cells of the others. Lingg was first, and was ordered to a different cell to wait while the turnkeys hauled out all of his belongings and deposited them on a bright spot in the corridor under a skylight.

This took some time as Lingg had collected a great thicket of "books, pamphlets, papers, fruit baskets, cigar boxes, candy boxes, hundreds of pages of manuscript, writing paper, envelopes, underclothing, pipes, cigars, tobacco, handkerchiefs, poems in German and English, love letters, checks from George Francis Train, telegrams and letters by the score admonishing him to be firm . . ." In one of those cigar boxes jailers discovered four iron pipe bombs, six inches long and about five-eighths in diameter. Lingg, true to form, just grinned when asked about them.

Though the anarchists' advocates immediately accused the police of planting the bombs in Lingg's cell, this was not given much credence at the time and years later was overthrown entirely when Dyer Lum confessed to having smuggled the bombs to Lingg.[21]

The coincidence of there being four bombs and four men who refused to sign the petition pressed on them the previous day was not lost on the press who freely speculated that the four were planning on going out together in a blaze of glory. But Spies was clearly at odds with his death row comrade as was evident in a note he slipped to his friend William Salter marked "Strictly Confidential:" "Lingg has often expressed his satisfaction with our conviction—that he would be hung a dozen times if we were hung with him. I am confident that he placed those bombs there when he saw that public sentiment was changing in our favor. He ought to be examined by a commission de lunatico inquirendo."[22]

The day before the execution Dr. Theodore Bluthardt, a former county physician, was escorted to Lingg's cell. It couldn't have taken Lingg long to realize what the purpose of the German doctor's visit was as he began peppering him with questions about his family history, his beliefs, and his feelings. But he didn't realize until Dr. Bluthardt told him so that he his fellow condemned comrades were the ones who had raised the issue of his sanity. Bluthardt reported that at this moment Lingg "seemed annoyed," insisted he wasn't insane, and said "I never had such a thing said to me." Clearly insulted and disturbed, Bluthardt said it took Lingg "a few minutes" to calm down and "talk pleasantly again." The doctor reported that in his opinion Lingg was simply a highly intelligent young man, "of pure ideas" that he believed in "as much as any man believes in his religion."

The prisoners' last full day of life dawned and a few minutes before nine in the morning Louis Lingg lay back on his cot and gritted a blasting cap between his teeth. A dull muffled noise, more like a pop than a blast, echoed through the stone structure. A jail guard arrived and saw Lingg thrashing on his bed, surrounded by splashes of blood on the walls and a steady dripping from the bed to the floor. The sight of him, his face but a ragged mass of flesh, what one guard described as a "piece of liver blown up" was shocking and sickening. After a minute of convulsing Lingg's body went limp. Thinking he was dead, perhaps relieved that the horror was at an end, a brace of deputies lifted him up and carried him to the nearest bathroom and deposited him on the cold, hard floor. After Lingg had been carried away a deputy found a two inch piece of Lingg's jaw bone in his bed. There was movement, Lingg was alive! Surgeons arrived and had Lingg lifted onto a wooden bench.[23]

A Dr. Moyer entered the cell and began probing the wound. The upper jaw through to the base of the nose was completely torn away and Lingg was having trouble breathing as what was left of his tongue had fallen back into his throat. Dr. Moyer tied a string around it and pulled it forward to clear the airway. He sewed up the lingual artery that had been torn but so much of the flesh of his face had been damaged that the whole field continued to ooze and hemorrhage. With a large glass hypodermic the doctor injected Lingg with 16 ounces of 1 percent saline solution. He chose not to splint Lingg's thumb that had been broken both above and below the first joint, but merely dressed his left hand in cotton gauze.

For a time Lingg seemed to rally and Dr. Moyer threaded a tube down his throat and poured in some puréed food.

Just before ten o'clock Captain Black arrived and was shown into the bathroom where Lingg lay. He sat on a wooden bench that had been brought into the room and asked, "Do you know me, Lingg?" Lingg opened his eyes and nodded. Black exclaimed, "Poor, poor boy! O what made you do this?" but of course, Lingg could say nothing.

Outside the jail, talking to reporters, Black did his best to exploit Lingg's act. ". . . I knew he was a desperate man, but had no idea that he would attempt to take his own life. That he did so only goes to show that he was insane. I always believed in that theory, for he has always been the paragon of monomaniacs on the subject of anarchy. The rest of the prisoners, however, were not in the least surprised."[24]

While Lingg lay dying in a jailhouse bathtub attorney V.V. Hunt rapped on a heavy Ellis avenue mansion door and woke Judge Frank Baker. Hunt requested a stay of Lingg's execution on the grounds that he was insane. Baker wearily chided Hunt for bringing his petition to his home rather than his court and told him to appear properly later that morning. At ten o'clock Baker gavelled his court into session, called Hunt and heard his argument until Grinnell pointed out that the petition was out of order because it did not state whether Lingg was insane prior to his trial or had left his senses since. This was a critical legal distinction because in the former case the finding of insanity would overturn his conviction while in the later case it only carried the possibility of mitigating his sentence. Once again an important legal document drafted by the defense lawyers was rejected because it was improperly composed. Judge Baker displayed patience with Hunt and allowed him to redraw his petition and submit it to him again after his lunch.

Hunt used part of this time to hedge his bets by submitting the same petition to Judge Richard Prendergast who quickly rejected it on the grounds that he had no jurisdiction in the matter. Hunt then located Dr. James Kiernan, but the physician refused to swear that Lingg was not insane prior to his conviction. At one o'clock a dejected Hunt conceded to Judge Baker that his docter failed him and he withdrew his petition. While leaving the courtroom and declaring to reporters that he would submit a new plea, a mandamus, injunction, or "something" to get his case heard, he was informed that Lingg had died.[25]

With just 48 hours left before the state of Illinois was due to hang the seven anarchists, Samuel McConnell made preparations to make his last plea for clemency to the governor. McConnell, a longtime Chicago judge, a colleague of Gary who had followed the Haymarket case closely and came to the conclusion that the trial had been unfair, was walking through a corridor of the Illinois capitol when he was approached by Captain William Black, the lawyer who had been in charge of the condemned men's defense. According to McConnell's recollections more than 40 years later, Black said, "I want to talk with you, McConnell. I have heard that you are to have an interview with the Governor this afternoon. Won't you do what you can for Parsons? If he is hanged I shall be responsible for his death." Black broke down "shedding tears and part of the time his talk was broken with sobs," McConnell recalled. Black unburdened himself to the judge: "I have blundered ... I believed too much in the court ... But, oh God, I have blundered clear through! Their conviction and their execution if it happens will be on my shoulders and will always be on my heart. I should never have taken the case. It was not in my line ..."[26]

McConnell was inclined to agree. Looking back, he felt that had the anarchists been defended by an expert and able legal team, "there would have been no conviction." Even their appeals had been "bungled." McConnell commented on the Illinois Supreme Court's upholding of the men's convictions: "... knowing as I did the lawyers who represented the condemned men, I doubt whether the court had the questions involved properly or luminously presented."[27]

In the eleventh hour the amnesty committee finally produced the affidavit from Otis Favor that they had been unable to procure for over a year. For his part, Favor refused to discuss the matter and simply signed an affidavit alleging that Ryce, the man designated to dragoon hundreds of candidates to jury duty, told him, "I am managing this case, and know what I am about. Those fellows are going to be hanged as certain as death. I am calling such men as the defendants will have to challenge peremptorily and waste their time and challenges. Then they will have to take such men as the prosecution wants." With Favor's sworn statement the leaders of the amnesty movement thought they had a chance to at least postpone the execution.[28]

The discovery of the bombs in Lingg's cell crushed all such hopes. One of the amnesty committees' leaders in Springfield, C.G. Dixon, a member of the United Labor Party in the state house, declared, "If the Anarchists are hanged Lingg will be responsible for it, and there is a theory that this was what he has wanted all along. ... If Lingg wanted to contrive a way which all of them would be hanged could he have devised a better one than this? He has been wanting to hang and has called, it is said, those who do not traitors to the cause. What better means could he have contrived to secure the hanging not only of himself but the others than this? The bombs were certain to be discovered because there never was a time when a man's cell was not examined days before he was hanged."[29]

That last week the governor's office reported receiving about 200 letters per day and that the sentiments of their authors ran two-to-one in favor of clemency. The governor also reported receiving a total of seven death threats by letter and postal card. But as the week wore on the winds of public sentiment seemed to shift and by Wednesday the governor's office reported receiving 450 letters "the remonstrances were again in excess of the appeals for clemency." Govenor Oglesby granted a private audience with Samuel Gompers, leader of the American Federation of Labor. He received Henry Demearest Lloyd who brought with him three important documents. Lloyd presented the governor with a clemency petition signed by "leading Chicago citizens," a letter from Michael Schwab acknowledging his crime and asking forgiveness, and a letter from Judge Gary commenting positively on Schwab's recantation. A.C. Cameron representing the Chicago Trades and Labor Assembly was followed by the mournful mother and wife of Spies, and the wives of Engel, Fischer, as well as Lingg's German girlfriend.[30]

Neither State's Attorney Grinnell nor Judge Gary was prepared to block clemency for Schwab or Fielden. This was not a new development as Grinnell had indicated during his closing summary of the trial that he thought Schwab, Fielden, and Neebe were less culpable than the others. After the Illinois Supreme Court had rendered its decision the prosecutor's office leaked to the press that it would not oppose clemency for Fielden or Schwab.[31] Judge Gary had recently come around to supporting a lessening of the sentence for Samuel Fielden, and wrote to the governor, "As there is no evidence that he knew of any preparation to do the specific act of throwing the bomb that killed Degan, he does not understand even now that general advice to large masses to do violence . . . nor that being joined by others in an effort to subvert law and order by force makes him responsible for the acts of those others . . . In short, he was more a misguided enthusiast than a criminal, conscious of the horrible nature and effect of his teachings, and of his responsibility therefor [sic]."[32]

Astute legal observers accurately predicted a few days before the execution date that Fielden and Schwab would be reprieved while Lingg, Spies, Parsons, Fischer, and Engel would be passed over, both because they refused to sign any petition to the governor that asked for anything short of a full pardon and because Judge Gary and prosecutor Grinnell only put in a good word for Fielden and Schwab.[33]

The day before the scheduled execution, November 10, Governor Oglesby cleared his entire appointment calendar and sequestered himself in his mansion. He told his secretary not to interrupt him and not even to open the day's mail. George Schilling and others of the amnesty committee waited on the sidewalk outside and were heartened when that afternoon two typewriters were delivered, a sign they felt that the governor must be preparing official orders of some sort and the only sort that needed to be issued that day were writs of commutation. In the afternoon, the governor's son Robert appeared at the door and announced to the small crowd outside that the governor would make a formal statement later that evening. But before seven o'clock when Robert again appeared in his father's stead to announce that the death sentences of Fielden and Schwab had been commuted to life in prison, it was already old news as word had already arrived from Chicago where the governor had telegraphed Sheriff Matson an hour earlier. Disappointed, the representatives of the amnesty association refused to speak to reporters and boarded a midnight train back to the city.[34]

Sheriff Matson had received a telegram from the governor around six in the evening commuting the death sentence of Fielden and Schwab and confirming that of all the others. Matson later told reporters that all the men, both those saved and those condemned took the news without any expression of emotion. Forty-eight hours later Fielden and Schwab stood in the special receiving cells new arrivals in Joliet were placed their first day and night in prison. These cells had inscriptions cut into the stone floor that read, "It is never too late to mend."[35]

Matson allowed Spies to see his mother for the last time in the relative comfort of the jail library. The sight of his grieving mother, weeping so deeply that she could not compose herself to speak, finally shattered Spies' stoic mask and he broke down promising her he was innocent but would "die like a man." Following his mother, Spies was next visited by the woman he had married while in jail, Nina Van Zandt. Observers thought Spies was unusually chilly toward her and were concerned when she kissed him goodbye and said "I will meet you to-morrow," which they interpreted as a suicide threat. Spies replied, "I hope so," and seemed unmoved, lighting a cigar.

Fischer too was allowed to meet his wife in the library and she brought him a letter written in English from some family friends that she couldn't read. It offered her their support and care but Fischer told her to go back to Germany and live with his mother. The last thing he told her was to "Bring our children up and tell them their father died a martyr to capital and a thirst for blood by the people." By this time the deputies in the room were crying as well.

Engel was given the use of Sheriff Matson's office for his final visits and said his goodbyes to his wife, the words he shared with her whispered close to her ear and inaudible to the watchful deputies.

Only Parsons was kept in his cell as Lucy, for some reason not recorded, arrived too late at the jail to be admitted and was left yelling for her husband on the wrong side of the locked gate.

As the condemned men were served their last suppers, Fischer and Engel eating oysters, Parsons a steak, and Spies chops and fried eggs, down the hall Lingg's corpse lay in the bathtub where he died. At eight-thirty the coroner finally arrived and his assistants carried a plain pine coffin into the bathroom, lifted Lingg's body from the tub to the box, and covered it with crushed ice. The coffin was then lifted onto the bloody bathtub and left there for the night.

No one but Engel, who dozed for a time before midnight, slept during their last night. Sleeping could not have been easy with one deputy sheriff assigned to sit outside each cell and another standing suicide watch inside with each condemned man. All the county deputies shunned such duty and they eventually drew papers from a hat, the loser drawing a slip with the words "death watch" written on it. After their final family visits, all the prisoners were carefully searched and then marched to new cells as a further precaution against a repeat of the Lingg horror. Carpenters had been banging the scaffold together all that day and it wasn't until around one in the morning that the sheriff and an assistant hauled heavy bags of sand onto the platform and tied them up for the gibbet's final test. The rasping sound and bang of the drop could be heard throughout the jail causing deputy sheriff Baumgartner to shiver but apparently not disturbing Parsons who coolly smoked a cigar through the process.

Deputy Charles W. Peters who spent the night with Engel reported later that he told him that he had no regrets and would do everything over again the same way if given the opportunity. Engel, Peters thought, harbored bitterness toward Spies and remembered Engel saying, "Any man who is a true socialist, thoroughly imbued with its glorious principles, can go bravely to the scaffold and die for them. I am afraid that there are one or two of us who have not the principles of socialism deep in their hearts." Engel told Peters that through the hardest part of the last visit of his wife and daughter, he took comfort that he had told them from the beginning not to hold out any hope for him. As deputy Peters spoke to a reporter he let slip that he had a wad of notes Engel wrote to his family and friends in his pocket. When asked what they contained Peters loyally replied, "They are sacred: I can not divulge them." He did, however, reveal the last words Engel wrote in his diary: "For liberty and right we made a good fight."[36]

A number of newspapers reported that late in the night the soulful voice of Albert Parsons echoed along the stone walls of the cell block as he sang the old Scottish ballad "Annie Laurie," a detail that soon became fixed in the literature of the event. But in 1941, Otto Eisenschiml wrote a letter to the *Chicago Tribune* in which he revealed that the story was a hoax. He reported that Clara E. Laughlin was a reporter for the *Inter Ocean* and was dispatched to the county jail to pick up a story for the following day's paper. The jail was utterly dark and quiet and when she returned and told her editor that she had nothing to file, he hammered his fist on the desk and ordered her to bring him some copy. Laughlin then dreamed up the story about Parsons singing "Annie Laurie" so beautifully that all the other prisoners and even the guards joined in. Her invention made the front page and was syndicated around the country. Eisenschiml wrote, "As the years passed, Miss Laughlin tried hard to set things right. It was no use. The story was too good to let truth spoil it."[37]

At 9:15 in the morning the death warrants arrived and the four condemned men dressed in the smocks provided by the jailer. They were given spirits to ease their nerves and then taken from their cells, their demeanor "cool, indifferent, or sullenly resigned." Pickets standing observantly on the roof gripped their Winchester rifles against the possibility of some desperate assault on the building. Fischer and Engel sang the "Marseillaise." Spies chatted with his jailer about literature while Parsons stood mute, weakening rapidly. The warden read aloud each of their death warrants. Marched to the gallows they were positioned on their traps. Sheriff Matson shook hands with Spies and bid him goodbye and then tied his arms at the elbows behind his back. More ropes and shrouds were positioned. Famous last words were uttered. Spies: "The time will come when our silence will be more powerful than the voices you strangle today!" Fischer: "Hurrah for Anarchy!" Engel: "This is the happiest moment of my life." Parsons: "Will I be allowed to speak, O men of America? Let me speak, Sheriff Matson! Let the voice of the people be heard!" The executioner brought his axe down on the tensed rope holding the traps upon which the four men stood.[38]

Either the executioner botched his job or exacted a vicious revenge. All four men kicked and twitched and heaved for minutes before their struggles ceased. The sheriff and attending physicians thought it prudent to let the men dangle until they were absolutely certain the men were dead, which, apparently, they were not until 26 minutes after they dropped. A postmortem revealed that none of the men's necks were broken and all had died by strangulation. The county physician told a reporter later that he still felt Fischer's pulse nearly eight minutes after the noose tightened.[39]

CHAPTER 9

THE PARDON

THOUGH THE EXECUTIONS HAD BEEN MARCHING STEADILY NEARER FOR A YEAR AND A HALF, the fact that they were actually carried out came as a deep shock to many. Two days after the executions a cop stopped a drunken man stumbling down Eighth avenue. Without warning the man swung at him wildly, yelling "I'm an anarchist!" "I'm an anarchist!" It took two other officers to subdue the man and drag him to the closest station. The 23-year-old carpenter told the desk sergeant his name was George Wolfe and that he was Adolph Fischer's foster brother, which prompted the police to thoroughly rifle his clothes looking for bombs. Wolfe was taken to one of the basement cells. A suspicious jailer rounded back on him early and found Wolfe swinging from his own suspenders, still choking. Wolfe was cut down, revived, and placed in a strait jacket.[1]

Across town, standing at their martyrs' gravesite, leaders of Chicago's radicals eulogized their dead heroes. All the sad and trenchant things said that day reflected two opposing understandings of this tragedy. Among those gathered in Waldheim Cemetery were a small number who lauded their fallen heroes as having died in obedience to their principles, while others portrayed them as innocent victims. Those who kindled the flame of revolutionary action seemed fewer in number but bolder in voice. Someone interrupted a speaker by shouting "Throttle the law!" the very cry that supposedly triggered the police to storm out into the street on May Fourth. Robert Reitzel, editor of the Detroit anarchist literary magazine, *Arme Teufel* ("Poor Devils"), thundered not against the government that murdered his friends, but the cowards who failed to pick up their black flag and carry it onward: "I shall not enter a complaint . . . against the hangman . . . nor against the jury, or the judges, but against the workingmen of Chicago, because they have permitted five of their best men to be murdered . . . In such a moment self-preservation is a crime . . ." Reitzel leaned dangerously close to inciting violence himself when he railed, "We have a right to say what we want, and we have a right to demand that this blood shall be atoned for. Which one of us has a heroic character like Louis Lingg?"[2]

But aside from these, most who made speeches that day maintained the fiction that the men laying in their crypts were martyrs to free speech, to the right of workers to organize, and to the eight hour day. Trade union leader Thomas Morgan, who before the Haymarket bombing had fought the anarchists tooth and nail, now co-opted their memory as martyrs to free speech and free assembly. "Here in the United States . . . they have set a precedent in the law that men can be hung for talking . . . Giving voice to the misery of the working people, here in this glorious country flowing with milk and honey, yet starving for the necessaries of life." Likewise, Capt. Black redefined their anarchism as a reformist, gradual socialism. "They were called anarchists. They were painted and presented to the world as men loving violence, riot, and bloodshed for its own sake, as men full of an unextinguishable and causeless hatred against existing order. Nothing could be further from the truth. They were men who loved peace, men of gentle instincts, men of gracious tenderness of heart . . . the anarchy of which they spoke and taught—what was it? But an attempt to answer the question, 'After the revolution, what?' " Cryptically, Black concluded, "I say that a mistake may well be forgotten in the glory of the purpose which we condemn, it may be, through undue haste. Whatever of fault may have been in these men, these the people whom they loved and in whose cause they died, may well close the volume and seal up the record, to give our lips to praise of their heroic deed and their sublime self-sacrifice."[3] Was Black trying to absolve himself of his own guilt for his legal failures?

Once all the legal appeals and pleas for clemency had failed and the executions became a terrible fact, a few anarchists who had for practical purposes downplayed their militancy and denied their revolutionary aspirations since the riot briefly rediscovered their ferocity. Speaking over the martyrs' graves on the first anniversary of their internment, Paul Grottkau, the anarchist who assumed leadership of the Chicago movement, concluded "We are heirs to the principles for which these heroes fell . . . Carry on the peaceful agitation and let the war of revolution sweep the streets of Chicago, carrying everything before it." Under the nervous eyes of a squad of Chicago police at the West Twelfth street Turner Hall on the occasion of the fourth anniversary, Grottkau reached the peroration of his speech and proclaimed "I will not say or do not wish to be understood as saying that Spies did not throw the bomb. If he or any of his fellows threw that bomb they did perfectly right." And the crowd erupted in cheers while the police commander, Inspector George W. Hubbard, a survivor of the bombing, warned the speaker that he would clear the room if more "incendiary" language was used. Grottkau's fiery rhetoric, focused on the martyrs' revolutionary sacrifice rather than their supposed defense of "free speech," was more in keeping with the original spirit and ideas espoused by the executed anarchist leaders.[4]

A few militant holdouts favored decisive action over speech making. John Hronek, one of Lingg's old friends from Vienna who liked hanging around the *Arbeiter Zeitung* office before the Haymarket and contributed a few pieces to the *Alarm*, was arrested as he left his home by detectives acting on the tip of an informer. The snitch told police that Hronek was the leader of a trio plotting to murder former State's Attorney Grinnell, Judge Gary, and Inspector Bonfield. Hronek's accomplices were Frank Capek, who was convicted of rioting for his part in the Haymarket meeting but given a suspended fine on his promise of good behavior, and Frank Chleboun, a Bohemian baker and a member of the Lehr und Wehr Verein. Chleboun had second thoughts after Hronek laid out his plan to take revenge for the execution of the Haymarket anarchists and asked him to avenge his own death if he was later executed. Hronek's plans advanced far enough to include walking around Grinnell's upscale neighborhood and scoping out his house. A search of Hronek's apartment and that of one of his accomplices turned up weapons, bombs, several pounds of dynamite, and pictures of Grinnell, Gary, and Bonfield clipped out of the paper. Hronek was found guilty and sentenced to twelve years in the penitentiary. Judge Collins in denying Hronek's motion for a new trial expressed his regret that the sentence was so harsh, intimating that if Hronek had waived his right to trial by jury he would have given him a lighter sentence.[5]

A few days after Hronek was sent to Joliet prison, his informer, Frank Chleboun was beaten in an Eighteenth street saloon. Chleboun had just saddled up to the bar when someone called out, "Be careful what you say; here is that low-born spy. Beware of the informer." Chelboun made the mistake of whirling around and daring the man who said that to step up. A "large-boned, burly fellow" named Thomas Hula did and pounded Chelboun's face until both eyes were purple while the rest of the bars' patrons coolly looked on. Hula's bartender defended him at his hearing, saying Chelboun was drunk and had called the other patrons "oxen" but the judge fined Hula 10 dollars all the same.[6]

Such outbursts of revolutionary anarchist spirit as Hronek's (and Hula's) became rarer as time went on. After the sensation of the Haymarket trial, journalists throughout the country paid more attention to the small groups of anarchists in their own cities. In New York a series of intrepid journalists disguised themselves (Henry Guy Carleton "put on a woolen shirt, a pair of greasy trousers, old . . . slouch hat, and by smirching my face with soot, and oil and dirt . . .") in order to attend anarchist meetings and hang around anarchist saloons, surreptitiously interviewing their secretive members. These reporters found that in the wake of the executions anarchists had turned even more secretive and dampened their radical fires. A New York anarchist admitted to one reporter that "we have secret meetings at which only the chosen are invited. The word is conveyed personally and not by any circular or letter. We used to drill at these secret meetings, but since that affair in Chicago we have been so watched by the police that we have had no drills and the muskets have been put away."[7]

On the first anniversary of the hangings, Joseph Pulitzer tasked his *New York World* correspondents around the nation with assessing the strength of anarchism in their cities. Chicago's *World* reporter filed a detailed examination of the state of the movement in its now most famous city. He noted that the *Arbeiter Zeitung* continued to publish but that its tone was much muted from its pre-Haymarket fire breathing. As an institution, the anarchist publishing company was rent with factional in-fighting and its leaders seemed to spend more time "quarrelling among themselves . . . than against society." Since the Haymarket blast the ranks of the hardcore revolutionaries had steadily dwindled to fewer than 100. Many more socialists and anarchists in the city before the executions "had a vague idea that their doctrines were to triumph by force" but since had come to "believe in education and peaceful agitation" as the best means to achieve their dreams.[8]

Within a couple of years of the execution, both William and Lizzie Holmes bemoaned the waning interest in the memory of the martyrs. Lizzie wrote in 1889, "I am reluctant to say that the old spirit of devotion—the determination, desperate courage, and whole-souled anxiety to *work* in the cause—that fearlessness of conventionalism, and utter disregard of the opinions of the 'respectable' element, which characterized the agitators of twelve, seven, and four years ago—have utterly died out." She was especially disgusted that "one of our oldest and ablest agitators" spoke at a society meeting chaired by Julius Grinnell on the subject of labor in society. How was it, she wondered that any of their movement could "address that atrocious perjurer and murderer with calmness or patience on any subject." Clearly, time's balm was soothing quickly.

Lizzie's husband, William, tried to kindle the flame of the martyrs' memory by urging everyone to wear a special symbol on their lapels or dresses. "Some of us here in Chicago have already taken the initiation, and wear as badges a miniature gallows with a noose hanging from the cross-beam. Comrades all over the world should do likewise." Holmes predicted this symbol would march on and soon rival the crucifix in popularity.[9]

But Holmes' gallow lapel pins didn't catch on and the event itself continued to dim as a memory. One of the early historians of the city wrote in 1895 that the event had faded from the public mind and was only kept alive by the anarchists' "admiring disciples in feeble demonstrations on the anniversary of their execution." With each passing year fewer gathered in Waldheim Cemetery to lay wreaths at the graves of the Haymarket martyrs.

At Joliet prison, Schwab, Neebe, and Fielden settled into their different monotonies. Neebe worked as a nurse at the hospital. The bookish Schwab was given a job in the prison library. Fielden, in keeping with his experience while a free citizen, was allowed to work for stone contractors who employed prison labor.[10] Prison's dulling routines damped their revolutionary ardor. In 1891, a correspondent for the anarchist magazine, *Liberty*, reported upon his recent visit to the Joliet Prison where he had the opportunity to visit Fielden, Schwab and Neebe. "Schwab and Fielden, I can state positively (and, I think, Neebe also), now realize the utter idiocy of the revolutionary programme of the "whoop-her-ups" and have lost all faith in the absurd method of the revolutionary Communists."[11]

While the three anarchists marched in lockstep to and from their jobs, out of public sight a nucleus of amnesty activists quietly continued working for the prisoners' release. They grasped at some very slight legal straws. In the summer of 1892, they engineered another day in court for Schwab and Fielden by once again arguing that their rights were denied when an appellate court upheld their convictions without the accused in court. Even though the U.S. Supreme Court had ruled decisively in 1887 that there was no precedent and no Fifth Amendment right for defendants to be present before an appellate court when upholding their sentencing, Capt. Black and Sigmund Zeisler managed to get one more bite at this apple, but, predictably, lost again.[12]

Their disappointment proved short lived as an election the next year brought to the governor's office a reformer who many amnesty leaders believed was secretly in favor of pardoning the imprisoned radicals. John Peter Altgeld, a former municipal judge and popular progressive Democrat moved in the same social and political circles as many of the leaders of the amnesty movement. The amnesty leaders knew Altgeld and had come to trust him.

John Peter Altgeld's law partner, Clarence Darrow, took credit for nudging the governor toward granting a pardon to all the anarchists. Darrow was a warm friend of George A. Schilling, the leader of the amnesty movement almost since the day the smoke rose from Desplaines street. Darrow described Schilling in his memoirs as "about the first man I met when I came to Chicago, and he has been a close friend ever since." Darrow later recalled Altgeld telling him, "I haven't had time to go over that case yet, but I am going over the record carefully and if I conclude those anarchists ought to be freed I will free them. But make no mistake about its being a popular move—if I do it I will be a dead man politically." On June 26, 1893, Altgeld signed pardons for all three imprisoned anarchists.

The timing of Altgeld's sudden decision was prompted by a confluence of events. In April of 1893, a leading monthly magazine published an article by his archenemy, Judge Joseph E. Gary, defending his decisions in the Haymarket trial. A few weeks later, a monumental sculpture memorializing the Haymarket martyrs was dedicated in Waldheim Cemetery. With one stroke Altgeld trumped both.

For seven years Judge Gary had been sphinx-like in refusing to comment on the trial. Many were surprised when his history of the trial appeared in the *The Century Magazine*, a leading monthly that built its large circulation with the memoirs of Civil War generals and excerpts from Mark Twain's novels. Through pages of twisting, serpentine, even stilted prose common to that era, Gary upheld his reputation for judicial poise, but obscured his main purpose: to put down the idea that had grown steadily since the publication of Dyer Lum's *Concise History* that the Haymarket eight had been tried and convicted for their words and not their deeds. More upsetting to Gary was the praise he received from his more bellicose supporters who argued that society had the right to defend itself from dangerous ideas and that Gary in "straining the law" had performed a great service. "I protest against any such commendation," wrote Gary, "and deny utterly that I have done anything that should subject me to it." Perhaps realizing that his prose was murky, Gary highlighted his thesis in italics for the benefit of those readers he had confused: "The motive, then, or at least the principal motive, of this paper, is *to demonstrate . . . that the verdict of the jury in the case of the anarchists was right; that the anarchists were guilty of murder; that they were not the victims of prejudice, nor martyrs for free speech . . .*"[13]

The common misunderstanding about the case was that the anarchists merely advocated revolution as a principle or a hope. Had this been the case then there would not have been any grounds for prosecution. Gary pointed out that the men brought to his court had formed an organization that didn't merely preach anarchy but prepared to create it by stockpiling weapons and making plans to turn the eight-hour strikes into a general uprising. Spies participated in the "very serious riot" that broke out at the McCormick factory. This provided the excuse to lay a trap for the police and they planned their protest meeting "near a police station at which they knew a large force was concentrated." Once the police were lured into the open the bomb could do its work.

Gary structured his essay in an odd way. He began by dismissing the idea that the anarchists were in fact convicted for their speeches and writings, but demonstrated by reference to Illinois law, legal precedents, and voluminous quotations from anarchist newspapers, that the eight men *could* have been convicted on those grounds alone. Only toward the end of his essay did the judge mention that any of the evidence went beyond this standard and connected the defendants to the bomber. Rather, while Gary initially seemed bent on framing the trial as having hinged on the difference between speech and conspiracy, the line he drew still lay in the nature of the anarchists' words rather than in their deeds:

> There is nothing criminal in a combination of few or many to induce and persuade the people of the United States to change our form of government to a monarchy, or to abandon all government for anarchy; the criminality of the anarchists was not in the ultimate end they proposed, but in the means by which they proposed to attain it. Those means—by violence and slaughter—changed what otherwise might have been merely a faction in politics into a band of criminals.[14]

Was this merely an inconsistency of Gary's thought at the time or was it a reflection of his intentions all along? Perhaps Gary, while publicly adhering to what he understood to be a conservative interpretation of the law during the trial personally believed that this construction was too restrictive. Perhaps Gary's essay reveals that underneath his legal sensitivity to the requirement that the state connect the conspirators to the act of bombing in his heart he didn't actually think this was necessary and merely proving that they preached violence and bloodshed should have been enough to hang them all.

It is also possible that the seven years that had passed since the trial, years filled with spectacular industrial battles such as the Homestead Strike in Pennsylvania, could have pushed Gary to rethink the trial's meaning and reframe its (and his) legacy as having delivered a blow against violent conspiracies. Whatever caused Gary' to downplay the direct evidence uncovered at the trial connecting some of the defendants with the bombing in favor of quoting their most inflammatory statements, his doing so ultimately contributed to the same distortions in the common memory of these events that he had begun his article complaining of.

A week or so after the article appeared Clarence Darrow surprised his audience at the University club with a slashing attack on Judge Gary. Darrow repeated Lum's old canard that the men had been convicted on the theory that their speech making incited some stranger to throw his bomb. "Never, until the Anarchist case . . . did a court of law hold that those who talked and wrote and preached for a change of government, peaceful or forceful, were guilty of murder . . . It is this making of new law to make criminal that which was never so regarded in the past that constitutes what Judge Gary calls the beauty of common law . . ." Sitting to Darrow's left at the head table while Darrow let fly his impassioned attack was Judge Gary. When Darrow was finished Gary, "with great dignity" replied:

> It is nearly seven years since, upon an occasion more solemn than this, I said that every man had full right to entertain and advocate personally or in print such opinion as he thinks right. But if he proposed murder he puts his life at stake, and no talk of free speech, wrongs to be righted, or reforms to be promulgated can shield him from the consequences of that act. Since that time I have had no reason to alter that opinion.

And Gary took his seat to a burst of applause.[15]

Gary made the same mistake in responding to Darrow that he made in his essay in *The Century Magazine*. He didn't make clear that by "proposing murder" he meant not only advocating force in a general sort of way, but specifically laying plans to incite, attack, and kill.

Six weeks later, 8,000 people, many having come to Chicago for the World's Fair but deciding to spend part of their day instead to watch a radical spectacle, gathered at Waldheim Cemetery for the unveiling of a monument to the memory of anarchist martyrs. No red flags were carried by the throngs who paraded to the graveyard under an agreement with the police. The statue itself, pointedly the same height as the one depicting a police officer standing in Haymarket Square, was shrouded under a deep crimson cloth. When the cloth dropped the 200 voices of the International Socialist Mannerchor broke into "Wacht Auf" (Wake Up) a song composed for the occasion.[16]

The next day Altgeld called on his secretary, a young Brand Whitlock who would go on to his own distinguished progressive political career, and told him to make out three pardons. By that evening, Schwab, Fielden, and Neebe were free and on a train steaming back to Chicago.[17]

On the day of their release Neebe, Schwab, and Fielden were served a sumptuous lunch by the warden of Joliet prison, given new suits of clothes, and driven in the warden's carriage to the station where they would catch the train that would take them back to Chicago and their families, reporters peppered them with questions and the three men did not shy from the limelight. Schwab made no attempt to claim his innocence. "Perhaps I should have suffered some punishment, but I have suffered enough . . ." Schwab swore off anarchy, saying he was "an individualist with perhaps socialistic tendencies . . . I don't believe there are any Anarchists or that there ever will be." Fielden continued to deny he ever fired at the police and revealed that Governor Oglesby once visited him in prison and told him he didn't believe it either. But Fielden also hinted that there may have been more to the charge of conspiracy than many credited. "As a matter of fact, if people hadn't been stirred up to such a point there never would have been a riot. During the time prior to May 4 there had been a lot of strikes and considerable talk . . . Then things got stirred up worse and there was talk of anarchy and all that sort of thing, which forced a state of belief tending that way amongst certain labor organizations, which belief before had not even existed. . . . I got mixed up with a lot of people that believed they were mistreated, and being a spouter I naturally voiced their sentiments. All that, I hope, has passed away forever. If I have made a mistake it was one of associations."

Even Edward Dreyer, who had labored strenuously for years as a leader of the amnesty movement and jubilantly carried their pardon to the prison, felt compelled the day Neebe, Schwab and Fielden were released to say that he did believe that they were guilty to some degree. "I do not believe that Fielden and Schwab were innocent, under the laws of the State of Illinois, but I do believe that their punishment was far greater than the crime which was not proven directly against them warranted."[18]

But there were no such doubts about the anarchists' innocence in Altgeld's pardon message. Altgeld's justification for his pardon begins with a plain misstatement of the facts of the case: "The prosecution could not discover who had thrown the bomb and could not bring the really guilty man to justice, and, as some of the men indicted were not at the Haymarket meeting and had nothing to do with it, the prosecution was forced to proceed on the theory that the men indicted were guilty of murder . . ." It was true that for the first few days the police had no idea who the bomber was, but once Harry Gilmer identified Rudolph Schnaubelt's picture, the police were sure he was the bomber and tried their best to capture him. Nor was it true that the prosecutors only pursued the conspiracy theory of murder when they could not lay their hands on Schnaubelt. Spies, Fischer, and Schwab were all arrested the day after the bombing, Fielden, Neebe, and Engel not long afterward, and well before Schnaubelt's trail had run cold the prosecutors announced their intention of trying them all for murder, sure that they could connect them all in one way or another to the conspiracy and the bombing.

Altgeld took pains to declare that his pardon was not being granted because the men who had spent the last eight years in prison had suffered enough. It was not an act of mercy. Rather, Altgeld boldly said his pardon was because the original trial was unfair—the judge was biased, the jury packed, and the evidence insufficient to sustain the charge of murder.

More than half of Altgeld's statement dealt with the issue of the selection of jurors. At one point Altgeld invented a novel account of the experiences of Otis S. Favor, that old coworker of the amnesty leader William Salter and anarchists William and Lizzie Holmes, who submitted an affidavit accusing Bailiff Ryce of expressing his intention to handpick a hanging jury. Altgeld claimed that Favor was originally a member of the jury pool but was dismissed for cause for being prejudiced against the anarchists. But Bailiff Ryce's actions were so outrageous that they moved even Favor, a successful businessman with a large wholesale company on Wabash avenue and a home in Hyde Park, to step forward. According to Altgeld, Favor was dragooned to the jury pool by Ryce but was excused because during his examination he revealed his bias against the anarchists and was excused for cause.

However, the trial record does not support Altgeld's version of Favor's relationship to the trial. Otis Favor was the two hundred and ninety-ninth man quizzed as to his fitness to serve on the jury and Judge Gary did grant the defense's motion to excuse him for cause. But Favor never said anything under questioning opposed to anarchism or socialism. Favor was excused because he told the court that he knew several people who were present that awful night and had heard from them accounts that he believed and that he would find it difficult to forget in order to render a verdict on the evidence alone. Favor was never asked nor did he offer his opinion about whether his belief leaned toward the men's guilt or their innocence.[19]

The governor leaned heavily on Otis S. Favor's tardy affidavit but put even more weight on a wishful reading of an Illinois Supreme Court decision that Algeld claimed reversed the juror selection rule laid down in *Spies v. Illinois* but in fact upheld it.[20] *Coughlin v. The People* was a case that paralleled and even intersected with that of the anarchists in many ways. Like *Spies v. Illinois*, it involved a group of men tried together as members of a conspiracy that resulted in murder. Both cases brought to the bar men belonging to secret radical organizations, though in *Coughlin* the defendants were Irish militants bent on sending bombs to England. As was true for the anarchists, a raft of sensational pretrial publicity combined with the unpopularity of the men's beliefs made empanelling a jury a difficult prospect. Just as Judge Gary did for the anarchists, Judge Samuel McConnell appointed a special bailiff to bring to the court veniremen by the hundreds. Their lawyers, like those who had appealed the anarchists' case, petitioned for a new trial on the grounds that the jury that convicted them was handpicked and biased, and that the judge had allowed plainly biased jurors to be empanelled over the objections of the defense.

The Supreme Court of Illinois examined the cases of two jurors, Bontecou and Clark, who were challenged for cause but were deemed acceptable by the trial judge after the defense had exhausted all of its preemptory challenges. Both Bontecou and Clark admitted that they had firm opinions that the defendants were guilty and they had gathered their conclusions from the extensive newspaper coverage of the murder. However, after extensive questioning, the trial judge, Samuel McConnell, deemed both men to be capable of setting aside their opinions and deciding the case strictly on the evidence presented in the courtroom. The majority of the Supreme Court reversed McConnell on the grounds that both Bontecou and Clark not only testified as to their having an opinion about the facts of the case, but had revealed that their ideas about the case were "fixed and positive" thus failing the legal litmus test for qualification as jurors.

According to the Illinois justices the test of the suitability of a juror was not whether swore that he could set aside his biases and beliefs and look solely to the evidence, but whether the biases and beliefs that he had were "fixed and positive." Judge McConnell stepped over a bright line in questioning the two critical jurors in the case by badgering them into pledging that they would be neutral and could make their judgments on the testimony alone. It wasn't only McConnell's intensive questioning that bothered the high justices, it was that none of all that probing revealed that their biases and prejudices were anything but "fixed and positive." Had the judge interrogated either venireman with the clear purpose of revealing the nature of his bias and found it provisional, tentative, or unsure, then he was perfectly within his discretion to overrule the objection to him. "His statement that he can render a fair and impartial verdict does not tend to show that he is not partial, since it does not tend to show the nonexistence of the fixed and decided opinion to which he has already confessed."

The majority of the court also placed great weight on the record that showed Judge McConnell had badgered each venireman until he "forced from the mouth of the juror" a declaration that they could decide the case fairly on its merits and set aside his prejudices. Rather, the justices ruled, it was essential that a prospective juror's "impartiality should appear before he is permitted to take ... [an] oath. If he is not impartial then, his oath can not be relied on to make him so."

By contrast, in the Haymarket trial the state's examination of Harry T. Sandford, the venireman upon whose qualification the anarchists' appeal rested, clearly was not intended to compel the witness to swear to something he did not truly believe. The relatively few questions posed were aimed at understanding Sandford's true state of mind, rather than maneuvering him to swear an oath and would have been just as acceptable to the Illinois Supreme Court in 1893 as it was in 1887. Sandford did express his belief that the anarchists were involved in some way but he also revealed a degree of uncertainty about it. Sandford said he was biased against socialism and anarchism but in the next breath added "Well, as I know so little about it in reality at present it is a pretty hard question to answer." Sandford admitted he'd read the newspapers and formed a belief about the anarchists' guilt but then added uncertainly, "Well, suppose I have an opinion in my own mind that they encouraged it?"[21]

The panel of justices took pains to distinguish the case of the Irish revolutionaries before them to that of the anarchist revolutionaries of the past and to show that Judge Gary and his earlier rulings would have passed their new sniff test as well:

> The opinion of the juror challenged in the Spies case did not appear to be fixed or positive. He answered that, from all he had read and heard, he had an opinion as to the guilt or innocence of some of the defendants; that his opinion was made up from random conversations, and from newspaper reading, but from nothing reliable, or that he regarded as in the nature of sworn testimony; that he had never talked with the witnesses, or with any one having knowledge of the facts; and that he could listen to the evidence fairly and impartially and render a fair, impartial, unprejudiced and unbiased verdict. He never expressed his opinion, nor did it appear that evidence would be required to remove it ... The case therefore was one properly governed by the statute ...

In deciding to grant Coughlin a new trial, the court pointedly reconfirmed its earlier opinion in the anarchists' case. Noting that the juror qualification statutes of Illinois were tested by the anarchists in 1887, they had no doubts about the provisions now. "The constitutionality of this statute was directly in question in *Spies et al.* v. The People, 122 Ill., 1, and we there held it to be constitutional, and we are still disposed to adhere to the conclusion announced in that case."

Judge Magruder, writing for the minority, had a different reading of the court transcript, finding that neither Bontecou nor Clark's opinion were actually "fixed and positive." Where the majority thought that the judge's leading questioning of the veniremen compromised the value of their subsequent claims of competence, Magruder believed that a trial judge should be given great latitude to examine and probe a juror's mind. Essentially, Magruder argued that a trial judge's ruling that a juror was competent cannot be determined by any single statement of a prospective juror but needed to be judged in the context of his entire testimony. "Though some of the answers of a juror taken separately may perhaps establish a disqualification, yet if the effect of all that he says is to show that he is a proper juror, he ought not to be excluded."

Throughout his review of the examination of the jurors, Altgeld twisted and distorted quotes to the point where they were but his own fabrications. Here, for example, is Altgeld's version of Sandford's examination:

Q: Do you believe that that prejudice would influence your verdict in this case?
A: Well, as I know so little about it, it is a pretty hard question to answer. *I have an opinion in my own mind that the defendants encouraged the throwing of that bomb.*

Whereas this is how the transcript that Altgeld claimed to have used reads:

A: [You have a] decided prejudice against them? Do you believe that that would influence your verdict in this case, or would you try the real issue which is here, as to whether these defendants were guilty of the murder of Mr. Degan or not, or would you try the question of socialism and anarchism, which reality has nothing to do with the case?
A: Well, as I know so little about it in reality at present it is a pretty hard question to answer.
Q: You would undertake, you would attempt of course to try the case upon the evidence introduced here upon the issue which is presented here?
A: Yes sir.
Q: Now, that issue and the only issue which will be presented to this jury, unless it is presented with some other motive that to arrive at the truth, I think, is, did these men throw the bomb which killed officer Degan? . . .
A: Well, suppose I have an opinion in my own mind that they encouraged it?[22]

Among the bits of evidence Altgeld relied on to reach his conclusion that the trial was unjust were affidavits alleging serious police abuses. These affidavits were supplied by amnesty leader George Schilling and it is unlikely that Altgeld knew anything about the men who swore to them. Victor Djmek and Jacob Mikolanda swore that they were picked up by the police, beaten, and threatened with summary execution unless they agreed to turn state's witnesses and testify.[23]

What neither Djmek, Mikolanda, nor Altgeld thought to mention was that Victor Djmek was actually Vaclav Dejnek, an employee of the Bohemian anarchist newspaper *Budoucnost* that Jacob Mikolanda owned. Mikolanda was the more famous of the pair, having been one of the founders of the Czech socialist movement before immigrating to Chicago. Mikolanda attended the great Pittsburgh Congress that founded the Black International in 1883 and was designated its corresponding secretary for the Bohemian language.[24]

Dejnek and Mikolanda's courage and militancy was tested the day of the McCormick riot when the two men led a mob that cornered and attempted to hang a police officer from a nearby pole. Two Chicago cops later fingered Mikolanda as a man who pulled a "large revolver" and fired on their patrol wagon after they had rescued their fellow patrolman from the mob. Vaclav Dejnek was convicted of assault with intent to kill and was sentenced to a year in the penitentiary by Judge Gary for looping a rope around a cops' neck. Jacob Mikolanda was found guilty of assault and also spent one year in jail. Both men were released several years before they wrote their affidavits at the request of amnesty association leader George Schilling.[25]

Probably aware that pardoning the anarchists on a legal technicality alone was too politically dangerous, Altgeld ventured a theory that, if true, collapsed the basis of the state's conspiracy theory. Altgeld theorized that the bombing was the work of a deranged workman seeking revenge for a previous police beating. Unlike those who had earlier pointed their fingers at Pinkerton spies or police agents, Altgeld offered a theory as to why he believed the assailant must have acted alone and for reasons of his own. Governor Altgeld reasoned that if there had been a conspiracy, as alleged: "there would have been many bombs thrown; and the fact that only one was thrown shows that it was an act of personal revenge." The prosecution did view this as a flaw in its case but explained this inconsistency by holding that the bomb was either a signal for other anarchists to open fire or one of many bombs held in pockets that night that would have been thrown had it not been for the quick action and fortitude of the police in holding their ground and returning fire.[26]

Altgeld heaped scorn on Judge Gary, selectively quoting from Gary's own recent article on the case to make it seem that Gary admitted that he had purposely rail-roaded the men to their deaths. Even Altgeld's closest advisors thought he went too far. Whitlock later wrote of his "regret that so great a soul should have permitted itself to mar the document by expressions of hatred of the judge who tried the case." Darrow thought Altgeld "was wrong in laying all the blame to Judge Gary." In fact, Darrow wished that Altgeld had consulted him before writing such a lengthy state-ment for had he just pardoned the men without taking the extraordinary step of writing a brief against the prosecution, Darrow thought he would have escaped the political immolation he suffered. But Darrow also thought Altgeld "seemed almost to court the opposition of the world."[27]

Chicago's politicos had long whispered that Algeld's hatred of Judge Gary sprung not from his treatment of the anarchists but from his casting the deciding vote on a three-judge appeal panel that cost Altgeld a small fortune. Altgeld had sued the city seeking 26,000 dollars in damages because the city built a new bridge across Jackson street, adjacent to a parcel of land Altgeld was holding in speculation. Altgeld felt he was due 60,000 dollars in damages, but as a sitting judge, Altgeld realized the politi-cally sensitive nature of his making a claim on the city's treasury and so he attempted to cut a quiet deal with the city attorney for 26,494.60 dollars. Just as he was on the verge of collecting his judgment the city's corporation counsel, a tool of his political rivals, challenged the deal in open court and accused Altgeld of influence peddling. Altgeld lept to his feet, waved his fist, and called the lawyer "a damned liar." The judge ordered Altgeld to apologize and then later found him guilty of contempt and fined him 100 dollars. The whole episode was a political embarrassment for the aspiring politician and was exuberantly splashed across the front pages of newspapers loyal to his opponents. As if this experience was not wounding enough, Judge Gary and a fellow appellate judge ruled Altgeld's settlement inappropriate and ordered a rehearing in the case, an order that resulted in Altgeld ultimately settling for 16,000 dollars.[28]

Never one to quietly swallow what he considered an affront, Altgeld sent the appellate justices a letter claiming that he would "not complain of your decision, although it is true that you do not settle a single question in the case..." Under the guise of asking the judges to delete from their opinion a reference to his good character, saying "I do not want your praise," Altgeld told the judges just what he thought of them: "...I have long thought that your court simply picked at the bark with its finger nails, and seemed almost incapable of deciding a case on its merits..." Altgeld charged them with "frequently reversing meritorious cases on ground that nobody cared about or thought of..." Claiming that "I will not complain," Altgeld concludes by calling the decision in his case "a moral outrage" and their decision an effort "to patronize me."[29]

Altgeld's animus toward Gary reappeared a few months later as the governor took the unusual step of coordinating the local Chicago campaign against the judge. One of the campaign sheets distributed by the campaign pictured wood cuts of the anarchist martyrs surrounding likenesses of Capt. and Hortensia Black over the inscription, "This is the Issue of the Present Campaign." But Gary's solid bipartisan support was formidable and he easily defended his seat.[30]

More damaging to the way this event would be written about in later history books, was Altgeld's distorted characterization of the legal theory pursued by the prosecution. Altgeld presented the prosecution as proceeding entirely on the theory that anyone who advocated murder was guilty as an accomplice if some entirely unknown person was then inspired to follow their advice. Thus, Altgeld alleged, "...because it was claimed they had at various times in the past uttered and printed incendiary and seditious language, practically advising the killing of policemen, of Pinkerton men and others acting in that capacity, and that they were therefore responsible for the murder of Mathias Degan." This idea was the same one popularized by famous critics of the trial such as the giant of literature, William Dean Howells, who wrote, "The historical perspective is that this free Republic has killed five men for their opinions."[31]

Altgeld's predecessor, Oglesby, would not criticize the pardoning of Schwab, Neebe, and Fielden, but could not contain his anger at Altgeld's attempt to whitewash the whole affair. "Is there any 'reasonable doubt' in the mind of any living man that the members of the association knew Lingg was making bombs? Is there any 'reasonable doubt' that they knew what the bombs were for? They did all know, from the fact that Ling [sic] was their associate, from the fact that he was a bomb-maker, from the fact that he manufactured bombs for the occasion, and that the bombs he manufactured had been distributed only a short time before the meeting of that night. There could be no reasonable doubt that they knew bombs were to be used . . ." Oglesby observed that Altgeld's pardon message had largely been written by a lawyer for the anarchists and further charged that Altgeld's only contribution was his self-serving attack on Judge Gary.[32]

Nevertheless, Altgeld's pardon message profoundly influenced the memory of this event. It was immediately embraced by the same labor leaders who had six years before carefully distanced themselves from the anarchists' trial. Labor journals and magazines reprinted lengthy excerpts. When the American Federation of Labor held its annual convention in Chicago in 1893, as each delegate passed into the meeting hall they were given a recently published pamphlet entitled "Reasons for Pardoning Fielden, Neebe, and Schwab," by John P. Altgeld.[33]

Altgeld had not only freed the remaining anarchists and vindicated the slain revolutionaries, he had laid the basis for generations of historians to misinterpret the Haymarket events and domesticate the wild ideas of the revolutionaries. Those who believed that the anarchists had once meant what they said, who remembered that there was once a time when their slogans and activities spread fear, that there was once a moment when mottos of force took form and became a bomb arcing through the cool night air, and men died, those who remembered these things had lost the battle for history.

CONCLUSION

WHILE FALLING FAR SHORT OF WHAT COUNTS AS FAIR AND JUST TODAY, the Haymarket defendants were accorded the rights and protections generally recognized by courts in the Gilded Age. Many details of the court proceedings that today would prompt an immediate reversal on appeal—the use of evidence seized without warrant and of undocumented provenance, the inflammatory display of anarchist flags and placards, the seating of jurors who openly voiced their dislike of anarchists—were common practice in that era. Other questionable practices, such as extensively using speeches and publications as evidence, viewing coconspirators as equal to principals, granting accomplices who turn state's witnesses lighter sentences, and condemning men to execution, remain features of the judicial order in the twenty-first century.

The political nature of the Haymarket trial undoubtedly influenced its outcome. It drove the prosecution to use every considerable legal means at hand to achieve a conviction while tempting the anarchists to use the trial as a platform from which to expound their social theories even at the risk of compromising their defense. Inevitably, the glare of publicity distorted the behavior of all the actors in this legal drama, while the insistence by all sides to view the trial as a symbol of something greater—as evidence of class rule and the inherent injustice of the state or as the vindication of the rule of law and republican justice—ensured its history would be written by partisans.

Casting a lingering doubt over the entire episode (and nothing opens the door to fanciful interpretations like a vexing mystery) was the fact that the man who threw the bomb was never brought to justice. Without a bomber the full scope of the conspiracy was harder to grasp both at the time and increasingly in hindsight, and no amount of lawyerly explanation could ever make a conspiracy trial without the main perpetrator in the conspiracy seem completely legitimate. The bomber's escape also fed innumerable rumors that the bombing was an accident or the bomber was settling a private score and had no connection to the anarchists or the bombing was the work of an agent provocateur bent on providing a pretext for smashing the labor movement. Even though the preponderance of the evidence presented at the trial clearly pointed to only one man, Rudolph Schnaubelt, defendant Michael Schwab's brother-in-law, as long as the bomber remained at large those who advocated for clemency, pardon, or even just a particular heroic memory for the Haymarket anarchists, cherished hope that the truth would accompany discovery of the true bomber's identity.

Between the public's hunger for sensational stories and the anarchist defenders' hope for redemption by discovering a bomber who was a loner or a police agent, the number of suspects quickly multiplied. Prosecutor Grinnell told reporters that he had been flooded with hundreds of letters from tipsters claiming to have discovered who "really" threw the bomb and from troubled souls confessing to the crime.[1] A Pennsylvania carpenter who fell off a roof and broke his neck reportedly claimed on his deathbed that he was at the Haymarket Riot and he was the one who threw the bomb.[2] Lawyers for the defense included among their petitions for a new trial an affidavit from an Indianapolis saloonkeeper who swore that a stranger entered his bar, ordered a whiskey, and pointed to his suspiciously heavy satchel saying, "I come from New York and I guess I will go to Chicago. You will hear of some trouble there very soon."[3]

On the day of the executions Captain William Perkins Black waved before reporters a telegram just wired from New York offering "proof" that the true bomber was in that city and had no connection to Chicago's condemned men.[4] Black's information came from a man, Franz Maykopf, aka George Mayer, who was locked in Sing Sing for insurance fraud. Maykopf was part of a ring of "firebugs" who burned down crowded tenement buildings to reap a modest sum on the furnishings and clothes they had insured. Maykopf was convicted on the testimony of the man he claimed masterminded the scheme, Kleeman Schultz, while Schultz was rewarded with immunity and freedom. Maykopf swore vengeance and told his lawyer that Schultz boasted of having thrown the bomb that killed policemen in Chicago. A reporter interviewed Maykopf later but none of the details of his story—that Maykopf threw the bomb from behind the speakers' wagon, that a man on the wagon served as the spotter and gave him a signal for throwing the bomb, and that this man also successfully escaped the dragnet—are consistent with other witnesses' testimony. Schultz himself later admitted that he lived in Pullman at the time of the bombing, but insisted that he never came near the site of the Haymarket Riot.[5]

A week after the executions, Fred Gerhardt locked himself in his Indianapolis hotel room and tried hacking his hand from his wrist. At his commitment hearing it was revealed that Gerhardt had been overheard boasting of having thrown the bomb in Chicago, and he was declared insane.[6]

Amidst the cloud of bomb thrower rumors the whereabouts of Rudolph Schnaubelt, the man identified from a photograph by two trial witnesses as having thrown the bomb, remained unknown. Schnaubelt sightings were reported frequently while the Haymarket prisoners awaited the outcome of their appeals. Schnaubelt was reportedly seen in Pittsburgh, Santo Domingo, California, Mexico, and Germany by the spring of 1887. The *Arbeiter Zeitung* published a letter claiming to be from Schnaubelt postmarked Christiania, Norway. In it Schnaubelt denied that he was the bomber while taunting the authorities, "If I had really thrown this bomb, surely I would have nothing to be ashamed of, but in truth I never once thought of it."[7] One unrelated report offers some support to this letter being genuine. In 1889, a Norwegian sailor, Knute Arnoldsen, reported that he had encountered Rudolph Schnaubelt on a ship in northern seas. Arnoldsen reported that Schnaubelt was embarking on a whaling voyage to the Arctic; he had "admitted that anarchy was a failure..."[8]

Nearly a decade after the bombing a number of reports placed Schnaubelt either visiting his mother in Vallejo, California, or begging the streets in Honduras. One reporter claimed to have interviewed Schnaubelt in Mexico:

> Asked whether he threw the bomb in the Haymarket, he remained silent a long time and afterward tried to turn the conversation to another subject, but the correspondent insisted. Then he admitted he saw the bomb fall and the police killed and heard the wounded cry. He seemed even to gloat over the cries and suffering which his memory recalled, but would neither deny nor admit he had thrown the bomb. He did say he had taken an active part in the anarchists' work in Chicago. Further he said that the anarchists of Chicago were obliged either to kill or be killed and spoke earnestly of revenge in the future...[9]

After the passage of a decade, the state's attorney in Chicago let it be known that he no longer thought it possible to bring Schnaubelt to trial, even were he to be found. Some key witnesses were dead, evidence would be hard to recover, and the prospect of a new trial at this late date was nearly impossible. In June 1895 a foreign correspondent wired that Schnaubelt had been shot and mortally wounded in a fight at Pinalajo Villa, Honduras, and later offered to provide to the Associated Press a full transcript of his deathbed confession for an undisclosed price.[10]

Schnaubelt was again reported to be dead a year later, this time of tuberculosis in San Bernardino, California, though his mother and sister told reporters that the dead man was more likely his brother Henry, who had long suffered from the disease and was known to live in the area. Other dispatches around the same time noted that Schnaubelt may indeed have visited California but only for a brief time before returning to Rio de Janeiro, where he had been living for some years. A generation later Schnaubelt's relatives confirmed that he lived out his days raising a family and prospering as a successful farm machinery manufacturer, in Buenos Aires, Argentina.[11]

In spite of recent historians' reluctance to credit the fact, the weight of historical evidence presses on the likelihood that the bomber was a member of the inner circle of Chicago anarchists and that Schnaubelt was most likely the perpetrator.[12]

Max Nettlau, a pioneering chronicler of the nineteenth-century anarchist movement, had no doubt that the bomber was an anarchist and an associate of the men tried for the crime. Nettlau, who knew personally most of the leading anarchists of the day, related how in the summer of 1888 he had a conversation with Victor Dave, an internationally renowned "physical force" anarchist of the 1880s. Dave confided in Nettlau that London socialist William Morris had shared with him a letter from Chicago anarchist William Holmes in which Holmes admitted that the accused Chicago anarchists had intended to respond violently to police attempts to break up their meetings. However, one of the men who had agreed to meet the police with bombs left the city on the morning of May 4 to spend the day in the countryside, enjoying life and nature before the battle to come. In the meantime, the earlier plans were changed but word did not reach this man before it was too late. When the police marched up and ordered the crowd to disperse, this individual threw his bomb fully expecting others to do the same.[13]

Unfortunately, no independent confirmation of Dave and Holmes' story can be found. Nettlau did add that he had heard the same story independently from another anarchist, though he admitted that he couldn't be sure this man had not heard it from Dave as well. Similarly, Dyer Lum, a close associate of August Spies and his successor as editor of the *Arbeiter Zeitung*, wrote in 1891 that the bomber was an anarchist who disobeyed his orders not to bring arms to the demonstration. America's most famous anarchist, Emma Goldman, was also reported to have confided to one of her many lovers that the bomber was indeed an anarchist.[14]

In November 1886, Henry Jansen, a member of the anarchist "North Side Group," the same militant cell that Engel and Fischer led, was arrested after attacking his wife. It was the second time he had stabbed her, having slashed her in the stomach years earlier. But this time her wounds were deeper and she lingered near death for four days before succumbing. Weak and struggling for breath, Mrs. Jansen told police that her husband took part in the Haymarket Riot and that he had stood near the man who threw the bomb and had told her the man's name. She couldn't remember the name distinctly but thought it sounded like "Shurbeld."[15]

In 1935, Ernest Zeisler, whose father was Sigmund Zeisler, one of the lawyers who had represented the Haymarket anarchists, met with Dr. Otto Schmidt, whose father was Dr. Ernst Schmidt, a longtime associate of many of the anarchists and the leader of the amnesty and clemency movements on their behalf. They talked about their recently deceased fathers, Zeisler recounting how his father told him that Schmidt's father knew the identity of the Haymarket bomber and that Schmidt had promised to share this secret at some future date, but died before he could reveal the name. The junior Zeisler asked the younger Schmidt if his father had confided the bomber's identity to him and Schmidt replied, "Inasmuch as my father promised your father he would tell him and he did not keep his promise, and the man is undoubtedly dead by now, I think I should tell you. Yes, I will tell you. It was Schnaubelt."[16]

Over time other people with direct knowledge of the event eventually confided their beliefs about the bomber. George Schilling, who was the one labor leader in Chicago who bridged both the trade union and anarchist camps at the time of the eight-hour strikes in 1886 and who took the lead in raising money for the anarchists' legal defense, late in life corresponded with a young librarian then accumulating materials for an archive of anarchism at the University of Michigan. Schilling told her that he believed that Schnaubelt "did the job" and later told historian Henry David the same thing. Chicagoan John F. Kendrick, who was only 12 in 1886 but later was a neighbor of Oscar Neebe who served eight years in Joliet prison for his part in the bombing, told historian Henry David that Neebe emphatically told him that he believed that Schnaubelt threw the bomb.[17]

The Haymarket Bombing and Trial rightfully deserves its place in history as a symbol of its age but not as a simple morality tale of the oppression of labor leaders or the corruption of justice. Undoubtedly Parsons, Spies, Fischer, Engel, Schwab,

Lingg, Fielden, and Neebe were not equally involved in the planning or the actions that unfolded so tragically on May 4, 1886. But among them there were those who the legal system proved to the standards of its day had foreknowledge of the deadly moment and in acts both small and large contributed to its bloody conclusion. Had the anarchists had more competent lawyers and cared less about propounding their ideas, advancing their movement, or securing their legacies, and more about saving their own necks, the judicial outcome may have been different. Stubbornly they trod to their own demise, achieving behind bars and in nooses the impact of the "propaganda by the deed" that had eluded them in freedom. In this sense they were martyrs—men who refused to compromise their principles at all costs.

One of the men who had known the condemned anarchists longest and worked hardest for their freedom, George Schilling, never forgot who the Haymarket anarchists really were, though he shared this knowledge only with fellow movement insiders. Schilling spent a decade publicly claiming that these radicals were bluffers who never seriously believed their own rhetoric about dynamite or about sparking a revolutionary uprising but in a private letter to Lucy Parsons, he dropped all such pretenses and scolded her for continuing to peddle the old slogans of force and murder. "Your agitation conducted at time[s] with great vigor and more than ordinary intellectual power [has] been a wasted force ... The open espousal of physical force—especially when advocated by foreigners as a remedy for social maladjustments can only lead to greater despotism. When you terrorize the public mind and threaten the stability of society with violence, you create the conditions which place the Bonfields and Garys in the saddle, hailed as the savior of society. Fear is not the mother of progress and liberty, but oft times of reaction and aggression." Schilling then remembered whom he was lecturing and summed up the meaning of the Haymarket bombing in a way that rings with sincerity and deep insight:

> At Waldheim sleep five men—among them your beloved husband, who died in the hope that their execution might accelerate the emancipation of the world ... but I do not believe the time will ever come when the judgment of an enlightened world will say that their methods were wise or correct. They worshiped at the shrine of force; wrote it and preached it; until finally they were overpowered by their own Gods and slain in their own temple.[18]

To his confidants Schilling refused to bury the truth that the anarchists were revolutionaries under the gauzy romanticism of their victimization as so many who understood them less well have done for so long.

NOTES

1. Chicago *Times*, May 5, 1886, p. 1; Chicago *Herald*, May 5, 1886, p. 1.
2. Good accounts of the aftermath of the riot can be found in *Chicago Tribune*, May 5–6, 1886, p. 1; *Chicago Herald*, May 5, 1886, p. 1.
3. *Chicago Tribune*, June 14, 1888, p. 2.
4. *Chicago Tribune*, May 4, 1887, p. 3; *Chicago Times*, May 8, 1886, p. 2; May 12, 1886, p. 8. On Daly see *Chicago Inter-Ocean*, May 7, 1892, p. 1; Sept. 30, 1896, p. 4.
5. Even after 125 years of discussion and research about this event, there are still wildly conflicting statements as to the number of people killed or wounded around the Haymarket Square that night. Estimates of casualties among the protesters vary even further, from one civilian killed to a death toll of as many as "fifty or more workers" (James Green, *Taking History to Heart: The Power of the Past in Building Social Movements* (Amherst: Univ. of Massachusetts Press, 2000), p. 121). Both Paul Avrich and Henry David agree that the proper total of deaths on the police side should be seven, though they differ as to the total among civilians. David counts one dead and more than 50 wounded, while Avrich estimates "seven or eight dead and thirty to forty wounded" on the belief that some victims were secretly buried (Henry David, *The History of the Haymarket Affair: A Study in the American Social-Revolutionary and Labor Movements* (New York: Russell & Russell, 1936, 2nd ed., 1958), pp. 206, 234, n. 20; Paul Avrich, *The Haymarket Tragedy* (Princeton, NJ: Princeton Univ. Press, 1984), p. 208). These numbers have since then been recycled endlessly through undergraduate textbooks and general treatments of the era.

   Neither David nor Avrich consulted the authoritative source of information about deaths in Chicago, the Coroner's Records of Inquest, all of which exist for the year 1886. According to these records, a total of three men were killed in the melee following the bombing near the Haymarket Square on May 4: Carl Kiester, who died that night; Mathias Lewis, who lingered until May 9; and Charles Schumacher, who succumbed the day after Lewis (*Coroner's Inquest Records*, Nos. 1557, 1569, 1583 (all 1886), Illinois Regional Archives Depository, Northeastern Illinois University, Chicago).

   In order to arrive at his total of "seven or eight," Avrich counts "four civilians...definitely known to have been killed"; they include Lewis, Kiester, and Schumacher. Emil Lutz, whom he includes as his fourth, was apparently injured, but his shoulder wound did not lead to his death according to the Coroner's records for 1886, or state death certificates. To claim Lutz in his body count, Avrich cites William Adelman's *Haymarket Revisited*, who does state that Lutz was killed but provides no source for this claim other than to mention that Lutz's death was "verified by death certificates," which is not true (Adelman, *Haymarket Revisited*, p. 38). None of the death records of the state of Illinois list an "Emil Lutz" or any variant spelling of that name (see *Pre–1916 Illinois Statewide Death Index*, Illinois Regional Archives Depository). Adelman may have mistaken Emil Lutz for Nelson Lutz, a different man, who did die in July 1886 of causes not related to the riot. (*Chicago Tribune*, July 15, 1886, p. 2.) To this already shaky total,

Avrich adds Reinhold Krueger, who was shot to death in a police shootout in a saloon the day after the Haymarket Riot. He then adds an "unidentified Bohemian . . . who was killed in the affray" but fails to mention that this man was only unidentified by the initial press reports and was later revealed to be Kiester. Of Avrich's total count of the dead, one is a man who was injured but did not die, another is a man who was killed the following day in a different place, and a third is a man counted twice. (Avrich, p. 210.) Even with this degree of padding, Avrich is still left a few bodies short of his total of "seven or eight." To fill the gap, Avrich then claims that the exact number of civilian dead cannot be known because many of the victims were secretly buried out of fear of arrest. To sustain this claim Avrich relies not on a primary source, but on an unattributed rumor mentioned in Harry Barnard's *Eagle Forgotten: The Life of John Peter Altgeld* published in 1938. Indeed, in this highly readable account of the Haymarket drama, Barnard does refer to rumors of secret burials, but writes, "The story was that many of the civilians were killed but 'the anarchists stole their dead away and buried the bodies secretly.' This probably was not true." (Avrich, p. 210. Harry Barnard, *"Eagle Forgotten": The Life of John Peter Altgeld* (New York: Bobbs-Merrill Co., 1938), p. 106.)

While it was certainly possible for individuals to be secretly buried in 1886, even in established cemeteries (as some cemeteries would inter bodies on the strength of a physician's certificate and not a permit from the health department), it is highly unlikely that this was done in the wake of the Haymarket episode for two reasons. First, considering the intense media focus on the case, with all manner of rumors printed first and retracted later, and the number of people who would have had to be part of such a midnight burial, the fact that no such burials were reported, even as a "newspaper yarn," or evidence for them turned up in the 125 years since, strongly suggests that none occurred. (See *Chicago Tribune* article on "newspaper yarns" about the Haymarket case, May 12, 1886.) Second, and more importantly, those individuals who were most seriously wounded were also least able to flee from the police. In order for anyone to escape that night, they had to outrun the police for a distance of at least three blocks within a few minutes after the blast; police reinforcements secured an area three blocks in radius from the point of the blast. Most of the citizens who were most gravely injured lay in the street until picked up by police after the riot. For example, Charles Schumaker, the young tailor who lingered a week until succumbing to an infection of the heart, lay in the street near the speaker's wagon for half an hour before being picked up by Officer John O'Dowd and carried back to the Desplaines street station, which, by that time, was filled with injured rioters unable to flee the area. (*Chicago Tribune*, May 13, 1886, p. 2.)

If we wish to apply normal standards of scholarship to this incident, then we must conclude that in addition to the seven police officers slain that night (as well as the one who died a year later of complications arising from his injuries), there were three citizens, Carl Kiester, Mathias Lewis, and Charles Schumacher, who were shot and killed. Several dozen other citizens were wounded.

6. Robert W. Glenn, *The Haymarket Affair: An Annotated Bibliography* (Westport, CO: Greenwood Press, 1993).

7. Joseph R. Conlin, *The American Past: A Survey of American History*, vol. 2 (Boston: Wadsworth Publishers, 9th ed., 2009), p. 453.

8. G.L. Doebler, "The Contest for Memory: Haymarket through a Revisionist Looking Glass," *Fifth Estate*, #352 (Winter 1999), pp. 3–8.

9. *The New York Times*, Sept. 15, 2004, p. 16.

10. David, 541.

11. Avrich, 456.

12. James Green, *Death in the Haymarket: A Story of Chicago, the First Labor Movement and the Bombing that Divided Gilded Age America* (New York: Pantheon Books, 2006), pp. 10, 12.

13. Foster Rhea Dulles and Melvyn Dubofsky, *Labor in America: A History* (Harlan Davidson, 4th ed., 1984), p. 118.
14. *In the Supreme Court of Illinois, Northern Grand Division, March Term, A.D. 1887. August Spies et al., vs. The People of the State of Illinois. Abstract of Record*, 2 vols., Chicago, 1887.
15. Avrich notes in his bibliography, "The Chicago Historical Society houses a rich collection ... [including] a complete transcript of the trial, of which the *Abstract of Record* is a two-volume abridgement" (p. 517). However, none of his footnotes reference the full transcript, only the *Abstract of Record*. William P. Black, Moses Salomon, and Sigmund Zeisler, eds. *Abstract of Record* (Chicago: Barnard & Gunthorp, 1887). Volume 1 deals with procedural motions, jury selection, and evidence. Volume 2 contains excerpts and abridgements of trial testimony.

CHAPTER 1

1. Keith Inman and Norah Rudin, *Principles and Practice of Forensic Science: The Profession of Forensic Science* (Boca Ratan, NJ: CRC Press, 2001), Appendix A.
2. *Chicago Journal*, May 5, 1886, p. 1.
3. *Chicago Mail*, May 5, 1886 (11 A.M. edition), p. 1; *Chicago News*, May 5, 1886, p. 1.
4. *Chicago Tribune*, May 5, 1886, p. 1; *Chicago Mail*, May 5, 1886 (10 A.M. edition), p. 1.
5. *Chicago Tribune*, May 6, 1886, p. 1.
6. Philip S. Foner, ed., *The Autobiographies of the Haymarket Martyrs* (New York: Humanities Press, 1969), pp. 131–160; *Chicago Tribune*, Aug. 11, 1886, p. 1.
7. Testimony of James Bonfield, Haymarket Affair Digital Collection (HADC), Chicago Historical Society, Vol. I, pp. 361–362, 458–459.
8. *Chicago Tribune*, May 7, 1886, p. 2.
9. Paul Avrich, *The Haymarket Tragedy* (Princeton, NJ: Princeton Univ. Press, 1984), p. 123; Foner, p. 67.
10. Details of Spies family can be found at U.S. Census for 1880, Series T9, Roll 196, p. 382, subpage B.
11. For insight into the schisms within the SLP see Thomas Morgan to NEC, July 19, 1880, Morgan to Van Patten, July 20, 1880, M. Schalck to NEC, Aug. 4, 1880, Incoming Correspondence, Records of the Socialist Labor Party of America, State Historical Society of Wisconsin. See also Mark A. Lause, *The Civil War's Last Campaign: James B. Weaver, the Greenback-Labor Party & the Politics of Race and Section* (Lanham, MD: Univ. Press of America, 2001).
12. Admittedly, this summary of the origins of Chicago anarchism is far too cursory. For a fuller treatment, see my *The Haymarket Conspiracy: Transatlantic Anarchist Networks* (Champaign Urbana: Univ. of Illinois Press, 2012).
13. *Chicago Tribune*, July 21, 1884, p. 5; July 26, 1884, p. 8; Aug. 1, 1884, p. 8.
14. *Chicago Tribune*, May 7, 1886, p. 2; Dyer Lum, "Pen-Pictures of the Prisoners," *Liberty*, Feb. 12, 1887, p. 1.
15. Elliot J. Kanter, "Class, Ethnicity, and Socialist Politics: St. Louis, 1876–1881," *UCLA Historical Journal*, 3 (1982), pp. 36–60.
16. *Chicago Tribune*, Nov. 14, 1887, p. 2. Interestingly, aside from one brief mention in his autobiographical sketch, Fischer was mute about his time in St. Louis, a fact that is remarkable because he actually spent the majority of his life in America in that city. Fischer steamed to America in 1873. He and his brother moved to St. Louis in time for the great railroad strikes of 1877 and then lived in that city for another six years before moving on. It was clearly the place he was most attached to as when he last met with his friend William Holmes in his jail cell just a month prior to his scheduled execution, both men suspecting that this would be the last time they would ever see each other, his friends

in St. Louis were all Fischer wanted to talk about. As Holmes recalled later: "Comrade Fischer took me to one side, and with his face close to the meshes of the 'cage' he talked to me of his former home in St. Louis and gave me his last message to his comrades whom I should find there. "Tell them," he said, "that I gladly die for my principles. Tell them that I shall not falter or hesitate; that they must not weep for me or mourn me dead, but that they must carry on the good work, and be prepared, if necessary, also to give up their lives for our great cause." " William Holmes, *Free Society*, Nov. 6, 1898, quoted in *Haymarket Scrapbook*, p. 41.

17. Foner, pp. 74–75; Avrich, pp. 151–153; Kanter, "Class, Ethnicity, and Socialist Politics," pp. 36–60.
18. Dyer Lum, "Pen-Pictures of the Prisioners," *Liberty*, Feb. 12, 1887, p. 1.
19. Testimony of James Bonfield, HADC, Vol. I, pp. 347, 366–367, 378, 453–454. *Chicago Tribune*, May 6, 1886, p. 2; Testimony of John Aschenbrenner, HADC, Vol. J, pp. 351–352.
20. Testimony of James Bonfield, HADC, Vol. I, pp. 347, 366–367, 378, 453–454; *Chicago Tribune*, May 6, 1886, p. 2.
21. Max J. Kohler, "Admissibility of Evidence Illegally Obtained," *The Albany Law Journal*, Sept. 30, 1899, p. 205.
22. See David J. Bodenhammer, *Fair Trial: Rights of the Accused in American History* (New York: Oxford Univ. Press, 1992). Samuel Dash, *The Intruders: Unreasonable Search and Seizures from King John to John Ashcroft* (New Brunswick, N.J.: Rutgers Univ. Press, 2004). Erwin N. Griswald, *Search and Seizure: A Dilemma of the Supreme Court* (Lincoln: Univ. of Nebraska Press, 1975). Testimony of Edmund Furthmann, HADC, Vol. I, pp. 498–499. The only time between the famous Boyd case of 1886 and the Weeks decision in 1914 that the issue even came up before the U.S. Supreme Court, was in the anarchists' case.
23. *Chicago Times*, May 6, 1886, p. 1; Testimony of Bartholemew Flynn, HADC, Vol. J, p. 120, Testimony of August Spies, HADC, Vol. N, p. 66. Paul Avrich omits any mention of the explosives found in Spies' desk, though he describes the search itself and some other objects seized: "Spies's locked desk was broken open and emptied of its contents. Copies of the 'Revenge Circular' were found, as well as of the circular summoning the Haymarket meting" (p. 226). Later, when describing some of the evidence introduced at the trial, Avrich makes use of his earlier omission: "In a further effort to inflame the emotions of the jury, the state exhibited bombs, fulminating caps, shells, melting-ladles, and other paraphernalia of the dynamiter's craft, although they had not been traced to any of the defendants . . . " (p. 276). Likewise, Henry David also chose not to detail the evidence gathered at the Socialistic Publishing Company offices, saying only that "bombs were discovered all over Chicago . . . Most of the bombs were either non-existent or had been planted by the police . . . " David provides no sources or citations to support his assertion that any evidence was "planted" by the police (Henry David, *The History of the Haymarket Affair: A Study in the American Social-Revolutionary and Labor Movements* (New York: Russell & Russell, 1958, org. 1936), pp. 222–223). James Green vaguely indicates that some sort of bomb making materials were found: " . . . the police searched the *Arbeiter-Zeitung* office, where they found 100 copies of the call for the Haymarket meeting, and in the room adjoining Spies's office they seized some material they believed was to be made into bombs" (James Green, *Death in the Haymarket: A Story of Chicago, The First Labor Movement, and the Bombing that Divided Gilded Age America* (New York: Pantheon Books, 2006), p. 195).
24. Testimony of James Bonfield, HADC, Vol. I, pp. 355–356, Testimony of John D. Shea, HADC, Vol. J, pp. 51, Testimony of William Jones, HADC, Vol. J, pp. 92–93, Testimony of James Duffy, HADC, Vol. J, pp. 107–108, Testimony of Louis Haas, HADC, Vol. J, pp. 269–270; *Chicago Times*, May 6, 1886, p. 1. The first issue of the *Arbeiter Zeitung* to appear after the bombing carried a curiously tepid denial that dynamite was actually

found in its offices. "It is claimed that in the office of the *Arbeiter Zeitung* dynamite was found; but this claim seems to be untrue, as after the arrest of the editors the building was thoroughly searched and nothing was found. A short time afterward the police appeared again, arrested the whole force of compositors down to the proof boys, and also found dynamite" (Translation from *Chicago Times*, May 8, 1886, p. 2).

25. *Chicago Times*, May 6, 1886, p. 1; Dyer Lum, "Pen-Pictures of the Prisioners," *Liberty*, Feb. 12, 1887, p. 1.

26. Testimony of Fred L. Buck, HADC, Vol. J, pp. 75–76, Testimony of Timothy McKeough, HADC, Vol. J, pp.115–116.

27. Paul Avrich writes, "In two days more than fifty gathering places of anarchists and social-ists were raided ... " Even assuming that not all locations searched were listed in the newspapers, a thorough examination of the daily papers turns up a total of 17 places that were raided on May 5 and May 6. The total from May 5 through May 8 is 27 (Avrich, p. 221). Avrich also quotes State's Attorney Grinnell as encouraging police law-lessness. Here is Avrich's text: "In two days more than fifty gathering places of anarchists and socialists were raided and persons under the slightest suspicion of radical affiliation arrested, in most cases without warrant and with no specific charges lodged against them. 'Make the raids first and look up the law afterward!' counseled Julius S. Grinnell, the state's attorney for Cook County, who was to prosecute the anarchists' case" (Avrich, p. 221). Avrich cites the May 6 edition of the *Chicago Times* as his source for Grinnell's dramatic statement. But this issue of the *Times* carries no such remarks. The only reference close to this is a report of what Grinnell told the police officers who had summoned him before searching the *Arbeiter Zeitung* offices: "The attorney told the officers to make the raid first and they could look up the legal points afterward; that the search was a lawful one he had no doubt." Grinnell was not offering a blanket encouragement for raids throughout the city, but offering his legal judgment about the raid on these particular offices.

28. *Chicago Herald*, May 6, 1886, p. 1; Testimony of William Jones, HADC, Vol. J, pp. 94–95.

29. *Chicago Journal*, May 5, 1886, p. 1.

30. Melville E. Stone, *Fifty Years a Journalist* (Garden City, New York: Doubleday, Page & Co., 1922), p. 173. *Chicago Tribune*, May 6, 1886, p. 1. Both Paul Avrich and James Green greatly exaggerate the role of Melville Stone, editor of the *Chicago Daily News*, in crafting the prosecution's legal strategy. Avrich writes, "Before the trial, he had dis-cussed with friends and associates the difficulty of proceeding against accessories when the principal had not been identified or apprehended. Among those with whom he had consulted was Melville E. Stone ... " (Avrich, p. 275). Green goes even further, writing, " ... Grinnell had been reluctant to try the defendants for homicide without charg-ing someone with actually committing the murder. However, the newspaper publisher Melville E. Stone met privately with the state's attorney and convinced him to take the case to trial anyway ... " (Green, p. 215). In fact, neither did Stone claim to have met "pri-vately" with Grinnell, nor did he claim to have given Grinnell advice on how to proceed to trial.

31. *Chicago Tribune*, May 6, 1886, p. 1; *Chicago News*, May 7, 1886, p. 1. Lum calls it a "suspicious omission" that a man by the name of Brazelton, though listed on the prosecution's list of witnesses who testified before the grand jury, was not produced at the trial. Brazelton, Lum asserted, was an important witness who could have confirmed Thompson's account of his movements around the Haymarket prior to the rally. But this not only overestimates Brazelton's value (all he would have testified to is that Thompson was where he said he was) but ignores other reasons why the prosecution may have hesitated to put him on the stand. Of all the reporters interviewed by the Grand Jury, Brazelton was the only one who thought it possible that the police had fired first after the bomb exploded. Lum, p. 157; *Chicago Tribune*, May 20, 1886, p. 2.

32. *Chicago Times*, May 6, 1886, p. 4.
33. *Chicago News*, May 7, 1886, p. 1.
34. *Chicago Tribune*, Dec. 11, 1887, p. 25. Snyder confirmed some of this story in his testimony for the defense. He mentioned leaving the note at Lucy Parsons' home and being confronted with it at the Central Police Station. Testimony of William Snyder, HADC, Vol. M, pp. 113–114.
35. *Chicago Tribune*, Dec. 11, 1887, p. 25.
36. Michael J. Schaack, *Anarchy and Anarchists* (Chicago: F.J. Schulz & Co., 1889), p. 175; *Chicago Tribune*, June 5, 1886, p. 6; Jan. 8, 1888, p. 15.
37. *Brooklyn Eagle*, May 9, 1886, p. 9.
38. Foner, pp. 93–98. Avrich, pp. 153–156. *Alarm*, Jan. 28, 1888, p. 3.
39. *Chicago Tribune*, May 7, 1886, p. 2.
40. Testimony of Herman Schuettler, HADC, Vol. K, pp. 517–528, Testimony of Jacob Lowenstein, HADC, Vol. K, pp. 529–547; *Chicago Times*, May 16, 1886, p. 6. Details of the discovery of the bolt on Desplaines street are in *Chicago Tribune*, May 6, 1886, p. 1.
41. *Chicago Tribune*, May 8, pp. 1–2; Schaack, pp. 246–247.
42. Fremont O. Bennett, *Politics and Politicians of Chicago, Cook County, and Illinois* (Chicago: The Blakely Printing Co., 1886), p. 463; Schaack, pp. 249–250. Schaack's account of Thielen's arrest differs from Bennett's in that he claims that Thielen was caught spying on the Larrabee street station. Testimony of Michael Hoffman, HADC, Vol. K, p. 583; Testimony of Michael Schaack, HADC, Vol. K, pp. 592, 601.
43. Testimony of Herman Schuettler HADC, Vol. K, pp. 516–517; Testimony of Jacob Lowenstein, HADC, Vol. K, pp. 530–531. Schuettler and Lowenstein had slightly different accounts of the way Lingg phrased his appeal to them to kill him. I've combined them in this quote rather than giving each separately.
44. *Chicago Tribune*, May 20, 1886, p. 2.
45. Foner, pp. 176–177.
46. *Illinois Staats-Zeitung*, Mar. 2, 1886, p. 4. According to one of the officers of this union Henry Witt, who later testified for the defense at the Haymarket trial, the German "lumber shovers' union" was first organized on April 4 at a small meeting on the southwest side whose main speaker was none other than the militant anarchist Louis Lingg. Testimony of Henry Witt, HADC, Vol. M, p. 220. The organizing meeting was held in a "Mr. Letker's saloon" located on the corner of Blue Island avenue and 20th street (five blocks from where the lumber rally of May 3 took place and the same distance in the opposite direction from where Witt lived). Frederick Breest, the recording secretary of this union, also testified that the German lumber shovers' union had existed only since April 4, though his answer as to where it held its meeting is confused, saying the April 4 meeting was held at "Blue Island Avenue, 550, Greif's Hall." Greif's Hall is located miles away from Blue Island avenue at the corner of Clinton and Lake. Testimony of Henry Witt, HADC, Vol. M, pp. 218, 224, Testimony of Frederick Breest, HADC, Vol. M, p. 232.
47. Testimony of Michael Hoffman, HADC, Vol. K, pp. 581–583.
48. Testimony of Michael Schaack, HADC, Vol. K, pp. 599–605.
49. Testimony of Frederick Drews, HADC, Vol. K, pp. 634–636; *Chicago Tribune*, July 31, 1886, p. 1; Testimony of Michael Whalen, HADC, Vol. K, pp. 636–640.
50. Testimony of Thomas McNamara, HADC, Vol. K, pp. 661–664.
51. Gustav Lehman, an anarchist and a union brother of Lingg, testified that Lingg gave him three bombs, an assortment of fuses, and a full tin of dynamite and told him to hide them on May 4, prior to the riot. That two witnesses both swore to this fact would seem to strongly connect these bombs to Lingg; however, some doubt creeps in because of a discrepancy in their testimony. The bomb found by fireman Miller was also tied to Lingg by one of the trial's most important witnesses, William Seliger, who claimed to have helped Lingg make bombs. Indeed, Seliger described how, on the day of the Haymarket Riot, he

laboriously drilled the bolt holes through the top and bottom halves of the bombs. Seliger testified that after the riot he saw Lingg discard one of his bombs under the sidewalk on Siegel street. Testimony of William Seliger, HADC, Vol. I, pp. 514–516, 529.

52. John H. Dodson, "Walter Stanley Haines," *Bulletin of the Society of the Medical History of Chicago*, 3:2 (Oct. 1923), pp. 271–276. *Chicago Tribune*, Mar. 15, 1871, p. 3.

53. In the court, Haines and Delafontaine testified as to the percentages of tin, explaining that the rest of the sample was lead with other traces. They found that the four samples they took from a bomb linked to Lingg contained mostly lead, with significant amounts of tin and traces of antinomy, zinc, and in one case, copper. Only the tin content was quantitatively measured, and this was found to vary in the four samples from 1.9 to slightly less than 7 percent of the total. The other trace metals, each, were estimated to constitute less than 1 percent of the sample. Testimony of Walter S. Haines, HADC, Vol. K, pp. 670–671.

54. It is unclear from the court records whether "Officer Murphy" was Lawrence Murphy, who sustained wounds to his neck, leg, and foot, or whether it was Bernard Murphy, who sustained wounds to his thigh, head, and chin. Most likely, it was Lawrence Murphy as his foot was amputated—the police captain heading the investigation recorded that a large piece of shell, "two inches square," was taken from his leg. Schaack, pp. 152–155.

55. Howard E. Boyer and Timothy L. Gall, eds., *Metals Handbook: Desk Edition* (Metals Park, Ohio: American Society for Metals, 1985), sec. 12, p. 1.

56. The *Tribune* later reported that a short time prior to the labor strikes of May 1886, the *Arbeiter Zeitung* purchased a new "dress" of type from the Barnhart Brothers. It attempted to sell its old type, which had also been made by the Barnhart Brothers, but the amount offered was so puny that it declined and simply dumped the old type into a box in its office. The *Tribune* noted that the chemical composition reported by the chemists consulted in the Haymarket bombing case was the "identical combination of metals used by their [the Barnhart Brothers] foundry" (*Chicago Tribune*, Nov. 10, 1887, p. 3).

57. *Chicago News*, May 22, 1886, p. 1; Testimony of James Bonfield, HADC, Vol. I, pp. 375, 379. Paul Avrich alleges that police routinely beat confessions out of their radical prisoners. Avrich writes, "Detectives at the central station . . . conducted a 'sweating shop' without precedent in Chicago history, employing methods, in Lucy Parsons' words, that 'would put to shame the most zealous Russian blood-hound.' Prisoners were beaten, sworn at, threatened, and subjected to 'indignities that must be seen to be believed' " (p. 221). Avrich provides two sources for this extravagant claim: an article written by Lucy Parsons and published in the May 17, 1886, edition of the Denver *Labor Enquirer* and the brief memoir of anarchist lawyer Sigmund Zeisler ("Reminiscences of the Anarchist Case," *Illinois Law Review*, 21:3 (Nov. 1926), pp. 224–250).

In the May 22, 1886, edition of the *Labor Enquirer* (Denver), Lucy Parsons wrote, "Since that date a reign of terror has been inaugurated which would put to shame the most zealous Russian blood hound." She then listed the terrors meted out in those days of rage: the suspension of radical newspapers, the searching of private homes, and the subjection of their occupants to "indignities that must be seen to be believed." Parsons did not make any claims that prisoners held by the police were tortured or confessions beaten out of them, only that people whose homes were invaded by the police suffered unspecified abuses. She goes on to denounce the "indignities" she suffered after her arrest, but keeps the details of them to herself.

Sigmund Zeisler, who was one of the lawyers for the anarchists, wrote the following in his reminiscences 40 years after the event: "Captain Michael Schaack, in charge of the Chicago Avenue Police Station . . . in conjunction with Assistant State's Attorney Edmund Furthmann . . . conducted a sweating shop at his police station." The term "sweating" generally refers to the intense and prolonged interrogation of a prisoner. Zeisler did not use the common term "third degree" or some other reference to the practice of beating confessions out of prisoners that had become common in the early twentieth century. None of the anarchist defendants in their testimony, affidavits, appeals, or posttrial memoirs alleged physical mistreatment at the hands of their captors.

Avrich also repeats the claims of two men, Vaclav Djenek (Avrich incorrectly lists his name as "Djemek") and Jacob Mikolanda, who said that they were beaten while in police custody. Avrich states as a fact that "Djemek" was "kicked, cursed, and threatened with hanging." Likewise, Avrich writes that Mikolanda was "dragged" from a saloon to his home, which was ransacked. In jail, Mikolanda said, he was promised a job and money for his testimony and was then held "for a prolonged period before being released for lack of evidence" (Avrich, p. 222). However, there is more to the story than Avrich lets on. First, Djenek and Mikolanda's charges were not made in 1886, but in affidavits they were solicited to produce by Governor Altgeld's staff in 1893 as part of their drafting of his pardon message. Also, it worth noting that both Djenek and Mikolanda were participants in the McCormick riot, Mikolanda later prosecuted for "intent to do bodily harm" to a police officer and Djenek for "assault with a deadly weapon with intent to commit murder" (John Peter Altgeld, *Reasons for Pardoning Fielden, Neebe, and Schwab* (Springfield, IL: n.p., 1893), pp. 53–54; *Chicago Tribune*, Sep. 25, 1886, p. 7; Dec. 18, 1886, p. 8; Schaack, p. 128; *Chicago Times*, May 11, p. 1).

Charles Siringo, the "cowboy detective" who wrote a series of exposes of the Pinkerton agency beginning in 1912, began his detective career in Chicago about the time of Haymarket. Siringo claimed that a former Pinkerton he met in Denver said that other men told him that Rudolph Schnaubelt, the presumed bomber, never fled the city as supposed but was actually accidentally murdered by police while being put through the "third degree" and his body disposed of. There is no further evidence to support Siringo's third-hand account. Charles A. Siringo, *Two Evil Isms: Pinkertonism and Anarchism* (Chicago, 1915; reproduced by Steck-Vaughn Co., Austin, Texas, 1967), p. 6.

58. Testimony of Godfried Waller, HADC, Vol. I, pp. 123–124, Testimony of William Seliger, HADC, Vol. I, pp. 543–544.

59. *The Accused, the Accusers: The Famous Speeches of the Eight Chicago Anarchists*... (Chicago, IL: Socialistic Publishing Society, 1886), pp. 1–2; also reprinted in Lucy Parsons, *Famous Speeches of the Eight Chicago Anarchists* (Arno Press, 1969, org. 1910), p. 11.

60. On Folz's Hall, *Chicago Tribune*, Feb. 1, 1910, p. 12. On Schoeninger, see *Chicago Tribune*, Nov. 1, 1893, p. 21, Dec. 14, 1900, p. 5. On Nettlehorst, see Steven A. Riess and Gerald R. Gems, eds., *Chicago Sports Reader: 100 Years of Sport in the Windy City* (Urbana: Univ. of Illinois Press, 2009), p. 3; *Chicago Tribune*, May 20, 1888, p. 11, June 28, 1888, p. 3; Testimony of Godfried Waller, HADC, Vol. I, pp. 126–129, 134–135.

61. Testimony of Godfried Waller, HADC, Vol. I, p. 137; *Der Fackel*, May 16, 1886, p. 8.

62. Testimony of William Seliger, HADC, Vol. I, pp. 550, 577–578.

63. Schaack, pp. 231–234.

64. One of the reasons Schaack's book has been overlooked by historians is a false story implicating him and the other Haymarket investigators in a corruption scandal. Henry David established this myth on the basis of a very selective use of sources, concluding, "In 1888–1889, leading officers of the department were accused of corrupt practices, and in 1888 Ebersold was removed from the force. A year later, three officers, Captains Bonfield and Schaack included, were suspended." David cites only *The Alarm* for Feb. 25, 1888, and an obscure clipping from an even more ephemeral paper, the *Ohio Valley Budget*, for Feb. 9 (David, p. 485, esp. note 504). While the Chicago police were no strangers to accusations of corruption, it is not true that Ebersold was removed in 1888. Ebersold retired and drew his pension in 1891.

Paul Avrich wisely chose not to repeat David's mistake about Ebersold but fabricates an equally spurious account of corruption charges that swirled around Bonfield and

Schaack in 1889, claiming that both Bonfield and Schaack were dismissed in disgrace from the police force after an investigation found them taking payoffs, including stolen goods. "Following the investigation, Bonfield and Schaack were both cashiered in disgrace" (Avrich, pp. 415–416). In support of this claim, Avrich cites the autobiography of Henry Demarest Lloyd, Browne's biography of John Peter Altgeld, William Adelman's guidebook to anarchist Chicago, Ashbaugh's biography of Lucy Parsons, and issues of the *Chicago Times* for Jan. 5 and 15, 1889, as well as of *The Alarm* for Jan. 12 (Avrich, p. 510). Had Avrich consulted a wider array of sources he would have discovered that neither Bonfield nor Schaack was "cashiered" but that both were in fact cleared of all charges. Moreover, these charges never included general charges of graft or racketeering. It is true that Bonfield did resign and start his own successful detective agency, though it appears he did so for the usual political reasons that rendered his position a continual rotation of nepotism. Schaack never resigned or retired, but instead was promoted to inspector and died in uniform of pneumonia in 1898 (on Schaack see *Chicago Tribune*, Apr. 16, 1889, p. 7, and May 19, 1898, p. 4; on Bonfield see Oct. 20, 1898, p. 7).

Most recently, James Green regurgitated Avrich's errors nearly verbatim: " . . . a scandal that broke in 1889 when Captain Schaack was removed from the Chicago police force as a result of wrongdoing. The case also involved Inspector John Bonfield and two other commanders of the divisions that marched into the Haymarket on May 4" (Green, pp. 282–283).

65. For instance, the statement of Ernst Huber concludes: "This statement I make of my own free will and accord in the presence of the officers named, and it is true and correct. And I furthermore will say that I will not take any bribe to change my statement or make denials; neither will I leave the city or the State as long as this case is pending in court, unless I have the consent of Capt Schaack; that I always will be ready to give testimony for the people, whenever I am called on in this case, and that I will never make a second statement, that is to say, to a notary public or a justice of the peace, in writing or verbally; that I will only make a statement under oath for the grand jury of the Criminal Court, or Capt MJ Schaack" (Michael Schaack, *Anarchy and Anarchists* (Chicago: F.J. Schulte & Co., 1889), p. 282).

66. Carl Smith first pointed out the likelihood that Schaack's book was ghostwritten. Carl S. Smith, *Urban Disorder and the Shape of Belief* (Chicago: Univ. of Chicago Press, 1995), ft. 13, p. 333. McEnnis was also said to be the clever publicist who invented the famed "Abbott Kiss," where he wrote a report that the leading lady Emma Abbott, during the third act of her performance of "Paul and Virginia," lustily kissed the tenor full on mouth to mouth, scandalizing the audience and selling many newspapers. John Joseph Jennings, *Theatrical and Circus Life* (St. Louis: Sun Publishing, 1883), p. 303; on the "Abbott Kiss" see James W. Morrissey, *Noted Men and Women* (New York: Klebold Press, 1910), pp. 62–63. Fellow newspaper man Frank M. Gilbert called McEnnis "a splendid writer and thorough newspaper man in every sense of the word." Frank M. Gilbert, *City of Evansville and Vanderburg County Indiana* (Chicago: Pioneer Publishing Company, 1910), vol. 1, p. 248.

67. Walter Barlow Stevens, *St. Louis: The Fourth City, 1764–1911* (St. Louis: S.J. Clarke Co., 1911), p. 185.Theodore Dreiser, *Newspaper Days: An Autobiography*, T.D. Nostwich, ed. (Philadelphia: Univ. of Pennsylvania Press, 1991), p. 86; *Chicago Tribune*, July 21, 1896, p. 5.

68. John T. McEnnis, *The Clan-Na-Gael and the Murder of Dr. Cronin* (San Francisco: G.P. Woodward, 1889); John T. McEnnis, *The White Slaves of Free America, Being an Account of the Suffering, Privations, and Hardships of the Weary Toilers in Our Great Cities* (Chicago: R.S. Peale & Co., 1888); Thomas O. Thompson, "The Tariff, Its Use and Abuse" (1884), available in *Pamphlets in American History*, Tariffs, T 336 (Sanford, N.C.: Microfilming Corp. of America, 1979).

69. John Cameron Simonds and John T. McEnnis, *The Story of Manual Labor In All Lands and Ages* (Chicago: R.S. Peale & Co., 1887), p. 466.

70. Ibid., p. 649. Curiously, McEnnis does not mention the Haymarket bombing though he has several chapters that deal with the 1886 strikes. In fact, his book on labor is notable for its studious avoidance of discussions of socialism or anarchism. Only Terence Powderly in his essay "Strikes and Arbitration" mentions anarchism in venturing a theory that might very well have been written about the events in Chicago in the spring of 1886:

> Until recently very few workingmen dared to express their opinion in public on the subject of labor, for the reason that they were almost certain of an immediate dismissal from the service of the man or company they worked for, if it became known that they in any way favored the association of workingmen for mutual protection. With such a sentiment existing in the breasts of workingmen they could not be expected to feel very kindly toward the employer who so jealously watched their every movement, and who, by his actions, made them feel that they were regarded rather as serfs than freemen. While the real bone and sinew of the land remained in enforced silence, except where it could be heard through the medium of the press and rostrum, through chosen leaders, another class of men who seldom worked would insist on "representing labor," and in making glowing speeches on the rights and wrongs of man, would urge the "abolition of property," or the "equal division of wealth;" such speakers very often suggesting that a good thing to do would be to "hang capitalists to lamp posts." The employer of labor who listened to such speeches felt that in suppressing organization among his workmen he was performing a laudable act. Yet he was by that means proving himself to be the most powerful ally the anarchist could wish for. He caused his employees to feel that he took no interest in them other than to get as many hours of toil out of them for as few shillings as possible. The consequence was that the employer, who was himself responsible for the smothering of the honest expression of opinion on the part of labor, became possessed of the idea that the raw-head-and-bloody-bones curb-stone orator was the real representative of labor, and determined to exercise more vigilance and precaution than ever in keeping his "help" out of the labor society. The speaker who hinted at or advocated the destruction of property or the hanging of capitalists to lamp posts, was shrewd enough to speak very kindly, and in a knowing manner, of labor associations, giving out the impression that he held membership in one or more of them. Workingmen who were denied the right to organize, very frequently went to hear Mr. Scientific lecture on the best means of handling dynamite. And when the speaker portrayed the wrongs of labor, the thoughtful workman could readily trace a resemblance between the employer painted by the lecturer and the man he himself worked for. Workmen employed by those who frowned on labor organizations became sullen and morose; they saw in every action of the superintendent another innovation on their rights and they finally determined to throw off the yoke of oppression, organize and assert their manhood. The actions of the superintendent, or boss, very often tended to widen the breach between employer and employé . . . Not being drilled in organization, and feeling that the employer would not treat with them, the only remedy suggesting itself was the strike . . . Thus we find the organization in its infancy face to face with a strike or lockout.

T.V. Powderly, "Strikes and Arbitration," in Simonds and McEnnis, *The Story of Manual Labor In All Lands and Ages* (Chicago: R.S. Peale & Co., 1887), pp. ix–x.

71. Schaack, p. 358; Testimony of Johann Gruenberg, HADC, Vol. M, pp. 257–263. Gruenberg was called by the defense to testify to having been sent to Warner and Kline's printing office the morning of the riot to retrieve the Haymarket handbills that included the words "Workingmen Arm Yourselves and Appear in Full Force" and order the printer

to strike this line from the remainder of the print run. Gruenberg's story is suspicious as he was not an employee of the *Arbeiter Zeitung*. The usual practice of the paper seemed to be to send its own workers on such errands. On Monday evening, the day before, when the "Revenge Circular" was printed, a young employee of the paper ran the form over to the printers, according to George Schuler (Testimony of George Schuler, HADC, Vol. J, pp. 290–291, Testimony of August Goeke, HADC, Vol. J, pp. 389–393). August Spies could not even recall his name when asked about him on the witness stand, even though he had testified just two days earlier: "Greunberg or Gruenbog—I don't know which. I have seen the man. I know him but I don't know his name" (Testimony of August Spies, HADC, Vol. N, pp. 32–33). During his testimony, Gruenberg stumbled over a key point. Prosecutor Ingham asked him "Did you see Fischer at the Arbeiter Zeitung Office on Monday or Tuesday the 4th of May?" Gruenberg at first couldn't recall what he had just a moment earlier stated with clarity:

A: Maybe—I can't tell positively.
Q: When was it you saw him there in regard to this circular?
A: Yes, I was mistaken in the day, I was there that day the same day. (HADC, Vol. M, p. 259)

Warner and Kline printer August Kuhn confirmed that someone had ordered the last line to be struck off from the plate that morning, but did not know who it was (Testimony of August Heun, HADC, Vol. K, p. 366).

72. Seliger also says that a third man, "Heumann," was there as well. Testimony of William Seliger, HADC, Vol. I, pp. 512. Schaack, pp. 279–282, 314–316. It is also interesting that Seliger stated from the witness stand that he had given his statement to Inspector Schaack and attorney Furthmann at the Chicago avenue station after having been locked up for a week. Schaack prefaces his transcription of Seliger's jailhouse statement saying that he was present when Seliger confessed his part in the plot (Schaack, *Anarchy and Anarchists*, p. 237.).

73. Schaack, p. 246; Testimony of William Seliger, HADC, Vol. I, pp. 506–546. Captain Schaack's fame and high reputation for having broken the anarchist case took a tumble three years later when one of his detectives, Daniel Coughlin, was discovered to have been involved in the conspiracy and murder of the leader of a rival faction within an Irish secret society. On the witness stand at Coughlin's trial, Schaack admitted to having so trusted his detective that at his urging he ignored certain orders from his superiors and delayed usual steps in the investigation. His reputation in tatters, Schaack was then temporarily suspended from the police force. Ironically, one of the lawyers representing one of the defendants alongside Coughlin was none other than William Foster, who, years before, had defended the anarchists. Henry M. Hunt, *The Crime of the Century: Or, The Assassination of Dr. Patrick Henry Cronin. A Complete and Authentic History of the Greatest of Modern Conspiracies* (Chicago: People's Pub. Co., 1889), p. 239; John T. McEnnis, *The Clan-Na-Gael and the Murder of Dr. Cronin: Being a Complete and Authentic Narrative of the Rise and Development of the Irish Revolutionary Movement* . . . (San Francisco: G.P. Woodward, 1889), p. 290. Coughlin was convicted and sentenced to life in prison in 1889, but in 1893 was granted a new trial on the grounds of two jurors being biased against him, which led to his acquittal. Coughlin followed the usual route of ex-cops in Chicago in those days and opened a saloon and did private detective work for the railroads. Soon, he was indicted for attempting to bribe jurors hearing railroad liability cases and he reportedly skipped the country for Honduras. Thomas Samuel Duke, *Celebrated Criminal Cases of America* (San Francisco: The James H. Barry Company, 1910), p. 418. At the time of the Haymarket case, Coughlin was but a patrolman in Schaack's East Chicago station. M. L. Ahern, *Political History of Chicago* (Chicago: Donohue & Henneberry, 1886), pp. 231–232. William Holmes exaggerated Coughlin's role in the

Haymarket investigation when he predicted that Coughlin's prosecution would reveal great secrets about how Schaack conducted the investigation. " ... many of us hoping that disclosures of great value would be made, and a way opened for us to present the Anarchist case to the people in a new light" *The Commonweal* (London), Jan. 11, 1890, p. 13.

74. David, p. x.

CHAPTER 2

1. Samuel P. McConnell, "The Chicago Bomb Case: Personal Recollections of an American Tragedy," *Harper's Magazine*, May 1934, p. 734.
2. *Chicago Tribune*, Sept. 8, 1882, p. 6.
3. *Chicago Tribune*, May 26, 1886, p. 6; Feb. 17, 1891, p. 7; Nov. 11, 1892, p. 3; Mar. 19, 1897, p. 7; June 5, 1897, p. 2.
4. *Chicago Tribune*, Apr. 6, 1897, p. 5; Jan. 14, 1900, p. 5; Feb. 20, 1900, p. 12; obituary Jan. 4, 1911, p. 2.
5. *Chicago Tribune*, June 5, 1931, p. 7; Jan. 25, 1930, p. 1. Fannie Bloomfield's legend is repeated as late as the 1930s: *Chicago Tribune*, Jan. 1, 1950, p. E4. Zeisler died at age 71. A year and a half before his death, Zeisler married Amelia Spielman, a woman 34 years his junior.
6. *Chicago Tribune*, May 9, 1886, p. 2.
7. Howard Louis Conard, "The Bench and Bar of Chicago, VIII," *Magazine of Western History*, 13:4 (Feb. 1891), p. 483.
8. Sigmund Zeisler, "Reminiscences of the Anarchist Case," *Illinios Law Review*, 21 (Nov. 1926), p. 233.
9. *Chicago Tribune*, May 23, 1886, p. 9. (Note this quote is a reporter's paraphrasing of Zeisler's remarks.)
10. William P. Black did meet with Robert Ingersoll in November 1886 to persuade him to lead the defense in its appeals of the anarchists' convictions. *Chicago Tribune*, Nov. 4, 1886, p. 8.
11. *Chicago Tribune*, May 25, 1886, p. 3; May 28, 1886, p. 3. Sigmund Zeisler, "Reminiscences of the Anarchist Case," *Illinios Law Review*, 21 (Nov. 1926), p. 233.
12. Herman Kogan, *The First Century: The Chicago Bar Association, 1874–1974* (Chicago: Rand McNally, 1974), p. 70.
13. *Chicago Tribune*, May 28, 1886, p. 3.
14. *Chicago Tribune*, May 30, 1886, p. 10; June 1, 1886, p. 5.
15. *Chicago Tribune*, June 11, 1886, p. 8.
16. *Chicago Times*, May 9, 1886, p. 2; *Illinois Stats-Zeitung*, May 12, 1886, p. 4; Virginia G. Drachman, *Sisters in Law: Women Lawyers in Modern American History* (Cambridge, MA: Harvard Univ. Press, 1998), pp. 92–93; *Chicago Legal News*, June 28, 1890; Leila J. Robinson, "Women Lawyers in the United States," *The Green Bag* (Boston), Vol. II, 1890, pp. 10–32; Karen Berger Morello, *The Invisible Bar: The Woman Lawyer in America, 1683 to Present* (New York: Random House, 1986), p. 178; *Chicago Tribune*, Oct. 5, 1886, p. 2.
17. *Chicago Times*, May 12, 1886, p. 8; May 13, 1886, p. 10; May 14, 1886, p. 6.
18. *Chicago Tribune*, May 14, 1886, p. 2; May 16, 1886, p. 9.
19. *Chicago Tribune*, May 11, 1886, p. 2; May 14, 1886, p. 2; May 16, 1886, p. 9.
20. *Chicago Tribune*, May 13, 1886, p. 2.
21. Paul Avrich hints at Black's leanings toward anarchism, but downplays them. He notes that Black was "vaguely liberal in outlook" and that he "had become interested in socialism ... though he was far from being 'a deep student' of their ideas ... " (Paul Avrich, *The Haymarket Tragedy* (Princeton, NJ: Princeton Univ. Press, 1984), p. 250). Henry

David likewise writes that Black "had an earlier interest in Socialism" and was "a man of liberal tendencies . . . he fervidly believed in an ideal justice" (Henry David, *The History of the Haymarket Affair: A Study in the American Social-Revolutionary and Labor Movements* (New York: Russell & Russell, 1958, org. 1936), p. 231).

22. In 1893, attorney W.S. Forrest remembered that he was "requested to defend those men . . . " Interestingly, Forrest's recollection implicated Spies by revealing that he had foreknowledge of the bombing: "From information which I received in a professional way, when requested to defend those men, I was led to believe that, as a matter of fact, Spies and others did all they could to prevent the throwing of the bomb." *Chicago Tribune*, June 27, 1893, p. 2.

23. Kogan, p. 70; *Chicago Tribune*, Jan. 5, 1929, p. 13.

24. *Chicago Tribune*, Apr. 7, 1890, p. 3.

25. *Chicago Tribune*, on Greeley see Aug. 19, 1872, p. 5; Suffrage: Dec. 3, 1876, p. 8; Railroad chapel: Aug. 28, 1874, p. 2; Temperance: Nov. 18, 1877, p. 3; Anti-Monopoly: Oct. 4, 1882, p. 6; Incurables: June 20, 1880, p. 13; Humane: May 7, 1882, p. 7; Vegetarian: Mar. 12, 1899, p. 30; Garibaldi: June 12, 1882, p. 8.

26. *Chicago Tribune*, Oct. 29, 1882, p. 10; *Journal of Speculative Philosophy*, 15:2 (April 1881), p. 195; *Chicago Tribune*, May 29, 1882, p. 2.

27. *Liberty*, 2:3 (Nov. 11, 1882), p. 4.

28. *Chicago Tribune*, Oct. 31, 1881, p. 7.

29. *Chicago Tribune*, Oct. 29, 1882, p. 10; Jan. 29, 1883, p. 8; Nov. 20, 1886, p. 1; Nov. 7, 1881, p. 8. Liberal League "Constitution and By-laws Adopted Nov. 6, 1881," in George Schilling Papers, Agnes Inglis Collection, Labadie Library, University of Michigan.

30. *Chicago Tribune*, Oct. 5, 1882, p. 6; Oct. 19, 1882, p. 6.

31. *Chicago Tribune*, Oct. 28, 1882, p. 6.

32. *Chicago Tribune*, Oct. 29, 1882, p. 10.

33. *Chicago Tribune*, July 24, 1882, p. 10. Black may have once served as treasurer of the SLP. At a meeting of the American section of the SLP in July1878, it was said that the "ex-Treasurer," a man by the name of "Black," was gone to the "National mass-meeting on market street," by which it was implied that this individual had defected to the Greenback Labor Party. *Chicago Tribune*, July 18, 1878, p. 5.

34. *Chicago Tribune*, Mar. 24, 1884, p. 8.

35. *The Commonweal* (London), Oct. 2, 1886, p. 211.

36. *Chicago Tribune*, Oct. 29, 1882, p. 10; Jan. 29, 1883, p. 8; Nov. 20, 1886, p. 1; Nov. 7, 1881, p. 8. Avrich cites *Alarm*, May 16, 1885, for IWPA invitation to Black, Avrich, 111–112. *Arbeiter Zeitung* for Feb. 22, 1886, quoted in *Chicago Tribune*, Aug. 1, 1886, p. 10.

37. *Labor Enquirer* (Denver), Jan. 9, 1886, p. 1.

38. *Chicago Tribune*, Apr. 14, 1886, p. 1.

39. *Inter-Ocean*, June 12, 1886, p. 6. On Neebe's bail, *Inter-Ocean*, June 3, 1886, p. 6; June 4, 1886, p. 8.

40. For some unknown reason, the leading historians of the Haymarket trial have misrepresented this crucial motion. Paul Avrich wrote, "On the first day, William A. Foster, on behalf of the defense, moved that each of his clients be tried separately . . . " James Green, followed suit: "Black moved to quash the indictments and to hold separate trials for each defendant, but both motions were denied." Such inaccuracies are all the more curious because Henry David, in his earlier seminal work on the case, correctly notes that the defense had "some hope that separate trials for some of the defendants might be granted" and so sought "to secure a separate trial for Spies, Schwab, Fielden and Neebe." By wrongly insisting that the defense moved for separate trials for *each* defendant, Avrich and Green find nothing more of interest to say about the issue after noting that Judge Gary denied this reasonable and just request, thereby skipping past one of the most important

and revealing actions of the defense (Avrich, p. 263; James Green, *Death in the Haymarket: A Story of Chicago, The First Labor Movement, and the Bombing that Divided Gilded Age America* (New York: Pantheon Books, 2006), p. 211; David, p. 238).

41. It is important to note that this admission runs counter to the claims of scholars who say that Lingg did not participate in the Monday night conspiracy meeting. Some testimony, as will be seen, did place him there.

42. *Chicago News,* June 19, 1886, p. 5.

43. *Chicago Journal,* June 21, 1886, p. 1. Both Avrich and David depict Judge Gary's denial of the motion for severance as an example of his prejudice toward the accused. Avrich dresses up Gary's ruling saying "the motion was brusquely overruled," while David merely says that though "there was some hope that separate trials might be granted...Judge Gary...refused the request of the defense." The facts show, however, that the defense only contemplated splitting the trial into two, and once it had made arrangements to have Parsons surrender himself, even this weak motion was only pursued half-heartedly. Hardly the clear evidence of judicial prejudice these historians have claimed.

44. *Andrew J. Johnson, Cornelius F. Backus, and Edgar L. Morse v. The People* Supreme Court of Illinois, 22 Ill. 314; 1859 Ill. Lexis 79, April 1859.

45. *United States v. Marchant & Colson,* 25 U.S. 480; 6 L. Ed. 700; 1827 U.S. Lexis 400; 12 Wheat 480, Mar. 12, 1827.

46. *The Albany Law Journal,* Oct. 22, 1887, p. 321.

47. *Chicago Tribune,* Nov. 24, 1889, p. 10.

48. *Reminiscences of the Anarchist Case,* p. 237; Lewis F. Mott to Sigmund Zeisler, Mar. 14, 1927, Box 3, Folder 41, Zeisler Papers, Newberry Library.

49. *Chicago Herald,* June 21, 1886, p. 1; *Chicago Tribune,* June 22, 1886, p. 1.

50. *Chicago Tribune,* June 21, 1886, p. 1; Clipping of Lucy Parsons' letter to the Federated Press, Feb. 27, 1922 (printed in Federated Press, Mar. 2, 1922), in George Schilling Papers, Agnes Inglis Collection, Labadie Library, University of Michigan; Samuel McConnell, "The Chicago Bomb Case: Personal Recollections of an American Tragedy," *Harper's Magazine* (May 1934), p. 736.

51. *Chicago Tribune,* Nov. 11, 1887, p. 2.

52. *The Albany Law Journal,* Oct. 22, 1887, p. 339.

53. *Chicago Tribune,* Nov. 24, 1889, p. 10.

54. *Chicago Inter-Ocean,* Nov. 12, 1887, p. 2.

55. The story, as commonly told, is confusing in its particulars but is most elegantly condensed into a few lines by James Green: "Because the normal, random process of selecting jurors had broken down, a special bailiff was charged to find jurors. The process went on for three weeks, and it went badly for the defendants, because the jurors who were seated seemed utterly biased against them" (Green, p. 212). Note how Green avoids mentioning by this passive construction that the defense had requested the special bailiff and expressed confidence in Bailiff Ryce (Avrich, p. 264; David, p. 238). James Green also writes that the jury "did not constitute a group of the defendants' peers [because]... not one of them was an immigrant, a manual laborer or a trade union member, and, of course, none was a radical." According to Green, channeling the research of Avrich and David, most members of the jury were "salesmen" or "clerks." Paul Avrich described the jury as "thoroughly middle class in composition" (Green, p. 213; Avrich, p. 267). (Green is apparently unaware that since the indictment charged that the IWPA was a criminal conspiracy, any person who could be shown to have been a member or a supporter of the IWPA or its affiliated organizations could be legally dismissed from the jury pool. He seems also unaware that Spies and Neebe were members of wealthy families or that Engel and Fielden owned their own businesses.)

56. Avrich describes it this way: "After eight days of fruitless examination, an unusual expedient was adopted. The candidates for the jury were not to be selected in the customary

manner, by drawing names at random from a box. Instead they would be handpicked by a special bailiff, nominated by the state's attorney . . . While this procedure was sanctioned by the defense, it soon became apparent that the bailiff . . . was exercising his powers in a grossly unfair manner . . . " (Avrich, p. 264).

57. *Illinois vs. August Spies et al.* Trial Transcript no. 1, court discussion regarding the appointment of a special bailiff, June 29, 1886. Vol. C., p. 186.

58. As the Illinois Supreme Court observed of the calling of special venire just months prior to the Haymarket trial, "Unless something in the record disclosed the contrary, it will be presumed the discretion with which judges of courts of record are clothed in such matters has been well exercised in the interest of public justice." *Mackin v. People*, 115 Ill. 312; 3 N.E. 222; 1885 Ill. LEXIS 555, Nov. 14, 1885.

59. *Davison v. People*, 90 Ill. 221; 1878 Ill. LEXIS 192, Sept. 1878.

60. *Hanna v. People*, 86 Ill. 243; 1877 Ill. LEXIS 124, Sept. 1877. The 1874 case was upheld numerous times prior to 1886. See *White v. People*, 81 Ill. 333; 1876 Ill. LEXIS 330, Jan. 1876; *Empson v. People*, 78 Ill. 248; 1875 Ill. LEXIS 348, Sept. 1875; *Blemer, alias, v. People*, 76 Ill. 265; 1875 Ill. LEXIS 617, Jan. 1875; *Barron v. People*, 73 Ill. 256; 1874 Ill. LEXIS 333, Sept. 1874; *Clawson v. U. S.*, 114 U.S. 477; 5 S. Ct. 949; 29 L. Ed. 179; 1885 U.S. LEXIS 1784, Apr. 20, 1885. David notes that the calling of a special bailiff while "not commonly resorted to" was a "procedure [that] was entirely legal" and "was in full accord with the statutory law of Illinois, Act of February 11, 1874, chapter 78, sec. 13 of the laws of Illinois" (David, 238, 251). Avrich doesn't mention the legal basis for appointing a special bailiff but instead implies that it was an entirely novel maneuver: "After eight days of fruitless examination, an unusual expedient was adopted. The candidates for the jury were not to be selected in the customary manner . . . instead they would be handpicked by a special bailiff . . . " (Avrich, p. 264).

61. Seymour D. Thompson, "Challenge to the Array," *The American Law Review*, Nov. 1881, pp. 699–717.

62. S.S. Gregory, "Trial and Procedure," *Proceedings of the Illinois State Bar Association . . . for the Year 1888* (Springfield, 1888), *History of Cook County, Illinois*, Weston A. Goodspeed and Daniel D. Healy, eds. Vol. 2 (Chicago: Goodspeed Historical Assoc. 1909), pp. 51–61, 513–514; Sigmund Zeisler, "Unanimity of Juries," *Proceedings of the Illinois State Bar Association . . . at its Thirteenth Annual Meeting* (Springfield, 1890), p. 54.

63. Robert. E Jenkins, "The Selection of Juries Grand and Petit," *The Albany Law Journal*, Aug. 8, 1896, p. 90.

64. *Lippincott's Magazine of Popular Literature and Science*, June 1882, p. 627.

65. *The Progressive Age* (Chicago), Dec. 10, 1881, p. 1.

66. *The Soldier of Indiana in the War for the Union* (Indianapolis: Merrill & Co., 1864), p. 140; *Chicago Tribune*, July 22, 1908, p. 5.

67. This fact is particularly salient as it was obvious from the defense's use of peremptory challenges and from published accounts in the daily press that defense lawyers wished to keep those of Irish or Scandinavian descent from serving on the jury. Men with Irish or Scottish surnames composed approximately 23 percent of the venire but were the recipients of nearly 30 percent of the defense's peremptory challenges. No other ethnic group was singled out for special treatment by the defense, though the prosecution likewise worked to exclude Germans by a similar proportion (33 percent of prosecution peremptory challenges were used to exclude Germans though they constituted 19 percent of the venire). Both benches of lawyers also pursued a strategy of packing the jury box on a class basis. Prosecutors used 27 percent of their peremptory challenges to excuse a disproportionate number of industrial wage workers, who constituted 7 percent of the jury pool. The defense burned 15 percent of their challenges to exclude brokers, investors, and bankers, a group totaling just 3 percent of all prospective jurors. In sum, there is little evidence in the record of jury selection to accuse Bailiff Ryce of any misconduct

other than taking the path of least resistance to obtaining his daily quota of 50 literate English-speaking citizens and residents of Cook County.

68. In a revealing argument after the trial was over, Black as much as admitted that the defense had intentionally squandered its remaining challenges. Black's admission came as he was introducing Favor's affidavit as part of his effort to lay the groundwork for a new trial. Judge Gary skeptically noted that even if Favor's allegations were true, such actions couldn't be shown to have harmed the defense as it didn't use all its peremptory challenges.

> *Judge Gary*: ... it is a matter perfectly well known to everybody who was present at the trial, that the last 50 of your peremptory challenges you exhausted simply for the purpose of exhausting them.
> *Captain Black*: What difference does that make if your Honor please?
> *Judge Gary*: Your complaint there is, that by the action of Ryce you are compelled to exhaust your peremptory challenges.
> *Captain Black*: Yes, sir; that is our position.
> *Judge Gary*: Well, it is perfectly well known to everybody who was present at the trial, that the last 50 you exhausted without at all referring to the character of the men that were being examined.
> *Captain Black*: Now, if your Honor please, with reference to that: From the rulings which were adopted by your Honor in the beginning of this case, there was left to us upon our side, simply a choice among prejudiced men. That is all ...

Black did not deny Gary's charge but instead justified the defense's actions. Had the defense not intentionally burned up its remaining challenges, Black probably would not have responded to Gary's charge in this way. HADC, Vol. O, pp. 70–71.

69. *Thomas Mimms v. The State of Ohio*, Supreme Court of Ohio, 16 Ohio St. 221; 1865 Ohio LEXIS 63, Dec. 1865; *James W. Erwin v. The State of Ohio*, 29 Ohio St. 186; 1876 Ohio LEXIS 384, Dec. 1876.

70. Samuel P. McConnell, "The Chicago Bomb Case: Personal Recollections of an American Tragedy," *Harper's Magazine*, May 1934, p. 734.

71. Paul Avrich charged, "Most of the veniremen called by the bailiff admitted to having a prejudice against the defendants or a preconceived opinion that they were guilty. To Judge Gary, however, this was insufficient reason to exclude them from the jury ... Time and again Gary refused to disqualify a prospective juror who had openly admitted his prejudice against the defendants." James Green followed in the same vein: "Black objected over and over to jurors who seemed clearly prejudiced against his clients, but again and again Judge Gary refused to accept Black's challenges for cause ... " (Avrich, p. 265; Green, p. 212). Over the course of the generations of writing on this landmark case, scholars' appreciation of the legal context in which Judge Gary ruled noticeably declined. In 1936 Henry David admitted that it seemed as though Judge Gary followed the law of his own day. David writes, "It could be argued that in the strictest legal sense, each of these rulings by Judge Gary was justifiable ... ," and quotes the relevant text of the 1874 statute. But he overstates the case when he continues, "This plainly places vast discretionary powers in the hands of the trial judge." David also grasped the importance of the distinction between positive and hypothetical opinions, charging not that Gary made up this distinction but that he was "either unable to distinguish between positive and hypothetical opinions, or ... was so prejudiced that he refused to see a difference between the two" (David, pp. 240–241).

72. (Ch. 78, Sec. 14 of the Illinois code) in Harvey B. Hurd, ed., *The Revised Statutes of the State of Illinois* ... (Chicago: Chicago Legal News Co., 1887), p. 814 (Ch. 78, Sec. 14 of the Illinois code).

73. As one of the anarchists' own lawyers observed of a different murder trial that transfixed Chicago, "With the exception of illiterates, I do not believe you could fine one out of a thousand men who has not eagerly scanned the newspapers every day throughout the trial for evidence produced in court, and who has not formed a decided opinion as to the guilt of the accused . . . " Sigmund Zeisler wondered in that case, "How many men in cook county—nay how many men in Illinois, would be competent for jury service in . . . a new trial?" Sigmund Zeisler, "Unanimity of Juries," *Proceedings of the Illinois State Bar Association . . . for the Year 1890* (Springfield, 1890), p. 64.

74. *Jack Cooper v. The State Of Ohio*, Supreme Court of Ohio, 16 Ohio St. 328; 1865 Ohio, LEXIS 72, Dec. 1865. *Sidney A. Frazier v. The State of Ohio*, Supreme Court of Ohio, 23 Ohio St. 551; 1873 Ohio, LEXIS 147, Dec. 1873. *Hopt v. Utah*, Supreme Court of the United States, 110 U.S. 574; 4 S. Ct. 202; 28 L. Ed. 262; 1884 U.S. LEXIS 1719, Submitted January 4, 1884, March 3, 1884, Decided. Avrich chose not to mention either the existing statute law on jury selection or the legal precedents that drew the line between positive and fixed opinions and general ones. Avrich intentionally clouds the law and court precedents by implying that Gary's standard for accepting veniremen was simply one of their testifying to their own ability to weigh the evidence impartially. Judge Gary's rulings were "quite out of the ordinary" Avrich claims, in that he "was very rigid in his rulings as to cause, holding that even if a venireman acknowledged that he had formed an opinion regarding the guilt of the accused, he was acceptable if he said he could change it if the testimony warranted" (Avrich, pp. 264–265).

75. *Archimedes Smith v. Timothy D. Eames*, Supreme Court of Illinois at Springfield, 4 Ill. 76; 1841 Ill. LEXIS 33; 3 Scam. 76, July, 1841.

76. *William D. Noble v. The People*, Supreme Court of Illinois at Vandalia, 1 Ill. 54; 1822 Ill. LEXIS 12; 1 Breese 54.

77. *Chicago Tribune*, Oct. 7, 1900, p. 41.

78. One frequently made claim is that one of the members of the jury was in fact a relative of one of the murdered police officers; it is one of those ideas that seem to have experienced a slow exaggeration over the years. In Henry David's 1936 book, *The History of the Haymarket Affair*, is the following observation: "Judge Gary . . . overruled a challenge for cause where a venireman admitted . . . kinship to one of the policemen fatally wounded by the bomb" (p. 245). Later, Paul Avrich in his 1984 *The Haymarket Tragedy* wrote, "Gary went so far as to pronounce fit for service M.D. Flavin, a relative of one of the slain policemen . . . " (p. 265). Sidney Lens, writing the opening piece in Dave Roediger and Franklin Rosemont's *Haymarket Scrapbook* (1986), places Flavin squarely on the jury: "The trial in Judge Joseph E. Gary's courtroom was a travesty. Candidates for the jury had been chosen by a special bailiff, instead of being selected at random. One of those picked, after the defense had exhausted its peremptory challenges, was a relative of a police victim" (p. 19). (Lens' erroneous piece is the centerpiece of *The Lucy Parson's Project* website: www.lucyparsonsproject.org.) Most recently, James Green repeated this idea in *Death in the Haymarket* (2006), " . . . Judge Gary refused to accept Black's challenges for cause, even in the case of a juror who admitted kinship with one of the slain policemen" (Green, p. 212).

The slippage in terminology from 1936 to 2006 is significant. David correctly identifies the man in question as a "venireman," indicating that he never made it onto the jury panel. Avrich loosens his language in describing the man as being "pronounced fit for service" and not clearly stating that he was actually challenged and removed from consideration. (Avrich does list the names of all the jurors several pages later, but the casual reader may not remember the names from one place to the next.) Finally, Green completes the slide into misrepresentation by calling this questionable man "a juror" and not listing the names of the jury panel in his book, thus leading the reader to think that this man may have actually sat in judgment. (Interestingly, Green cites David as his only source for this passage.)

According to the record of the trial, M.D. Flavin was examined and during the course of his questioning noted that Officer Flavin was a "distant relative." The defense challenged him for cause and Judge Gary did overrule the challenge; the defense then used one of their 180 peremptory challenges to remove Flavin from the jury pool. Flavin did not serve on the jury that convicted the anarchist defendants (*Abstract of Record*, Vol. 1, pp. 84–85).

79. David, p. 249; Avrich, p. 266.
80. *Illinois vs. August Spies et al.* Trial Transcript no. 1, Examination of S. G. Randall, June 24,1886. Volume B, 19–26.
81. *Illinois vs. August Spies et al.* Trial Transcript no. 1, Examination of Theodore Denker, June 24, 1886. Volume B, 112–122.
82. *Chicago Tribune*, July 15, 1886, p. 2; July 14, 1886, p. 8.

CHAPTER 3

1. *The American Architect and Building News*, Mar. 3, 1877, pp. 68–74; May 8, 1880, p. 198; Apr. 30, 1881, p. 205; May 14, 1881, p. 233; Apr. 11, 1885, p. 178. Trinity Church in Boston and the U.S. Capitol were the top two. June 13, 1885, p. 282. See also Robert Bruegmann, *The Architects and the City: Holabird & Roche of Chicago, 1880–1918*, vol. 1 (Chicago: Univ. or Chicago Press, 1997). *Chicago Tribune*, Oct. 30, 1881, p. 11.
2. Alfred T. Andreas, *History of Chicago*, vol. 3 (Chicago: 1886), p. 597.
3. Linda Mulcahy, "Architects of Justice: The Politics of Courtroom Design," *Social Legal Studies*, 16:3 (2007), pp. 383–403. *Chicago Tribune*, Dec. 31, 1880, p. 8; Placement of jurors varied widely across American courtrooms at the time. In Richmond County Court-House, Virginia, built at the same time as the Cook County Court-House, jurors sat alongside the judge on a raised semicircular bench. *The American Architect and Building News*, June 23, 1877, p. 199.
4. *Chicago Times*, July 17, 1886, p. 1. When the last juror was accepted, a reporter was close enough to hear every word Capt. Black whispered to his fellow attorney, Foster, "Challenge for cause any good man the State accepts. We want that for a point when we take the case to the Supreme Court, for we can't show error in the record unless we show also that we were out peremptories." *Chicago Tribune*, July 16, 1886, p. 2.
5. *Chicago Journal*, July 16, 1886, p. 1; *Chicago Tribune*, July 17, 1886, p. 1. Contemporary scholars unfamiliar with the history of the development of courtroom architecture have interpreted the lack of clearly defined spaces within the bar as a "chaotic" or "circus-like" atmosphere. Paul Avrich interpreted the presence of ladies sitting with Judge Gary to mean the judge lacked seriousness and decorum (Paul Avrich, *The Haymarket Tragedy* (Princeton, NJ: Princeton Univ. Press, 1984), p. 263). Likewise, James Green writes "Judge Gary . . . contributed to the theatricality of the event by filling the seats behind his chair with well-dressed young ladies who clearly enjoyed the spectacle" (James Green, *Death in the Haymarket: A Story of Chicago, The First Labor Movement, and the Bombing that Divided Gilded Age America* (New York: Pantheon Books, 2006), p. 217). There is no evidence that Gary gave precedence in use of these chairs to "young ladies." It should be noted that sitting behind or beside the judge was a common practice at this time. During a capital trial two years earlier, chief defense counsel William P. Black, who did not take part in the proceedings, was observed to sit beside Judge Gardner on the bench and Captain Black's wife Hortensia was allowed to sit next to the defendant (*Chicago Tribune*, Dec. 2, 1882, p. 7).
6. *Chicago Tribune*, July 20, 1886, p. 1.
7. *Chicago Tribune*, July 17, 1886, p. 1. *Chicago Legal News*, July 31, 1886, p. 387.

8. *Chicago Tribune*, Oct. 21, 1906, p. F4; Nov. 1, 1906, p. 4; Dec. 6, 1903, p. 26; Nov. 20, 1903, p. 5.
9. *Chicago Journal*, July 16, 1886, p. 2.
10. *Chicago Tribune*, July 11, 1886, p. 8.
11. *Chicago Tribune*, July 11, 1886, p. 8.
12. *American State Trials*, John David Lawson, ed., vol. 12 (St. Louis: F. H. Thomas Law Book Co., 1919), pp. 24–25.
13. *American State Trials*, p. 26.
14. *American State Trials*, pp. 36–38.
15. Grinnell has been consistently misquoted by historians. Henry David opens his chapter entitled "The Evidence" by misquoting from Grinnell's opening statement. David presents the following in quotations:

> For the first time in the history of our country are people on trial for endeavoring to make anarchy the rule, and in that attempt for ruthlessly and awfully destroying human life. (Henry David, *The History of the Haymarket Affair: A Study in the American Social-Revolutionary and Labor Movements* (New York: Russell & Russell, 1958, org. 1936), p. 253)

But David's source reads differently (differences indicated in italics):

> For the first time in the history of our country are people on trial for *their lives* for endeavoring to make Anarchy the rule, and in that attempt for ruthlessly and awfully destroying human life.
> (*American State Trials*, vol. 12, p. 24)

Henry David is then misquoted in turn by James Green whose claims Grinnell said:

> "for the first time in the history of our country people are on trial for endeavoring to make Anarchy the rule," and "to ruthlessly and awfully destroy human life" to achieve that end.
> (Green, p. 214. Green also cites the wrong page from David placing his source on p. 217 when it is, in fact, on p. 253.)

James Green further deviates from the original source when purporting to quote Grinnell's legal theory of the case:

> it is not necessary in this kind of case . . . that the individual who commits the particular offense—for instance, the man who threw the bomb—to be in court at all.
> (Green, p. 214)

Green cites David as his source but David provides yet a different version of this passage:

> it is not necessary in *a case of this kind* . . . that the individual who commits the . . . particular offense—for instance, the man who threw the bomb—*should* be in court at all.
> (David, p. 256)

16. *American State Trials*, pp. 27–32.
17. James Green claims that after Grinnell finished his opening address "The next day Judge Gary outlined the state's position in his charge to the jury" (Green, p. 215). Judge's instructions to jurors were, then as now, delivered at the very end of the trial after the hearing of all evidence. Had Gary given "a charge" to the jurors out of this proper order, the defense would have had an excellent basis on which to appeal on purely procedural grounds. Rather, Gary issued a ruling on an objection raised by the defense.
   More importantly, Gary's ruling did not contain any of the words that Green attributes to him. Green quotes Gary as saying "[The prosecution would prove] the existence of a

general conspiracy to annihilate the police force and destroy property [and show that the] defendants who were instigators of it [were therefore liable for the act,] even if committed without their specific sanction at that particular time and place." (Green provides no citation for this quotation. Apparently, it comes from a summary of the days proceedings published in the *Chicago Tribune*, July 17, 1886, p. 1: "The ruling of Judge Gary was in substance that the existence of a general conspiracy to annihilate the police force and destroy property rendered the defendants, who were the instigators of it, liable for an act looking to such annihilation, even if committed without their specific sanction at that particular time and place.")

What Judge Gary actually is documented to have said is substantially and fundamentally legally different from what Green purports he "charged." In his ruling on the defense objection, Gary said in part: "if there was this combination and agreement among a great number of people, *and preparation for it*, to assault and kill the police upon some occasion which might occur in the future, and whether the proper occasion had occurred was left to the parties who used the violence at that time, and then that violence was used and resulted in the death of the police, everybody who is a party to that combination and agreement is guilty of the results" (HADC, Vol. I, p. 93. Italics added). Gary clearly saw that the prosecution had to connect the conspiracy to the act, both in terms of intention and actual actions (*"and preparation for it"*) taken to see it to completion. Nowhere in his ruling did Gary imply that conspirators could be guilty if an act was committed that was unintended by them. The whole point was that the bombing or some other act of violence was anticipated and planned for by those who were in on the conspiracy.

18. Biographical details in Schaack, pp. 287–288.
19. HADC, Vol. I, pp. 97–98, 101–102.
20. Avrich, p. 192; Testimony of Godfried Waller, HADC, Vol. I, pp. 58–61, 63, 73.
21. Testimony of Godfried Waller, HADC, Vol. I, p. 63.
22. Testimony of Godfried Waller, HADC, Vol. I, pp. 60, 63. Historians have stubbornly refused to accurately describe Waller's testimony. Henry David writes that nothing in Waller's testimony established a "causal connection" between the Greif's Hall meeting and the Haymarket bombing. "There was nothing said about the [Haymarket] meeting," said Waller on the witness stand. "There was nothing [*sic*] expected that the police would get to the Haymarket" (David, p. 261). David conveniently places a period after the word "Haymarket" but Waller's sentence didn't actually end there but continued. His actual sentence was "There was nothing expected that the police would get to the Haymarket, only if strikers were attacked then we should shoot the police" (Testimony of Godfried Waller, HADC, Vol. I, p. 67).

Paul Avrich writes that "as both Waller and Schrade admitted, nothing was said at the Greif's Hall meeting about any action to be taken at the Haymarket. If a conspiracy had indeed been set afoot, the incident of May 4 was in no way connected with it" (Avrich, p. 273). James Green follows suit and writes, "Waller . . . testified that nothing was said about preparing for the Haymarket event because no one expected the police to intervene. No one at the meeting said anything about using dynamite" (Green, p. 216). Waller did in fact say that everyone at the meeting presumed there would be a fight in the city, and the conspirators positioned a "committee" at the Haymarket to signal the troops when this occurred. Waller also said that Engel urged the use of bombs against police stations.

23. Testimony of Godfried Waller, HADC, Vol. I, pp. 102–103.
24. Testimony of Godfried Waller, HADC, Vol. I, pp. 110–111.
25. Testimony of Godfried Waller, HADC, Vol. I, p. 111.
26. *Chicago Tribune*, Aug. 21, 1886, p. 1.
27. The nature of Foster's objection has been grossly mischaracterized in the existing literature. Henry David misquotes Foster's objection: "If you show," pertinently asked Mr. Foster, "that some man threw one of these bombs without the knowledge or authority,

or approval of any of these defendants, is that murder?" (David, p. 260) Judging by his citations, David did not copy Foster's quote from the actual trial transcriptions, but from anarchist Dyer Lum's work in defense of the accused, *The Great Trial of the Chicago Anarchists* (Chicago: 1886). According to the trial transcript, what Foster actually said is: "Allow me to ask a question. Suppose that all you say is true; yet without the authority, and without the knowledge of any of the defendants, and without their consent, and without their approval, some man throws a bomb into the ranks of the police and Mr. Degan is killed; are they guilty of murder? Do you say that they are guilty of murder?" (HADC, Vol. I, p. 84) The difference is subtle but profound. Foster begins by saying, "suppose that all you say is true..." This after Ingham had just laid out the framework of the prosecution's legal theory: "we can show that these men have not only been preaching these doctrines, but that they have been preparing themselves by arming... [and that] some of their dupes—some of the men who were their accomplices and connected with them—threw this bomb as a result of this general conspiracy..." (HADC, Vol. I, p. 83). In other words, Foster was conceding the existence of a general conspiracy that included actual preparations between the leaders on trial and the "dupe" who threw the bomb. His legal point, then, was far less extensive than David implies; Foster was arguing that even if the bomber was connected to this general conspiracy but threw the bomb at a time and place that had not been previously agreed upon, could that still be considered conspiracy murder? Judge Gary ruled that it was if the bomber's act was in furtherance of the purposes of the conspiracy.

28. *Chicago Tribune*, July 17, 1886, p. 2.
29. HADC, Vol. I, p. 91.
30. *Chicago Tribune*, July 17, 1886, p. 1.
31. HADC, Vol. I, p. 91.
32. *Brooklyn Eagle*, Aug. 22, 1886, p. 9.
33. *Chicago Tribune*, July 28, 1886, p. 9.
34. Testimony of Bernardt Schrade, HADC, Vol. I, pp. 142–144, 153.
35. *Chicago Tribune*, July 18, 1886, p. 10.
36. See testimonies of officers Edward J. Steele, Martin Quinn, James P. Stanton, H.F. Krueger, John Wessler, Peter Foley, James Bowler, Louis C. Baumann, Edward John Hanley, John E. Doyle, Charles Spierling, and James Bonfield. HADC, Vol. I, pp. 168–274, 288–309, 325–380.
37. Testimony of Edwin Steele, HADC, Vol. I, p. 182; Testimony of Martin Quinn, HADC, Vol. I, pp. 189, 192.
38. Testimony of Luther V. Moulton, HADC, Vol. I, pp. 277–280.
39. Testimony of HADC, Vol. I, p. 281; Testimony of George Schook, HADC, Vol. I., p. 286.
40. Testimony of James K. Magie, HADC, Vol. I, pp. 310–324; Testimony of Henry E.O. Heinemann, HADC, Vol. I, p. 383.
41. Testimony of J. A. West, HADC, Vol. I, pp. 388–392.
42. Cook County Coroner's Records, May 4, 1886.
43. Waller testified that the agreement had been that "it was not to be in the papers until the revolution should actually take place." Waller said he saw the word "Ruhe" in the *Arbeiter Zeitung* around 6 P.M. on May 4 (Testimony of Godfried Waller, HADC, Vol. I, pp. 112–113). Typesetter Theodore Fricke testified that the copy containing the word "Ruhe" was written in August Spies' handwriting (Testimony of Theodore Fricke, HADC, Vol. I, p. 468). Haymarket historians have chosen not to speculate upon the meaning of these codes. Avrich avoids analyzing it by saying "Why it was inserted, however, remains a mystery" (Avrich, p. 192). David asks, "Who sent the request for its insertion to Spies? And what was the motive? These questions are no more answerable today than they were in the dingy courtroom where Judge Gary presided in 1886" (David, p. 262). But this is

no great mystery. In fact, the only source distancing August Spies from these codes is his own testimony. James Green avoids the whole issue by not mentioning the coded signals at all.

44. Testimony of Theodore Fricke, HADC, Vol. I, p. 477.
45. *Chicago Tribune*, July 22, 1886, p. 1.
46. *Chicago Tribune*, July 22, 1886, p. 1.
47. Testimony of William Seliger, HADC, Vol. I, pp. 515–519.
48. Testimony of William Seliger, HADC, Vol. I, pp. 526–529.
49. Testimony of William Seliger, HADC, Vol. I, pp. 526–527.
50. Testimony of Bertha Seliger, HADC, Vol. I, pp. 582–585.
51. Testimony of Moritz Neff, HADC, Vol. J, pp. 277–279.
52. *The New York Times*, Feb. 13, 1887, p. 3. *Chicago Tribune*, Aug. 15, 1887, p. 8. In 1920, approaching his seventieth birthday, Neff, still single, rented a room at the Madison Bridge Hotel and earned his living as a weaver. *Twelve Census of the U.S.*, 1900, Manhattan Borough, New York, New York, Series T623, Roll 1088, Page, 219; *Fourteenth Census of the U.S.* 1920, Manhattan, New York, New York, Series T625, Roll 1186, Page 162.
53. Testimony of Gustav Lehman, HADC, Vol. J, pp. 205–215.
54. *Thirteenth Census of the United States*, 1910, Chicago, Cook County, Illinois, Series T624, Roll 243, p. 310. *Fourteenth Census of the United States*, 1920, Chicago, Cook County, Illinois, Series T625, Roll 313, p. 192.
55. Henry David claims that Thompson perjured himself on the basis that his testimony conflicted with other prosecution witnesses, including a police detective who followed Spies that night. David writes, "Testimony of police officers gave full reason for believing that Thompson's description of Spies' movements was inaccurate . . . two policemen . . . failed to see the meeting of the three men described by Mr. Thompson. . . . So overwhelming is the evidence on these points, that one must conclude that while Schwab was present in the Haymarket before the meeting really began, he did not meet and converse with Spies and Schnaubelt . . . " David quotes Officer McKeough as testifying "there was a man with him [Spies] who I think was Schwab, but I am not sure of that . . . " (David, pp. 270–271). In fact, David takes this quotation out of context as McKeough was only saying he couldn't be sure he saw Spies and Schwab when he spotted Spies on the corner of Desplaines and Randolph. But McKeough was quite certain that he had seen Spies and Schwab together near the speakers' wagon. McKeough stated that he saw Schwab "got on the wagon I think before the meeting started, and tapped Mr. Spies on the shoulder and said something to him." Spies then got off the wagon and went looking for Parsons. Later McKeough spotted Schwab again, first talking to Parsons, and then talking with Spies by the side of the speakers' wagon. Testimony of Timothy McKeough, HADC, Vol. K, pp. 189, 201.
56. Philip S. Foner, ed., *The Autobiographies of the Haymarket Martyrs* (New York: Humanities Press, 1969), pp. 120–121.
57. *Chicago Tribune*, July 29, 1886, p. 1.
58. *Inter-Ocean*, June 23, 1879, p.8.
59. Under cross-examination Gilmer admitted he was 'acquainted' with a "Fanny Hubble," a woman whose reputation was implied to be less than respectable. However, this author could find no trace of Ms. Hubble and discover just what business she engaged in. Testimony of Harry L. Gilmer, HADC, Vol. K, p. 488.
60. Testimony of Harry L. Gilmer, HADC, Vol. K, pp. 407–408. James Green describes Gilmer's testimony as being "absurd" and "filled with inconsistencies and contradictions" but cites no sources for this judgment and provides none of these supposed contradictions (Green, p. 220).
61. *Chicago Tribune*, Aug. 21, 1886, p. 1.

62. See testimonies of John Bonfield, HADC, Vol. K, pp. 503–511; Martin Quinn, pp. 498–503; Herman Schuettler, pp. 515–529; Jacob Lowenstein, pp. 529–547; John B. Murphy, pp. 551–72; Michael Hoffman, pp. 581–585; Michael Schaack, pp. 587–617; Walter S. Haines, pp. 664–674; Mark Delafontaine, pp. 674–581; Michael Hahn, pp. 445–452.

63. Testimony of John Degan, HADC, Vol. K, pp. 699–700.

64. *The Commonweal* (London), Aug. 21, 1886, p. 163; Aug. 28, 1886, p. 174.

CHAPTER 4

1. John D. Lawson, ed., *American State Trials* (St. Louis, Missouri: F.H. Thomas Law Book Co., 1919), vol. 12, p. 129.

2. *American State Trials*, vol. 12, p. 128.

3. Notes, p. 2, Albert R. Parsons Papers, State Historical Society of Wisconsin, US MSS 15A.

4. Ibid.

5. *American State Trials*, vol. 12, p. 128.

6. *American State Trials*, vol. 12, p. 129.

7. *Chicago Tribune*, Aug. 1, 1886, p. 9.

8. *Chicago Tribune*, Aug. 3, 1886, p. 1.

9. Testimony of Carter H. Harrison, HADC, Vol. L, p. 32.

10. Testimony of Carter H. Harrison, HADC, Vol. L, p. 44.

11. Testimony of Carter H. Harrison, HADC, Vol. L, pp. 48–50. James Green paraphrases only a portion of the mayor's statements making it appear as though Bonfield betrayed his orders: "The mayor . . . testified that after listening to the speakers he told Chief Inspector Bonfield nothing dangerous seemed likely to occur and that he should send the police reserves home" (James Green, *Death in the Haymarket: A Story of Chicago, The First Labor Movement, and the Bombing that Divided Gilded Age America* (New York: Pantheon Books, 2006), p. 221).

12. Testimony of Carter H. Harrison, HADC, Vol. L, p. 51.

13. Testimony of Carter H. Harrison, HADC, Vol. L, p. 50.

14. Testimony of Barton Simonson, HADC, Vol. L, pp. 80–81. According to Capt. Schaack, Simonson's employer, the Rothschild Clothing Co., fired Simonson immediately after he had finished his testimony (Michael Schaack, *Anarchy and Anarchists* (Chicago: F.J. Schulte & Co., 1889), p. 488).

15. Testimony of John Ferguson, Testimony of John Ferguson, HADC, Vol. L, pp. 126, 132–133; Testimony of William Gleason, HADC, Vol. L, pp. 362, 364, 368, 372, 374–375.

16. Testimony of William Gleason, HADC, Vol. L, pp. 368, 375.

17. Testimony of Friedrich Liebel, HADC, Vol. L, pp. 210–216, 219–220.

18. Testimony of Friedrich Liebel, HADC, Vol. L, pp. 216, 219.

19. Mention of jurors taking notes and discussing the case in HADC, Vol. O, pp. 97–98; *Chicago Tribune*, Aug. 21, 1886, p. 1. Jurors in this era were generally allowed to confer prior to the formal conclusion of the case. On history of jury procedure see Douglas G. Smith, "The Historical and Constitutional Contexts of Jury Reform," *Hofstra Law Review*, Winter 1996 (25 Hofstra L. Rev. 377); juror note taking was generally allowed in 1886 on the basis of a Georgia Supreme Court precedent, *Tift v. Townes*, 1879 (71 Ga. 535, 540).

20. Testimony of Michael Schwab, HADC, Vol. N, p. 12.

21. Testimony of Edgar Owen, HADC, Vol. K, pp. 214–215, 230–231; Testimony of Carter Harrison, HADC, Vol. L, p. 28.

22. HADC, Vol. N, pp. 1–4; Testimony of Hermann Becker, HADC, Vol. M, pp. 209–212.

23. Testimony of Edward Preusser, HADC, Vol. M, pp. 200, 205.

24. Testimony of Michael Schwab, HADC, Vol. N, p. 4, Schwab's route that night as he rode out Clybourne avenue toward the Deering factory took him past the hall where his anarchist group, the North Side Group, held their meetings and socials, Neff's saloon. According to Schwab's own accounting of his time, he left the Deering meeting between ten and ten-thirty, took a horsecar back down Clybourne to the Willow street stop, and walked the remaining mile home, arriving at 11 P.M. But had he instead stayed on his horsecar a few stops further he could have gotten off at Neff's and arrived in time to meet his comrades arriving from the riot.

25. Testimony of William Snyder, HADC, Vol. M, pp. 97, 101; Testimony of Thomas Brown, HADC, Vol. M, p. 123; Testimony of Lizzie Holmes, HADC, Vol. M, p. 284; Testimony of Samuel Fielden, HADC, Vol. M, pp. 310–313, 345; Testimony of Joseph Bach, HADC, Vol. M, pp. 404–405; Testimony of Albert Parsons, HADC, Vol. N, pp. 109–111; Testimony of Michael Schwab, HADC, Vol. N, p. 11.

26. Testimony of Albert Parsons, HADC, Vol. N, pp. 109–110; Testimony of Lizzie Holmes, HADC, Vol. M, p. 282; Testimony of William Snyder, HADC, Vol. M, pp. 97, 101; Testimony of Henry H. O. Heinemann, HADC, Vol. M, p. 280.

27. Testimony of William Snyder, HADC, Vol. M, p. 101; Testimony of Lizzie Holmes, HADC, Vol. M, p. 282; Testimony of Samuel Fielden, Vol. M, p. 312; Testimony of Joseph Bach, HADC, Vol. M, pp. 404–405; Testimony of William Patterson, HADC, Vol. M, p. 42.

28. R.S. Barnum, an advertising clerk for the *Chicago Daily News*, was called to the witness chair and given a scrap of paper. He recognized some marks he had made on it and said that it was advertising copy he was given by another clerk between 10 and 11 on the morning of May 4. The scrap of paper Barnum held in his hand had earlier been identified by Theodore Fricke, the business manager of the *Arbeiter Zeitung* as bearing the handwriting of Albert Parsons. Parsons confirmed he wrote and placed the ad. Testimony of Albert Parsons, HADC, Vol. N, p. 109; Testimony of R.S. Barnum, HADC, Vol. J, pp. 384–386; Testimony of Theodore Fricke, HADC, Vol. I, p. 478.

29. Testimony of R.S. Barnum, HADC, Vol. J, p. 385.

30. *Chicago Mail*, May 4, 1886, p. 1; Testimony of Lizzie Mae Holmes, HADC, Vol. M, p. 294. *The Alarm* (Chicago), Apr. 24, 1886, p. 4; Testimony of Max Mitlacher, HADC, Vol. M, p. 433.

31. Testimony of Albert Parsons, HADC, Vol. N, pp. 109–111; Testimony of Samuel Fielden, HADC, Vol. M, pp. 310–313, 345; Testimony of Michael Schwab, HADC, Vol. N, p. 11; Testimony of Lizzie Holmes, HADC, Vol. M, p. 284; Testimony of Joseph Bach, HADC, Vol. M, pp. 404–405; Testimony of William Patterson, HADC, Vol. M, p. 42; Testimony of John F. Waldo, Vol. M, p. 172; Testimony of William Snyder, HADC, Vol. M, 97, 101; Testimony of William Snyder, HADC, Vol. M, p. 98.

32. Testimony of Godfried Waller, HADC, Vol. I, pp. 73–74.

33. Testimony of August Krueger, HADC, Vol. M, pp. 159–160.

34. Schaack, *Anarchy and Anarchists*, p. 339.

35. Testimony of August Krueger, HADC, Vol. M, p. 166.

36. Testimony of Michael Schaack, HADC, Vol. K, p. 612.

37. Henry David wrote, "During Fielden's address, Parsons went over to his wife, children, and Mrs. Holmes who were seated in another wagon a few feet away from the one that was used as a rostrum . . . " Similarly, Paul Avrich recounted: "Stepping down from the speakers' wagon, Parsons went to another wagon a few paces north of it, on which sat his wife and children . . . " (Henry David, *The History of the Haymarket Affair: A Study in the American Social-Revolutionary and Labor Movements* (New York: Russell & Russell, 1958, org. 1936), p. 280; Paul Avrich, *The Haymarket Tragedy* (Princeton, NJ: Princeton Univ. Press, 1984), p. 204). In both these statements, and in many more based on them, the

presence of Parson's children that chilly May night is stated as fact. But apart from Parson's own claim, made after he was convicted and faced the gallows, there is no evidence that they were there and much that casts doubt upon it.

38. Philip S. Foner, ed., *The Autobiographies of the Haymarket Martyrs* (New York: Humanities Press, 1969), p. 49.

39. Testimony of Henry E. O. Heinemann, HADC, Vol. M, p. 280.

40. Testimony of Lizzie Mae Holmes, HADC, Vol. M, p. 286.

41. Testimony of William A. Patterson, HADC, Vol. M, p. 52.

42. Testimony of Joseph Bach, HADC, Vol. M, p. 404.

43. Testimony of Samuel Fielden, HADC, Vol. M, p. 312.

44. Testimony of Albert R. Parsons, HADC, Vol. N, p. 111.

45. Testimony of Lizzie Mae Holmes, HADC, Vol. M, p. 286.

46. Testimony of William Snyder, HADC, Vol. M, p. 102.

47. Testimony of Whiting Allen, HADC, Vol. K, p. 167.

48. Testimony of William Sahl, HADC, Vol. L, p. 380.

49. Testimony of Albert R. Parsons, HADC, Vol. N, p. 112.

50. Testimony of Lizzie Mae Holmes, HADC, Vol. M, p. 286.

51. Testimony of Thomas Brown, HADC, Vol. M, pp. 130–132.

52. Testimony of M. D. Malkoff, HADC, Vol. M, p. 5.

53. Testimony of Sleeper T. Ingram, HADC, Vol. M, p. 454.

54. Testimony of Henry Schultz, HADC, Vol. M, p. 389.

55. *Chicago Tribune*, Nov. 1, 1887, p. 6.

56. Testimony of G. P. English, HADC, Vol. K, pp. 303–304. Note the ellipsis in this passage marks the removal of an interruption and further question from an attorney and not the excising of any portion of English's record of Fielden's speech.

57. Testimony of Albert R. Parsons, HADC, Vol. N, pp. 115–116.

58. Testimony of M. D. Malkoff, HADC, Vol. M, pp. 4, 10–11, 20. Malkoff was committed to the Milwaukee County Insane Asylum in 1900 and choked to death on his dinner there in 1902. *Chicago Tribune*, Apr. 28, 1902, p. 5.

59. Testimony of Lizzie Mae Holmes, HADC, Vol. M, p. 299.

60. *Chicago Times*, May 5, 1886, p. 2. Testimony of Whiting Allen, HADC, Vol. K, pp. 164–5.

61. Testimony of W.M. Knox, HADC, Vol. J., p. 309.

62. Testimony of August Spies, HADC, Vol. N, pp. 28–29.

63. Testimony of August Spies, HADC, Vol. N, pp. 66–67.

64. Testimony of August Spies, HADC, Vol. N, pp. 83–84. Procedural references have been omitted from this excerpt.

65. Testimony of August Spies, HADC, Vol. N, pp. 94–95.

66. Testimony of August Spies, HADC, Vol. N, pp. 105–108.

67. Testimony of Henry Spies, HADC, Vol. M, p. 139; Testimony of August Spies, HADC, Vol. N, p. 33.

68. Testimony of Henry Spies, HADC, Vol. M, p. 149; Testimony of August Spies, HADC, Vol. N, p. 72.

69. Spies provides a different account of these moments surrounding the bombing in his published memoirs (*Reminiscenzen von August Spies*, Albert Currlin, ed. (Chicago: Christine Spies, 1888)) recounts the critical moment of the blast: "...I had just reached the ground when a terrible detonation occurred. 'What is that?' asked my brother. 'A cannon, I believe,' was my reply. In an instant the fusilade of the police began." Having just stepped foot on the sidewalk, Spies was standing erect about 40 or 50 feet away and with his left side toward the blast. He does not report being thrown to the ground, nor does he report turning his head to look at the grisly effects of the "detonation" which would have been easily seen from his vantage point, but instead reports

having a discussion with his brother in which he speculates that perhaps a cannon had gone off.

Would a man who kept explosives in his office, who wrote editorials about the uses of dynamite to combat the police, and had set off homemade bombs in the woods outside of the city really have any doubts about what had caused the sound he had just heard? Within the range that Spies was to the explosion, he would have been hit with a powerful shockwave and the air would have instantly been acrid with the distinctive smell of TNT. At the very least, his hearing would have been momentarily impaired, especially his left ear, facing the blast, would have been ringing violently. The noise level immediately after the blast would have also been deafening as the gravely injured screamed in pain, commanders shouted their commands above the din, and the crack of gunfire rang out. Is it likely, in that moment, that Spies and his brother could have heard each other, let alone have a seven word conversation? Only later in the next paragraph of his narrative does Spies describe the bomb as having "a loud report."

At this point Spies narrative encounters an even more puzzling disjunction. "Turning aside when I had answered, 'It's a cannon, I believe,' [which are not the same words he remembered in the previous paragraph] his brother beheld the muzzle of a revolver deliberately aimed at my back. Grasping the weapon, the bullet struck him in a vital part." According to Spies this occurred as the police fusillade began and "Everybody was running . . . I lost my brother in the throng and was carried away toward the north." Half an hour later he took a streetcar and rode home "to see if my brother had been hurt."

If an assassin held a gun to Spies' back at the moment he had been talking to his brother, wouldn't his brother have to reach behind Spies to seize the weapon? How could Spies have not witnessed the desperate struggle between his brother and a mysterious assailant and not known of this until he returned home? His brother, being struck in a "vital part" must have had the strength to run away, though if he did so, why would the assassin, having shot him once, allow him to flee?

And just who tried to assassinate August Spies? Spies explains in a footnote that "There is no question at all but that detectives had been stationed in the crowd to kill the obnoxious speakers at the instant the police would charge upon the crowd." They must have been very poor shots, because they failed to kill any of the anarchist speakers. Moreover, what detective would stand in plain clothes, undercover, in the midst of a crowd that they knew was about to be fired upon by a phalanx of police just to get off an additional shot at one of the speakers? If assassination was the plan, wouldn't it have been better to station a shooter on one of the rooftops and pick them off without danger to themselves? Or better, to wait a block up by Lake street in the direction the crowd would flee to set up a deadly crossfire? Tactically, Spies' assassin story is clearly questionable.

70. Testimony of Henry Spies, HADC, Vol. M, p. 153.
71. Testimony of Henry Spies, HADC, Vol. M, p. 155.

CHAPTER 5

1. Testimony of Frank Stenner, HADC, Vol. L, pp. 285–286; Testimony of John Wessler, HADC, Vol. I, pp. 250–251; Testimony of Peter Foley, HADC, Vol. I, pp. 266–274.
2. Testimony of Daniel Scully, HADC, Vol. N, pp. 157–163. Testimony of John B. Ryan, HADC, Vol. N, pp. 164–166. The defense attempted to question a different lawyer who was present in Judge Scully's courtroom and who they thought was going to say that he heard a police officer accuse Stenner of shooting from the wagon, but William Weimers could not remember which police officer he heard make the remark and he was not allowed to swear to it unless he could indicate who he allegedly made the remark.

Grinnell suggested at the time that the defense call Scully or Ryan to the stand instead
and they must have decided not to. Testimony of William F. Weimers, HADC, Vol. M,
pp. 185–189.

3. Testimony of Frank Stenner, HADC, Vol. L, p. 296.
4. Testimony of Samuel Fielden, HADC, Vol. M, p. 318.
5. Testimony of E. G. Epler, HADC, Vol. K, p. 573.
6. Testimony of Frank Stenner, HADC, Vol. L, pp. 293–294.
7. Testimony of Friedrich Liebel, HADC, Vol. L. p. 202.
8. Testimony of Ludwig Zeller, HADC, Vol. L, p. 151.
9. Testimony of Friedrich Liebel, HADC, Vol. L, p. 202.
10. Testimony of William Gleason, HADC, Vol. L, p. 373.
11. Testimony of Robert Lindinger, HADC, Vol. L, p. 487.
12. Testimony of George W. Hubbard, HADC, Vol. J., p. 81.
13. In fact, newspaper reports indicated that the Chicago Telephone Company had begun
    removing lines and poles in December of 1885 that were no longer needed. *Chicago
    Tribune*, Dec. 14, 1885, p. 8.
14. Testimony of Andrew J. Baxter, HADC, Vol. K, pp. 618–619. Paul Avrich categori-
    cally claimed, "The eighth fatality, Timothy Sullivan, died from the effects of a bullet
    wound" (Paul Avrich, *The Haymarket Tragedy* (Princeton, NJ: Princeton Univ. Press,
    1984), p. 208). Avrich's primary source for this statement is police captain Michael
    J. Schaack's work, *Anarchy and Anarchists* (Chicago: F.J. Shulte & Co., 1889), a work that
    Avrich otherwise dismisses as an apology for the prosecution lacking credibility. Though
    Schaack claimed that he compiled his detailed inventory of the police officer's wounds
    from medical reports, his list is inconsistent with the testimony of four surgeons who actu-
    ally treated the men. It is possible that Schaack exaggerated the extent of bullet wounds
    as his book left no room for doubt as to the coordinated character of what he referred to
    as the "Haymarket Massacre." By inflating the number of bullet wounds, Schaack made
    the anarchist conspiracy appear larger than even the prosecution claimed it to be (See
    Schaack, pp. 146, 150–155).
15. Testimony of H. F. Kruger, HADC, Vol. I, pp. 231–246.
16. *Chicago Tribune* reprinted in *Labor Enquirer* (Denver), July 10, 1886, p. 1.
17. Paul Avrich uses this anonymous source as grounds to write, "Another fact is equally
    noteworthy. All or nearly all of the policemen who had suffered bullet wounds had been
    shot by their fellow officers and not by civilians in the crowd. . . . nearly all sources agree
    that it was the police who opened fire; and while it is possible that some civilians fired
    back, reliable witnesses testified that all the pistol flashes came from the center of the street,
    where the police were standing, and none from the crowd" (Avrich, pp. 208–209). James
    Green likewise uses this anonymous tipster selectively, mentioning only his allegation of
    friendly fire and not his equally insistent claim that the crowd fired first from all sides
    (James Green, *Death in the Haymarket: A Story of Chicago, The First Labor Movement, and
    the Bombing that Divided Gilded Age America* (New York: Pantheon Books, 2006), p. 189).
    Green also twists the testimony of Captain Ward to make him appear to be uncertain as
    to whether the crowd or the police fired first. "Captain Ward said he heard gunshots
    immediately after the explosion, but could not be sure who fired first because the firing
    was indiscriminate" (Green, p. 188). Green provides a citation for this statement that
    sources the *Chicago Tribune* for May 5 and 6, 1886. Ward did not make any comments in
    the *Tribune* issued on May 5, so Green must be referring to Ward's testimony before the
    Coroner's Jury on May 6 where his remarks were paraphrased as follows: "At that moment
    the bomb exploded and an indiscriminate firing began. . . . He (Capt. Ward) was ten feet
    or more in front of the police line when the bomb was thrown. He did not give any
    order for his men to fire. There was a great deal of confusion among the officers after the
    bomb exploded" (*Chicago Tribune*, May 6, 1886, p. 1). Actually, Ward's only documented

statement on this issue, from the witness stand and under oath, contains no such doubts about who began the shooting:

A: Well, a few seconds after he said "We are peaceable", I heard the explosion.
Q: In your rear?
A: In my rear.
Q: Then what happened?
A: I turned and looked to see and pistol firing began from in front and on both sides of the street.
Q: Was the pistol firing begun by the crowd?
A: By the crowd, yes; it came from in front of us and on each side of the street, immediately afterwards. (HADC, Vol. I, p. 430)

18. *Labor Enquirer* (Denver), May 22, 1886, p. 2.
19. *Labor Enquirer* (Denver), May 29, 1886, p. 2.
20. Testimony of Adolph Temmes, HADC, Vol. Vol. M, pp. 267–273.
21. Testimony of Sleeper T. Ingram, HADC, Vol. M, pp. 447–487. *Chicago Tribune*, Aug. 8, 1886, p. 11.
22. Testimony of Carl Richter, HADC, Vol. L, pp. 191–192; Testimony of Frank Raab, HADC, Vol. L, p. 313; Testimony of Konrad Messer, HADC, Vol. L., pp. 402–405. Testimony of August Krumm, HADC, Vol. L, p. 454.
23. Contemporary defenders of the anarchists eagerly repeated Spies' charges. Lum, p. 157; Leon Lewis, *The Facts Concerning the Eight Condemned Leaders* (Greenport, N.Y., 1887), pp. 26–27.
24. *The Accused, the Accusers: The Famous Speeches of the Eight Chicago Anarchists* . . . (Chicago, IL: Socialistic Publishing Society (1886), pp. 1–2; also reprinted in Lucy Parsons, *Famous Speeches of the Eight Chicago Anarchists* (Arno Press, 1969, org. 1910)), p. 11.
25. *Chicago Tribune*, Oct. 9, 1886, p. 1.
26. Schaack, pp. 382–383.
27. *Chicago Tribune*, Nov. 5, 1887, p. 2.
28. Spies testimony on this point is found in HADC, Vol. N, p. 48. *Chicago Tribune*, Nov. 8, 1887, p. 2.
29. Most historical accounts of the bombing conclude that the bomb was thrown from behind a tall stack of boxes that stood on the sidewalk 35 to 40 feet south of Crane's alley. "It was established, in any case, by the testimony of reporters, policemen, and other witnesses, that the bomb was thrown not from the alley but from a point on the sidewalk of Desplaines Street a considerable distance to the south of it." Avrich, p. 270; "Careful consideration of the evidence leads to the conclusion that the bomb was probably thrown from a point some fifteen paces south of Crane's alley." Henry David, *The Haymarket Affair* (New York: Russell & Russell, 1936, 1958), p. 266.

    The bomber had to consider where to stand so as to be able to light the fuse and toss the bomb without being interfered with. Obviously, if this was done within sight of policemen, they might very well interrupt the process. As the crowd on Desplaines street that night, by all accounts, consisted of a large number of apolitical curious onlookers, there was also a danger that a bystander might gather up the courage to grapple with the bomber. Since every murderer would prefer to remain anonymous given the choice, it only made sense to light and throw the bomb from a hidden or sheltered spot. There were only a few places on the southerly end of Desplaines street where a man could hide with room to light, stand and throw a heavy lead bomb. There was a vestibule at the very southwestern corner of the block, but this was about one hundred feet from where the bomb landed, a mark far too long for even a strong man to reach. It was also possible for a man to crouch down behind one of the wheels of the speakers' wagon itself, though the apparent trajectory of the bomb would rule out any spot north of Crane's alley. Of course, the deep shadows in the narrow alley afforded excellent cover. Somewhere between Crane's alley and that vestibule was a stack of fish crates, nearly as tall as a man.

The fish crates did, indeed, make an excellent blind from which to light and throw the bomb, but that being so, why didn't the bomber throw the bomb in the direction of the police as they were marching up the street, rather than waiting to throw it after they had passed him? Throwing it before they came up had many advantages, especially in making it more likely that he could escape, for once the police marched past the fish crates the bomber was effectively surrounded and his likely routes of flight were blocked. Moreover, testimony of both witnesses for the state and for the defense described how as the police marched shoulder-to-shoulder, curb to curb, the crowd was pushed both back up the street and onto the sidewalks, particularly the eastern sidewalk. This meant that the closer the police came to the fish crates, the more crowded was the sidewalk and therefore the less private was the hiding spot behind those fishy boxes. Unless the bomber planned to throw the bomb before the police reached his position behind the crates, the crates were just a lousy place from which to launch the attack.

The only good ambush-spot on that particular street, one that satisfied all three tactical concerns, that of safety to friends, cover, and escape, was the alley. It was shadowy, it held a number of people, it provided a good view of the street and a safe zone in which to throw the explosive. It was also the best place from which to escape. Crane's alley made a right turn after about 40 feet and led directly out to the always-busy Randolph street and the streetcars that ran along it. Crane's alley also fits the facts as the bomber's hiding place in one other important way—had someone been hunkering down in the alley, waiting to attack, because the alley was so narrow, the police would not have come into range until they had marched clear up the block, right past the alleyway pushing the crowd ahead of them, just as they did before the bomb was thrown.

30. The Olympic world record in the shot put is held by Ulf Timmermann, who heaved the shot put seventy-three feet, eight and three-quarters inches at the 1988 games.

31. Testimony of August Krumm, HADC, Vol. L, p. 419, 458–459.

32. Testimony of August Krumm, HADC, Vol. L, p. 460.

33. *Chicago Tribune*, Aug. 8, 1886, p. 11. Testimony of John Bernett, HADC, Vol. M, p. 491.

34. Testimony of James D. Taylor, HADC, Vol. L, p. 238.

35. Testimony of James D. Taylor, HADC, Vol. L, pp. 231, 247, 254, 222. Beyond the inconsistencies with the defense's lone-bomber-behind-the-boxes theory, there was another small but important matter. The bomb had to not only be thrown, but it had to be lit as well. The portable lighter had not yet been invented and the state of the art in matches made lighting a match with one hand very difficult, if not impossible.

In the 1880s two types of matches were commercially available. One variety, known popularly as "Lucifers," were manufactured with a coating of white phosphorous and could be struck against any very rough surface. But Lucifers were notoriously unstable and prone to combustion at unwanted times and places, such as a man's coat pocket, and were carried in metal match-safes that prevented such accidents. Match-safes were manufactured in a wide variety of styles, from finely sculptured jeweled cases to simple tin boxes. All match-safes had a rough striking plate on one side upon which to scrape the stubborn, thick-headed Lucifer matches.

Also available by the 1880s were red-phosphorous "safety" matches that were safer in two important ways. They could not ignite by being jostled together and they did not contain the white phosphorous that was so poisonous that a common method of suicide was to swallow a handful of match-heads. Safety matches could only be ignited by striking on the chemically impregnated strip located on the side of a safety-match box. (M.F. Crass, "A History of the Match Industry," *Journal of Chemical Education*, Vol. 18 (1941), pp. 277–282, 316–319, 380–384, 428–431.)

If the bomb was lit by a match, it was probably struck by an accomplice rather than by the bomber himself. Whether using a match-safe or a matchbox, lighting a match required holding the box with one hand and the match in the other. It would have been possible for someone to strike a Lucifer match against the wall of a building, but not against the street or the sidewalk as both of these were made of wood, rather than brick or stone. Moreover, unlike modern "strike-anywhere" matches that only require a slight flick off the head to ignite, older Lucifers required a longer draw with more friction to ignite and were fickle once lit. Mayor Harrison when he was on the stand happened to note that he tried lighting his cigar earlier that night and said in an offhand way, "I use more matches than I do cigars a good deal—I struck it, and the first one went out. I put two together, and the flame was wide and it made quite a blaze in my face" (Testimony of Carter Harrison, HADC, Vol. L, p. 32). If the bomber was crouching behind the fish-boxes, as the defense argued, he would have been a dozen feet from the wall of building behind, and had he stepped away from the boxes to light his Lucifer he would no longer have been concealed from the view of the police.

If striking the match was a two-handed operation, it is most unlikely that the bomber would set the bomb on the ground to light it. Fuses were of fickle duration and the bomb was a sphere and so the bomber would have had to have been concerned about getting a handle on the bomb and picking it up smoothly before the fuse had burned down too far. Also, striking the match, setting down the match-safe or matchbox and then picking up the bomb would have been difficult for two reasons. Either the bomber would have had to have struck the match with his off-hand, or passed the bomb from his off-hand to his favored hand after it was lit, because unless the bomber was ambidextrous, the natural tendency would have been to handle the match and throw the bomb with whichever hand was customary. It is, of course, possible that the bomber could have lit a cigar, returned his matchbox to his pocket and then, carefully flicking off ash to keep the tip as hot as possible, used it to light the bomb. But the bomber would still have to have lit his cigar at some point and this was, apparently, not easily done that night. Moreover, not a single witness for either the prosecution or the defense, who claimed to have seen the bomber, described a man with a cigar.

Compounding the bomber's task was the weather. According to both prosecution and defense accounts of that evening's weather, the wind had come up just before the police marched down Desplaines street. With the clouds gathering overhead and the wind gusting, the match-striker would have had to cup the match between his hands or duck down behind a wind-break to even light a match, and the prospect of lighting one then holding it burning while the other hand put down a matchbox and picked up a bomb seems rather unlikely. One defense witness, August Krumm, explained that he had trouble lighting his pipe about the same time the police moved up the street. Krumm's solution was to duck into Crane's alley to avoid the wind. He and his friend "went back a little ways in the alley, and lit my pipe. He gave me a pipe of tobacco, and lit the match and both of us had fire from that match, a couple of steps back in the alley maybe" (Testimony of August Krumm, HADC, Vol. L, p. 415). The prosecutor clarified, "Q: Why did you withdraw to the alley to light your pipes? A: There was a kind of a draft on the sidewalk, and we stepped back into the alley." (Testimony of August Krumm, HADC, Vol. L, p. 418.) Once their pipes were lit Krumm and his companion left the alley. With the wind kicking up, it would have only made sense for the bomber too to duck into the alley to get his bomb lit.

36. Testimony of W.C. Metzner, HADC, Vol. K, p. 239.
37. Testimony of W.C. Metzner, HADC, Vol. K, p. 238.
38. Testimony of George W. Hubbard, HADC, Vol. J, p. 79.
39. Testimony of John Wessler, HADC, Vol. I, p. 253.
40. Testimony of James P. Stanton, HADC, Vol. I, p. 225.

41. Stanton's guess that the bomb had come from north of the alley would have put the bomber near to Officer H.F. Krueger who was on the right next to the curb in the very first rank of the police. Krueger did not see either the bomb or the bomber. See Testimony of H.F. Krueger, HADC, Vol. I, pp. 240–242.

42. Testimony of James P. Stanton, HADC, Vol. I, pp. 221, 226–227.

43. Testimony of John Holloway, HADC, Vol. M, p. 59.

44. Testimony of John Holloway, HADC, Vol. M, p. 60.

45. Testimony of Joseph Schwindt, HADC, Vol. L, p. 563.

46. Testimony of Lucius M. Moses, HADC, Vol. L, pp. 267–273; Testimony of Austin Mitchell, HADC, Vol. L, pp. 274–279.

47. Testimony of B.P. Lee, HADC, Vol. L, pp. 280–281; Testimony of John O. Brixley, HADC, Vol. L., pp. 326–335.

48. Testimony of Mary Grubb, HADC, Vol. M, pp. 37–40; Testimony of Phineas H. Adams, HADC, Vol. M., pp. 213–217; Testimony of Edward H. Castle, HADC, Vol. M, pp. 263–266; Testimony of H.S. Howe, HADC, Vol. M, pp. 266–267. Testimony of J.W. Gage, HADC, Vol. M, pp. 487–489. Paul Avrich exaggerates both the quality and quantity of witnesses when he writes that "ten prominent Chicago citizens... testified that Gilmer was an inveterate liar whom they would not believe under oath" (p. 270).

49. Testimony of Richard S. Tuthill, HADC, Vol. N, pp. 173–180. Carolyn Ashbaugh writes, "One of the persons who testified to Gilmer's *good* character was Joshiah B. Grinnell, first cousin of the prosecutor." In fact, no one by that name appears on the inventory of the full trial transcript, nor anywhere in the 17 volumes or in the daily newspaper accounts of the trail (Ashbaugh, p. 272).

50. Testimony of Charles A. Dibble, HADC, Vol. N, pp. 181–186.

51. John D. Lawson, ed., *American State Trials* (St. Louis, Missouri: F.H. Thomas Law Book Co., 1919), vol. 12, p. 155. *Chicago Tribune*, Aug. 12, 1886, p. 1. In his haste Walker mistakenly described *Lamb v. Illinois* as the case of a man who was killed by a mob in which the Supreme Court of Illinois underscored the rule that "all who were engaged in the unlawful proceedings were guilty... as well as the one who threw the stone." That description is actually part of another conspiracy case, *Kern Brennan, et. al., v. Illinois* (15 Ill. 511; 1854 Ill. Lexis 53, June 1854). In the Brennan case the Illinois Supreme Court stated that "The prisoners might well be convicted of the homicide, if the fatal blow was given by a person not named in the indictment, provided they were present aiding or abetting him, or, if absent, had advised or encouraged him to do the act." Lamb's case involved a burglar who wasn't present when his fellow thieves shot and killed a Chicago police officer in October of 1878 while transporting their loot. The trial judge refused to instruct the jury that unless Lamb was present at the killing or in planning the crime had advised or agreed that deadly force be used to conceal their activities, he should be acquitted. The Illinois Supreme Court in a close decision thought this instruction should have been given and granted Lamb a new trial. See also *John Lamb v. The People of the State Of Illinois*, Supreme Court of Illinois, 96 Ill. 73; 1879 Ill. Lexis, 48.

52. *American State Trials*, vol. 12, pp. 158–159, 240.

53. Frederick Trevor Hill, "The Chicago Anarchists' Case," *Harper's Monthly Magazine*, 114, Dec, 1906-Jan. 1907, p. 898.

54. *Chicago Tribune*, Aug. 15, 1886, p. 6; *American State Trials*, vol. 12, pp. 201, 206, 208, 218.

55. *American State Trials*, vol. 12, pp. 231, 235.

56. *American State Trials*, vol. 12, p. 167.

57. *American State Trials*, vol. 12, p. 171.

58. HADC, Vol. M, pp. 74–81. *American State Trials*, vol. 12, p. 169. Officers Duffy (HADC, Vol. J, pp. 106–114) and McKeough (HADC, Vol. J, pp. 115–117) testified to finding the package of dynamite in the closet.

59. *American State Trials*, vol. 12, pp. 167, 169.
60. *American State Trials*, vol. 12, pp. 175–176, 239, 242.
61. *American State Trials*, vol. 12, pp. 245, 246.
62. *American State Trials*, vol. 12, pp. 250, 252. Among the more frequently repeated quotes from the Haymarket trial is this portion of prosecutor Grinnell's concluding remarks. Many scholars have quoted Grinnell as "thundering" or "shouting" to the jury: "Law is on trial. Anarchy is on trial. Gentlemen of the jury, convict these men, make examples of them, hang them and you save our institutions, our society." However, Grinnell never made this speech. It is a complete fabrication.

The historian most responsible for spreading this spurious quotation is Philip Foner (*History of the Labor Movement in the United States*, vol. 2 (New York: International Publishers, 1955), p. 109). Foner cites as his source for this quotation not the widely available newspaper or legal reprints of Grinnell's speech, but defendant Albert Parson's recollections of the trial as published in his *Anarchism: Its Philosophy and Scientific Basis* (Chicago, 1887), p. 53. In his recollection, Parson does not attribute this quote to Grinnell, but indicates that these remarks were a compilation of statements of the "prosecution." Foner ignores Parson's own qualifications and simply misattributes Parsons' contrived montage of recollections to Grinnell and places them authoritatively in quotation marks. From there, it seems, many scholars have been eager to repeat Foner's invention without consulting the actual source.

This false quotation has appeared regularly in literature on the Haymarket. Here are some of the scholars who have included it in their own works: Saku Pinta, "Anarchism, Marxism, and the Ideological Composition of the Chicago Idea," *Working USA: The Journal of Labor and Society*, Vol. 12 (Sept. 2009), pp. 421–450; Melinda M. Hicks, Charles Belmont Keeney, *Defending the Homeland: Historical Perspectives on Radicalism, Terrorism, and State Responses* (Charleston: West Virginia University Press, 2007), p. 10; Kristian Williams, *Our Enemies in Blue: Police and Power in America* (Rev. Ed., Boston: South End Press, 2007; org. New York: Soft Skull Press, 2004), p. 172; Kenneth E. Foote, *Shadowed Ground: America's Landscapes of Violence and Tragedy* (Austin: University of Texas Press, 2003), p. 135; Marco D'Eramo, Graeme Thomson, *The Pig and the Skyscraper: Chicago a History of Our Future* (London: Verso, 2003), p. 190; Robert Justin Goldstein, *Political Repression in Modern America from 1870 to 1976* (Urbana: University of Illinois Press, 2001), p. 40; Donald L. Miller, *City of the Century: The Epic of Chicago and the Making of America* (New York: Simon & Schuster, 1997), p. 477; Bruce C. Nelson, *Beyond the Martyrs: A Social History of Chicago's Anarchists, 1870–1900* (New Brunswick: Rutger's Univ. Press, 1988), pp. 192–193; Carolyn Ashbaugh, *Lucy Parsons, American Revolutionary: American Revolutionary* (Illinois Labor History Society, Chicago: Charles H. Kerr Pub. Co., 1976), p. 96; Andrew S. Berky, James Patrick Shenton, *The Historians' History of the United States* (New York: Putnam, 1966), p. 966; Sidney Lens, *Radicalism in America* (New York: Crowell, 1969), p. 170.
63. *American State Trials*, vol. 12, pp. 258–259.
64. *Chicago Tribune*, Aug. 21, 1886, p. 1.
65. *Chicago Tribune*, Aug. 20, 1886, p. 1.

CHAPTER 6

1. Existing Haymarket scholarship misrepresents the nature of the trial by claiming that it was "the defendants' ideas alone that were to be the basis of their guilt" as Bryan Palmer puts it. Paul Avrich in describing the trial gives the impression that Judge Gary's

instructions to the jury simply emphasized that the defendants could be convicted if their words encouraged the throwing of the bomb. "At no other point in the trial... were Gary's rulings more injurious to the defendants. If, he now declared, they conspired to overthrow the law by force, and if, in the pursuance of such a conspiracy, a bomb was thrown by a member of the conspiracy... then the defendants were accessories... whether or not the identity of the bombthrower had been established." This overlooks the fact that several other instructions required that there be proven a more direct connection between the conspiracy and the bombing (Paul Avrich, *The Haymarket Tragedy* (Princeton, NJ: Princeton Univ. Press, 1984), p. 275).

2. Court's Instructions to the Jury, HADC, Vol. O, pp. 35–38. As far as I can determine, no historian who has written about the Haymarket trial in the past century has mentioned or quoted these instructions given to the jury by Judge Gary.

3. *Illinois vs. August Spies et al.* trial transcript no. 1, Illinois Supreme Court: Writ Of Error Decision, Sept. 14, 1887, 7-v, 8-v. Reproduced in HADC, Vol. O, pp. 186–187.

4. *Chicago Tribune*, Aug. 21, 1886, p. 1.

5. Defendants Instructions to the Jury, HADC, Vol. O, p. 11.

6. Court's Instructions to the Jury, HADC, Vol. O, p. 34.

7. *Chicago Tribune*, Aug. 26, 1886, p. 2.

8. *Chicago Tribune*, Aug. 20, 1886, p. 1.

9. *Chicago Tribune*, Aug. 21, 1886, p. 1; *Liberty*, Sept. 18, 1886, p. 4.

10. *Chicago Tribune*, Aug. 21, 1886, p. 1.

11. *Chicago Tribune*, Aug. 21, 1886, p. 2; Aug. 26, 1886, p. 2.

12. Motion by Defense for a New Trial, HADC, Vol. O, pp. 53–54.

13. Affidavits of the Defendants and E. A. Stevens, HADC, Vol. O, p. 62.

14. *Chicago Tribune*, Oct. 29, 1882, p. 10; Jan. 29, 1883, p. 8; Nov. 20, 1886, p. 1; Nov. 7, 1881, p. 8. *The Open Court: A Quarterly Magazine* (Chicago), Feb. 17, 1887, p. 1; Nov. 24, 1887, p. 592; Liberal League "Constitution and By-laws Adopted Nov. 6, 1881," in George Schilling Papers, Agnes Inglis Collection, Labadie Library, University of Michigan; *Chicago Daily Tribune*, Nov. 20, 1886, p. 1 and Stevens letter to editor, Nov. 23, 1886, p. 10a.

15. *The Alarm*, Jan. 13, 1885, May 16, 1885; "Annual Convention of the Union of Ethical Culture Societies," *The Open Court*, Nov. 24, 1887, p. 592; Favor is listed as "trustee" and "treasurer" of the society in *The Open Court*, Feb. 17, 1887, p. 1.

16. Affidavits of the Defendants and E. A. Stevens, HADC, Vol. O, p. 69.

17. Sigmund Zeisler, "The Prevalence of Perjury," May 14, 1894, Zeisler Papers, Newberry Library, Box 4, Folder 62; Affidavits of John Phillip Deluse, Jacob L. Biehler and Oscar Sputh, HADC, Vol. O, pp. 92–93.

18. Affidavits of Thomas J. Morgan, Thomas S. Morgan and Michael Cull, HADC, Vol. O, pp. 75–79; Ralph Scharnau, "Thomas J. Morgan and the Chicago Socialist Movement, 1876–1901," Ph.D. Diss. Northern Illinois Univ., 1967, p. 102.

19. Affidavit of Albert P. Love, HADC, Vol. O, pp. 119–123; *Chicago Tribune*, Oct. 2, 1886, p. 1.

20. Sigmund Zeisler, "The Prevalence of Perjury," May 14, 1894, Zeisler Papers, Newberry Library, Box 4, Folder 62.

21. Affidavit of Thomas H. Currier, HADC, Vol. O, pp. 90–91,

22. *Chicago Tribune*, Oct. 5, 1886, p. 2.

23. Lucy Parsons, *Famous Speeches of the Eight Chicago Anarchists* (New York: Arno Press, 1969; 2nd ed. org. 1910), pp. 82, 68, 106.

24. *Chicago Tribune*, Oct. 8, 1886, p. 2. *The Accused, the Accusers : The Famous Speeches of the Eight Chicago Anarchists in Court...* (Chicago: Socialistic Publishing Co., 1886), pp. 8, 23.

25. *Chicago Tribune*, Oct. 9, 1886, p. 1.
26. *Chicago Tribune*, Oct. 9, 1886, p. 1.
27. *Inter-Ocean*, Oct. 8, 1886, p. 6.
28. *Chicago Tribune*, Oct. 8, 1886, p. 2.
29. *Liberty: Not the Daughter but the Mother of Order*, Sept. 18, 1886, p. 4.
30. *Brooklyn Eagle*, Sept. 24, 1886, p. 4.
31. James Green misquotes his sources in discussing the press response to the verdict. Green writes that the *Inter-Ocean* said, "Anarchism has been on trial ever since May 4; and it now has got its verdict. Death is the only fitting penalty" (James Green, *Death in the Haymarket: A Story of Chicago, The First Labor Movement, and the Bombing that Divided Gilded Age America* (New York: Pantheon Books, 2006), p. 229). But the source he cites, Henry David's *History of the Haymarket Affair*, reads very differently: "Anarchism has been on trial ever since May 4; and it has now got its verdict . . . The verdict . . . is unquestion-ably the voice of justice, the solemn verdict of the world's best civilization . . . " (Henry David, *The History of the Haymarket Affair: A Study in the American Social-Revolutionary and Labor Movements* (New York: Russell & Russell, 1958, org. 1936), p. 319). While the first line of the quote is accurate, the second appears to have been appended from another page in David, where David quotes a different editorial from another day's *Inter-Ocean*. On page 320 of David's book can be found the following: "This thought was repeated the following day by the *Inter-Ocean*. 'Anarchism is treason and when any undertake to substitute it in place of law, it becomes a crime of the deepest dye. Death is the only fitting penalty.'" Apparently, Green combined a portion of a quote from one day with a portion of a quote from another day's paper to construct a more lurid passage.

    Green misquotes other newspapers' remarks on the verdict as well. He writes of the *Chicago Tribune*: "The *Tribune* reported 'universal satisfaction with the verdict' because 'the law had been vindicated.'" (Green, p. 229) But the actual wording in the *Tribune* is significantly different: "The universal satisfaction with which the verdict of the jury was received yesterday was based upon this very point—namely: that the law had been vindi-cated and had shown itself amply able to cope with Anarchism and strangle it" (*Chicago Tribune*, Aug. 21, 1886, p. 4).
32. *The Commonweal* (London), Oct. 2, 1886, p. 211.
33. *Chicago Tribune*, Aug. 21, 1886, p. 2.
34. *Inter-Ocean*, Dec. 5, 1887, p. 5; Dec. 6, 1887, p. 7.
35. *Chicago Tribune*, Oct. 11, 1886, p. 1.
36. *Brooklyn Eagle*, Oct. 12, 1886, p. 4.
37. *Brooklyn Eagle*, Oct. 12, 1886, p. 4.

CHAPTER 7

1. *Inter-Ocean*, Apr. 25, 1887, p. 3.
2. John D. Lawson, ed., *American State Trials* (St. Louis, Missouri: F.H. Thomas Law Book Co., 1919), vol. 12, p. 202; *Chicago Tribune*, Aug. 22, 1886, p. 15.
3. *Chicago Tribune*, Mar. 18, 1887, p. 1.
4. *Chicago Tribune*, Mar. 15, 1887, p. 3. Swett was retained in late November 1886, *Chicago Tribune*, Nov. 24, 1886, p. 1.
5. *Chicago Tribune*, Jan. 21, 1887, p. 3.
6. *Chicago Inter-Ocean*, Nov. 28, 1886, p. 8. In 1897, Captain Black appeared on a cam-paign platform with Eugene Debs and stumped for the "Social Democracy." Black roused the crowd by arguing that the Declaration of Independence did not give any rights to property. *Chicago Tribune*, Aug. 2, 1897, p. 3.

7. *Chicago Tribune*, Nov. 26, 1886, p. 1; Engels interviewed in *Inter-Ocean*, Nov. 11, 1887, p. 2.
8. *Chicago Tribune*, Mar. 19, 1887, p. 1.
9. *The University Magazine* (New York) 9:4 (October, 1893), p. 713. *The Green Bag* (Boston), Vol. 3, 1891, pp. 236–237.
10. Illinois Supreme Court Decision, HADC, Vol. O., p. 15.
11. Illinois Supreme Court Decision, HADC, Vol. O., pp. 16–25.
12. Ibid.
13. Illinois Supreme Court Decision, HADC, Vol. O., p. 36.
14. Illinois Supreme Court Decision, HADC, Vol. O., p. 52.
15. Illinois Supreme Court Decision, HADC, Vol. O., p. 64.
16. Illinois Supreme Court Decision, HADC, Vol. O., p. 72.
17. Illinois Supreme Court Decision, HADC, Vol. O., p. 73.
18. Illinois Supreme Court Decision, HADC, Vol. O., pp. 94–95.
19. Illinois Supreme Court Decision, HADC, Vol. O., pp. 125–126.
20. Illinois Supreme Court Decision, HADC, Vol. O., p. 164.
21. Testimony of August Spies, Haymarket Affair Digital Collection, Chicago Historical Society (HADC), Vol. N, p. 104.
22. *August Spies et. al. v. The People*, Supreme Court of Illinois. 122 Ill. 1; 12 N.E. 865; 1887 Ill. LEXIS 969. Paul Avrich selectively quotes the first bit of Mulkey's opinion but not the part in which he compliments the conduct of the trial (Paul Avrich, *The Haymarket Tragedy* (Princeton, NJ: Princeton Univ. Press, 1984), p. 334). *The Bench and Bar of Illinois*, John M. Palmer, ed., Vol. 1 (Chicago: Lewis Pub. Co., 1899), p. 63.
23. *The Albany Law Journal*, Oct. 29, 1887, p. 341.
24. *The Central Law Journal*, Nov. 12, 1887, p. 457.
25. *Chicago Tribune*, Sept. 16, 1887, p. 1.
26. *Brooklyn Eagle*, Oct. 16, 1886, p. 4.
27. *Chicago Tribune*, Oct. 23, 1887, p. 11
28. *Chicago Tribune*, Sept. 23, 1887, p. 2.
29. *Chicago Tribune*, Oct. 27, 1887, p. 3.
30. *Chicago Tribune*, Oct. 2, 1887, p. 11.
31. James Wilton Brooks, *History of the Court of Common Pleas of the City and County of New York* (New York: Werner, Sanford & Co., 1896), pp. 127–128; Robert S. Holzman, *Adapt or Perish: The Life of General Roger A. Pryor, C.S.A.* (Hamden, CO: Archon Books, 1976).
32. Norman K. Risjord, *The Old Republicans: Southern Conservatism in the Age of Jefferson* (New York: Columbia Univ. Press, 1965); Henry W. Scott, *Distinguished American Lawyers* (New York: Charles L. Webster & Co., 1891), pp. 681–682.
33. Chester G. Hearn, *When the Devil Came Down to Dixie: Ben Butler in New Orleans* (Baton Rouge: Louisiana State Univ. Press, 1997); Howard P. Nash, *Stormy Petrel: The Life and Times of General Benjamin F. Butler, 1818–1893* (Rutherford, N.J.: Fairleigh Dickinson Univ. Press, 1969); *Chicago Tribune*, Oct. 19, 1887, p. 1.
34. James Green devotes three paragraphs to the Supreme Court appeal, James Green, *Death in the Haymarket: A Story of Chicago, The First Labor Movement, and the Bombing that Divided Gilded Age America* (New York: Pantheon Books, 2006), pp. 253–254. Paul Avrich sums it up in two, writing, "The court, as Benjamin Butler had foreseen, ruled that it lacked jurisdiction in the case because no Federal issue was involved" (Avrich, pp. 335–336). Incredibly, neither author cites nor seems to be aware of the chapter Henry David devoted to the Supreme Court case in his otherwise closely scrutinized *The History of the Haymarket Affair: A Study in the American Social-Revolutionary and Labor Movements* (New York: Russell & Russell, 1958, org. 1936), ch. 18, pp. 375–392. *Chicago Tribune*, Sept. 21, 1887, p. 2.

35. *Chicago Daily Tribune*, Nov. 7, 1887, p. 1; June 9, 1898, p. 12. Grinnell was elected judge of the circuit court in June 1887 and stood for election as judge of the superior court that November. Grinnell served as county judge for the next four years before resigning to take up the more lucrative job of general counsel of the Chicago City Railway. *Chicago Tribune*, June 7, 1887, p. 1; Oct. 5, 1887, p. 3.

36. *The New York Times*, Nov. 1, 1887, p. 3.

37. *Brooklyn Eagle*, Oct. 16, 1886, p. 4.

CHAPTER 8

1. *Lucifer*, June 18, 1886.

2. Testimony of Godfried Waller, Haymarket Affair Digital Collection, Chicago Historical Society (HADC), Vol. I, p. 60.

3. *In the Supreme Court of Illinois, Northern Grand Division. March Term, 1887. August Spies et. al., vs. The People of the State of Illinois, Abstract of Record* (Chicago, 1887), vol. 2, p. 4.

4. Dyer D. Lum, *A Concise History of the Great Trial of the Chicago Anarchists in 1886* (Chicago: Socialistic Publishing Co., 1887; reissued by Arno Press, New York, 1969), p. 69.

5. Lum, *A Concise History*, p. 174.

6. Howell's letter to George William Curtis, Aug. 18, 1887, quoted in Clara and Rudolf Kirk, "William Dean Howells, George William Curtis, and the 'Haymarket Affair'," *American Literature*, 40:4 (Jan. 1969), pp. 487–498. See also Howard A. Wilson, "William Dean Howells' Unpublished Letters About the Haymarket Affair," *Journal of the Illinois Historical Society*, 61:1 (Spring 1963), pp. 5–19.

7. *Chicago Tribune*, Nov. 7, 1887, p. 2; Nov. 8, 1887, p. 2.

8. *The American Law Review*, Vol. 21 (1887), p. 992.

9. New York *World*, Nov. 20, 1888, p. 2.

10. *Chicago Tribune*, Nov. 7, 1887, p. 1; Nov. 8, 1887, p. 4.

11. *Chicago Inter-Ocean*, Nov. 9, 1887, p. 2. The numbers reported varied slightly from paper to paper. See also *Chicago Tribune*, Nov. 10, 1887, p. 6.

12. *Chicago Tribune*, Nov. 9, 1887, p. 4.

13. *Chicago Inter-Ocean*, June 4, 1887, p. 12; June 5, 1887, p. 1; June 6, 1887, p. 1.

14. *Chicago Inter-Ocean*, June 7, 1887, p. 2.

15. New York *Evening World*, Nov. 5, 1887, p. 4; *Chicago Tribune*, Nov. 6, 1887, p. 10.

16. Henry David, *The History of the Haymarket Affair: A Study in the American Social-Revolutionary and Labor Movements* (New York: Russell & Russell, 1958, org. 1936), p. 428. James Green mischaracterizes the petitioners' apology for advocating "aggressive force" instead writing that "All three prisoners wrote that they had never advocated the use of force, except in the case of self-defense . . . " (James Green, *Death in the Haymarket: A Story of Chicago, The First Labor Movement, and the Bombing that Divided Gilded Age America* (New York: Pantheon Books, 2006), p. 254).

17. *Chicago Tribune*, Nov. 2, 1887, p. 1.

18. *Chicago Tribune*, Sept. 23, 1887, p. 2.

19. *Chicago Tribune*, Nov. 5, 1887, p. 1; Nov. 6, 1887, p. 10.

20. New York *Evening World*, Nov. 7, 1887, p. 1. Most historians have completely ignored reports of Engel's suicide attempt and those few who do, such as Henry David, doubt that it is true but provide no evidence to support their skepticism. However, anarchist supporter Henry F. Charles, writing for *The Commonweal* of London from Chicago, while freely questioning other official statements, such as claiming the four bombs found in Lingg's cell were "a miserable police plot to make sure of hanging Lingg," but he repeats reports of Engel's attempted suicide without such criticism. *The Commonweal*

(London), Dec. 24, 1887, p. 413. Engel's lawyer, Capt. Black, told reporters he didn't believe Engel tried to kill himself but just "drank a little too much bad whiskey." *Chicago Tribune*, Nov. 7, 1887, p. 1. The *Chicago Tribune* investigated the story of Engel's supposed suicide and concluded there was nothing to it but a "drunk." *Chicago Tribune*, Nov. 8, 1887, p. 1. However, Engel confessed a second time to a reporter the day of his execution that he had indeed tried to kill himself. *Chicago Inter-Ocean*, Nov. 12, 1887, p. 1.

21. The eccentric George Francis Train claimed to have interviewed a man, Adam Cottam, who was responsible for cleaning Lingg's jail cell and thought there was no way he could have concealed anything from his view. Train could not later find Cottam when reporters asked to speak to him. *Chicago Tribune*, Nov. 10, 1887, p. 3.

22. *Chicago Tribune*, Nov. 16, 1887, p. 3.

23. *Inter-Ocean*, Nov. 10, 1887, p. 1.

24. *Inter-Ocean*, Nov. 11, 1887, p. 2.

25. *Chicago Daily Tribune*, Nov. 11, 1887, p. 6.

26. Samuel P. McConnell, "The Chicago Bomb Case: Personal Recollections of an American Tragedy," *Harper's Magazine*, May 1934, pp. 735–736.

27. Ibid.

28. John P. Altgeld, *Reasons for Pardoning Fielden, Neebe and Schwab* (Chicago, IL: s.n., 1893), p. 8.

29. *Chicago Tribune*, Nov. 8, 1887, p. 1.

30. *Chicago Tribune*, Nov. 8, 1887, p. 1; Nov. 10, 1887, p.1.

31. *Chicago Tribune*, Sept. 16, 1887, p. 1.

32. M.M. Trumbull, "Judge Gary and the Anarchists," *The Arena*, Oct. 1893, p. 544.

33. *Chicago Tribune*, Nov. 10, 1887, p. 1.

34. *Inter-Ocean*, Nov. 10, 1887, p. 1.

35. *Chicago Tribune*, Nov. 15, 1887, p. 2.

36. *Inter-Ocean*, Nov. 11, 1887, p. 2; New York *World*, Nov. 11, 1887 (3 o'clock ed.), p. 1.

37. *Chicago Tribune*, Sept. 16, 1941, p. 14.

38. New York *World*, Nov. 11, 1887 (3 o'clock ed.), p. 1. *Chicago Tribune*, Nov. 12, 1887, p. 1.

39. *Chicago Inter-Ocean*, Nov. 12, 1887, p. 1.

CHAPTER 9

1. *Brooklyn Eagle*, Nov. 13, 1887, p. 16.

2. *Chicago Tribune*, Nov. 14, 1887, p. 1.

3. *Inter-Ocean*, Nov. 14, 1887, p. 2; *Chicago Tribune*, Nov. 14, 1887, p. 1.

4. Chicago *Daily News*, Nov. 12, 1888, p. 1; Nov. 12, 1891, p. 1.

5. *Chicago Inter-Ocean*, July 18, 1888, p. 1; July 19, 1888, p. 3; Nov. 28, 1888, p. 9; Dec. 1, 1888, p. 9; Dec. 2, 1888, p. 1; *Chicago Tribune*, June 9, 1888, p. 2; July 18, 1888, p. 2; July 20, 1888, p. 8; July 26, 1888, p. 2; Nov. 28, 1888, p. 3; Nov. 29, 1888, p. 6; Dec. 1, 1888, p. 9; Dec. 2, 1888, p. 9. Judge Collins on sentencing, *Chicago Inter-Ocean*, Jan. 3, 1889, p. 7. Hronek unsuccessfully appealed his case to the Illinois Supreme Court on two grounds: that the newly passed statute forbidding the manufacture of dynamite for nefarious purposes was defective and that witnesses against him were allowed to testify without swearing an oath on the Bible. *John Hronek v. The People*, Supreme Court of Illinois, 134 Ill. 139; 24 N.E. 861; 1890 Ill. LEXIS 952, June 12, 1890.

6. *Chicago Inter-Ocean*, Jan. 10, 1889, p. 2; Jan. 16, 1889, p. 7.

7. New York *World*, Sept. 25, 1887, p. 1.

8. New York *World*, Nov. 20, 1888, p. 2.

9. *The Commonweal* (London), June 29, 1889, p. 204; Apr. 12, 1890, p. 117.

10. *The Open Court* (Chicago), Sept. 25, 1890, p. 2538; *Chicago Tribune*, Nov. 15, 1887, p. 2.
11. *Liberty: Not the Daughter but the Mother of Order*, Mar. 7, 1891, p. 4.
12. *Schwab v. Berggren*, Supreme Court of the United States, 143 U.S. 442 S. Ct. 525; 36 L.Ed. 218; 1892 U.S. LEXIS 2034, Feb. 19, 1892.
13. Joseph E. Gary, "The Chicago Anarchists of 1886. The Crime, The Trial, and the Punishment. By the Judge Who Presided at the Trial," *The Century Magazine* (New York), XLV, p. 809.
14. Gary, p. 832.
15. *Chicago Tribune*, Apr. 30, 1893, p. 5.
16. *Chicago Tribune*, June 26, 1893, p. 7.
17. Clarence Darrow, *The Story of My Life* (New York: Charles Scribner's Sons, 1932), p. 103; Ernest L. Bogard, Charles M. Thompson, *The Industrial State, 1870–1893*, Vol. IV of *The Centennial History of Illinois*, Clarence Walworth Alvord, ed. (Chicago: A.C. McClurg & Co., 1922), p. 187. In his autobiography Darrow seems unaware of the great controversy in the trial over where the bomber stood and writes, "a bomb was thrown from an alley into the Square, which landed in the midst of the policemen . . . " (Darrow, *The Story of My Life*, p. 97). Darrow also notes that William Penn Nixon, editor of the *Inter-Ocean* was chairman of the amnesty committee (p. 99).
18. *Chicago Tribune*, June 27, 1893, p. 2.
19. *Spies et. al. v. State of Illinois*, Supreme Court of Illinois, Illinois State Archives, microfilm roll 30–1831, vol. 1, pp. 361–364.
20. Historians have consistently claimed that *Coughlin v. The People* overturned one of the key principles upholding the anarchists' convictions. Paul Avrich writes: "In January 1893, only days after the governor took office, the Illinois Supreme Court, reversing its stand in the Haymarket case, ruled in The People v. Coughlin (sic) that a prospective juror who had read about a case in the press and had formed an opinion as to the defendant's guilt was ineligible to serve. Justice Magruder, who had delivered the unanimous opinion in Spies v. Illinois (sic), now conceded that, if the court was right in the Coughlin case, then it erred in regard to the anarchists" (Paul Avrich, *The Haymarket Tragedy* (Princeton, NJ: Princeton Univ. Press, 1984), p. 418. See also Henry David, *The History of the Haymarket Affair: A Study in the American Social-Revolutionary and Labor Movements* (New York: Russell & Russell, 1958, org. 1936), p. 494).

But *Coughlin v. The People* did not break with the precedent set by *Spies et al. v. The People* nor did anything in Judge Magruder's dissent even imply that the majority opinion in any way overturned it. Rather, throughout both majority and minority opinions the anarchist precedent was repeatedly restated in support of the decision made in this case. As the majority opinion expressly stated: "The conclusions to which we have arrived in relation to the competency of the jurors in this case are not, in our opinion, in conflict with the decisions in . . . *Spies et al. v. The People* . . . " (*Coughlin v. The People*, 144 Ill. 140; 33 N.E.1; 1893 Ill. Lexis 1120, Jan. 19, 1893).

The claim that *Coughlin v. The People* cast doubt upon the Haymarket case because it broke with the principles of juror disqualification used in *Spies et al. v. The People* was first made by Governor Altgeld in defending his pardon. They were then repeated uncritically by Edgar Lee Masters in 1925, by Harvey Wish in his 1938 history of Altgeld's pardon, and by Harry Barnard in his biography of Altgeld of the same year, and from there to Avrich and others (Harry Barnard, *"Eagle Forgotten": The Life of John Peter Altgeld* (Indianapolis: Bobbs-Merrill, 1938), pp. 225–227). In this way what began as an opportunistic interpretation of a decision that really upheld the original appellate interpretation of the anarchist case over time became twisted into one that historians used to question it.

The original source for the idea that Magruder "conceded . . . [he] had erred in regard to the anarchists" is not to be found in the *Coughlin* decision itself, but in a tale told by George Schilling, the leading activist for a pardon, who claimed that Magruder confronted his fellow jurists about the case, exclaiming, "If this is the view of the court, it is a pity that those anarchists were hanged!" Schilling told this story to Harry Barnard, Altgeld's biographer, and he used it in his account, though even Barnard didn't believe it was true, describing it in his own book as "an apocryphal story" (Barnard, p. 226).

21. Examination of Harry T. Sandford, Haymarket Affair Digital Collection, Chicago Historical Society (HADC), Vol. H, p. 302.

22. Altgeld quote from HADC, "Reasons for Pardoning," p. 26; Examination of Harry T. Sandford, HADC, Vol. H, pp. 301–302. Altgeld's version of the examination of juror Theodore Denker is just as fanciful:

> He was then asked further questions by the defendants' counsel, and said: "I have formed an opinion as to the guilt of the defendants and have expressed it. We conversed about the matter in the business house and I expressed my opinion there; expressed my opinion quite frequently. *My mind was made up from what I read and did not hesitate to speak about it.*"
>
> Q: Would you feel yourself in any way governed or bound in listening to the testimony and determining it upon the pre-judgment of the case that you had expressed to others before?
> A: Well that is a pretty hard question to answer."

The similar portion of Denker's actual testimony reads:

> "Q: In the conversations that you have had there at the store you say you have expressed the opinion which you have formed before?
> A: Yes sir.
> Q: Is that a frequent occurrence—that you have expressed the opinion which you formed?
> A: Well, I think I have expressed it pretty freely.
> Q: As to the number of times—as to whether it was frequent or not?
> A: Oh, no; we did not bring the matter up in conversation very often, but when we did we generally expressed our opinions in regard to the matter.
> Q: Your mind was made up from what you read, and you had no hesitancy in saying it—speaking it out?
> A: I don't think I hesitated.
> Q: Would you feel yourself any way governed or bound in listening to the testimony and determining it upon the pre-judgment of the case that you had expressed to others before?
> A: Well, that is a pretty hard question to answer.
> Q: I will ask you whether acting as a juror here you would feel in any way bound or governed by the judgment that you had expressed on the same question to others before you were taken as a juryman? Do you understand that?
> A: I don't think I would." (Examination of Theodore Denker, HADC, Vol. B, pp. 112–122).

23. Bernard, pp. 208–209.

24. *Chicago Tribune*, Sept. 25, 1886, p. 7; Avrich, p. 133; Bruce C. Nelson, *Beyond the Martyrs: A Social History of Chicago's Anarchists, 1870–1900* (New Brunswick, NJ: Rutgers University Press, 1988), pp. 118, 159–160. Though Nelson mentions that Dejnek and Mikolanda were convicted, somehow he fails to mention what it was they were sent to jail for. See Nelson, p. 199.

25. *Chicago Inter-Ocean*, Dec. 22, 1886, p. 11; July 9, 1887, p. 6; Officer Casey was later cashiered from the force for proposing to marry a young widow; the news of impending

nuptials came a surprise to his wife. *Chicago Inter-Ocean*, July 8, 1887, p. 3. *Chicago Tribune*, Sept. 26, 1886, p. 16, Sept. 24, 1886, p. 8; Dec. 18, 1886, p. 8,

26. "Reasons for pardoning Fielden, Neebe and Schwab," by John P. Altgeld, governor of Illinois (Chicago, IL: s.n., 1893), p. 50.

27. Brand Whitlock, *Forty Years of It* (New York: D. Appleton, 1914), p. 74; Darrow, p. 102.

28. *Chicago Tribune*, Oct. 28, 1893, p. 9; Bernard, *Eagle Forgotten*, pp. 135–143.

29. Bernard, p. 141; *Chicago Tribune*, June 29, 1893, p. 1.

30. *Chicago Tribune*, Oct. 30, 1893, p. 10.

31. Howard A. Wilson, "William Dean Howell's Unpublished Letters About the Haymarket Affair," *Journal of the Illinois State Historical Society*, 56:1 (Spring 1963), p. 8. If Altgeld's characterization of the trial were correct it would not have been necessary for Prosecutor Grinnell to swear in dozens of material witnesses. Judge Gary specifically instructed the jurors that merely advocating violence was not enough to convict these men but that "a direct connection [must be] established by credible testimony between the advice and the consummation of the crime..." ("Reasons for Pardoning Fielden, Neebe and Schwab," John P. Altgeld, HADC, p. 4). Though Samuel Fielden urged the throng in the Haymarket to "throttle the law" minutes before the bomb sailed, prosecutor Grinnell called witness after witness to tell how he ducked behind the wagon and blazed away with his revolver, a completely unnecessary bit of testimony were Altgeld's theory correct.

32. *Chicago Tribune*, July 6, 1893, p. 4. Oglesby referred to a letter that Captain Black sent to Altgeld the previous summer that provided many of Altgeld's arguments. *Chicago Tribune*, July 18, 1893, p. 4

33. *Chicago Tribune*, Dec. 16, 1893, p. 6.

CONCLUSION

1. *The Washington Post*, Nov. 30, 1888, p. 1.

2. Henry David, *History of the Haymarket Affair: A Study in the American Social-Revolutionary and Labor Movements* (New York: Russell & Russell, Rev. ed., 1958, org. 1936), p. 519.

3. Affidavit of John Phillip Deluse, HADC, Vol. O, p. 92.

4. *Chicago Tribune*, Nov. 11, 1887, p. 2.

5. New York *Sun*, Nov. 11, 1887, p. 2; *Chicago Tribune*, Nov. 11, 1887, p. 7.

6. *The New York Times*, Nov. 16, 1887, p. 1.

7. *Chicago Tribune*, Apr. 11, 1887, p. 8; Apr. 21, 1887, p. 2.

8. *The Washington Post*, Sept. 6, 1889, p. 4.

9. *San Francisco Call*, May 23, 1895, p. 3.

10. *Chicago Tribune*, May 14, 1895, p. 8; May 20, 1895, p. 7; June 7, 1895, p. 1; June 24, 1895, p. 3.

11. *Chicago Tribune*, Oct. 20, 1896, p. 1; Oct. 21, 1896, p. 7; *New York Observer*, May 16, 1895, p. 666; Paul Avrich, *The Haymarket Tragedy* (Princeton, NJ: Princeton Univ. Press, 1984), p. 440; Paul Avrich, *Anarchist Voices: An Oral History of Anarchism in America* (Oakland, CA: AK Press, 2005), p. 22.

12. Historians have shown a great reluctance to acknowledge the obvious—that Schnaubelt was the likely bomber. Arbitrarily sweeping aside the testimony of eyewitnesses, circumstantial evidence, and the reminiscences of many principals in the affair, Paul Avrich writes, "There is not a shred of evidence that Schnaubelt hurled the explosive..." (Avrich, *Haymarket Tragedy*, p. 439). Rather, Avrich finds more credible the secondhand reminiscences of the granddaughter of a Chicago anarchist, George Meng, who remembered her mother describing how, when she was a girl, a strange man named "Rudolph" hid out at their suburban Chicago farm and her mother being sure that "he was the one" (Paul Avrich, "The Bomb-Thrower: A New Candidate," *Haymarket Scrapbook* (Chicago:

Charles Kerr Co., 1986), p. 71). Without examining the evidence, James Green in *Death in the Haymarket* likewise breezily dismisses the idea that Schnaubelt had anything to do with the bombing, saying "... the evidence against him was not credible" (James Green, *Death in the Haymarket: A Story of Chicago, the First Labor Movement, and the Bombing that Divided Gilded Age America* (New York: Pantheon Books, 2006), p. 291).

13. Max Nettlau, *Anarchisten und Sozialrevolutionäre : die Historische Entwicklung des Anarchismus in den Jahren 1880–1886* (Berlin: Asy-Verlag, 1931), p. 387.

14. Jack McPhaul, "Who Hurled the Haymarket Bomb?" *Chicago Sun-Times*, May 5, 1957.

15. *Chicago Tribune*, Nov. 27, 1886, p. 2; Nov. 28, 1886, p. 9; Dec. 2, 1886, p. 6; Mar. 16, 1887, p. 1. Henry Jansen claimed insanity but was tried, sentenced to life, and sent to Joliet prison.

16. Ernest Bloomfield Zeisler, *The Haymarket Riot* (Chicago: Alexander J. Isaacs, 1956), p. 105. See also Axel W.-O. Schmidt, *Der Rothe Doktor von Chicago: Ein Deutsch-Amerikanisches Auswandererschicksal: Biographie des Doktor Ernst Schmidt, 1830–1900* (Frankfurt am Main: Peter Lang, 2003), p. 372.

17. Schilling was interviewed by Henry David and told him that he thought that Schnaubelt was the bomber (David, p. 509, ft. 5, p. 525); Agnes Inglis, in her own research notes, indicates that Schilling told her the same story. File on "George Schilling," Agnes Inglis Papers, Research and Notes (Box 30), George Schilling, Labadie Collection, University of Michigan Library. Neebe's neighbor, John F. Kendrick, was also interviewed by David (David, p. x).

18. Schilling to Lucy Parsons, Dec. 1893, George Schilling Papers, Labadie Collection, University of Michigan Library. Schilling concludes, "The revenge circular of August Spies was met by the revenge of the public mind, terrorized by fear until it reeled like a drunken man, and in its frenzy swept away the safeguards of the law and turned its officers into pliant tools yielding to its will."

INDEX

CPSIA information can be obtained
at www.ICGtesting.com
Printed in the USA
LVOW13s1743090317
526683LV00006BA/12/P